Jaguar Books on Latin America

Series Editors

WILLIAM H. BEEZLEY, Professor of History,
   University of Arizona
COLIN M. MACLACHLAN, Distinguished Professor of History,
   Tulane University

Volumes Published

John E. Kicza, ed., *The Indian in Latin American History: Resistance, Resilience, and Acculturation* (1993; rev. ed., 2000). Cloth ISBN 0-8420-2822-6 Paper ISBN 0-8420-2823-4

Susan E. Place, ed., *Tropical Rainforests: Latin American Nature and Society in Transition* (1993). Cloth ISBN 0-8420-2423-9 Paper ISBN 0-8420-2427-1

Paul W. Drake, ed., *Money Doctors, Foreign Debts, and Economic Reforms in Latin America from the 1890s to the Present* (1994). Cloth ISBN 0-8420-2434-4   Paper ISBN 0-8420-2435-2

John A. Britton, ed., *Molding the Hearts and Minds: Education, Communications, and Social Change in Latin America* (1994). Cloth ISBN 0-8420-2489-1   Paper ISBN 0-8420-2490-5

David J. Weber and Jane M. Rausch, eds., *Where Cultures Meet: Frontiers in Latin American History* (1994). Cloth ISBN 0-8420-2477-8 Paper ISBN 0-8420-2478-6

Gertrude M. Yeager, ed., *Confronting Change, Challenging Tradition: Women in Latin American History* (1994). Cloth ISBN 0-8420-2479-4 Paper ISBN 0-8420-2480-8

Linda Alexander Rodríguez, ed., *Rank and Privilege: The Military and Society in Latin America* (1994). Cloth ISBN 0-8420-2432-8 Paper ISBN 0-8420-2433-6

Darién J. Davis, ed., *Slavery and Beyond: The African Impact on Latin America and the Caribbean* (1995). Cloth ISBN 0-8420-2484-0 Paper ISBN 0-8420-2485-9

Gilbert M. Joseph and Mark D. Szuchman, eds., *I Saw a City Invincible: Urban Portraits of Latin America* (1996). Cloth ISBN 0-8420-2495-6 Paper ISBN 0-8420-2496-4

Roderic Ai Camp, ed., *Democracy in Latin America: Patterns and Cycles* (1996). Cloth ISBN 0-8420-2512-X   Paper ISBN 0-8420-2513-8

Oscar J. Martínez, ed., *U.S.-Mexico Borderlands: Historical and Contemporary Perspectives* (1996). Cloth ISBN 0-8420-2446-8 Paper ISBN 0-8420-2447-6

William O. Walker III, ed., *Drugs in the Western Hemisphere: An Odyssey of Cultures in Conflict* (1996). Cloth ISBN 0-8420-2422-0 Paper ISBN 0-8420-2426-3

Richard R. Cole, ed., *Communication in Latin America: Journalism, Mass Media, and Society* (1996). Cloth ISBN 0-8420-2558-8 Paper ISBN 0-8420-2559-6

David G. Gutiérrez, ed., *Between Two Worlds: Mexican Immigrants in the United States* (1996). Cloth ISBN 0-8420-2473-5 Paper ISBN 0-8420-2474-3

Lynne Phillips, ed., *The Third Wave of Modernization in Latin America: Cultural Perspectives on Neoliberalism* (1998). Cloth ISBN 0-8420-2606-1   Paper ISBN 0-8420-2608-8

Daniel Castro, ed., *Revolution and Revolutionaries: Guerrilla Movements in Latin America* (1999). Cloth ISBN 0-8420-2625-8 Paper ISBN 0-8420-2626-6

Virginia Garrard-Burnett, ed., *On Earth as It Is in Heaven: Religion in Modern Latin America* (2000). Cloth ISBN 0-8420-2584-7 Paper ISBN 0-8420-2485-5

Carlos A. Aguirre and Robert Buffington, eds., *Reconstructing Criminality in Latin America* (2000). Cloth ISBN 0-8420-2620-7 Paper ISBN 0-8420-2621-5

The Indian
in
Latin American
History

The Indian
in
Latin American
History

Resistance, Resilience, and Acculturation

Revised Edition

John E. Kicza
Editor

Jaguar Books on Latin America
Number 1

A Scholarly Resources Inc. Imprint
Wilmington, Delaware

© 2000 by Scholarly Resources Inc.
All rights reserved
First published 1993
Printed and bound in the United States of America

Scholarly Resources Inc.
104 Greenhill Avenue
Wilmington, DE 19805-1897
www.scholarly.com

Library of Congress Cataloging-in-Publication Data

The Indian in Latin American history : resistance, resilience, and
   acculturation / John E. Kicza, editor. — Rev. ed.
       p.   cm. — (Jaguar books on Latin America : no. 1)
       Includes bibliographical references.
       ISBN 0–8420–2822–6 (cloth : alk. paper). — ISBN 0–8420–
   2823–4 (pbk. : alk. paper)
           1. Indians—History. 2. Indians—Ethnic identity. 3. Indians—
   Cultural assimilation. 4. Acculturation—Latin America. 5. Latin
   America—Politics and government. I. Kicza, John E., 1947–   .
   II. Series.
   E65.I45   1999
   980-dc21   99–29755
                                                                              CIP

♾ The paper used in this publication meets the minimum requirements of
the American National Standard for permanence of paper for printed library materials, Z39.48, 1984.

Grateful acknowledgment is made to the publishers and authors of the following selections for their permission to reprint:

Thomas C. Patterson, "The Inca Empire and Its Subject Peoples," in *The Inca Empire: The Formation and Disintegration of a Pre-Capitalist State* (New York: Berg Publishers), 98–116. Reprinted by permission of Berg Publishers.

Steve J. Stern, "The Rise and Fall of Indian-White Alliances: A Regional View of 'Conquest' History," *Hispanic American Historical Review* 61, no. 3 (August 1981): 461–91. © 1981 by Duke University Press. Reprinted by permission of Duke University Press.

Nancy M. Farriss, "Maya Society under Colonial Rule: The Collective Enterprise of Survival," in *Maya Society under Colonial Rule: The Collective Enterprise of Survival* (Princeton: Princeton University Press, 1984), 12–25. ©1984 by Princeton University Press. Reprinted by permission of Princeton University Press.

Robert Charles Padden, "Cultural Adaptation and Militant Autonomy among the Araucanians of Chile," *Southwestern Journal of Anthropology* 13, no. 1 (Spring 1957): 103–21. Reprinted by permission of *Southwestern Journal of Anthropology* and Robert Charles Padden.

Robert Haskett, "Coping with the Cultural Conquest," in *Indigenous Rulers: An Ethnohistory of Town Government in Colonial Cuernavaca* (Albuquerque: University of New Mexico Press, 1991), 161–95, 259–72. Reprinted by permission of the University of New Mexico Press.

Paul Charney, "Negotiating Roots: Indian Migrants in the Lima Valley during the Colonial Period," *Colonial Latin American Historical Review* 5, no. 1 (1996): 1–20. Reprinted by permission of the *Colonial Latin American Historical Review*.

William B. Taylor, "Patterns and Variety in Mexican Village Uprisings," in *Drinking, Homicide, and Rebellion in Colonial Mexican Villages* (Stanford, CA: Stanford University Press, 1979), 113–51. © 1979 by the Board of Trustees of the Leland Stanford Junior University. Reprinted by permission of Stanford University Press.

About the Editor

John E. Kicza is the Edward R. Meyer Distinguished Professor of History at Washington State University. He is the author of several books, including *Colonial Entrepreneurs: Families and Business in Bourbon Mexico City* (1983) and *La Vida social en Hispanoamérica* (1998). He also composed "The Peoples and Civilizations of the Americas Before Contact," American Historical Association Essays on Global and Comparative History (1998). His current research includes book projects on the impact of early colonization in the Americas on the native societies, and a comparative synthesis of patterns in Spanish overseas conquest expeditions to 1600 and the reasons for their success or failure. Professor Kicza has enjoyed research grants from the Organization of American States, the Fulbright Program, and the National Endowment for the Humanities.

Contents

Introduction

John E. Kicza

The history of Latin America does not begin in 1492. Some tens of millions of peoples organized into distinct polities and ethnic groups had already lived in this vast region for thousands of years before Europeans reached the hemisphere. Nor are we dependent just on archaeology and oral traditions for our knowledge of the history and culture of many of these societies. The more elaborate among them—most notably, the Maya and the Aztecs—had developed writing and mnemonic systems that recorded aspects of their pasts and their beliefs. Further, soon after the arrival of the Europeans, some members of these cultures learned to write their language using the Spanish alphabet. They then composed versions both of their histories and of contemporary events in their societies, sometimes with very little Spanish intervention.

The native peoples of the Americas have displayed remarkable cultural resilience in the face of demographic catastrophes; loss of lands and local political autonomy; recurrent infusions of outside technologies, animals, foods, and procedures over the centuries; and disrespectful treatment of their values and ways of life by the governments and citizens of those nations into which they have been merged. To the extent possible, Indian peoples have been selective about what aspects of the outside world they incorporate into their cultures. The indigenous communities have not been without resources. They have used their internal unity, under dedicated local leaders in many cases, to incorporate the changes forced upon them on the best terms that they could muster. Nor were they cowed or passive before the impositions of colonial and national governments. Both individual Indians and Indian corporations commonly initiated petitions and lawsuits to demand remedies for perceived injustices. Local rebellions by native peoples were endemic in large parts of Latin America over the centuries; some indigenous communities had well-earned reputations for insurrection. Occasionally, these rebellions became widespread and threatened major regions and even national governments. Through a combination of selective adaptation and peaceful (or sometimes violent) resistance, the native peoples of Latin America, even those subjugated by the Europeans, have been making their own histories for five hundred years.

Latin American Indians have been so successful in drawing upon their own resources and capacities that today their numbers are growing and they constitute a majority of the population in countries such as Guatemala and Bolivia and a substantial plurality in Mexico, Ecuador, and Peru. Even in countries where they do not make up a large part of the population—Brazil, Colombia, and Chile, for example—native peoples have been able to assert their rights and claims and make the national societies come to grips with the issues of native autonomy and control over land and other resources.

Clear evidence of human habitation in the Americas dates from at least 12,000 B.C., and some findings hint at a human presence in this continent perhaps twenty thousand years earlier. Whatever the actual date of humanity's arrival in this part of the world, undoubtedly the next great transforming development was the emergence of agriculture in the centuries before 1500 B.C. Indications are that native peoples of Mexico, Guatemala, Colombia, and Peru commenced the cultivation of crops—instead of continuing their practice of hunting and gathering—autonomously and at roughly the same time. By 1500 B.C. villages of full-time farmers were proliferating. Maize, beans, and squash constituted the primary crops cultivated, but potatoes and manioc dominated some major agricultural zones in South America.

The intensive, permanent cultivation of crops had immense consequences for the native peoples' way of life. It promoted a vast increase in the population and required practitioners to remain settled in communities surrounded by their fields. This sedentary existence facilitated occupational differentiation as farmers routinely produced food surpluses that they were willing to trade for the finished goods fashioned by local artisans. Social distinctions also emerged. With time, ruling classes, sometimes complete with royal families, appeared, as did a priesthood. In fact, religious practice became more elaborate, and large ceremonial complexes were constructed for the first time. Hundreds of ethnic groups worshipped similar sets of gods, though each group gave its local versions distinct names and, understandably, saw its own gods as the rightful and effective ones, unlike those of the other peoples.

These hundreds of ethnic groups practicing agriculture eventually formed themselves into political entities, organized as provinces in which a head town—where the ruling dynasty resided—controlled a complex of subject villages; in turn, in each village there was a set of families who governed local society. It was from among these sedentary agricultural societies, with their labor surpluses, local craft specializations, and large armies, that empires developed. These entities could be found in Mesoamerica (the sedentary zone of Central America, roughly the southern two-thirds of Mexico, all of Guatemala, and most of El Salvador, Honduras, and Nicaragua) and in the Andean highlands in the modern nations of Ecuador, Peru, and Bolivia at least a millennium and a half before the arrival of Europeans in the hemisphere. No other true empires would appear in indigenous America, for the hundreds of other ethnic groups, totaling in the millions of people, did not practice fully sedentary agriculture and hence lacked the attributes needed for the long-term conquest of other societies (although warfare was common among these peoples).

Mesoamerica and the Andean zone witnessed the rise and fall of a series of empires over the centuries. The conquerors typically demanded labor service from the subjugated peoples and, in the case of Mesoamerica, formal tribute payments also. The Incas and the Aztecs were the last examples—though certainly dramatically successful ones—of such polities, and in most aspects they replicated the institutions and practices of their predecessors. Characteristically, all of these empires permitted the inhabitants of their subjugated provinces to retain their own languages, sets of gods, local rulers, and separate ethnic identities, as Thomas Patterson illustrates in Chapter 1. These long-surviving empires did not destroy the ethnic distinctiveness of the subordinated peoples, who were quick to rebel whenever they saw any chance of success.

Many other peoples practiced some agriculture, but their environments were sufficiently unaccommodating that they had to move their settlements within a certain zone every few years and perhaps supplement their crops with substantial amounts of other foods. Most of the Maya of the Yucatán Peninsula and Guatemala practiced this slash-and-burn, or swidden, agriculture. Such agriculture dictated lower population densities and made enduring empires harder to attain—these peoples were more difficult to organize into large polities and had fewer surplus resources that they could transfer to an imperial power. Besides living in the southern zone of Mesoamerica, substantial numbers of semisedentary peoples resided on the major Caribbean islands and in highland Colombia, Brazil, Paraguay, and Chile.

Hunting-and-gathering peoples who practiced no agriculture remained in the desert, mountain, and tropical areas of Latin America. Organized into many small ethnic groups, they actually totaled far fewer persons than did either the sedentary or semisedentary societies. Without agriculture but with a need to migrate over considerable distances in order to gain sufficient resources to survive, these bands had to remain rather small in order to function effectively. Understandably, there was little political or craft differentiation among these peoples; the primary distinction in labor roles was based on gender. The artistic achievement of these peoples was rudimentary, and they used natural sites rather than constructed arenas as their religious centers. There were no empires among such societies, but they were especially adept fighters, utilizing ambushes and rapid retreats and advances as tactics and bows and arrows, sometimes poisoned, as weapons.

The best estimates indicate that the total native population of the Americas approached 75 million people on the eve of the Europeans' arrival. Of these native peoples, around 8 million lived in North America, more than 22 million in Mexico, some 8 million in Central America, another 8 million in the Caribbean, about 17 million along the Andes, and perhaps 12 million in lowland South America. The vast numbers in Mexico and the Andes resulted from the dominance of agriculture and densely settled permanent villages in these areas.

It is only to non-natives that these peoples can be classified into a collective population termed "Indian." They were as distinct from each other in language and ethnic identity as their counterparts were in Europe—and often as contentious. In fact, the major differences between native Americans and the peoples of Europe, Africa, and Asia (for the peoples of these three continents shared broadly similar characteristics) were largely accidents of history and geography. The native Americans lacked metal tools and weapons, did not have draft animals, and did not use the wheel in manual labor. They also were insulated from most of the epidemic diseases that regularly ravaged the Old World.

The Americans routinely refined gold, silver, and copper, which they shaped into ornaments. However, they had not developed industrial metals, especially iron, which are harder and thus appropriate for making tools. As a consequence, they largely relied on hard, sharp stones as tools and weapons. Flint and obsidian functioned as projectile points and were placed along the edges of swords and clubs. Overall, the lack of industrial metals led to a certain technological stagnation among these peoples. The tools of the Aztecs and the Incas varied little from those of the peoples who preceded them by a millennium and a half.

The Western Hemisphere lacked horses, oxen, and other suitable beasts of burden. It also did not have cattle, pigs, goats, or chickens. The plains of North America were the home of millions of buffalo, which provided abundant meat, hides, and other necessities of life, but buffalo are totally unsuitable as beasts of burden. Llamas constituted the only useful animals of size in South America, and, although they yielded some meat and could bear some weight, they could not pull plows or wagons. Without draft animals, native Americans had little use for the wheel. They certainly knew of it and incorporated it into small implements, but they could not use it in sizable undertakings without large animals to provide power.

In most respects the Spaniards resembled other European colonists of the Americas. Unlike the others, however, the Spaniards rarely just established trading bases in new lands; instead, they sought to settle the lands fully and permanently. This process entailed the significant immigration of people (commonly an appreciable minority of the immigrants were women) and importation of animals, the establishment of cities, the setting up of rural enterprises to supply the urban sector, the incorporation of the local native peoples into a dependent labor force, and a rigorous effort to locate and work deposits of precious metals. These people went to the Americas not out of some compelling need for adventure but rather to make a better life for themselves and their descendants. Hardly any of them possessed a strong curiosity about Indian thought and culture. They wished merely for the native peoples to be peaceful, to provide them with unskilled labor, and to convert to Christianity. The actual conversion effort was left largely to members of religious orders with the support of wealthier colonists who financed a good bit of the process. Precious metals were pursued because they constituted the commodity that could be exported most profitably to Europe and thereby underwrite the long-term prosperity of a colony. (Eventually, in some areas in the Americas, commodities such as sugar, tobacco, dyewoods, and furs would also support elaborate colonial societies.)

The defeat of the great imperial armies of the Aztecs and the Incas by small Spanish expeditions seems quite beyond belief until systematically examined. Of course, the Spanish forces did not have to fight all of the millions of peoples who made up these massive empires. In fact, most of the subordinated peoples already within these empires welcomed the Spaniards as potential liberators from the demands of their traditional oppressors. Thus, Hernán Cortés and Francisco Pizarro were able to get many ethnic groups to agree either to remain outside the fight or even, sometimes, to support the invaders. The Spaniards also benefited immensely from their technological superiority over the Indians. Firearms and cannon were not too important, for they were slow to fire, inaccurate, and inappropriate for the battles in open country that characterized warfare between the Spaniards and the sedentary empires. Far more decisive were the metal weapons and armor and the small contingent of horses that each expedition usually had with it. Lacking armor, the native armies could not defend themselves against the crossbow fire, swords, and lances of the Spaniards. The Spanish cavalry was virtually unstoppable, able to disperse or outflank any formation assembled against it.

The technological advantage of the Spaniards was maximized by the style of warfare practiced by the imperial societies. Making only minimal use of bows and arrows, imperial soldiers preferred close engagement with their opponents. They were equipped with wooden clubs commonly edged with obsidian chips, and they typically fought in the open rather than from cover, stressing capture over the killing of their opponents. The imperial armies presented themselves in tight formations in which only the front rank could actually fight, and they remained under strict hierarchies. When commanders were killed or captured, their forces would fall out of action.

Finally, the Spaniards, as did all the European colonists, unwittingly brought with them virulent epidemic diseases with which the American peoples had no experience and against which they had no resistance. Smallpox, measles, and typhus seem to have had the worst impact. These diseases were so contagious that smallpox was already sweeping through the Aztec capital when Cortés had it under siege. Both an Aztec and an Incan emperor died from this disease even though no European was in their vicinity at the time.

After the defeat of their empires, the Indians tried to explain these catastrophic defeats to themselves. Because they were very religious peoples who believed that the gods determined all outcomes, they asserted that their defeats had been prefigured by omens and that they had viewed the Spaniards as returning gods. However, the evidence indicates that this perspective developed after the fact and did not affect the course of the actual conquests.

The Spaniards never saw it as in their interest to destroy the structure of native society. Rather, they sought to use the structure that was already in place to govern effectively, to mobilize cheap Indian labor, to funnel resources into the Hispanic sector of the society, and to Christianize the population. Steve Stern (Chapter 2) describes the Spanish reliance on indigenous systems and traditional relationships in the decades just after the conquest of Peru and how the elaboration of a large-scale market economy and the declining native population brought an end to this practice.

Against native peoples who were not fully sedentary and organized into empires, the Spaniards' technological advantages faded. Nancy Farriss (Chapter 3) shows some of the difficulties the Spaniards faced against the loosely confederated Maya in the Yucatán Peninsula. The Spaniards had to fight nearly every individual settlement in this region—a difficult tropical environment in which Spanish mobility was restricted and that the Maya could utilize to their advantage. Mayan settlements could withdraw into the countryside in the face of Spanish advances, and, when beleaguered, Mayan fighters could retreat into difficult country to fight another day.

Robert Padden, in Chapter 4, analyzes one of the most dramatic cases of successful resistance by native peoples. The Araucanians of southern Chile remained independent of outside control until they finally were defeated by the Chilean army around 1880. Mobility, flexibility, and adaptability explain how they were able to retain their autonomy prior to their defeat. The Araucanians adopted the horse and even changed their settlement and eating patterns to enhance their ability to resist. Over the decades they studied the Spanish way of fighting and developed suitable responses. But in the late nineteenth century the introduction of the repeating rifle and of such developments as barbed wire and the telegraph gave the Chileans the means to subdue the Araucanians. (The Araucanians who controlled southern Argentina also were defeated at this time by an Argentine army utilizing the same advances.)

The Spaniards faced immense difficulties in overcoming the hunting-and-gathering peoples located in northern Mexico, at the Amazon headwaters, in eastern Bolivia, and elsewhere. Often the colonists abandoned their efforts to subdue these native groups, which fought them so effectively using bows and arrows and hit-and-run tactics. These Indians held little promise as a usable labor force and generally controlled no resources that the Spaniards considered lucrative. It was in this setting that the Spaniards would establish missions in an effort gradually to convert the natives and to attract them to a European style of life. In northern Mexico, however, the Spaniards discovered major silver deposits and thus had to protect the region's mining towns and shipping routes from attack. During the second half of the sixteenth century their attempts either to subjugate the local peoples or to run them off were notably unsuccessful. The Spanish viceroys finally resorted to offering the local groups annual shipments of supplies to be provided by the colonial government if they would agree to cease their raids, settle in permanent villages, and accept missionaries among them. The natives generally accepted such offers because the alternative was continued warfare in which the native societies suffered losses and dislocation even when they prevailed in a particular campaign. Consequently, much of the north was opened to colonization.

Until roughly 1650 the factor that most transformed Indian life in Latin America was the collapse of the population brought about overwhelmingly by the new epidemic diseases that arrived with the colonists. As these diseases were most virulent in temperate settings where there was heavy population density, central Mexico suffered as badly as, if not worse than, any other region. In a little over a century, successive waves of epidemics reduced the native population by about 95 percent, from more than 20 million people to fewer than 1.5 million. The indigenous community in the Spanish Caribbean literally had been eliminated by 1550. Central America and the Andean region were also badly hit. It must be stressed that the Spaniards neither encouraged nor understood the catastrophe. They sought to utilize local native populations, not to eradicate them.

The primary consequence of this enormous die-off was to skew the native-colonist population ratios so greatly that the surviving Indians were more fully acculturated to the European way of life (as described by Robert Haskett in Chapter 5) and could be more closely regulated by Spanish priests and administrators. Great expanses of agricultural land that had become depopulated were thus available for cultivation by colonists. Without this demographic catastrophe, modern Latin America would more closely resemble Africa or India, where the European impact, although certainly significant, was not as transforming of native cultural, social, and political patterns as it was in the Western Hemisphere.

The introduction of Old World animals and tools affected the indigenous way of life as well. Horses, oxen, cattle, pigs, and chickens were brought to the Americas in great numbers. Overall, Indian villagers did not incorporate draft animals into their agricultural practices in a systematic fashion, but pigs and chickens became staples in their diets. Tools, pans, and knives of metal became integral parts of native existence. Firearms, however, seem to have been used rarely by Indians, even in hunting.

The Christianization of the Indians is a controversial and poorly understood development. An appreciation that there was always a shortage of Catholic priests available to work in native communities and that the Indians often were inclined to adopt major components of the religion of their conquerors—even before the arrival of the Europeans—helps to explain much of what transpired. A Spanish cleric typically set up his parish in the head town of an Indian province. He would be able to visit the many villages within the province only two or three times each year. Church marriages, baptisms, and the like thus had to wait for such occasions. Of course, the priest could teach religious doctrine, say Mass, and hear confessions only at these times also. Understandably, then, the form of Catholicism that emerged stressed community values and public celebrations, which did not require a priest's continued presence. Individual towns adopted patron saints and shrines that they promoted in their festivities. Neighborhoods and other community groups organized themselves into religious brotherhoods (*cofradías*) to sustain such activities and to provide benefits to the membership. Over time, assumption of the burden of sponsoring community religious celebrations became the primary avenue by which an individual could rise in respect and responsibility within the society, and the men who sacrificed their interests to those of the community through such endeavors became eligible to hold the highest civic offices. This set of practices has become termed the "cargo system."

Spanish priests commonly located their churches and chapels upon sites that the Indians already considered sacred. For their part, the Indians often merged the Catholic church's spectrum of saints with their own enduring pantheon of gods. The result of such practices was a certain combining of systems of belief, called syncretism, that has lasted in many areas to the present day.

It would be misleading, however, to argue that Spanish priests—or colonial officials, for that matter—acted as the primary agents of change in native culture. Rather, that honor goes to the colonists themselves, who, by their continuing interaction with the Indians, generally in the most informal and unstructured ways, engendered new practices and relationships. For despite laws against it, Indians interacted incessantly with Spaniards in colonial towns, mining camps, and rural estates. Sometimes natives would fulfill a labor shift at such a location, during which time they would be exposed to European material culture and customs, and then would return to their home community. Other natives, however, remained and became permanent members of Spanish colonial society, as Paul Charney shows in Chapter 6. Nor did Spaniards and, later, the persons of mixed blood (mestizos) who resulted from the matings between Spaniards and Indians, stay out of Indian communities. Few of these individuals chose to live in such communities in the colonial period (though later a scattering would reside interspersed in Indian villages with regularity), but they passed through as peddlers, labor recruiters, and the like.

Early in the colonial period, Indian communities were expected to supply a portion of their adult male populations—generally around one sixth—on a rotating basis to work in the Spanish sector of the economy. Such labor gangs were organized by the villages' headmen (caciques), and they remained under the immediate supervision of their own leaders during their period of labor. But the fruit of the natives' efforts, of course, directly assisted the Spanish sector of the society. With time, as the colonial economies became more elaborate, this form of temporary unskilled labor became less useful, and, characteristically, it endured only in the more backward parts of Latin America. Instead, Spanish entrepreneurs attracted particularly skilled and industrious Indians as permanent workers in their enterprises by offering them improved terms of employment. Many natives accepted such offers because of the considerable deterioration that had taken place in their own communities from population decline and Spanish demands for labor service and tribute payments. Working for individual Spaniards provided them with a degree of security and protection from the worst of these demands. Over the long term, then, a considerable number of Indians came to reside permanently in Spanish colonial society, and their children were born to this, rather than to the traditional village way of life. As the Indians interbred with Spaniards and blacks in the cities and on rural estates, a large community of persons of mixed blood emerged with whom urban Indians interacted on a regular basis.

The eighteenth century was a time of considerable economic growth in Latin America. Previously peripheral regions were incorporated into the world market economy for the first time and prospered as a result. In already heavily settled and economically developed regions, such as Mexico and Peru, market-oriented estates proliferated throughout the countryside, occupying virtually all of the land suitable for cultivation and grazing. Indian communities were increasingly restricted to just the lands they traditionally controlled—lands that the colonial governments had recognized as theirs and now helped to protect. Both Indian communities and their individual members now enjoyed little opportunity to expand their land holdings.

This situation might not have been harmful except for the sizable growth in the indigenous population that took place during the same era. Whereas the native population in the Americas would never again approach what it had been upon the arrival of the Europeans, it did increase rapidly as the natives built up resistance to the several epidemic diseases that periodically had ravaged their population over the previous two centuries. For example, indications are that Mexico's native population roughly doubled, to a total of about 3.7 million over the hundred years before 1810. But the Spanish and mixed-blood populations were growing as well and at nearly comparable rates at this time. Heightened competition for the limited resources in these societies resulted.

As Indian communities experienced little improvement in productivity, they had to send out their members, either temporarily or permanently, to be laborers in the Spanish sector of the economy. Some natives thus lost their connections with their communities of birth and became permanent dwellers in cities or on rural estates. Others returned to their villages, using their external earnings to help their communities survive economically. (This pattern has endured to the present day, and one may inquire whether modern Indian communities could survive without the continuing outmigration of their young combined with an influx of part of the money that is earned.)

As demonstrated by William Taylor (Chapter 7), village uprisings increased greatly in frequency in both Mexico and Peru during this period. However, these uprisings typically addressed local grievances and therefore rarely developed into regional or crossethnic revolts against the government. Nonetheless, in 1780, an Andean cacique named José Gabriel de Condorcanqui, who himself lived and operated regularly within the Spanish sector of the society, initiated a revolt that was joined by great numbers of people in the highlands. He gave himself the name Tupac Amaru II, claiming descent from the last autonomous Inca ruler, Tupac Amaru, who was executed in 1572. His movement dominated the highlands around Cuzco for some months, even attracting active support from people of mixed blood and from lower-class Spaniards, until a military expedition dispatched from Lima defeated the insurgents. Tupac Amaru, his wife (a Spaniard who functioned as one of his primary lieutenants), and other commanders were captured and executed. But the Andean highlands remained in an unsettled state for another half century, with periodic regional revolts breaking out throughout Peru and Bolivia.

Members of Indian communities had surprisingly little involvement in the Latin American independence movements from 1808 to 1825. By and large, the leaders of these movements belonged to local elites, and their complaints simply did not address the place of native peoples in their societies, except for arguing that equality before the law should prevail in the new nations and that ethnic designations should be eliminated. Furthermore, neither the patriots nor the royalists saw a need to mobilize the Indian masses in their warfare against each other.

Although the vast number of Indians who lived in traditional villages under the authority of their ethnic leaders stayed out of the independence struggle (if anything, they seem to have favored the status quo), in Mexico that substantial minority of Indians who had left their communities to live permanently in the Spanish sector of the society strongly backed the initial uprising against the colonial order. This uprising was led by Father Miguel Hidalgo and began in the prosperous agricultural and mining region north of Mexico City. Tens of thousands of lower-class Spaniards, people of mixed blood, and acculturated Indians joined Hidalgo's army as it captured important regional centers and advanced on Mexico City. To the extent that we can determine the intentions of those Indians who participated, it seems that they resented the discrimination they endured under the prevailing social and political order as well as the requirement that they continue to pay tribute to the government even though most of them had long abandoned their association with native communities. When Hidalgo's army was crushed in a battle that took place about six months after the start of the insurrection, most of the priest's supporters tried to resume their civilian lives, but a substantial minority organized themselves into small regional gangs—often not very different from bandits—and remained active for years.

The new national governments, usually dominated by liberals, thought that Indians should lose both the special protections afforded them and the obligations placed upon them during the colonial period and become full and equal citizens. They also believed that Indian lands should no longer be held in common but instead should be distributed to individual members of the communities who then would either work their private plots or sell them, as they saw fit. But these early governments were so weak and politically unstable that none could organize an effective campaign to achieve these ends. They were desperate for revenue, and some nations therefore retained the Indian tribute system for several decades after independence, renaming the impost an "indigenous contribution" in an effort to distinguish it from its colonial precedent. Residents of many Indian communities in Central America and in the Andean republics were expected to contribute several days of free labor each year to maintain local roads.

Village uprisings occurred in the early national period much as they had in the late colonial one, but now the Indian communities were commonly on the offensive rather than seeking to protect themselves from threatening initiatives. Encountering politically divided elites, failing national economies, and ineffective governments, many Indian communities undertook to take lands away from nearby haciendas. In Mexico, in the late 1840s, several of these movements turned into widespread regional revolts in which the Indians organized into interethnic coalitions and acted jointly to drive all non-Indians (and thus the national government) from their provinces.

The most notable and enduring of these insurrections took place in the Yucatán and was called the "Caste War." Casualties ran into the thousands, and many thousands more fled the region. The non-Indian population had to abandon virtually the entire countryside and cluster in several cities, and the Yucatán's market economy simply collapsed. Within a couple of years, the Mexican government was able to take the offensive against the insurgents, but vast parts of the peninsula remained firmly under rebel control. A belief that a divine cross located in a remote cave spoke to their leaders, directing them to continue the revolt, helped to maintain unity among the insurgents. The rebel commanders demanded heavy labor and military service from their followers but fought among themselves, with assassinations sometimes the result. The insurrection also benefited from the rebels' ability to purchase arms from traders in British Honduras. Finally, in the first years of the twentieth century, the development of henequen plantations in the Yucatán, the fortification of the boundary with British Honduras, and the continuous deteriorating conditions in "Chan Santa Cruz," the territory controlled by the rebels, killed off the organized vestiges of the uprising. Until after World War II, however, extensive parts of the Yucatán backcountry remained in the hands of indigenous villages, which were still autonomous and sought to rekindle the revolt.

Some governments in heavily Indian countries did seek to protect their native populations in the mid-nineteenth century. Perhaps the greatest success was in Guatemala, where for more than twenty-five years starting in 1838, the Conservative dictator Rafael Carrera insulated the communal holdings of native villages from Liberal demands that the collectives be broken up into small individual holdings. Carrera's government also enacted an "Indian Code" so that natives did not fall under the jurisdiction of the national legal system. Although Carrera promoted the use of indigenous languages, he still argued, nonetheless, that native peoples should eventually assimilate themselves into the larger Guatemalan nation and culture and that this should be a benign and gradual process.

The half century after about 1870 was perhaps the worst period since the initial conquest era for the Indian peoples of Latin America. Stimulated by a vastly heightened demand in the industrialized world for the commodities and minerals that they held in such abundance as well as by a tremendous influx of foreign capital and by the rapid development of railroad and utility systems and port facilities, Latin American countries installed governments oriented toward capitalist development and friendly to the large-scale projects attractive to individual investors. In Chapter 8, David McGreery enumerates the effects of the emerging coffee-plantation economy on the native communities of Guatemala. An atmosphere of disdain toward native peoples and their cultures proliferated throughout the hemisphere. Newly created national armies moved aggressively against those indigenous societies that sought to protect their lands and their traditional political autonomy. Evelyn Hu-DeHart (Chapter 9) recounts a central episode from one of the most enduring resistance movements, that of the Yaquis of northwestern Mexico. This unrelenting attack on native resources, culture, and autonomy continued in most countries well into the twentieth century.

The Mexican Revolution, which took place between 1910 and 1920, marks the first distinct break in this onslaught. The struggle to regain communally owned lands that had been alienated from indigenous villages over the previous half century played a major role within this movement. By the end of the violent stage of the revolution, its leaders had committed themselves to restoring these lands. In the early 1920s, vast amounts of land in central Mexico and in the Yucatán were returned to the native communities that had lost them. Establishing collectives became a central part of the revolutionary program, and their number and extent expanded in each decade through the 1970s.

Land reform was not, however, without its opponents and drawbacks. Both the Indian and non-Indian populations of Mexico had increased rapidly after the revolution to the extent that the number of landless rural dwellers continued to grow in absolute terms while a vast amount of land was being distributed to millions of people. The recipients of this land often did not produce surpluses sufficient to feed Mexico's massive urban population or to be sold abroad for badly needed foreign earnings. Nor was the government's protection of native lands totally successful. Local businesspeople, often with official connections, circumvented regulations in order to gain control of communal lands or became favored suppliers and marketers to the native communities.

Beginning in the late 1930s, the Mexican government has sought to protect the diverse Indian languages and cultures of the country. Traditional caciques and village councils have had some of their authority restored. Teachers now often endeavor to provide native children with a bilingual education rather than to eradicate indigenous languages. Powerful government institutes work to preserve Indian cultures and to develop handicraft practices that may earn the natives money in the larger national economy.

Conditions for the native peoples in much of Latin America outside Mexico stayed worse for a longer time. In countries such as Guatemala and Peru, Indian villages were required by statute to provide laborers for public works projects or large agricultural enterprises. Such laws generally were not changed until the World War II period. Even in recent times, native peoples are under duress—often with the compliance of government agencies or armed forces—to labor on plantations far from their homes. They typically are paid very low wages and may in fact owe money by the time that their obligation is over; these debts may be used to compel workers to return the following year. Wives and children often accompany the men during these periods. They live in squalid temporary housing where they are susceptible to dangerous diseases, and sometimes they too have to labor in the fields.

The native peoples of Bolivia, largely Aymara speaking, lost most of their lands early in the twentieth century to Hispanic Bolivians who used their privileged position in the economy and in the political system to their advantage. Most of these Aymara then became retainers on the large—and typically unproductive—estates that resulted. As Erick Langer demonstrates in Chapter 10, the indigenous populations were not passive before these offensives against them. In their resistance, they revealed their retention of ancient native rituals and beliefs and also their sensitivity to the expectations and procedures of the national Bolivian society in which they lived.

In 1952, appreciating the opportunity afforded them by a reformist coalition's overthrow of the government, Indian communities throughout Bolivia rose up, expelled estate owners, and reclaimed their traditional lands. Given the total collapse of the Bolivian military and government structures, the amount of violence involved was rather limited. The nascent reform government, recognizing the benefits to be gained from supporting the land seizures, passed a law the following year officially validating the land redistribution. Since that time, although Bolivia remains one of the most impoverished countries in Latin America, most rural villages have experienced an improvement in quality of life. The villagers have been able to grow crops for urban markets, retain authority over their internal affairs, and benefit from the extension of education and public health services into their communities. They also are connected to the larger political system and to developments at the national level to an unprecedented extent.

Despite some concerted efforts at improvement over the last twenty-five years, conditions for the Indian peoples of Peru continue to be worse than perhaps they are in any other nation of Latin America. Until the late 1960s, the Indians' land and labor situation closely resembled that of the Bolivian native communities before the 1952 land reform. But even more than the Indians of Bolivia, the Indians of Peru were seen as belonging to an inferior culture apart from mainstream life; this attitude and Indian isolation were reinforced because the majority of Indians dwelled in the Andean highlands, whereas the Spanish, internationally oriented sector of Peruvian society predominated in the coastal regions. By the early 1960s, Indian communities and Indian workers on the backward estates that dominated the highlands had begun to protest and sometimes to revolt. The military who repressed these movements became sensitized to the plight of these people and to the primitiveness prevalent in this vast region of the country.

The opportunity for systematic change appeared in 1968, when a reformist military regime seized power in Peru. The following year it implemented a large-scale agrarian reform that affected the majority of estates in both the highland and coastal zones. Many permanent workers became members of the collectives that took over these lands. However, the cultural and economic isolation of these regions was not broken. By the mid-1970s, when the country entered a deep and persistent recession, the utility and appropriateness of these collectives were called into question.

In the early 1980s a radical and ruthless terrorist movement, the Shining Path, began to attack exposed highland communities. By the end of the decade they effectively controlled extensive regions and even could attack in cities along the coast. Cocaine production had begun to expand dramatically in this otherwise depressed economic climate, and many communities could survive only by growing coca leaf for the international drug trade.

As this introduction and the readings that follow make clear, most native peoples of Latin America had continued contact with the Spanish sectors of their societies and in response made significant modifications in their cultures—often voluntarily, but sometimes forcibly. In fact, over time, though sometimes haltingly, the Spanish (or Western, if you will) sphere of Latin American society has tended to expand, and the portion of the economy and society that has remained Indian has shrunk. Thus the Indian population residing within modern national societies (which excludes only that small percentage of the overall Indian population that still lives along or beyond the frontiers of effective settlement by Latin Americans of European descent, such as the peoples of the upper Amazon) is very much a part of the larger culture—journeying routinely from their communities into provincial cities and economic enterprises and bringing new technology and practices back to their communities.

Nevertheless, as Alan Sandstrom illustrates in Chapter 11, these residents of rural villages remain distinctively Indian in culture through speaking unique languages and maintaining long-established belief systems and customs that distinguish them from practitioners of the larger national culture. However, those members who pass permanently into cities often have difficulty in retaining their native identity over the long term. The process of becoming a mestizo is as much cultural as it is racial. Unfortunately, many indigenous communities are so poor that they must send many of their youth to find work in the larger society. Sometimes these emigrants are expected to return part of their earnings to their home villages to help support those who remain.

Thus many Indian communities in modern Latin America find themselves caught in a dilemma. If they continue their traditional agricultural, landholding, and marriage practices, their internal economies will stagnate, and they will have to export many of their young people or relegate them to increasing poverty. If they encourage even greater integration into the national market economies, however, over time their populations are likely to lose their ethnic uniformity and their societies their cultural integrity. Either choice is unpleasant, but in the modern world the need to make such a choice may be unavoidable.

1

The Inca Empire and
Its Subject Peoples

Thomas C. Patterson

This selection depicts important aspects of life among the most advanced sedentary agricultural peoples of the Andes on the eve of the arrival of the Spaniards. The ayllu (kin-based community) served as the fundamental unit of social and labor mobilization. Ethnic identity and loyalty remained central, and ethnic lords were the primary mediators between their own groups and the outside world. To most Andean peoples, the Incas were alien invaders who exploited their local resources. Inca efforts to create a dominant state apparatus to manipulate and, in some cases, to relocate conquered ethnic groups were resisted. The Incas sought to reformulate local myths and traditions to make them more compatible with their imperial rule. Many of the subjugated groups would view the Spaniards initially as potential allies against this resented imperial power.

Land and human labor power were the two main sources of wealth in the central Andes, both before and after the Inca conquest. In many areas, agricultural land was owned by kin-based communities, even though it was held by individual households. While there was continuity in family holdings, there were also periodic reallotments of agricultural land to bring its distribution into accord with the changing needs of the various constituent households. Llama and alpaca herds were also owned, controlled, shared, or contested with other, similar groups. The animals were sheared for their wool, sacrificed, and occasionally eaten; llamas, the larger of the two camelid species, also served as beasts of burden.[1]

Labor-intensive tasks—like agriculture, house building, or the construction and repair of irrigation systems—were carried out by the community as a whole. The beneficiaries of these efforts were "expected to furnish the seeds or cuttings, to feed the workers and to provide them with maize beer."[2] There were technical divisions of labor that reflected age and gender differences: for example, teenagers typically watched over herds pastured in the puna, the high alpine grasslands; men plowed; and women planted seeds, spun thread, and made beer.[3] There was also some degree of craft specialization, as certain households or ayllus (kindreds) were renowned as silversmiths, potters, or dancers.[4] In many instances, they seem to have practiced their particular skills on a part-time or seasonal basis—after planting or harvesting, before the rainy season in the case of the potters, or when dancers were required for ceremonies or other special occasions. Their artisan activities were grafted onto food production; the goods they produced or the services they performed benefited the entire community.

While traditional land-tenure practices undoubtedly continued after local communities were encapsulated and incorporated into the imperial state, the Incas immediately imposed liens on the various sources of their wealth. The state expropriated portions of the producers' agricultural fields, pastures, unworked lands, and herds belonging to the communities. These were set aside for the benefit of the state, the imperial sun cult, and the royal corporations.[5]

The Incas also appropriated labor power from the conquered communities. Their demands took several distinct forms, each of which had its own implications for the encapsulated groups. First, the community members were required to cultivate the fields and tend the herds expropriated by the state for itself and the imperial cult. They planted, cared for, and harvested these fields before they worked on their own lands. The produce from these fields and the wool from these herds were destined for separate storehouses in the provincial capital.[6]

Second, the state also demanded other forms of labor service, collectively called the *mit'a* obligation. The needs of the state were both varied and extensive: building and repairing roads, maintaining rest stops, serving in the army, mining, and guarding fields are only a few of the tasks mentioned. Each year, the state requested labor time at one of its monthly feasts. After being feted and honored, the *kurakas*, the local chieftains, returned to their communities, laden with gifts and tasks to perform. The immediate goal of the chieftains, once they arrived in their villages, was to persuade, cajole, or beg the members of the community for their assistance. Once they consented, the lord assigned the chores equitably across the communities to ensure that enough members in each group remained at home to tend its fields and flocks. When their labor obligation was completed, the workers returned to their homes. When the next call for *mit'a* labor was issued by the state, they were exempt; they were replaced by another group of workers, since the burden shifted or rotated each year through the community. Since some communities were composed of artisans such as silverworkers, the state undoubtedly drew repeatedly on their labor resources to perform certain specialized tasks.[7]

The third category consisted of colonists, *mitaq* or *mitimae*, who were resettled with their families and leaders in provinces that were scarcely populated, recently incorporated into the empire, or whose inhabitants had rebelled against the state. The colonists were under the authority of the provincial officials in the new location. They were required to retain their own garb and customs; to provide the implements, seeds, and other goods they needed for their livelihood; and to defend frontiers and pacify rebel areas. The resettlement policies of the state were extensive. In some provinces, the colonists apparently outnumbered the original inhabitants, many of whom had been resettled among peoples whose loyalty to the state was not suspect.[8] The lands settled by the *mitimae* and the fields they planted had been confiscated by the state from peoples who either resisted its attempts to impose its will or rebelled against its domination.[9] They were detached from their kin and separated from their traditional means of production. Their capacity to produce a livelihood in their new homes was intimately linked with the continued generosity and intervention of the imperial state.

Finally, the state permanently removed certain categories of individuals from their natal communities, thereby depriving the groups of their productive and reproductive capacities. These were the *aclla*, chosen women, and *yana*, retainers. The former were the prepubescent girls selected each year by state officials, who were sequestered in the provincial capitals.[10] The latter, described by one chronicler as rebels left out of the census who were spared from death by the queen, worked on royal estates, in the households of local chieftains, and in the shrines of the state cult and other important *wak'as*. They apparently served the rulers, their wives, and families in various capacities that even included chieftainships in Chachapoyas and Collique.[11] The practice of removing *aclla* and *yana* from their communities gave the state a measure of control over the demographic and social reproduction of their natal communities. The autonomy of the communities and their ability to control their own destinies were diminished as their fortunes became inextricably intertwined with those of the state.

The thrust of Inca imperial expansion was to drain the encapsulated communities and polities of their means of production and to obscure the fact that the social relations of production and reproduction were being dramatically transformed in the process. While the Inca state attempted to intervene in the everyday lives of their members to ensure compliance with its demands, its capacity to do so effectively and successfully was hampered in significant ways by the virtual impossibility of rapid communication over the long distances separating the imperial capital from the provincial centers. This capacity was also limited by the political structures the state put together in the provincial areas. Although the governors were close allies and kinsmen of the ruler and members of the dominant class, layers of provincial administration immediately below them built on the existing local social and political hierarchies, incorporating them into the decimal organization of the state.

The position of the local chieftains, the *kurakas*, in these rapidly erected administrative and social structures was fraught with conflict. On the one hand, there were opportunities for both the chieftains and the communities they represented to benefit materially by supporting the Inca state. On the other hand, the *kurakas* simultaneously represented the interests of their subjects and served as provincial representatives of the state, conveying its requests for labor service to their subjects. Their ability to meet the demands of the state were only as good as their ability to persuade their subjects to provide labor service. To be persuasive, they had to be generous and hospitable. Their requests could not exceed those customarily expected by their subjects and kin. Chieftains whose demands were unreasonable or excessive risked being deposed or murdered by their subjects.[12] Ultimately, the state's claims were backed up by the threat of judicial or military force. The failure of a *kuraka* to respond to the state's request for labor service was a serious matter. It was the first step toward open rebellion, and he could lose his position or even his life.[13]

The state sought to retain the loyalty of the *kurakas* and to influence their actions in various ways. It held one lord hostage under the pretext that he fomented a rebellion; he was ultimately replaced by his son, who was loyal to the Incas.[14] The Inca ruler married the daughters of local chieftains incorporated into the state apparatus of the empire, and accepted these secondary wives into his household.[15] The sons of local chieftains and rulers, especially those responsible for large numbers of people, were taken to Cuzco, where they learned Quechua, Inca traditions, and the behavior expected from a loyal official of the state and a member of the emerging dominant class.[16] High-ranking *kurakas* were forced to maintain a residence in the imperial capital and live there four months each year; this also involved resettling retainers or subjects to act as servants.[17] The Incas brought provincial *wak'as* to Cuzco for long stays.[18] The presence of the provincial *wak'as* and the sons and heirs of the ethnic lords in Cuzco "made both past and future leaders of their communities hostages to the good behavior of their people, despite the honors with which both *wak'as* and young people were loaded."[19] Gifts of land and servants from the state also ensured the continued loyalty of *kurakas*, shrines, and communities that promoted its well-being.[20]

The Inca state demanded obedience from its subjects and employed various institutions and practices to ensure that it received their compliance and submission: the army, loyal *mitima* colonists, and a group of inspectors or overseers called *tokoyrikoq*, a term that can be translated as "those who see all."[21] They were sent to the provinces to check local conditions, to ensure that tax obligations were being met, and to determine that rebellions were not being fomented by dissatisfied chieftains or provincial governors. The *tokoyrikoq* were "faithful men whom the Inca could trust"; they may have been members of a royal corporation or personal retainers of the emperor, possibly even *yana* raised in the royal household.[22]

The legal code of the state was repressive, especially toward the lower classes—the members of encapsulated communities. Acquiescence rather than agreement was the desired goal. It attempted to achieve compliance through intimidation and the fear of retaliation for crimes against the state and its ruling class. The penalties were severe. For instance, the penalty for failing to perform work satisfactorily, lying to a census taker, moving the boundary markers delimiting state fields, traveling without permission, or not wearing clothing that allowed officials to identify an individual's natal community involved corporal punishment; the guilty were beaten with a stone or flogged. Individuals who failed to meet their labor obligations to the state not only were tortured for the first offense but also had their labor assessments increased; those who committed this offense a second time were threatened with execution. Foot-dragging, misrepresentation, deception, false compliance, evasion, desertion, traveling without permission, pilfering, and sabotage—which James Scott has called the "weapons of the weak"[23]—were also punishable crimes under the imperial legal code. Death was the penalty for those who stole from the state, the imperial cult, or the fields of the Incas as well as for those who spoke against the Inca, had intercourse with the *aclla*, or committed treason. Rebellious communities were deprived of their lands and herds, and their leaders were taken to Cuzco where they were publicly humiliated by the emperor himself before they were tortured, skinned, and executed. The emperor then had drinking mugs made from their skulls and drumheads from their skin.[24]

The state also used more subtle methods to gain the acquiescence of subjects. It attempted to recast the myths and practices of the encapsulated communities, which prescribed proper behavior, perpetuated socially acceptable explanations of everyday life, and maintained cohesion by asserting the power of local *wak'as* and ancestors. These attempts extended the traditional networks of mutual rights and obligations to include new groups. However, the mechanisms for transmitting this new ideology were

weak, because its interpretation remained in the hands of traditional intellectuals, the spokespersons of local shrines, rather than in the hands of
state functionaries or members of the emerging dominant class. The priests
who preserved and transmitted the traditional lore of their communities
and interpreted the local *wak'as* belonged to the groups that maintained
and served those shrines and that provided labor service to the state.[25]
The relation of these traditional intellectuals to the state and the emerging dominant class of the empire varied. Some, like the caretakers and
priests of Pachacamac or Pariacaca, saw their shrines derive significant
benefits from their relations with the state; others saw the traditional lore
of their communities suppressed.[26] Thus, the caretakers and spokespersons of the local *wak'as* were never completely assimilated into or sup-
portive of either the developing class or state structures.

The new ideological forms and practices of the state created new relations of exploitation. They linked together the Incas, the *kurakas* who
had allied themselves with the crown and the state, and state functionaries—groups that benefited materially from the labor service of the peasants and artisans. This was not, however, a homogeneous social category
characterized by tranquil and harmonious social relations; instead, the
relations among the various factions were wracked by competition, conflict, rivalries, and conspiracies. What united them was their exploitation
of the peasants and their dependence on them for labor service. This placed
their interests and those of the state in opposition to the interests of the
peasants. As long as the potential for dispute within the dominant class
was minimized and its demands, along with those of the state, were not
too excessive or abusive, the potential for rebellion could be contained.
When disputes surfaced or demands were excessive, however, the resentment and hostility of the encapsulated communities could erupt into open
dissent or even revolt.

In spite of the state's desire to ensure the loyalty of the *kurakas* as
well as the acquiescence of their subjects, it ultimately failed to create the
kind of society it wanted. While the settings in which the subject peoples
conducted their lives were only partly of their own creation, they were not
totally without some degree of power or control over their own lives. If
the subject communities had acceded to the wishes of the state, then the
inspectors and the terror of the harsh legal code would have been unnec-
essary. That the state found both inspectors and the terror of law necessary indicates how seriously it took threats posed by even petty acts of
insubordination.

Everyday forms of passive resistance, regardless of the motivation of
those who committed these acts of insubordination, require almost no
coordination or planning since they rely on implicit understandings and

informal networks. Passive resistance can also take a variety of forms. Scott has suggested that one way that subjugated classes attempt to penetrate, neutralize, and negate the hegemony of the dominant classes and the state is by using the values and rationale of the earlier social order to press their claims and to disparage those of their opponents.[27] However, they have no monopoly on these techniques, since both states and emerging ruling classes also rework and give new meanings to established institutions and practices to support their new forms of extortion by promoting the illusion of historical continuity. This is why tradition, the past, and heritage are so often contested terrains.

Archaeological evidence from the Ica Valley on the south coast of Peru provides insight into one instance where tradition was decomposed and reconstituted after its inhabitants fell under the sway of the Inca rulers. The local *kurakas* identified with the state and the emerging dominant class and benefited from the association, while their commoner peasant kin created and maintained an oppositional identity rooted in tradition and history. The use of Inca pottery vessels or pottery made locally in the Inca style and to Inca specifications was restricted to the higher levels of the local nobility; this was also true for pottery vessels that combined features of local and Inca styles. These three types of pottery vessels are found exclusively in distinctive structured tombs near Old Ica, the elite residential center of the valley, both before and after it was incorporated into the imperial state. Pottery fragments decorated in these styles are also found scattered on the surface of Old Ica and in nearby refuse deposits. The peasants, however, used only pottery vessels decorated with the traditional local designs rather than ones imitating the Inca style. They also looted tombs for antique pottery vessels of types that were manufactured and used in the valley when it was free of Inca domination; these vessels were used as sources of artistic inspiration, and fragments of them have been found in refuse deposits around the peasant villages and hamlets. They were not only collected and imitated, but used with some regularity during the period of Inca political control. When Inca control collapsed in the mid-1530s, the peasants reasserted the dominance of the local artistic tradition, purging it of all traces of Inca influence. This involved an artistic revival of the old styles—the ones preferred by the peasants, not those adopted by the nobility during the period of foreign domination.[28]

While acts like this may have had only a marginal impact on the state's capacity to extract labor, even such "protests within compliance" or "working the system to minimize disadvantage" issued challenges that were more than merely symbolic.[29] They mitigated or denied the claims of the state and its dominant class. What is ultimately threatening and dangerous about the "weapons of the weak" is that, under the right conditions, they can be transformed into a rallying point for more open defiance of authority or even direct confrontation against it. Such conditions did develop with some regularity in the Inca state, and not all opposition to its policies and practices was passive.

Border wars were a persistent feature of imperial expansion into new territories; rebellions erupted unexpectedly; and civil wars seem to have been an integral part of everyday life, especially after the death of an emperor. Clearly, not all of the communities on the margins of the state or even those already incorporated into it recognized the value of *pax incaica*, acknowledged the superiority of Inca beliefs and norms, viewed imperial demands in the same way as those of their traditional leaders, or were even particularly intimidated by the force the state could muster or the severity of its legal code. The consequence of the border wars and revolts engendered by imperial expansion and conquests, the civil wars produced by disputes over succession to the throne, and the rebellions and uprisings resulting from the desire of subject populations to reassert their autonomy was that the Inca state was engaged almost continuously in armed struggle from its inception in 1438 through the Spanish invasion in 1532 to its collapse in the 1570s.[30] Revolts in the frontier regions and rebellions in the core areas of the state were often sparked by rumors of the emperor's death and the civil disruption caused by the successional disputes that inevitably followed such an event. As a result, the state frequently had to reconquer people who had already been incorporated into the empire.[31]

Border Wars and Imperial Expansion

Through military conquest and negotiated incorporation, the Incas brought different kinds of societies into the imperial state. These included class-stratified kingdoms such as Chimor or the Lupaqa; kin-based communities with unstable or ambiguously defined social hierarchies such as the peoples of Huarochirí; and kin-based communities such as the Pastos, which showed no evidence for any overarching political authority before their encapsulation by the imperial state.[32] The Inca state was clearly more interested in some peoples and areas than others. Rich, well-populated countries were particularly intriguing because of their human and natural resources. It was considerably more cautious with groups like the Chiriguana, who were "poor and warlike."[33] While its policies toward subject peoples may have been uniform in theory, they varied in practice, depending on the economic and political importance of a given region, the circumstances under which it had been incorporated into the realm, and its existing organization at the time of incorporation.[34]

The Incas frequently intervened in frontier areas because local social and political dynamics created changes in existing arrangements, which they viewed as affecting their interests. The initial goal of the state was usually to establish cordial relations with at least one local group in order to gain and secure a foothold in the region.

Imperial expansion created continually shifting frontier areas and border societies. However, there was nothing automatic about the processes of encapsulation and incorporation that occurred on the frontiers of the Inca state. Communities confronted the expanding empire in various ways. Some abandoned their villages and fields, retreating to more remote, inaccessible locations where they reestablished their lives away from the immediate threat posed by the state. Other communities, finding it beneficial or desirable to establish or confirm relations with the Incas, received the imperial envoys, presented them with gifts, and negotiated their incorporation into the empire.[35] Some, like the Kingdom of Chimor, Huarco, or the inhabitants of Chachapoyas, waged war on the imperial armies sent to pacify them and were subdued only after a series of military campaigns spread over a number of years.[36] Others, like the Pastos in northern Ecuador, were more tentative in their response; they exchanged gifts with the state—cane tubes filled with lice for llamas—but continued to maintain close ties with their neighbors and kin who resided outside the frontier and still retained their autonomy and independence.[37]

From the perspective of the communities being encapsulated, the Inca state appeared in different forms at various stages in the process. During the initial stage, gift-bearing strangers—"spies and harbingers," to use [Pedro] Cieza de León's words[38]—began to appear on the frontier and establish contact with them; they came with llamas laden with food and other goods. These entourages of outsiders represented the state and, in some instances during and after the 1470s, represented its allies as well. For example, Topa 'Inka helped the caretakers of Pachacamac, the great oracle on the central coast, establish branch oracles in Mala and Chincha before those regions were incorporated into the state, and merchants from the coastal kingdoms of Chincha were active on the northern frontiers of the empire in the 1520s.[39] Besides their gifts, the strangers brought news about the aims of the Inca state. Some stayed to trade, talk further with the local people, and establish more intimate contact with their representatives or with the individuals who put themselves forward as important and influential personages; others from the entourage eventually left with information about local conditions and the prestations they had received for their gifts.

While the local peoples exchanged gifts and food with the outsiders, they retained firm control over their means of production, their labor power, and the goods they produced. But interpersonal relations were not quite the same as they had been earlier. In some instances, political authority came to reside more firmly in the hands of privileged members, chieftains, or self-proclaimed powerful individuals, who were able to gain increased control over the movement of goods created outside the subsistence sector through raiding and trade or through their enhanced ability to create and cement alliances with other peoples. Sometimes this consolidation of authority was accomplished subtly within the terms of the customary rights and obligations that prevailed in the community; their ability to make alliances and their control over exchange rested on their legitimacy, the authority they possessed in the eyes of their kin and subjects. In other instances, individuals who had gained prominence and followings through activities that were disconnected from customary practices of the community were able to propel themselves into positions of influence with the foreigners. Their capacity to make arrangements rested on both their relations with the foreigners and their ability to retain the loyalty of their followers in a milieu where some of the old constraints on action had been removed and new avenues for mobility were being paved.[40]

Soon, more strangers arrived. Some were refugees fleeing from the imperial army and the threat of Inca domination; others were deserters from the army, who were unable to return to their natal communities because of the death sentences that hung over their heads. Still another group of outsiders came from the region itself; they were transient merchants, the *mindaláes* or "those with the tattooed faces" in northern Ecuador, who brought food, raw materials, and finished goods from the region and beyond to trade with the local peoples, the new arrivals, and the remaining members of the imperial entourage.[41] The traders' presence benefited the local chieftains and persons of influence as well as the imperial state. In some instances, local leaders or individuals of renown were able to gain or consolidate control over the distribution of goods in circumstances where the local social structures and relations were slowly being distorted, deformed, and modified by the growing interference of the state. The presence of the *mindalá* traders also permitted the imperial state to acquire goods from people who were not under its direct control, and to spread its ideology and language to the independent communities beyond the frontier.

After a while, more strangers arrived from the empire. This time, its envoys came at the head of a column of soldiers, and a moment of decision had arrived for the inhabitants of the region. Should they accept the offers of the gift-bearing strangers and all that implied? Should they resist the invaders and fight them from *purcaras*, the hilltop fortresses and strongholds that had been prepared earlier? Or should they attempt to avoid the threat altogether by retreating to remote, relatively inaccessible areas or by fleeing across the frontier to lands and peoples whose lives were still unaffected by imperial control?

If they chose to resist, as the Huarco of coastal Peru did, then the state established garrisons, provisioned from the nearest provincial capital, to pacify the region.[42] Once resistance was crushed or the inhabitants acquiesced, acknowledging the balance of forces that prevailed, governors and *mitimae* colonists moved in and settled on lands expropriated from the indigenous peoples by the state. At first, the officials and colonists were also sustained by provisions from the provincial capital, but after the first harvests, they began to establish their self-sufficiency. They often fortified their settlements to ensure their own safety, and they brought whole hamlets and isolated homesteads down from the mountains and resettled their inhabitants in villages where they could be watched more easily.[43] The state did not want to deal with a potential enemy in relatively unknown terrain, where it would be almost impossible to prevent or defend against ambushes, hit-and-run attacks, or the destruction of isolated farmsteads initiated by rebel bands living in remote fortresses.

Pacification and incorporation into the imperial state meant that the local communities had to provide labor. Their members had to cultivate the fields expropriated by the empire and the imperial cult; and, during their *mit'a* obligation, they had to manufacture finished goods, according to imperial specifications, from raw material provided by the state.[44] The authority of the local leaders or persons of influence no longer rested solely on their abilities to distribute goods acquired from the *mindalá* traders, but rather on their connections with the imperial state and their abilities to provide the labor power required to produce the goods and services it demanded. Incorporation into the state diminished the autonomy of the local communities and their leaders, the importance of their contacts with other communities, and the role of local traders as the middlemen of frontier trade. Inca domination would be complete when the encapsulated communities became easily recognized, self-sufficient dependencies of the imperial state. The autonomy of these communities was even further diminished as they began to participate in state-sponsored institutions and practices, like the rituals associated with agricultural production or the *aclla*, which linked their reproduction with that of the empire.

At the same time, the connections between the frontier merchants and the communities and chieftains they once served were severed as the

Inca state restructured the traditional economies and became the main source of goods produced by distant peoples. The fate of the merchants now depended on their rather tenuous linkages with and dependency on the state in the borderlands and on their ability to forge new connections with other communities on the margins of or beyond the imperial boundaries.

Unrest or rebellions in the borderlands usually broke out when the state suffered setbacks in its domestic or foreign policies or when it attempted to impose new forms of surplus extraction. For instance, after Huarco successfully resisted Inca efforts to incorporate it into the imperial state in the late 1470s, other groups rebelled. The state was forced not only to continue its struggle with Huarco, which ultimately lasted three years, but also to suppress the unrest or revolts that appeared among other peoples. The state reproached these groups for the resistance they displayed and urged them to remain loyal friends or else they would be visited by a cruel war. At the same time, it enlarged the garrison located in the foothills on the edge of Huarco.[45]

The best-known rebellion was the one that occurred in northern Ecuador during Wayna Qhapaq's reign. While the imperial armies were completing the conquest of Chachapoyas to the south, the peoples on the northern frontier of the state—the Quitos, the Pastos, the Carangues, the Cayambia, and the Huancavelicas—revolted, killing the governors, the spies, and the tax collectors who had been left there to oversee their activities. The revolt probably began around 1510. It is not clear whether the revolt was precipitated by unrest in other parts of the empire, like Chachapoyas, or whether the state precipitated the uprising by attempting to transform what the native peoples viewed as gift exchange and what the state construed as tribute payments into regular *mit'a* labor obligations.

In either event the rebel tribes built fortresses and awaited the arrival of the imperial army, which included recruits from all quarters of the empire. When it entered the border areas, the army's goal was to conquer the Pastos. As the Incas and their allies approached, the Pastos men retreated. Old people, women, and children, guarded by a few warriors, remained to meet the imperial army. They were easily defeated, and, as the army began to celebrate its easy victory, the soldiers became careless. Guards were not posted as the soldiers drank and partied late into the night. Suddenly, under the cover of darkness, the Pastos warriors counterattacked, and the invading army, composed largely of Colla from the Lake Titicaca Basin, was slaughtered. The survivors escaped and made their way back to the encampments of their allies. Since an easy victory had eluded them, the Inca armies were forced to reenter the Pastos territory for the second time. On this occasion, the soldiers burned their fields and villages and killed rich and poor, men and women, young and old. After the Pastos were finally subdued, the emperor appointed a governor and saw that colonists were settled in the area, before turning his attention to the other groups that had participated in the revolt.[46]

The Inca army encountered stiff resistance when it attacked the other rebel groups, and casualties were heavy on both sides. As the war raged on, the imperial army initiated another scorched-earth policy, destroying the rebels' crops and villages and devastating a large area. Some of the rebels escaped to the fortified strongholds of the Carangues, where they were received as allies. The emperor himself led the army against one of the Carangue fortresses. The battle that ensued was fierce, and, during one of the rebels' counterattacks, the emperor was toppled from his litter and almost killed. He and his kin were humiliated by this turn of events. As the emperor walked back to the encampment, he let his kin and the troops know just how angry he was at the disrespect and lack of support he had received. This marked the beginning of a mutiny and a series of battles that would be waged over a period of several years.

Shortly after their defeat at the hands of the Carangues, several of the Inca nobles planned a mutiny. Their complaints were that the emperor was contemptuous of them, that he failed to provide them with adequate provisions, and that they were suffering from exposure. The mutineers, together with the troops they led, resolved to travel to Tumipampa, the provincial capital in southern Ecuador (Wayna Qhapaq's birthplace), to seize the *wak'as* that watched over and ensured the good fortunes of the army. When they arrived at the shrine, the emperor demanded to know their intentions. They told the emperor that they were going to take the *wak'as* back to Cuzco; this would restore its dignity as well as their own. Wayna Qhapaq then called upon the priests and priestesses of the state cult to intervene and take back the *wak'as* they had already appropriated. Ultimately, the emperor and his mutinous kin talked and resolved their differences. That night, the emperor sponsored an elaborate series of parties that lasted many days, in which loot, gifts, and *aclla* women were given to the soldiers.

Once the old army was placated and reinforced by new recruits, it undertook another assault on the Carangue fortresses. Once again, the soldiers carried out a scorched-earth policy, and eventually they torched the fortresses themselves, killing or capturing everyone who was inside. Some of the Carangues escaped and fled toward a lake where they attempted to hide in the reeds from the army pursuing them. A massacre ensued as the soldiers murdered thousands of men and adolescent boys.[47] Only a few successfully eluded the invading army.

One of the survivors was a Carangue named Pinto who escaped into the rugged, forest-covered mountains to the east. Here he met bands of roving Cañari rebels and exiles who had not been pacified earlier by Wayna Qhapaq and who had successfully resisted incorporation into the empire. While the Inca state was establishing garrisons and colonists in the area it had just conquered, Pinto and the Cañari rebels who had joined him were fomenting discontent for the state along the frontier. Given the decade-long revolt that was just coming to an end, the state was clearly not concerned at this point in time with bandits or groups plundering the countryside, but it focused on the real possibility that the rebels might make alliances with restless elements in the borderlands. Troops were dispatched to locate the rebel band and to eliminate the threat it posed. The army eventually found the rebel strongholds and starved them into submission. Wayna Qhapaq offered Pinto gifts if he would recognize and submit to Inca rule; the rebel leader refused and was executed.[48]

The Inca state's relation with the Chiriguana, who inhabited the mountain slopes east of Sucre, Bolivia, may help to explain this concern over the threat posed by Pinto and the renegade Cañaris.[49] The Inca army first invaded the lands of the Chiriguana during the reign of Topa 'Inka; it broke off the invasion of the country because of a lack of provisions and stiff resistance, what chroniclers described as "the savagery of its inhabitants."[50] After fortresses were built and garrisons were established along the frontier to protect its gains, the state turned its attention to potentially more productive expeditions and conquests in other regions. The Chiriguana once again attracted the attention of the Inca state in the early 1520s, while it was suppressing the frontier revolt in northern Ecuador and after it had expropriated extensive agricultural fields in the Cochabamba Valley, roughly one hundred twenty miles northwest of Sucre.[51] Wayna Qhapaq repaired the forts built during his father's reign and used Chiriguana troops in his campaigns against the Carangues.[52] Philip Means concluded from this that, while some Chiriguana seem to have been subject to the *mit'a* labor obligations of the state, a larger number, who resided outside the frontier, began to raid and plunder the Charcas borderlands east of Sucre.[53]

It is possible to discern two broad, loosely organized confederations on the eastern edge of the empire adjacent to Charcas. One consisted of the Chiriguana and their Guarani-speaking allies, some of whom lived as far away as the Paraguay River, roughly four hundred miles to the east. Their relations with the Inca state varied—depending on the time, the place, and the existing labor force—from sullen acquiescence to open hostility. Their relations with the Chanes and their allies, who were apparently on good terms with the Inca state, were also antagonistic and frequently erupted into raids for plunder and captives. When the Chiriguana raided along the imperial frontier, they took captives, metal utensils, and gold and silver jewelry, which quickly found its way as far east as the Paraguay River. However, groups like the Caracaras or the Candires, who were nominally under Inca control, also exchanged metal objects or precious metals with the lowland people—a practice that was frowned upon by the state, which attempted to control or restrict the distribution of metals.[54] The Chanes and their allies obtained metals through a group called the Payzunos in exchange for bows, arrows, and, by the early 1540s (if not before), slaves.

The Chiriguana resurfaced as a thorn in the side of the empire, especially after the state's military resources had been diverted to deal with the border insurrection in the northern provinces. The construction of the fortresses a generation earlier had indicated to the Chiriguana that the state intended to remain permanently in the borderlands, to secure the frontier, and to bring its inhabitants under the imperial rule. However, the state's policies for dealing with border populations were always narrowly developed: negotiation, intimidation, and the use of force covered the range of available options. When the troops were removed from the southern provinces, the state's capacity for controlling the movement of goods and people across the frontier was diminished. When the Chiriguana began to raid and plunder the borderlands under Inca control, the state could not respond merely by requesting that they desist; to do so would have alienated other frontier peoples, like the Chanes, who apparently had cordial ties with the Incas that counterbalanced their antagonistic relations with the Chiriguana.

The state's attempt to make the Chiriguana an economically self-sufficient, culturally distinctive enclave, like subject populations in the core area of the empire, was unsuccessful. The inhabitants of the state-administered areas continually constructed and reproduced close relations with Guarani-speaking communities in the hinterland, beyond the frontier. This had a number of implications. It meant that different political-economic relations prevailed in the administered and nonadministered sections of the Chiriguana social formation. The state appropriated surplus labor and possibly expropriated land from the inhabitants of the administered areas while their kin, who resided outside the imperial boundaries and retained their independence, had the ability to continue traditional use-rights and customary practices. It suggests that the Chiriguana, residing in the backcountry, probably received some of the goods that were distributed by the state to their kin on the other side of the border. This also meant they could raid communities in one area and exchange their spoils in another.

Class and state formation in frontier areas created contradictions and opportunities not only for the empire, but also for the indigenous peoples of those areas. These new conditions led to the constitution of new alliances, the merging of formerly independent communities into new groups, and even the appearance of border states where none had existed before, as people recognized their shared position in the emerging system of production and examined the implications of such infringements on their traditional use-rights and practices. This does not mean that all frontier communities automatically opposed the state either passively or actively; in a number of them, both the peasants and their leaders benefited materially, though differentially, from their new dependent relationship with the empire. Even though the frontier policies of the Incas were narrow, they succeeded, in many instances, in transforming customary use-rights, in separating traditional leaders from their kin and subjects, in linking the fortunes of subject groups with those of the state, and in recasting old enmities so that communities remained pitted against one another and their neighbors.

Notes

1. John V. Murra, "The Economic Organization of the Inka State," *Research in Economic Anthropology, Supplement 1* (Greenwich, 1980), 29–30, 51.
2. Ibid., 30–31.
3. Ibid., 50; John H. Rowe, "The Age Grades of the Inca Census," *Miscellanea Paul Rivet, octogenario dictata*, XXXI Congreso Internacional de Americanistas (Universidad Nacional Autónoma de México, 1958), tomo II, 512–513.
4. Francisco de Avila, *Dioses y hombres de Huarochirí: narración quechua recogida por Francisco de Avila* [1598?], translated by José María Arguedas (Lima, 1966); Karen W. Spalding, *Huarochirí; An Andean Society under Inca and Spanish Rule* (Stanford, 1984), 86.
5. Murra, "The Economic Organization," 37, 52, 54.
6. Ibid., 54; John H. Rowe, "Inca Culture at the Time of the Spanish Conquest," *Handbook of South American Indians*, edited by Julian H. Steward, vol. 2, *The Andean Civilizations, Bureau of American Ethnology Bulletin* 143 (Washington, 1946), 265–267.
7. John V. Murra, "The *Mit'a* Obligations of Ethnic Groups to the Inka State," *The Inca and Aztec States, 1400–1800: Anthropology and History*, edited by George A. Collier, Renato I. Rosaldo, and John D. Wirth (New York, 1982), 237–262; Rowe, "Inca Culture," 267–269; Spalding, *Huarochirí*, 86.
8. María Rostworowski de Diez Canseco, "Historia del Tawantinsuyu," *Historia Andina 13* (Lima, 1988), 221–224; Rowe, "Inca Culture," 269–270; "Inca Policies and Institutions Relating to the Cultural Unification of the Empire," *The Inca and Aztec States*, 105–107.
9. Murra, "The Economic Organization," 38.
10. Rowe, "Inca Culture," 269; "Inca Policies," 97–105, 107–108; Irene Silverblatt, "Andean Women in Inca Society," *Feminist Studies*, vol. 4, no. 3 (1978),

37–61; *Moon, Sun, and Witches; Gender Ideologies and Class in Inca and Colonial Peru* (Princeton, 1987), 80–108.

11. John V. Murra, "New Data on Retainer and Servile Populations in Tawantinsuyu," *Actas y memorias del XXXVI Congreso Internacional de Americanistas*, Seville, 1964, Instituto "Gonzalo Fernández de Oviedo" (Madrid, 1966), tomo 2, 35–45; Rostworowski de Diez Canseco, "Historia del Tawantinsuyu," 196–197, 224–226; Pedro Sarimiento de Gamboa, *Historia de los Incas* [1572], Biblioteca de Autores Españoles (Madrid, 1960), tomo 135, 256.

12. Patricia J. Netherly, *Local Level Lords on the North Coast of Peru* (Ph.D. dissertation in Anthropology, Cornell University, Ithaca, University Microfilms, Ann Arbor, 1977), 178–183.

13. Sally F. Moore, *Power and Property in Inca Peru* (New York, 1958), 66–72, 81–82; John V. Murra, "Social Structural and Economic Themes in Andean Ethnohistory," *Anthropological Quarterly*, vol. 34, no. 2 (Washington, 1961), 47–59; Spalding, *Huarochirí*, 82–83.

14. Miguel Cabello Valboa, *Miscelánea antártica; una historia del Perú antiguo* [1586], Instituto de Etnología, Facultad de Letras, Universidad Nacional Mayor de San Marcos (Lima, 1951), 330–331.

15. Juan de Betanzos, "Suma y narración de los Incas, señores que fueron de estas provincias del Perú . . . [1551]," *Colección de libros y documentos referentes a la historia del Perú*, edited by Horacio H. Urteaga, 2d ser., tomo 8 (Lima, 1924), 148–153; Pedro Cieza de León, *El señorío de los Incas* [1553] (Lima, 1967), 109, 201; Cabello Valboa, *Miscelánea antártica*, 315.

16. Rowe, "Inca Policies," 95–96.

17. John H. Rowe, "What Kind of Settlement Was Inca Cuzco?," *Ñawpa Pacha* 5 (Berkeley, 1967), 62.

18. Bernabé Cobo, *Historia del nuevo mundo* [1653], vol. 2, Biblioteca de Autores Españoles, tomos 91 and 92, Ediciones Atlas (Madrid, 1956), 109–111; Spalding, *Huarochirí*, 94–95.

19. Spalding, *Huarochirí*, 95.

20. Avila, *Dioses y hombres*, 109–111, 114–119, 131–135; Diego Dávila Brizeño, "Descripción y relación de la provincia de los Yauyos toda, anan Yauyos, y lorin Yauyos . . . [1586]," *Relaciones geográficas de las Indias*, edited by Don Marcos Jímenez de la Espada, Biblioteca de Autores Españoles, tomo 183 (Madrid, 1965), 155–165; Rowe, "Inca Culture," 260–261.

21. Rowe, "Inca Culture," 264.

22. Cieza de León, *El señorío de los Incas*, 42–44; Diego Gonzalez Holguin, *Vocabulario de la lengua general de todo el Peru llamada lengua quechua o del Inca* [1608], Ediciones del Instituto de Historia, Universidad Nacional Mayor de San Marcos (Lima, 1952), 38; Martín de Murúa, *Historia del orígen y genealogía real de los reyes Incas del Perú* [1590], edited by Constantino Bayle, Biblioteca "Missionalia Hispanica," vol. 2, Consejo Superior de Investigaciones Cientificas, Instituto Santo Toribio de Mogrovejo (Madrid, 1946), 206.

23. James C. Scott, *Weapons of the Weak: Everyday Forms of Peasant Resistance* (New Haven and London, 1985), xvi.

24. Cieza de León, *El señorío de los Incas*, 179–182; Cobo, *Historia del nuevo mundo*, 83; Sarimiento de Gamboa, *Historia de los Incas*, 254–256; Moore, *Power and Property*, 165–174.

25. Spalding, *Huarochirí*, 63–66.

26. Cabello Valboa, *Miscelánea antártica*, 319; Thomas C. Patterson, "Pachacamac—An Andean Oracle under Inca Rule," *Recent Studies in Andean Prehistory and Protohistory*, papers from the Second Annual Northeast Conference on Andean Archaeology and Ethnohistory, edited by D. Peter Kvietok and Daniel H. Sandweiss, Latin American Studies Program, Cornell University (Ithaca, 1985), 159–176; "Ideology, Class Formation, and Resistance in the Inca State," *Critique of Anthropology*, vol. 6, no. 1 (Amsterdam, 1986), 75–85.

27. Scott, *Weapons of the Weak*, 336.

28. Dorothy Menzel, "The Inca Occupation of the South Coast of Peru," *Southwestern Journal of Anthropology*, vol. 15, no. 2 (Albuquerque, 1959), 125–142; "Archaism and Revival on the South Coast of Peru," *Man and Culture: Selected Papers of the Fifth International Congress of Anthropological and Ethnological Sciences*, Philadelphia, September 1–9, 1956, edited by Anthony F. C. Wallace (Philadelphia, 1960), 596–600; *Pottery Style and Society in Ancient Peru: Art as a Mirror of History in the Ica Valley, 1350–1570* (Berkeley, Los Angeles, and London, 1976); Patterson, "Ideology, Class Formation, and Resistance," 75–85.

29. Scott, *Weapons of the Weak*.

30. This claim must be tempered to some extent by the fact that warfare probably had a distinctly seasonal character. It follows John Rowe's (1945) chronology of events based on the comparison and correlation of various documentary sources. From 1438 to roughly 1462, the Incas were either at war with the Chancas or allied with them as they conquered northward and ultimately established a garrison at Cajamarca. During the 1460s, the Inca state subordinated southern Ecuador and waged a prolonged war with the Kingdom of Chimor that probably ended about 1470 (Rowe, 1948:40). They subjugated the south coast of Peru in the early 1470s and then waged a three-year struggle with Huarco (Cañete) later in the decade (Menzel, 1959). The great Colla rebellion that erupted in the 1480s took twelve years to suppress (Avila, 1966:131). The civil strife following Topa 'Inka's death around 1493 lasted several years. Wayna Qhapaq's forces did not secure the areas around Quito until about 1500 (Frank Salomon, *Native Lords of Quito in the Age of the Incas: The Political Economy of North Andean Chiefdoms* [Cambridge, England, 1986], 146). This implies that the state's incursions further north occurred during the first quarter of the sixteenth century and were still taking place when the Chiriguana attacked the Bolivian frontier in the mid-1520s and at the time of Wayna Qhapaq's death in 1527 (Philip A. Means, "A Note on the Guarani Invasions of the Inca Empire," *The Geographical Review*, vol. 4, no. 6 [New York, 1917], 482–484; Erland von Nordenskiöld, "The Guarani Invasion of the Inca Empire in the Sixteenth Century: An Historical Indian Migration," *The Geographical Review*, vol. 4, no. 1 [New York, 1917], 103–121; Charles E. Nowell, "Aleixo García and the White King," *The Hispanic American Historical Review*, vol. 26, no. 4 [Durham, 1946], 450–466). The civil war and rebellions that accompanied the successional dispute between Washkar and 'Ataw Wallpa erupted almost immediately thereafter and continued until 1538, when the Spaniards defeated the last of the Inca armies in Bolivia. At that point, Andean resistance to the Spaniards became localized. However, in 1537, a civil war broke out among the Spaniards, which lasted until 1554. The Spaniards subsequently sent a series of military expeditions against Vitcos, the major pocket of Inca resistance, which was finally defeated in 1572.

31. John V. Murra, "La guerre et les rébellions dans l'expansion de l'état Inka," *Annales: Economies, Sociétés, Civilisations*, tome 33, no. 5–6 (Paris, 1978), 930.

32. Thomas C. Patterson, "Tribes, Chiefdoms, and Kingdoms in the Inca Empire," *Power Relations and State Formation*, edited by Thomas C. Patterson and Christine W. Gailey (Washington, 1987), 117–127; Franklin Pease, "The Formation of Tawantinsuyu: Mechanisms of Colonization and Relationship with Ethnic Groups," *The Inca and Aztec States*, 173–198.

33. Cabello Valboa, *Miscelánea antártica*, 383–384.

34. Craig Morris and Donald E. Thompson, *Huánuco Pampa: An Inca City and Its Hinterland* (London and New York, 1985), 24.

35. Cieza de León, *El señorío de los Incas*, 177.

36. Cieza de León, *El señorío de los Incas*, 162–164, 216; Inca Garcilaso de la Vega, *Comentarios reales de los Incas* [1609], vol. 1, Biblioteca de Autores Españoles, tomos 133–135 (Madrid, 1960), 291–303; María Rostworowski de Diez Canseco, "Guarco y Lunahuaná, dos señoríos prehispánicos, costa surcentral del Perú," *Revista del Museo Nacional*, tomo 44 (Lima, 1980), 187–188; John H. Rowe, "The Kingdom of Chimor," *Acta Americana*, tomo 6, no. 1–2 (Mexico, 1948), 26–59.

37. Pedro Cieza de León, *La crónica del Perú* [1553], Biblioteca de Autores Españoles, tomo 26, Ediciones Atlas (Madrid, 1947), 385–386.

38. Cieza de León, *El señorío de los Incas*, 177.

39. Patterson, "Pachacamac," 159–176; María Rostworowski de Diez Canseco, "Mercaderes del valle de Chincha en la época prehispánica: Un documento y unos comentarios," *Revista Española de Antropología Americana*, tomo 5 (Madrid, 1970), 135–177; "Pescadores, artesanos y mercaderes costeños en el Perú prehispanico," *Revista del Museo Nacional*, tomo 41 (Lima, 1975), 311–351; Frank Salomon, "Pochteca and Mindalá: A Comparison of Long-Distance Traders in Ecuador and Mesoamerica," *Journal of the Steward Anthropological Society*, vol. 9, no. 2 (Urbana, 1978), 231–246.

40. Thomas C. Patterson, "La creación de cultura en las formaciones sociales pre-estatales y no-estatales," *Gens: Boletín de la Sociedad Venezolana de Arqueólogos*, vol. 3, no. 1 (Caracas, 1987), 15–25.

41. Patterson, "Tribes, Chiefdoms, and Kingdoms," 121; "Merchant Capital and the Formation of the Inca State," *Dialectical Anthropology*, vol. 12, no. 2 (Dordrecht, 1987), 217–227; Salomon, "Pochteca and Mindalá," 231–246; Salomon, *Native Lords of Quito*.

42. Cieza de León, *El señorío de los Incas*, 194–197; John Hyslop, *Inkawasi, the New Cuzco, Cañete, Lunahuaná, Peru*, British Archaeological Reports, International Series, no. S234 (Oxford, 1985); Rostworowski de Diez Canseco, "Guarco y Lunahuaná," 153–214.

43. Craig Morris, "State Settlements in Tawantinsuyu: A Strategy of Compulsory Urbanism," *Contemporary Archaeology; A Guide to Theory and Contributions*, edited by Mark P. Leone (Carbondale, 1972), 393–401; "The Infrastructure of Inka Control in the Peruvian Central Highlands," *The Inca and Aztec States*, 153–171; Spalding, *Huarochirí*, 99–101.

44. Craig Morris, "Reconstructing Patterns of Non-Agricultural Production in the Inca Economy: Archaeology and Ethnohistory in Institutional Analysis," *The Reconstruction of Complex Societies*, edited by C. Moore (Philadelphia, 1974), 49–60; John R. Rowe, "Standardization of Inca Tapestry Tunics," *The Junius B. Bird Pre-Columbian Textile Conference*, edited by Ann P. Rowe, Elizabeth P. Benson, and Anne-Louise Schaffer, The Textile Museum and Dumbarton Oaks, Trustees for Harvard University (Washington, 1979), 239–264.

45. Cieza de León, *El señorío de los Incas*, 194–197.

46. Cobo, *Historia del nuevo mundo*, 91–93; Sarimiento de Gamboa, *Historia de los Incas*, 261–263.

47. Cieza de León, *La crónica del Perú*, 390.

48. Cabello Valboa, *Miscelánea antártica*, 382–383; Cobo, *Historia del nuevo mundo*, 91–93; Carl O. Sauer, *The Early Spanish Main* (Berkeley and Los Angeles, 1966), 261–263.

49. Brooke Larson, *Colonialism and Agrarian Transformation in Bolivia: Cochabamba, 1550–1900* (Princeton, 1988), 13–50; Means, "A Note on the Guarani Invasions," 483–484; Nordenskiöld, "The Guarani Invasion," 103–121; Nowell, "Aleixo García," 450–466; There are two accounts of the social conditions and relations that existed east of the Inca empire during the first quarter of the sixteenth century. Aleixo García, a Portuguese, was the first European to explore the Paraguay River and cross the Chaco. According to Erland von Nordenskiöld (1917:103–106), who based his account on the earlier work of Rui Díaz de Guzman ("Historia argentina del descubrimiento, población y conquista de las provincias del Río de la Plata" [1612], *Colección de obras y documentos relativos a la historia antigua y moderna de las provincias del Río de la Plata*, edited by Pedro de Angelis [Buenos Aires, 1910], 11–111), García left Santos on the coast of Brazil in the early 1520s to explore the interior. He and his companions, two to four other Portuguese and some friendly coastal Indians, set out overland. They crossed the Paraná River and eventually came to the Paraguay River. They were well received by the Guarani-speaking inhabitants of the villages and persuaded several thousand to accompany them on their explorations to the west. They fought their way across the Gran Chaco, the plain that lies between the river and the Andes Mountains. After many days, they reached the mountains between Mizque and Tomina. They attacked and plundered villages under Inca control and killed everyone they found. When the Charcas counterattacked, they retired to the lowlands, laden with the cloth, utensils, and gold, silver, and copper objects they had stolen. García was killed, but more Indians followed him to the territories where he had been, and settled on the frontier near Tarija.

Alvar Nuñez Cabeza de Vaca (*Comentarios de Alvar Nuñez Cabeza de Vaca, adelantado y governador del Río de la Plata* [1555] [Madrid, 1946], 555–556, 572–573, 579–580, 582–583) provides an overview of the conditions and complex social relations that prevailed east of Charcas in the early 1540s. The Chiriguana were Guarani-speaking peoples who maintained cordial relations with communities that spoke closely related dialects and lived on both sides of the Paraguay River, four hundred miles to the east. They had antagonistic relations with the Caracaras and Candires (groups that were under Inca control or that lived in the borderlands of Charcas), with the Chanes who resided along the imperial frontier to the south, and with the Chimenos, Tarapecocies, and Sacocies— tribes that inhabited areas to the south or east. The Guarani had attacked the villages of the Chanes, Tarapecocies, Sacocies, and Orejones for war captives, metal objects, and other kinds of plunder; some refugees from these raids had banded together and resided in a multiethnic settlement called Puerto de los Reyes on the Paraguay River. The Tarapecocies claimed that a group called the Payzunos who lived to the west gave them precious metals that its members had obtained from the Chanes, Chimenos, Caracaras, and Candires in exchange for bows, arrows, and slaves.

50. Garcilaso de la Vega, *Comentarios reales*, 270; Sarmiento de Gamboa, *Historia de los Incas*, 263.

51. Nathan Wachtel, "The *Mitimaes* of the Cochabamba Valley: The Colonization Policy of Huayna Capac," *The Inca and Aztec States*, 199–235.

52. Garcilaso de la Vega, *Comentarios reales*, 271–273; Fernando Montesinos, *Memorias antiguas historiales y politicas del Perú* [1644], *Colección de libros y documentos referentes a la historia del Perú*, edited by Horacio H. Urteaga, 2d ser., tomo 6, Librería e Imprenta Gil (Lima, 1930), 104–105; Sarmiento de Gamboa, *Historia de los Incas*, 263–264.

53. Means, "A Note on the Guarani Invasions," 482–484.

54. Moore, *Power and Property*, 40, 55–56, 116.

2

Early Spanish-Indian Accommodation in the Andes

Steve J. Stern

The Spanish conquest did not immediately transform social relationships and labor systems for many of the native peoples. Steve J. Stern demonstrates that for nearly a half century after their conquest in the Andes, the Spaniards depended heavily on traditional indigenous labor-delivery systems and on kurakas *(native lords) for their effective operation. In many ways, Spanish demands on the natives closely resembled those that the Incas had made on the peoples of the region of Huamanga.*

Initially, indigenous religious beliefs helped facilitate Spanish control, for the natives saw the lack of disruption in these early years as an indication that their gods looked benignly on the overthrow of the Incas. By the 1560s, however, when population decline and heightened labor demands placed great stress on indigenous communities, the natives responded with a religiously sanctioned revolt, the Taki Onqoy, that demanded restoration of the pre-Hispanic order.

The colonial history of Latin America usually begins with the drama of conquest, and this is, by and large, appropriate. Yet anyone who has read Bernal Díaz del Castillo knows that beneath the broad outline of conquest exploits lies a more subtle history of Indian-white alliances. The assistance of powerful regional kingdoms like Tlaxcala in Mexico, or that of the Huanca people in Peru, proved critical to the Spanish conquest of the Aztec and Inca empires. Such alliances expressed the internal contradictions and discontents that plagued Aztec and Inca rule and the failure of these empires to eradicate the independent military potential of resentful ethnic kingdoms. Yet we also know that mutually beneficial alliances between Spaniards and restive Indian peoples could prove short-lived. Spanish-Tlaxcalan relations soured after a "positive" early phase, and in 1564 the Huancas joined their former Inca enemies in a plot to throw off Spanish rule.[1]

This article explores the early history of Indian-Spanish relations in Huamanga, a highland region in the heartland of the former Inca empire.[2] The story focuses not on a major ethnic kingdom that emerged as a strategic power in its own right, but on the diverse region of Huamanga, which comprised numerous rival ethnic or tribal groups whose desires to secure political autonomy and economic resources frequently pitted them against one another and against the Incas. To understand better how the societies of Huamanga responded to the presence of the Spaniards who founded the city of the same name in 1539–40, we turn briefly to pre-Columbian history and social structure.[3]

Among Huamanga's local peoples, relations of kinship and reciprocity defined boundaries of social identity and economic cooperation. An ethnic group viewed itself as a "family" of ayllu lineages, related to one another by descent from a common ancestor-god. Within such "families," exchanges of labor created bonds of mutual obligation by which households and ayllus gained access to resources and labor assistance. Such cooperation enabled kin units, as coproprietors of the ethnic domain, to work ecologically diverse lands and resources scattered "vertically" in the Andean highland environment. As an economic institution, therefore, reciprocal labor exchange among "relatives" was a fundamental social relationship, governing production and distribution of goods. As an ideology, moreover, reciprocity defined relations between ayllu or ethnic *kurakas* (chiefs) and commoners. For the ethnic "family" as a whole, and for each of its many internal subdivisions, a *kuraka* symbolized the collective identity and interest of "his" people. In exchange for service as a guardian of local norms and interests, *kurakas* at the higher levels of social organization acquired special rights to labor services. A *kuraka* was expected, among other duties, to protect the group's domain against rivals, redistribute and enforce rights to land and other resources, organize work and ritual, and "generously" redistribute accumulated goods in the form of "gifts" from personal and community stores. In exchange, "his" people worked his fields, herded his animals, wove his cloth, and tended to household needs such as water and fuel. The exchange had to appear "balanced" to enjoy legitimacy.

Two consequences of this social and economic organization had important implications for the early colonial period. First, traditions of kinship and reciprocity imposed constraints on native "leadership." Only by building and maintaining a long-term exchange of mutual obligations, expectations, and loyalties did a *kuraka* acquire the prestige or "influence" that made ayllus or households responsive to his formal "request" for labor services. *Kurakas* who failed to fulfill the expectations of kin, or who consistently violated local norms, risked an erosion of prestige that undermined their authority. Second, the local mode of production tended to divide producers into competing, self-sufficient groups. The division of provincial society into autarkic, ethnically distinct networks of producer-relatives whose scattered properties often overlapped or were interspersed among the claims of other such networks, fostered fierce conflicts over lands and "strategic" ecological zones (coca fields, for example). Even within the bounds of an ethnic "family," decentralized networks of kinship and reciprocity bred competition between distinct kin groupings for self-sufficiency, prestige, and wealth. The very nature of local social and economic structure, therefore, tended to generate endemic rivalries between kindreds and ethnic groups.

The Incas conquered Huamanga around 1460. Their empire converted communities and ethnic groups into a peasantry whose surplus labors sustained an expansive state, but left intact traditional relations of production that assured local self-sufficiency. Despite the sophistication of Inca statecraft, loyalties remained fragile; local peoples proudly retained oral traditions of resistance to the invading Incas. To consolidate control over the region, the Incas implemented their standard policy of settling ethnic *mitmaq* (outsiders) in strategic zones of Huamanga. Inca domination thus left Huamanga a legacy of intensified ethnic fragmentation together with anti-Inca politics and attitudes and usurpations of local peoples' resources and labor, but without undermining the internal organization of local production and social identification. The disintegration of the Inca empire after 1532 brought a resurgence of small-scale community and ethnic societies whose economic vitality drew on centuries of local tradition and experience.

The confrontation of these peoples and the Spanish conquistadores gave rise to a complex pattern of alliances—negotiated primarily between encomenderos and Indian *kurakas*—in the new, post-Incaic era. As we shall see, both sides had good reasons to develop mutually acceptable relationships, but fundamental contradictions limited such relations to a transitory adaptation, and doomed the post-Incaic alliances to failure.

The Rise of Uneasy Alliances

The Europeans wanted riches and lordship. After the distribution of precious metals brought to Cajamarca to ransom the Inca Atahualpa, Francisco Pizarro and his fellow conquistadores set out southward to subjugate, plunder, and rule over an Andean colony. The European thirst for precious metals and the looting of religious shrines created the folk legend that Spaniards ate gold and silver for food.[4] Pizarro distributed encomiendas of Indian peoples to his conquistador allies. The encomendero was charged with serving the crown's military and political needs in the colony, and attending to the material and spiritual well-being of the Indians "entrusted" to his care. In exchange, he was free to command tribute and labor from them. As the personal representative of the crown in the field, the encomendero could use his authority over "his" people to enrich himself, but he also carried the burden of forging colonial relationships with the new Indian subjects.[5]

Military security quickly became a top priority, particularly after the puppet Inca emperor, Manco Inca, soured on his European friends and escaped to the *montaña* northwest of Cuzco in 1536. From his hidden jungle fortress, Manco organized raids that disrupted European commercial routes and harassed Indian societies allied to the Europeans. The resistance of Manco's "neo-Inca state" became so troublesome that Pizarro resolved to consolidate European control and expansion along the highland route between Jauja and Cuzco. The few Europeans who had set up a frontier town in Quinua (Huanta) held out precariously against Manco and the local groups who supported the Inca's cause. Pizarro sent Vasco de Guevara, a veteran of Nicaragua and Chile, and twenty-five Spaniards to the area in 1539, hoping to establish the Europeans more firmly in the region of Huamanga.[6]

In the interests of security, the more than twenty encomenderos centered in Huamanga decided in 1540 to move south from Quinua to a more defensible site.[7] The move was carried out under the leadership of Vasco de Guevara. Huamanga overlooked a strategic area west of the neo-Incas, and the conquistadores repeatedly sought to stabilize a European population in the new city to counter the threat of neo-Inca raids and local rebellions.[8] Those who settled in Huamanga saw the local Indian communities as a source of labor and plunder. Spanish settlers required Indian labor and tribute for the most basic necessities—food; transport of water, wood, and merchandise; construction of houses and public works such as churches, roads, and bridges.[9] Furthermore, the loyalty of the local Indians was essential to the Europeans if they were to resist Inca encroachments. The cabildo, a municipal council controlled by the European encomendero elite, sought to curb abuse of the natives in 1541 because it "would give the Indians reason to turn against us, killing Spaniards as they used to do."[10]

Fortunately for the conquistadores, local Andean societies had good reason to ally themselves with Europeans. The military prowess of the Spaniards, skilled masters of horse and sword, impressed the *kurakas* who accompanied Atahualpa in Cajamarca in 1532. As is well known, peasant societies are remarkably sensitive to changes in power balances important to their survival, and the Lucanas peoples of Andamarcas and Laramati quickly recognized the Spaniards as new masters. The *kurakas* of the Lucanas Laramati peoples proclaimed themselves "friends of the Spaniards" when the victorious entourage passed through Vilcashuamán en route to its historic entry into Cuzco. Once the Spaniards broke the Inca siege of Cuzco in 1537, such proclamations acquired additional credibility.[11]

Besides having a healthy respect for Spanish military skills, local societies of Huamanga saw positive benefits in an alliance with the Europeans. These local societies could finally break the yoke of Inca rule, and advance ethnic interests in a new, post-Incaic era. Some of the *mitmaq* populations settled in northern Huamanga by the Incas returned to their home communities. The Europeans were not the only people who plundered the Andean sierra in the early years. Local communities sacked warehouses once dedicated to the discredited Incas and major *huacas* (deities) associated with the state, and a mushrooming population of yanaconas—individuals who left ayllu society to become dependent retainers of the Europeans—joined their masters in the hunt for precious metals.[12]

Given these circumstances, the conquistadores got the help they needed, despite tenuous loyalties and occasional conflicts between Europeans and their native allies. Early in 1541, Indians from northeast Huanta, who bore the brunt of Manco Inca's assaults, came to Huamanga to warn of the Incas' plans to overrun the Spanish city. The cabildo sent Francisco de Cárdenas to lead an expedition of twenty Spaniards and "two thousand Indian friends" to forestall the attack and "to protect the natives."[13] Through the early 1550s, the continual turbulence of civil war among the Spaniards and fights with the neo-Incas put local societies and their *kurakas* in a difficult position.[14] Given the claims all sides made for logistic and military support, native peoples could not choose neutrality. They had to decide what kind of alliance would most benefit ethnic or communal interests. Robbed of the option of neutrality, local societies participated heavily in the early wars, which "[left] the Indians destroyed." While some Indians of Huamanga joined forces with the neo-Incas, most groups—including Incas settled in Huamanga—fought on the side of the Spanish crown. The strategic highway connecting Lima (founded in 1535), Huamanga, and Cuzco threw the burden of fighting upon the societies of the northern districts through which it passed—Huanta, Vilcashuamán, and Andahuaylas. In addition, Huanta and Andahuaylas bordered on the area controlled by the neo-Incas. A *kuraka* "guarding a pass out of fear of the Inca" sent urgent notice in 1544 that Manco Inca, with the help of dissident Spaniards, was planning an attack that threatened the encomienda Indians of Pedro Díaz de Rojas. But even the societies far to the south did not escape involvement. When Francisco Hernández Girón rebelled against the crown in the early 1550s, he raided the rich herds of the Soras and Lucanas peoples for supplies. The raids provoked Indian elites into supporting the royal campaign.[15]

The encomenderos knew that they needed favorable working relationships with "their" *kurakas*; the shrewdest sought to cement alliances with favors and gifts. Encomenderos and other Spaniards frequently came before the cabildo in Huamanga's first decade to ask for *mercedes* (land grants) for estancias or farms. Percipient encomenderos encouraged the cabildo to grant *mercedes* to their *kurakas* as well. The *kurakas* of Juan de Berrio received ten *fanegadas* (nearly thirty hectares) in the fertile Valley of Viñaca west of the city of Huamanga; one *kuraka* sponsored by Berrio received title to twenty *fanegadas*. Francisco de Balboa asked the cabildo to grant sixteen *fanegadas* in the rich Chupas plains south of Huamanga to his chief *kuraka* (*kuraka principal*).[16] Diego Gavilán claimed twenty *fanegadas* for himself in the Chigua Valley, and then had the cabildo grant the rest of the valley to his *kuraka*.[17] One of the most successful encomenderos, Diego Maldonado, showered gifts upon the *kurakas* of his Andahuaylas encomienda. The native elite received a black slave, mules, horses, livestock, and fine Inca and Spanish cloth. In a later dispute, a *kuraka* pointed out that such gifts were given "because [Maldonado] owed it to them for the services they would render him."[18]

Communities and ethnic groups hoped that alliances with Europeans would help them gain the upper hand in their own native rivalries. In 1557, for example, the Lucanas Laramati peoples complained that neighboring groups were intruding upon valuable hunting lands. With the help of their encomendero, Pedro de Avendaño, secretary of the viceroy and a resident of Lima, they obtained a viceregal ban on hunting directed against the Lucanas Andamarcas, Yauyos, Huancas, Parinacochas, and coastal peoples who surrounded the core settlement area of the Lucanas Laramati.[19] The Chancas of Andahuaylas, traditionally bitter rivals of the Incas, used European power against their enemies. When the neo-Incas kidnapped the Chanca guardians of coca fields in Mayomarca (between Huanta and Andahuaylas), ethnic groups from Huamanga threatened to take over the treasured fields. The Chancas solved their difficulty by persuading their encomendero to lead a military expedition to Mayomarca, which secured their control.[20] Collaboration with Europeans, despite the tolls of war, tribute, and labor, brought its advantages.

A closer look at the Chancas of Andahuaylas shows how astute encomenderos cultivated working relationships with native elites and societies. Diego Maldonado, one of the richest and most successful encomenderos, preferred negotiating agreements with the *kurakas* to resorting to brute force. Through one such agreement, Maldonado persuaded some natives who had lived in distant valleys and punas to resettle in a valley nearer the royal highway to Cuzco. Maldonado also avoided usurping treasured Chanca resources. Instead, he carved out lands and herds for his hacienda from the vast holdings once dedicated to the support of the Inca state. Initially, at least, Maldonado settled personal yanaconas on his lands rather than demand encomienda labor. When Indians complained that his expansive herds damaged their crops, he (or his administrator) inspected the claims and distributed corn, potatoes, *ají* (hot peppers), and other goods as compensation for damages incurred. Maldonado also negotiated agreements with the *kurakas*, specifying the tribute obligations of his encomienda. Maldonado customarily set aside a third of the tribute in foodstuffs for redistribution, and in lean agricultural years donated food and relieved his encomienda of various tribute obligations. He contributed the labor of African slaves and yanaconas to the construction of an *obraje* jointly owned by his Indians and a Spanish entrepreneur, and distributed European novelties such as scissors and glass cups. He preferred agreements to unsystematized plunder, and thus in a sense integrated himself into native society as a generous, "redistributive" patron, though Maldonado's son later exaggerated when he stated that his father's gifts were responsible for the *kurakas'* impressive wealth. Indian workers on his fields received, besides the customary payments, "gifts" of corn, coca, salt, *ají*, meat, sheep, and wool. During the twenty-two-day harvest of coca leaves, Maldonado would regale workers with eight baskets of coca.[21] In his will, he donated thousands of cattle to his Indians. During his lifetime, Maldonado sometimes acted as if he were a shrewd ethnographer applying Andean rules of "generosity" to create dependencies and "reciprocal" exchange obligations.

Alliance did not, of course, imply that life was free of conflict or abuse. Behind the negotiations often lay violence and the respective power and needs of both sides. At one point, Indians killed an African slave of Maldonado's, and the encomendero sometimes jailed the Chanca elites. A record of fines collected by Huamanga officials from 1559 onward documents the rough, violent episodes that marred many relationships. Among the encomenderos themselves, gambling and fighting seemed to be a way of life. The Indians were subject to whippings, looting, and rape by Spaniards, blacks, mestizos, and mulattoes. Labor conditions were crude and harsh. Construction of Huamanga in its original site cost the lives of many workers.[22]

As conquerors and aspiring commanders of the labor of their Indians, encomenderos saw themselves as agents personally responsible for basic public tasks. To construct a church, they assessed themselves a labor draft of 510 Indian workers. Later, they assumed responsibility for supplying Indians to carry water to urban Huamanga's households. In general, encomenderos and masters of yanaconas tended to treat their wards as personal property. For the native workers, such a relationship imposed harsh demands. For example, a lively business flourished around the rental of Indian workers and sale of Indian subjects.[23] Rental of Indian labor encouraged its exploiters, like some conquistadores bent on returning to Spain after a few years' plunder, to ignore the long-run survival of workers. The buyer of Indians who sought to squeeze out the most work in a short time period, as one observer put it, "enters like a hungry wolf."[24]

The abuses should not blind us, however, to facts that were so obvious to the native peoples themselves. Cooperation or alliance with the conquerors of the Incas offered at least the possibility of protection against extreme violence. Significantly, the majority of fines collected for personal abuse of Indians was not imposed on members of Huamanga's small circle of elite families, but on lesser Spanish, mixed-blood, and native residents. If alliance did not create an idyllic era, it nevertheless offered the advantages sketched above—continued freedom from Inca (or neo-Inca) rule, special privileges for the *kuraka* friends of the conquistadores, and valuable help in the endemic rivalries among local communities and ethnic groups.

Early relations, then, displayed an uneasy mixture of force, negotiation, and alliance. The parties to the post-Incaic alliances probed one another for weaknesses, testing the limits of the new relationship. In the early years, each encomendero—accompanied by soldiers, if necessary—"asked his cacique [*kuraka*] for what he thought necessary, and [the chief] bargained about what he could give." Ill-treatment and extortion varied "according to the care and greed of each [encomendero], and the skill that he had with his Indians."[25]

Sheer ignorance of the true resources available to local societies handicapped the conquistadores. The first inspection of the Huamanga region, in 1549, turned up only 12,179 native males between the ages of fifteen and fifty; several years later, when the population should have declined, Damián de la Bandera counted 12,771 tributaries. Despite his considerable skills and knowledge, Bandera had little choice but to rely on *kurakas* for much of his information.[26] Felipe Guaman Poma de Ayala wrote a scathing indictment of the European colonials around 1600. Significantly, this bitter Indian critic from Huamanga praised the first generation of encomenderos. The conquistadores "used to sit down to eat and gave all the clothes and textiles the [Indian] notables wanted, and if the crops froze or were lost, they pardoned the poor Indians [their tribute]." Francisco de Cárdenas, who had led two thousand Indians against the neo-Incas in 1541, left his Indians thousands of sheep on their punas in Chocorvos and Vilcashuamán. Don Pedro de Córdova, said Poma de Ayala, helped protect his Lucanas Laramati peoples from abusive priests and officials.[27] The Lucanas Laramati, who had always sought to be "friends of the Spaniards," granted Córdova a huge ranching estate "for the many releases of taxes and tributes which, as encomendero, he made and pardoned them."[28] The parties of the post-Incaic alliances understood very well that they needed one another.

The Early Commercial Economy

By securing cooperative relations with native elites and societies, an aspiring ruling class of encomenderos laid a foundation for the colonial economy and society in Huamanga. By the 1550s, Spanish-Indian relations entered a second phase as a corregidor and other appointed officials began to assume responsibility for many judicial and administrative tasks. The colonial state, centered in Lima, thereby began to intervene in a restricted way to limit the regional autonomy of Huamanga's leading families. Colonial officials, however, tended to enter into alliances with powerful local Spaniards; and, in the early years, the cabildo, dominated by encomenderos, had moved quickly to establish rules and guidelines for a colonial society.[29] The cabildo, almost immediately, had taken on the task of assigning *solares* (town lots) for homes, shops, gardens, and small farms, and of granting *mercedes* for farm and pasture lands.[30] During the years 1540 to 1543, the cabildo granted forty-two *mercedes* for estancias (grazing sites) and farm lands to twenty residents.[31] In 1546 the city appropriated common lands "that are around this town that are neither worked nor populated by Indians." It appears that eighteen notables of Huamanga received an average of eighty hectares each.[32] Twelve years later, the cabildo distributed thousands of hectares in the irrigated Chaquibamba plains to more than sixty *vecinos* and other residents.[33]

Leading citizens acquired lands and pastures for their own personal gain. Encomienda tributes already supplied Huamanga with food, cloth, artisanal products, and precious metals.[34] An encomendero who owned a fine home in the city and a productive encomienda had little reason to yearn for a huge estate to satisfy status pretensions. Commercial agriculture, however, offered lucrative possibilities. Lima, Cuzco, and the booming silver town of Potosí created markets for foodstuffs, cloth, wine, sugar, coca, tallow, hides, and artisanal items. Huamanga itself served as an economic pole attracting rural products. Corn and potatoes, for example, sold for twice the price in Huamanga that they fetched in faraway rural Lucanas.[35] Through cabildo *mercedes*, sales by *kurakas*, negotiations, or force, encomenderos and lesser European residents began to claim lands. Rather than consolidate holdings in a single large estate, the Europeans commonly carved out multiple holdings—often small- or middle-size— on lands whose fertility, suitability for marketable products such as coca or wine, or location near the city or major commercial routes (that is, the main highway in Huanta and Vilcashuamán) promised material reward. Herds of cattle, sheep, and goats; irrigated patches of wheat, corn, vegetables, and alfalfa; groves of fruit trees and carefully kept vineyards; and water-powered flour mills began to dot the valleys of Huatata, Yucay, and Viñaca near the city of Huamanga. Along the eastern edges of Huanta, aggressive entrepreneurs set up coca plantations.[36]

Commercial capital, understood as buying or producing cheaply to sell dearly, thus structured early patterns of investment and initiative.[37] The Europeans cast their entrepreneurial eyes not only toward agriculture but also toward mining, manufactures, and trade itself. Already in 1541, Pedro Díaz de Rojas had uncovered rich gold mines in the coca *montaña* of Mayomarca (eastern Huanta). The gold mines attracted fortune seekers fired with passion and dreams of glory; in 1545, the cabildo sent a leading citizen to restore order and authority to the violent, rough-and-tumble life of the miners.[38] The discovery of major gold and silver deposits in Atunsulla (Angaraes) in 1560, and of mercury in Huancavelica in 1563, made Huamanga a major mining region in its own right. The royal accountant in Huamanga joined encomenderos rushing to Atunsulla to extract minerals worth tens of thousands of pesos. On January 1, 1564, the encomendero Amador de Cabrera registered the fabulous mercury deposits of Huancavelica. Mercury soon circulated as a regional medium of exchange, along with gold and silver.[39] With the discovery of major mines, Huamanga's entrepreneurs began to build textile workshops and *obrajes*. Within fifteen years of Cabrera's discovery, encomenderos had established at least three major rural *obrajes* to supply the growing mining and commercial centers of Huamanga. In neighboring Andahuaylas, another *obraje* had been supplying the Cuzco market since the 1550s.[40] Huamanga's encomenderos had established trading networks with Lima very early, and the Vilcashuamán *tambo* (inn) on the Inca highway from Huamanga to Cuzco rapidly emerged as a major trading center.[41]

The Indians, rather than isolate themselves from these economic developments, usually sought to take advantage of new trends and opportunities. Individually and collectively, Indians searched for money and commercial advantage. To be sure, native societies had to find ways to acquire money if they were to pay tribute owed to the encomenderos. The early documentation, however, offers evidence that belies the conclusion that native societies participated reluctantly in the commercial economy just to gather money needed for tribute. On the contrary, communities displayed an open, aggressive—even enthusiastic—attitude that rivaled the boldness of Diego Maldonado's amateur ethnography in Andahuaylas. Long before the Spaniards gained control of Atunsulla around 1560, communities well over a hundred kilometers away had sent *mitmaq* representatives to mine "the hill of gold" abandoned by the Incas. The Lucanas Indians worked local gold and silver mines for their own benefit, but complained bitterly about demands that they work Spanish mines in faraway sites. *Kurakas* in Andahuaylas sent natives to set up ethnic outposts in the distant silver mines of Potosí.[42] Unhampered by Inca claims on coca fields, local societies expanded coca production and sales. One group used coca to pay "the tribute [they owed], and with what remained after paying tribute, they sustained themselves." Another group used the coca left after tribute to buy sheep and swine.[43] By the 1550s, the Chancas and Adrián de Vargas, a Spanish entrepreneur, agreed to build an *obraje* half-owned by the Indians, who sold some of the finished textiles to their encomendero in Cuzco.[44]

Individually, too, natives reacted innovatively to the new colonial economy. By 1547, Indian workers and traders captured an impressive share of the Mayomarca gold dust in exchange for their services and products.[45] Native merchants flocked to supply the dynamic mines and commercial centers of Huamanga, and artisans left ayllus to find opportunities elsewhere.[46] Silversmiths joined encomenderos in Huamanga, where their skills yielded handsome rewards. Stonemasons earned money in colonial construction, and skilled native artisans became indispensable specialists in the Huancavelica mines.[47] The brisk commerce in coca led Indian entrepreneurs, especially the *kurakas*, to join Spaniards in setting up private coca farms or plantations.[48] Andean ethnic "families" had always been plagued by internal tension and stratification; now, colonial society offered new possibilities to dissatisfied individuals willing to abandon or loosen ties with ayllu society. Some looked for alternatives in the city of Huamanga. In the mines, the loyalties of ayllu Indians sent to work distant ore deposits on behalf of their ethnic groups sometimes abated.[49]

The *kurakas*, in fact, were in some ways better equipped than the Spaniards to take advantage of new opportunities. The Europeans needed their cooperation to stabilize the early colony and to exact tribute and labor from ayllu society. The native elite, moreover, enjoyed special privileges precisely because their "kinfolk" recognized them as guardians of the collective welfare of their ayllus and communities. The long-run "reciprocal" exchange between peasant households and *kurakas* gave elites, as privileged leaders, the means to initiate rewarding activities in the colonial economy. One knowledgeable observer called the privately owned coca farms "their particular trade." The *kurakas'* power, complained the corregidor of Huamanga, allowed them "to rent [the natives] like beasts and to pocket the money themselves."[50] It was true that a *kuraka* who consistently violated his kinfolk's sense of a fair reciprocal exchange ran the risk of encouraging emigration or disloyalty. In extreme cases, Indians even turned to colonial authorities or patrons to denounce a *kuraka* or to challenge his authority. In 1559, Huamanga's officials fined one such chief 250 pesos for "certain torments and deaths of Indians."[51] In less extreme cases, however, or when native societies found alliance with European colonials beneficial to their interests, the *kurakas'* economic initiatives did not necessarily erode their traditional prestige or "influence" among ethnic "relatives."

Thus the Indians, impelled by the hunt for money and commercial profit, joined in the creation of a colonial economy. The native-white alliances did not only enhance the ability of Huamanga's colonials to create an impressive array of commercial production and relationships; they reinforced the natives' "open" attitude toward the newcomers, which focused on taking advantage of new opportunities rather than withdrawing sullenly from contact.[52] The goals of Indians and Spaniards were different and ultimately in contradiction, but joint participation in the commercial economy was, nevertheless, quite real. The Indians embraced the entry of commercial capital on the Andean stage; only later would they discover that the embrace was deadly. The encomenderos saw that alliance with local elites and societies could lay a foundation for colonial extraction; only later would they discover that the foundation was unstable and that it could crumble under pressure.

Labor and Tribute under the Alliances

The problem was that, under the terms of the early alliances, the colonial economy continued to depend for goods and labor almost wholly upon an Andean social system, managed and controlled by Andean social actors, relationships, and traditions. A colonial state apparatus had only partially rooted itself in Huamanga. Despite the presence of outside colonial officials and formal tribute lists by the 1550s, the colonials could not rely on the state to organize a new economic system that would funnel them native goods and labor. On the contrary, the natives went "over the heads" of local colonials to appeal for favorable rulings from metropolitan-oriented officials in Lima and Spain. The "state" in Huamanga in actuality remained the personal responsibility of about twenty-five encomenderos and a handful of cooperating officials who, as the king's representatives, sought to rule over the area.[53] Under such conditions, it was difficult to reorder the native economy.

Instead, it seemed more feasible to base colonial extraction upon long-standing Andean traditions. The more formal lists by officials in the 1550s and 1560s specified a large variety of items far more impressive than the short lists after 1570. Aside from the gold and silver, food, animals, and cloth of the post-1570 lists, the early tributes included items such as wooden plates and vases, washtubs, chairs, footwear, horse and saddle gear, large sacks and ropes, cushions and rugs, whips, and so forth.[54] The diversity not only attests to the capacity of native societies to incorporate new products and skills into their economic life, but it also dramatizes the dependence of Europeans upon indigenous communities, governed by Andean-style labor relations, for items that would later be supplied by a more Hispanicized artisan and handicrafts economy. The documents also hint that early encomenderos—to obtain their tributes—had to respect at least some of the traditional rules governing Andean labor and "taxes." Households continued to retain exclusive rights to crops produced on ayllu lands for local use; to pay tribute, households and ayllus contributed labor time on other lands specifically designated to satisfy outside claimants.[55] Traditionally, such practices protected ayllus and households from having to pay tribute in goods from subsistence crops or from reserves in years when crops fared poorly. A shrewd observer of Andean life commented that Indians would rather go as a community to work fifteen days on other fields than give up for tribute a few potatoes grown by the family for its own use.[56] Poma de Ayala's praise of Huamanga's early encomenderos for lightening the Indians' tribute burdens in bad years perhaps reflected the encomenderos' inability or unwillingness to overturn such cherished rules. In Andahuaylas, Diego Maldonado supplied the wool needed to make textiles the Indians "owed" him.[57] Such practices respected the rule that peasants supplied labor to claimants rather than raw materials or local subsistence products. Ethnic groups and communities distributed tribute obligations—including money tributes—by ayllu, in accordance with traditional practices.[58]

To obtain labor for public works, transport, and agriculture, the colonials had to pursue a similar policy. To replace worn fibrous cable bridges, the cabildo of Huamanga ordered "that all the caciques [*kurakas*] and Indians of this province come together [to say] who are obligated to make bridges . . . from old times, and their [European] masters are ordered to donate the Indians [thereby designated]."[59] To "rent" Indians to transport wares or to work lands, a European often had to make the arrangement with *kurakas* rather than hire the laborers directly. A contract as late as 1577 shows that the prominent Cárdenas family could not independently hire the workers they needed on their estancia in Chocorvos. Instead, a *kuraka* loaned twenty-seven kinsmen to the family and received the 162 pesos owed them after six months of labor. (Presumably the chief then distributed six pesos to each worker.)[60]

We should not exaggerate, of course, the dependence of the Europeans. They had alternatives and used them when they felt it necessary. Aside from an impressive population of yanaconas, they could draw on the services of slaves, mestizos, and other mixed-blood dependents, or exploit individual natives directly by extortion or agreement. For ambitious enterprises, however, these alternatives could only supplement rather than replace the labor of ayllu-based encomienda Indians. In the case of the Cárdenas estancia, the twenty-seven encomienda herders far outnumbered the "five *yanaconas* and four Indian cowboys" on the spread.[61] Furthermore, even if an encomendero wished to deal directly with individual natives to work various farms and estates, his ability to do so stemmed from a general spirit of cooperation with native societies as a whole, led by their chiefs. The Maldonados of Andahuaylas secured workers to tend to various herds, grow wheat and barley, harvest coca leaf, and so forth. Such relations sometimes carried the flavor of a direct interchange with native individuals, who earned food and money for their labors. Often, however, the Indians worked not to receive money, but to discharge collective tribute accounts settled upon with the *kurakas*. Even in the cases where encomienda Indians received individual payments in coin or in kind, Maldonado's access to their labors was facilitated by the *kurakas'* early approval, as spokesmen for communities and ethnic groups, of such relations. In the first year, *kurakas* had given Diego Maldonado llamas and Indian workers to transport items to Potosí and Lima. A tribute list in 1552 probably systematized earlier rules on the numbers of workers *kurakas* could spare to help out on Maldonado's farms, orchards, and ranches, and in domestic service.[62] As we saw earlier, Maldonado's success was related directly to a shrewd amateur ethnography. He rewarded cooperation with "gifts" and favors, negotiated agreements with the *kurakas*, and tended to respect traditional Andean prerogatives.

It is perhaps not surprising that the majority of the agricultural and artisanal surplus, and a considerable amount of the precious metal tributes, funneled to the Europeans rested heavily on the *kurakas'* ability to mobilize the labor of kinfolk in accordance with traditional Andean norms and expectations. More dramatic, however, is that even in the most dynamic sectors of the colonial economy—mining and textile manufactures—the Europeans could not transcend their reliance upon the *kurakas*. The mines and *obrajes* were strategic nerve centers crucial to the growth of a thriving commercial economy. Yet the voluntary flow of individuals or families to work the mines was not enough to ensure an adequate and regular labor force. In 1562 a special commission struggled unsuccessfully to reform Huamanga's mines and stabilize a labor force. Still, as late as 1569, Amador de Cabrera negotiated with the *kurakas* of his encomienda to contract Indians he needed to work the mines of Huancavelica. The corregidor complained that Huamanga's rich mine deposits were languishing "because of a lack of Indian workers."[63]

Well into the 1570s—a transitional decade—European entrepreneurs depended upon the *kurakas* to supply workers for *obrajes*. In 1567, Hernán Guillén de Mendoza reached an agreement with the Tanquihuas Indians of his encomienda to rotate a force of sixty Indians for his *obraje* "Cacamarca" in Vilcashuamán. Ten years later, in Castrovirreyna, the *kurakas* of the Cárdenas family agreed to provide forty adults and fifty children to run a new *obraje*. Only an agreement among the chiefs of the various lineages—tied to one another and to their people by the long-standing expectations and interchanges of local kinship and reciprocity—could commit ayllu Indians to labor in the *obraje*. One Huamanga contract recorded the formal approval of seven different chiefs; a similar contract from another region recorded the unanimous agreement of sixteen *kurakas* and *principales* (notables). Significantly, the *kurakas* of Cárdenas sent a minor chief to oversee production in the new *obraje*. In the 1570s, though not in later years, Antonio de Oré appointed prominent encomienda Indians instead of Europeans or mestizos to manage his *obraje* in Canaria (Vilcashuamán). The native elites oversaw labor relations with the *obraje* and adapted traditional Andean techniques to the manufacture of textiles.[64]

Excluded from the traditional web of reciprocities among "kinfolk," which mobilized labor and circulated goods in Andean ethnic "families," and unable to reorganize the native economy or control directly the basic elements of production, the colonials had little choice but to rely upon their alliance with the *kurakas*. Even if Europeans aspired to take on the precarious task of reordering internally the native economy, the limits of their position would force them to rely upon the *kurakas'* ability to persuade their kin to participate in this change. By cultivating working relationships with the managers of autonomous native economies, Huamanga's colonials could, at least, receive a portion of the wealth and labor available in dynamic local economies without having to try to organize a powerful state apparatus or reorder local society. Whether the alliance was more voluntary or forced in character, the chiefs would use their traditional prestige to mobilize a flow of labor and tribute to the colonial economy. Combined with an impressive show of Spanish military skill in Cajamarca and elsewhere, and some willingness to help local societies

promote ethnic interests, such a strategy seemed sensible at first. It is no
accident that the early decades produced figures like Juan Polo de
Ondegardo and Domingo de Santo Tomás. Experienced and shrewd
colonials, they urged the crown to base its exploitation of native economies upon a respect for the traditional relationships and prerogatives of
Andean society. To the greatest extent consistent with crown interests,
royal policy should siphon off surplus goods and labor from ongoing native economies rather than reorganize or control them directly.[65]

Extracting a surplus by allying with the chiefs of autonomous and
rather wealthy economic systems was for the conquistadores a realistic
path of least resistance, but it soon led to a dead end. The *kurakas* controlled the basic processes of production and reproduction that sustained
the colonials' economic, social, and political positions. If the *kurakas* were
not at all "inferior" to the Europeans, but in fact directed the social relations and dynamic economies crucial to the survival of colonial enterprise, why should they accept a subordinate position in colonial society?
On the contrary, their indispensable position tended to reinforce their
posture as collaborating allies rather than dependent inferiors. The
colonials remained foreign, extraneous elements superimposed upon an
autonomous economy in which they served little purpose. Such a limita-
tion did not augur well for an aspiring ruling class's hegemony, or for its
long-run capacity to dominate a society and capture the wealth it produced. As soon as the specific advantages of the *kurakas'* alliance with
the Spaniards began to run out—because the Europeans demanded too
much or because Andean kinfolk reacted against the alliance—the early
colonial system would enter a crisis. The dependence of Europeans upon
native elites for access to exploitable labor in agriculture, transport, public works, manufactures, and mining exposed the artificial character of
foreign hegemony. The economy erected by the post-Incaic alliances was
deeply vulnerable to changes in the natives' cooperative policies. Disillusion with the Europeans could spell disaster.

Contradiction and Breakdown

To understand why disillusion set in, we should remember that the native-
white alliances had always been uneasy and contradictory. The
encomenderos cultivated working relations with local chiefs and societies in order to rule over the Andes and to extract as much wealth as possible. The natives accepted an alliance with the victorious foreigners as a
way to advance local interests and to limit colonial demands and abuses.
The contradictions of the post-Incaic alliances thus bore within them the

seeds of severe disillusion. The violence and arrogance endemic in early relations warned of the limitations of such alliances for both sides.

In many ways, Huamanga's native societies had fared relatively well by allying with the Europeans. Their adaptations freed them of onerous bonds with the Incas, found them allies in ever-present struggles with rival native groups, and offered them the opportunity to accumulate wealth in the form of precious metals. The combined effects of epidemic disease, war, and emigration of yanaconas took their toll upon the several hundred thousand natives of Huamanga, but the decline was not as irrevocably devastating as that in other Andean areas. The Lucanas peoples, who in 1572 numbered about twenty-five thousand, claimed in the 1580s that their population had even increased since the turbulent reign of the Inca Huayna Capac (1493–1525).[66] For Huamanga as a whole, a high birth rate, the relative immunity of people in high-altitude areas to disease, shrewd politics, and good luck helped cut net population decline to an average rate of perhaps 0.5 percent a year, or some 20 percent over the 1532 to 1570 period.[67] Such a loss posed hardships for a labor-intensive system of agriculture, but was not by itself disastrous. Indeed, the rich herding economies of the high punas of Lucanas, Chocorvos, and Vilcashuamán served as a kind of "insurance" against a decline of labor available for agriculture.[68] Successful adaptation to colonial conditions had enabled Huamanga's Indians to maintain traditional relationships and economic productivity. Inspections of southern Huamanga in the 1560s turned up many local *huacas*, presumably supported by retaining rights to lands, animals, and ayllu labor.[69] Several years later, Viceroy Francisco de Toledo was so impressed with the wealth of the Lucanas Laramati peoples that he nearly tripled their tribute assessment.[70] Huamanga's *kurakas* joined other Andean chiefs in offering King Philip II a dazzling bribe to end the encomienda system—one hundred thousand ducats more than any offer by the Spanish encomenderos, who wished the system continued.[71]

Nevertheless, the alliance with the Europeans had created ominous trends. First, even though Huamanga's rural societies weathered the effects of epidemic, war, emigration, and population decline relatively well, these were disturbing events. Economically, unpredictable drops in the population available for local tasks augured poorly for the long-run dynamism of ayllu-based society. A certain expected level of available human energy was a prerequisite for the maintenance of the traditional economic prerogatives, relationships, and exchanges that tied producers together. Ideologically, Andean societies tended to interpret misfortune—especially disease or early death—as the result of poorly functioning, "imbalanced" social relationships within the community of kin groups and gods (many of them ancestor-gods). Disease was often considered the work of neglected or angry deities. War and epidemic disease raised the specter of fundamentally awry relationships, which could bring about a major catastrophe far more devastating than earlier trends.[72]

Second, colonial relationships created humiliations and dependencies that undercut the ethnic freedom gained by liberation from Inca hegemony. Aside from the individual abuses and extortions that natives confronted everywhere, local societies found themselves relying upon colonial authority to defend their interests. Using an alliance with Europeans to protect against encroachments by outside ethnic groups was one matter, but dependence upon Europeans to settle internal disputes or to correct colonial abuses was quite another. Unfortunately, such a dependence grew increasingly frequent. Given the internal strife that plagued decentralized ethnic "families," it was difficult to avoid turning to Europeans as a source of power in local disputes over land rights, tribute-labor obligations, and chieftainships. By the 1550s, Huamanga's Indians commonly traveled as far away as Lima to redress local grievances.[73]

Finally, the new relationships generated demands for labor that might go beyond what local societies were willing to offer in exchange for the benefit of alliance with the colonials. The number of Spaniards, of course, increased over the years. Moreover, the demands of any particular set of colonials did not necessarily remain static. Consider, for example, relations with Catholic priests. The *doctrineros* (rural priests) theoretically lived among ayllu Indians to indoctrinate them on behalf of the encomenderos; in practice, many were "priest-entrepreneurs" who sought to use their positions to promote commercial interests.[74] At first, many communities probably accepted the necessity of an alliance with the priests. To ally with the Europeans without cooperating with their gods was senseless from the Indians' point of view. The powerful Christian deities had defeated the major Andean gods at Cajamarca, and, like the native gods, could improve or damage the material well-being of the living. Since the Catholic priests mediated relations with the pantheon of Christian divinities (including saints) who affected everyday welfare, Indians did not rebuff the priests or their demands lightly. By the 1550s, churches and crosses—however modest—dotted rural areas, and their priests demanded considerable labor services, including those for transport, construction, ranching, and household service. By 1564, the rural priests' ability to extract unpaid native labor inspired jealousy among the urban encomenderos.[75] But as the priests' demands escalated, would native societies judge them far too excessive for the supposed advantages that favorable relations with Christian gods offered them?

The *kurakas*, as guardians and representatives of the community, could not ignore such evaluations of the relative advantages and disadvantages of cooperation with the colonials. The *kurakas* who mobilized labor for European enterprise did not, in the long run, enjoy complete freedom to will the activities of their peoples. The chiefs bolstered their privileges and "influence" by fulfilling obligations to guard the communitarian unity and welfare. The traditional interchanges of reciprocities that enabled chiefs to mobilize the labors of kinfolk created expectations that might be difficult to reconcile with a unilateral flow of goods, labor, and advantages to European society. Traditional reciprocities also placed limitations upon the kinds of requests a *kuraka* could make of his ayllus and households. Production of textiles for the Europeans through a "putting-out" system similar to accepted Andean practices was one matter. As we shall see, sending workers to distant mines was quite another. Natives would be reluctant to comply, and once at the mines might never return to the domain of local society.

Evidence shows that labor demands became a matter provoking resentment among Indians, even when the labor was sought for activities superficially similar to traditional Andean practices. If labor demands were originally the price for the relative advantages of working relationships with the encomendero elite, the advantages could dwindle over time and the price could rise unacceptably high. In local society, for example, canal cleaning had normally been an occasion for celebration on the agricultural and ceremonial calendars. In ritual led by the native elite, a community of "relatives" reaffirmed the importance of such tasks for the collective welfare of the group. But the same activity carried an onerous flavor if viewed as uncompensated labor to the exclusive benefit of others. The Huachos and Chocorvos Indians complained in 1557 that they were forced to sweep clean the great canal "with which the citizens [of Huamanga] irrigate their [farms]." The Indians did not benefit from or need the water.[76] Under such conditions, *kurakas* could not transfer the celebratory aspect of Andean work to colonial canal cleaning even if they had so wished. A *kuraka* who felt compelled to satisfy colonial labor demands could not assume that his call for labor would be accepted as justified.

In the 1560s, the contradictions inherent in the post-Incaic alliances sharpened. The growing dependency of Indians upon Europeans to settle disputes;[77] the economic shortages or hardships imposed by colonial extraction, emigration, or population decline;[78] the tendency of encomenderos, local priests, and officials to demand increasing shares of ayllu goods and labor—all these eventually would have provoked a reassessment of native policies toward the colonials. What made the need for a reevaluation urgent, however, was the above-mentioned discovery in the 1560s of gold and silver at Atunsulla and mercury at Huancavelica. The discoveries fired Spanish dreams of a thriving regional economy whose mines would stimulate a boom in trade, textile manufactures, artisanal crafts, construction, agriculture, and ranching. The only obstacle or bottleneck would be labor. If European demands escalated far beyond the supply of individual laborers, or of contingents sent by *kurakas*, how would the colonials stabilize an adequate labor force?

By 1562, the labor problem merited an official inquiry by the distinguished jurist, Juan Polo de Ondegardo. Polo investigated Indian complaints, set out to reform and regulate labor practices, and ordered native societies to turn over a rotating force of 700 weekly laborers for the Atunsulla mines. The labor regime imposed by the miners had been harsh. Miners sought to maximize their exploitation of native laborers. Natives personally hauled loads of fuel, salt, and other supplies from distant areas; in the mines themselves, laborers had to meet brutally taxing production quotas; after fulfilling their labor obligations, they faced a struggle to obtain their wages.[79] Small wonder that the Indians asked a noted defender, Fray Domingo de Santo Tomás, to inspect the mines. Santo Tomás found that "until now the Indians have been paid so poorly, and treated worse . . . that even if they went voluntarily, [these abuses] would wipe out [their willingness]." Hopeful that Polo's reforms—boosted by higher salaries—could attract enough voluntary labor, Santo Tomás warned that the Indians and *kurakas* would resist attempts to force natives to work under the abusive conditions of the past, "even if they knew they would have to spend all their lives in jail." Santo Tomás found the Indians restless about demands for mine labor. The Soras and Lucanas peoples, farther away than other groups from Atunsulla, were particularly vexed about working under abusive conditions current in distant mines.[80]

Polo's reforms changed little. The supply of native laborers forced or coaxed individually or through the *kurakas* remained irregular and insufficient. The corregidor of Huamanga complained in 1569 that work on the region's fabulous deposits faltered because of the labor shortage.[81]

The mines made obvious the limitations of previous relationships to both sides. For the Europeans driven by the international expansion of commercial capital, alliances with native societies meant little if they could not supply a dependable labor force for a growing mining economy. For the Indians—*kurakas* as well as their kinfolk—collaboration with the colonials offered few benefits if the Europeans insisted upon draining ayllu resources in a drive to develop a massive mining economy beyond the control of local society. The Europeans wanted favors that the *kurakas* could not or would not give them. Yet the colonials still lacked the organized state institutions and force that could compel the chiefs to turn over large contingents to the mines.

At this very moment, contradictions between metropolis and colony encouraged the Indians to rethink the necessity of cooperation with encomenderos. In Spain, the rulers had long debated whether to abolish the encomienda system and convert the Indians into direct vassals. By 1560, the crown had received impressive bribe offers from both encomenderos and the native *kurakas*, but had not reached a decision. A commission sent to report on the merits of the encomienda issue dispatched Polo (pro-encomienda) and Santo Tomás (anti-encomienda) to conduct an inquiry. The pair toured the Andean highlands in 1562. In Huamanga as elsewhere, they organized meetings of natives to participate in a public debate of the encomienda issue. The Indians sided with Santo Tomás.[82] Royal interests and moral sensibilities, honed by frictions between encomenderos and the church, created a spectacular debate. In the very years when mine discoveries made the basic antagonisms between natives and whites ever more weighty and ominous, the crown's distinguished representatives advertised political instability, divisions among the elite, and a receptivity to the idea that the encomenderos were dispensable to crown and native alike.

If growing disillusion with labor demands prompted sabotaging or discarding colonial relationships, the apparent vulnerability of such relationships to reform imposed by the metropolis could only give further impetus to such urges. Soon after 1560, native discontent expressed itself in the number of broken alliances. In 1563, *kurakas* in seven different Huamanga encomiendas refused to send Indians to the city plaza for corvée duty. The mines continued to suffer from an irregular labor supply. Many of Huamanga's peoples, especially the Soras and Lucanas, confirmed Santo Tomás's warnings by openly rejecting calls for laborers to work the mines. Indian shepherds cost their encomendero, Diego Maldonado, a claimed seven thousand sheep through robbery or neglect. Encomenderos blamed priests for the natives' growing tendency to ignore previously accepted obligations; one observer placed the blame on popular rumors that the Spaniards would kill natives for medicinal ointments in their bodies.[83] In an economy where the Europeans depended greatly upon alliances with native elites to gain access to exploitable labor, the spread of such disillusion and resistance poisoned enterprise. In a society where the neo-Incas maintained a military force in the *montaña* between Cuzco and Huamanga, and the colonials had not yet organized an impressive state apparatus, growing hostility posed strategic dangers as well. The corregidor of Huamanga warned the acting viceroy, Governor-General Lope García de Castro, that a rebellion might break out. In neighboring Jauja and in

Andahuaylas, alarming discoveries of stored arms confirmed that Indian-white relations were in jeopardy.[84]

Demands for mine labor on a new scale, the encomenderos' political vulnerability, and the neo-Incas' probable willingness to lead a revolt created a conjuncture that compelled second thoughts about the post-Incaic alliances. From the beginning, the inherent contradictions of the early alliances had created the likelihood of disenchantment. Despite the relative success of their adaptation to colonial conditions, Huamanga's native peoples confronted trends that threatened to undermine local autonomy, relationships, and production. Demographic decline and instability, humiliation and dependence, growing demands for labor—all tended to expose the erosive consequences of an alliance among partners whose fundamental interests clashed. The discovery of major gold, silver, and mercury deposits brought such contradictions to a head. The Indians' severe disaffection expressed itself in a radical millenarian upheaval, "Taki Onqoy," which inflamed Huamanga. The sect preached pan-Andean unity, proclaimed an end to all contact with Hispanic society, and pressured *kurakas* to cut off cooperation with colonials. The movement had exceptional appeal to peoples ethnically divided against themselves and deeply disillusioned by the consequences of cooperation with the Hispanic world. By the end of the decade, *kurakas* stubbornly refused to send Indians to the mines, and colonial relationships entered a crisis stage.[85]

Conclusion

The rise and fall of Indian-white alliances in Huamanga yield broad implications for the study of early colonial history. First, the activities of local Andean peoples had a decisive impact upon the particular texture of early relations and institutions "imposed" by Hispanic society (encomienda, tribute, labor drafts, Christianization, and the like). Yet a deeper understanding of the interests and motives behind native activity is elusive unless informed by an awareness of preconquest history and social structure. In this perspective, the line between pre-Columbian and colonial history becomes, in many respects, artificial and misleading. Second, the *kurakas'* importance as strategic mediators singled out for special favors by Spanish allies, and the impact of Andean ethnic rivalries upon native-white relations, indicate that divisions and tensions internal to local Andean societies played key roles in European success and failure, and the colonial process in general. We would be well advised, therefore, not to homogenize the "Indians" into a seamless social category, thereby ignoring internal contradictions that shaped events. Third, the crisis of the 1560s and its link to the mining economy illuminate the fundamental contradictions of purpose and interest that marred early native-white alliances and doomed them to failure. Indeed, the demise of the alliances meant that only a more effective, direct control of local native life and institutions, backed by a revitalized state, would truly serve Hispanic interests and develop the mining economy. It is in this sense that massive reorganization of the Andean colony, like that led by Viceroy Francisco de Toledo (1569–1581), was a historic necessity. Early alliances and cooperation represented not a "golden era" of native-white relations, but a transitory phase whose contradictions would eventually assert themselves with increasing force.

Finally, the Indian-white alliances might lead us to reassess the old distinction between sedentary native societies ruled by the Aztecs and Incas, and more independent or mobile peoples who had escaped subjugation by pre-Columbian empires. We normally observe that Europeans experienced little trouble dominating a sedentary peasantry already accustomed to rule from above, but encountered much more difficulty conquering stateless peoples undefeated by the Aztecs and Incas.[86] There is merit in the distinction, and we may certainly contrast the options and "moral economy" of peasants and those of free and independent "savages."[87] But the contrast misleads us in certain respects. It underestimates the degree to which stateless Indian people forged early alliances with Europeans, and the dynamics that drove such relations to disaster.[88] It overestimates the power of "habits of obedience" among peasantries exploited by the Aztecs and Incas. We presume that such habits generated a passive posture toward the Europeans, who simply filled the void left by Aztecs and Incas. By this line of reasoning, colonizers commanded surplus labor and products of peasants not because the latter (and their chiefs) had reason to comply, but because tradition dictated obedience. If the birth, evolution, and final demise of Huamanga's post-Incaic alliances tell us anything, however, it is that sedentary peasantries actively assessed their alternatives and made choices within the confines of their interests and power, and that, like many human beings, they could even change their minds.

Notes

1. For the history of these peoples' relations with Spanish conquistadores, see Charles Gibson, *Tlaxcala in the Sixteenth Century*, 2d ed. (Stanford, 1967); Waldemar Espinoza Soriano, *La destrucción del imperio de los Incas: La rivalidad política y señorial de los curacazgos andinos* (Lima, 1973); Manuel de Odriozola, ed., *Documentos históricos del Perú en las épocas del coloniaje después de la conquista y de la independencia hasta la presente*, 10 vols. (Lima, 1863–77), III: 3–9.

2. The Huamanga region corresponded roughly to the contemporary Peruvian departments of Ayacucho and Huancavelica. Huamanga's "core" districts included the *corregimientos* of Angaraes (Huancavelica), Huanta, Vilcashuamán, Chocorvos (Castrovirreyna), and Lucanas. Parinacochas and Andahuaylas were "swing" districts in many respects, oriented both to Huamanga and to Cuzco, and I cite data or patterns from these *corregimientos* when they accord with evidence from the "core" districts. For a convenient map of *corregimiento* districts, see Guillermo Lohmann Villena, *El corregidor de indios en el Perú bajo los Austrias* (Madrid, 1957), 200.

3. My understanding of pre-Columbian social and economic structure relies heavily on the pioneering studies of John V. Murra, *Formaciones económicas y políticas del mundo andino* (Lima, 1975). The following three paragraphs draw upon the much more extended discussion of Huamanga before the Spanish conquest in this author's "The Challenge of Conquest: The Indian Peoples of Huamanga, Peru, and the Foundation of a Colonial Society, 1532–1640" (Ph.D. diss., Yale University, 1979), 5–53. The largest ethnic groups of Huamanga probably number no more than thirty thousand individuals or five thousand to six thousand domestic units. Even within these groups, social identification, economic claims, and political authority were significantly varied along lines of kinship and ethnicity.

4. Felipe Guaman Poma de Ayala, *Nueva corónica y buen gobierno (codex péruvien illustré)* (Paris, 1936), 369–370.

5. For early encomienda grants by Pizarro, see U.S. Library of Congress, Harkness Collection (hereinafter HC), Stella R. Clemence, ed., *Documents from Early Peru: The Pizarros and the Almagros, 1531–1578* (Washington, DC, 1936), 154, 170. On the Peruvian encomienda, see Enrique Torres Saldamando, *Apuntes históricos sobre las encomiendas en el Perú* (Lima, 1967); Manuel Belaúnde Guinassi, *La encomienda en el Perú* (Lima, 1945); Manuel Vicente Villarán, *Apuntes sobre la realidad social de los indígenas ante las leyes de Indias* (Lima, 1964), 25–100; James Lockhart, *Spanish Peru, 1532–1560: A Colonial Society* (Madison, 1968), 11–33, and passim.

6. See Vasco de Guevara, as quoted by Marcos Jiménez de la Espada, ed., *Relaciones geográficas de Indias—Perú* (hereinafter cited as *RGI*), reprinted in *Biblioteca de autores españoles*, tomo 183 (Madrid, 1965), 181–182 n.2; James Lockhart, *The Men of Cajamarca: A Social and Biographical Study of the First Conquerors of Peru* (Austin, 1972), 424. For Inca *mitmaq* who fought against the Spanish, see "Autos criminales que siguieron Juan Tucabamba y Pedro Cachi, indios . . . 1567," Archivo General de la Nación, Lima (hereinafter cited as AGN), Derecho Indígena (hereinafter cited as DI), leg. 1, cuad. 9, fol. 5.

7. Raúl Rivera Serna, transcriber, *Libro del cabildo de la Ciudad de San Juan de la Frontera de Huamanga, 1539–1547* (Lima, 1966), 28–33.

8. See ibid., 47, 64–65, 68, 71, 91, 95, 100, 121, 128–129, 137, 165, 194.

9. See ibid., 21–22, 30, 31, 46–47, 54, 62, 64, 112, 189; Viceroy Francisco de Toledo to Corregidor of Huamanga, Valley of Yucay, May 26, 1571, HC, doc. 985; Don Pedro de la Gasca to ?, Jauja, Dec. 27, 1547, Biblioteca Nacional del Perú (hereinafter BNP), ms. A127.

10. Serna, *Libro del cabildo*, 64.

11. Luis de Monzón et al., "Descripción . . . de los Rucanas Antamarcas," *RGI*, 238; Monzón et al., "Descripción . . . de Atunrucana y Laramati," *RGI*, 226–227; Roberto Levillier, ed., *Gobernantes del Perú*, 14 vols. (Madrid, 1921–26), II:

103–104, 153, 183, 192. On the sensitivity of peasants to power balances, see, for example, Frances Fitzgerald, *Fire in the Lake: The Vietnamese and the Americans in Vietnam* (New York, 1973), 28–32, 397–398.

12. Serna, *Libro del cabildo*, 47, 69, 100; Juan Polo de Ondegardo, "Informe . . . al Licenciado Briviesca de Muñatones," *Revista Histórica* 13 (1940), 156. Some of the yanacona retainers of Europeans may have been yana retainers alienated from ayllu society before the Spanish conquest. On the preconquest yana, see Murra, *Formaciones*, 225–242; on yanaconas as an auxiliary arm of conquest, see Nathan Wachtel, *Sociedad e ideología: Ensayos de historia y antropología andinas* (Lima, 1973), 149–158; John Hemming, *The Conquest of the Incas* (New York, 1970), 136, 171, 180, 184, 186, 305–306, 362.

13. Serna, *Libro del cabildo*, 63.

14. For a concise history of the Peruvian civil wars, see Lockhart, *Spanish Peru*, 3–5; for the role of Huamanga in colonial politics, see Serna, *Libro del cabildo*, 71–72, 73–79, 85–88, 93–96, 98–99, 141, 142–145, 146–150, 152, 159–164, 168–174, 199; Domingo de Santo Tomás to King, Lima, May 20, 1555, in Emilio Lissón Chaves, ed., *La iglesia de España en el Perú*, 4 vols. (Seville, 1943–46), II:57.

15. Report by La Gasca, Lima, Sept. 25, 1548, BNP, ms. A127; Archivo Departamental de Ayacucho, Ayacucho (hereinafter cited as ADA), Protocolos Notariales (hereinafter cited as PN), Navarrette 1627, fols. 473–474; "Autos que siguieron don Melchor y don Salvador Ataurimachi . . . 1643," AGN, DI, leg. 6, cuad. 109, fols. 2r, 5v; Damián de la Bandera, "Relación general . . . de Guamanga," *RGI*, 178; "Provisión de los indios Cañaris de Vilcas . . . 1612," BNP, ms. B44, fol. 8r; Serna, *Libro del cabildo*, 121, 142, for quotations; Poma de Ayala, *Nueva corónica*, 431–433.

16. Serna, *Libro del cabildo*, 45, 50–51, 130. For other cases, see idem, 38, 45, 48, 61, 120, 124, 132. One *fanegada* is approximately 2.9 hectares.

17. Ibid., 61, 97, 100, 120; "Autos que sigue el Común de Indios . . . de Chiara . . . 1806," AGN, Tierras de Comunidades, leg. 3, cuad. 19, fols. 40v, 42r; "Libro de Cabildo . . . 1557," BNP, ms. A203, fol. 65v.

18. "Autos . . . contra Juan Arias Maldonado . . . 1573," AGN, DI, leg. 2, cuad. 17, fols. 195, 226.

19. Viceroy Marqués de Cañete to Indians of several repartimientos, Lima, Sept. 27, 1557, HC, doc. 1013. The Yauyos and Huancas mentioned in this document refer to those who lived in southern Huamanga (Chocorvos and Vilcashuamán) rather than the societies of the central sierra north of Huamanga.

20. "Autos . . . contra Juan Arias Maldonado . . . 1573," AGN, DI, leg. 2, cuad. 17, fols. 178r, 197r, 219v–220r.

21. Ibid., esp. fols. 179, 191–195 (son's exaggeration: 195v), 208–209, 226.

22. Ibid., fols. 195r, 208v, 215v; "Libros de penas de cámara . . . de Huamanga . . . 1559," BNP, ms. A336, passim; cf. Serna, *Libro del cabildo*, 30, 122.

23. Serna, *Libro del cabildo*, 21–22, 31, 64, 112; cf. Marie Helmer, "Notas sobre la encomienda peruana en el siglo XVI," *Revista del Instituto de Historia del Derecho* 10 (1959), 124–143.

24. José María Vargas, *Fray Domingo de Santo Tomás, defensor y apóstol de los indios del Perú: Su vida y escritos* (Quito, 1937), "Escritos" section, 10.

25. Polo, "Informe . . . al Licenciado Briviesca de Muñatones," 157. Polo's observations were probably based upon patterns in the greater Cuzco region. For similar data from Huamanga, see Monzón et al., "Descripción . . . de los Rucanas Antamarcas," 238.

26. See Bandera, "Relación general," 176; "Autos criminales que siguieron Juan Tucabamba y Pedro Cachi indios . . . 1567," AGN, DI, leg. 1, cuad. 9, fols. 20–22.

27. Poma de Ayala, *Nueva corónica*, 559.

28. Monzón et al., "Descripción . . . de Atunrucana y Laramati," p. 227; "Testimonio . . . y confirmación de la Hacienda de LOCCHAS . . . 1625," AGN, Títulos de propiedad, cuad. 747, fols. 4v (quotation), 16.

29. For juridical, economic, public works, and other cabildo policies and regulations, see Serna, *Libro del cabildo*, 21–22, 42–43, 46–47, 54, 62, 112, 126, 132, 145, 184, 185, 196.

30. Ibid., 35, 36, 38, 39–41, 43–46, 48, 51, 53, 54–59, 65, 72, 97, 121, 154.

31. Ibid., 40, 43, 46, 48, 52, 54, 56–61, 63, 73, 93, 120–122, 126–127, 130, 133, 153–155.

32. Ibid., 179 for quotation; 180–181, 182–183, for distribution.

33. "Libro de Cabildo . . . 1557," BNP, ms. A203, fols. 24–25.

34. For the incredible variety of items in pre-1570 tribute lists, see "Autos . . . contra Juan Arias Maldonado . . . 1573," AGN, DI, leg. 2, cuad. 17, fols. 179–180, 184–186; "Testimonio . . . que siguió doña María Carrillo . . . sobre . . . la mitad del repartimiento de ANDAMARCA . . . 1576," AGN, DI, leg. 1, cuad. 8, fols. 109–112.

35. "Testimonio . . . que siguió doña María Carrillo . . . sobre . . . la mitad del repartimiento de ANDAMARCA . . . 1576," AGN, DI, leg. 1, cuad. 8, fol. 110v, for prices in 1563.

36. In addition to notes 31–33 and 28, see Serna, *Libro del cabildo*, 62; Pedro de Cieza de León, *Parte primera de la crónica del Perú*, in *Biblioteca de autores españoles*, tomo 26 (Madrid, 1853), chap. 87; Juan López de Velasco, *Geografía y descripción universal de las Indias*, edited by Marcos Jiménez de la Espada (Madrid, 1971), 241; "Sobre la medición . . . de unas tierras en Yucay . . . 1578," BNP, ms. Z305; "Testimonio de los títulos . . . de Guatata, Churucana y Pacuaro . . . 1626," BNP, ms. B75, fols. 23v, 46r; "Copia de los títulos de las tierras de CHINCHE-PAMPA . . . 1568," AGN, Títulos de propiedad, cuad. 8; untitled *expediente* concerning Huanta lands disputed among various Europeans and Indians, 1678, ADA, Corregimiento, Causas Ordinarias, leg. 2 (provisional classification in 1977), esp. fol. 935; land registration of Monastery of Santa Clara, 1642, Registro de Propiedad Inmueble de Ayacucho, tomo 21, partida XXXIII, 330; "Libro de Cabildo . . . 1557," BNP, ms. A203, fol. 33v.

37. This definition of commercial capital refers to a profit mechanism based on: (1) "underpaying" producers by acquiring labor power or commodity goods for free (tribute) or at less than their market value; and (2) exploiting a position as intermediary between high-priced and low-priced markets. On the distinction between industrial capital or capitalist production, and commercial capital in precapitalist settings, see Karl Marx, *Capital*, edited by Frederick Engels, 3 vols. (New York, 1967), esp. III, chaps. 20, 36, 47. As Marx pointed out, it is important to distinguish between the dynamics of commercial capital within a capitalist economy and the commercial capital that predates the dominance of capitalist production. In the text, I refer to the later form of commercial capital.

38. Serna, *Libro del cabildo*, 50, 123, 142, 166; see Levillier, *Gobernantes*, 1, 190. On the social atmosphere of mining centers, see the fines collected in Atunsulla in the 1560s, as recorded in "Libro de penas de cámara . . . 1559," BNP, ms. A336.

39. See "Don Diego de Salazar pide que se le ampare . . . 1622," AGN, Minería, leg. 2, Ayacucho 1622, fols. 55, 169–172, 192; Fernando Montesinos, *Anales del Perú*, edited by Víctor M. Maúrtua, 2 vols. (Madrid, 1906), I, 278; *expediente* concerning mines of Amador de Cabrera, AGN, Minería, leg. 13, Huancavelica 1585–91, exp. 1, fol. 49; *expediente* regarding property and debts of Amador de Cabrera, AGN, Minería, leg. 11, Huancavelica 1562–72, fols. 254–255.

40. "Causa de cuentas dada por Dn. Diego Guillén de Mendoza . . . 1616," BNP, ms. Z313, fols. 164–165; ADA, PN, Romo 1557, fols. 202–204; "Para que el corregidor de Vilcashuamán . . . hara [haga] averiguaciones . . . 1600," BNP, ms. B1485, fols. 62r, 247r; "Autos . . . contra Juan Arias Maldonado . . . 1573," AGN, DI, leg. 2, cuad. 17, fols. 193v–194r.

41. See Lockhart, *Spanish Peru*, 23; Lockhart, *The Men of Cajamarca*, 297; López de Velasco, *Geografía*, 241.

42. "Don Diego de Salazar pide que se le ampare . . . 1622," AGN, Minería, leg. 2, Ayacucho 1622, fol. 79r; Santo Tomás to Royal Council of the Exchequer in Lima, Andahuaylas, Apr. 6, 1562, Archivo General de las Indias, Seville (hereinafter cited as AGI), V, Lima 313; "Autos . . . contra Juan Arias Maldonado . . . 1573," AGN, DI, leg. 2, cuad. 17, fols. 192v–193r.

43. Bandera, "Relación general," 177; "Autos criminales que siguieron Juan Tucabamba y Pedro Cachi, indios . . . 1567," AGN, DI, leg. 1, cuad. 9, fols. 1r (quotation), 3v.

44. "Autos . . . contra Juan Arias Maldonado . . . 1573," AGN, DI, leg. 2, cuad. 17, fols. 192–194.

45. Serna, *Libro del cabildo*, 112, 193; "Autos . . . contra Juan Arias Maldonado . . . 1573," AGN, DI, leg. 2, cuad. 17, fol. 192v; Polo, "Informe . . . al Licenciado Briviesca de Muñatones," 189.

46. See Viceroy Toledo to Regimiento of Huamanga, Yucay Valley, June 10, 1571, HC, doc. 983; Juan Polo de Ondegardo, "Ordenanzas de las minas de Guamanga," in *Colección de libros y documentos referentes a la historia del Perú*, 4 vols. (Lima, 1916), IV: 142; López de Velasco, *Geografía*, 241.

47. Bandera, "Relación general," 177; "Registro de escrituras públicas . . . 1592," BNP, ms. Z306, fols. 490, 491; ADA, PN, Padilla 1602/1613, fol. 339v; Marqués de Cañete to Garci Díez de San Miguel, Lima, Aug. 21, 1559, HC, doc. 1014; *expediente* regarding property and debts of Amador de Cabrera, AGN, Minería, leg. 11, Huancavelica 1562–72, fol. 258.

48. Polo, "Informe . . . al Licenciado Briviesca de Muñatones," 189.

49. ADA, PN, Peña 1596, fol. 311r; "Autos . . . contra Juan Arias Maldonado . . . 1573," AGN, DI, leg. 2, cuad. 17, fol. 193r.

50. Ibid.; Bandera, "Relación general," 180, for quotations.

51. "Libro de penas de cámara . . . 1559," BNP, ms. A336, entry for Oct. 13, 1559.

52. The "open" strategy of native society had religious and cultural dimensions as well, but space constraints limit my discussion to socioeconomic patterns. For the religious and cultural sides of the Indian-Spanish alliances, see Stern, "The Challenge of Conquest," 77–79.

53. The encomendero population was not completely stable in the first years after Huamanga's founding in 1539, but usually hovered around twenty-five.

54. For tribute lists in the 1550s and 1560s, see "Testimonio . . . que siguió doña María Carrillo . . . sobre . . . la mitad del repartimiento de ANDAMARCA

. . . 1576," AGN, DI, leg. 1, cuad. 8, fols. 109–112; "Autos . . . contra Juan Arias Maldonado . . . 1573," AGN, DI, leg. 2, cuad. 17, fols. 184–188.

55. Bandera, "Relación general," 179.

56. Polo, "Informe . . . al Licenciado Briviesca de Muñatones," 169.

57. "Autos . . . contra Juan Arias Maldonado . . . 1573," AGN, DI, leg. 2, cuad. 17, fol. 185r. For similar practices elsewhere, see Karen Spalding, "*Kurakas* and Commerce: A Chapter in the Evolution of Andean Society," *Hispanic American Historical Review* (*HAHR*) 53 (Nov. 1973), 586–588.

58. For clear examples from 1570 to 1572 in Andahuaylas and Parinacochas, see "Autos . . . contra Juan Arias Maldonado . . . 1573," AGN, DI, leg. 2, cuad. 17, fols. 181–183; "Libro común de sumas . . . por el tesorero Miguel Sánchez. Cuzco, 1572–1573," Yale University, Sterling Library, Department of Manuscripts, Latin America Collection, vol. 5, fol. 62v. Cf. "En la residencia secreta . . . a Dn. Francisco de Cepeda, Corregidor de Parinacochas . . . 1597," BNP, ms. A236, fols. 20r, 22r.

59. Serna, *Libro del cabildo*, 40.

60. Bandera, "Relación general," 180; ADA, PN, Romo 1577, fols. 331–332. Cf. three contracts recorded in Cuzco in 1560, in *Revista del Archivo Histórico* 4 (Cuzco, 1953), 25, 31, 32.

61. ADA, PN, Romo 1577, fol. 332v.

62. For the data above, see "Autos . . . contra Juan Arias Maldonado . . . 1573," AGN, DI, leg. 2, cuad. 17, fols. 179, 186–187, 191–192, 207, 213r, 216–217.

63. Guillermo Lohmann Villena, *Las minas de Huancavelica en los siglos XVI y XVII* (Seville, 1949), 28, 91–92; Polo, "Ordenanzas de las minas de Guamanga," 139–151; Vargas, *Fray Domingo*, "Escritos" section, 57–62; *expediente* regarding property and debts of Amador de Cabrera, AGN, Minería, leg. 11, Huancavelica 1562–72, fol. 62r; "Libro 50 del Cabildo . . . 1568," BNP, ms. A603, fol. 23v (quotation). See Levillier, *Gobernantes*, II: 573, 578.

64. "Causa de cuentas dada por Dn. Diego Guillén de Mendoza . . . 1616," BNP, ms. Z313, fols. 164–165; ADA, PN, Romo 1577, fols. 202–204, esp. 203; "Concierto en el asiento de Colcabamba . . . 1571," BNP, ms. A455; "Para que el corregidor de Vilcashuamán . . . hara [haga] averiguaciones . . . 1600," BNP, ms. B1485, fol. 61r; Miriám Salas Olivari, "El obraje de Chincheros. Del obraje a las comunidades indígenas, siglo XVI" (Bachelor's thesis, Pontífica Universidad Católica del Perú, 1976), 109–110 (courtesy of Scarlett O'Phelan).

65. Santo Tomás, an opponent of the encomienda, was the more extreme proponent of this view. On these two personalities, see Murra, *Formaciones*, 285–286, 306–311; Patricia J. Bard, "Domingo de Santo Tomás, a Spanish Friar in 16th Century Peru" (M.A. thesis, Columbia University, 1967).

66. Monzón et al., "Descripción . . . de los Rucanas Antamarcas," 238; Monzón et al., "Descripción . . . de Atunrucana y Laramati," 227.

67. See Noble David Cook, "The Indian Population of Peru, 1570–1620" (Ph.D. diss., University of Texas at Austin, 1973), 238; see John H. Rowe, "Inca Culture at the Time of the Spanish Conquest," in Julian H. Steward, ed., *Handbook of South American Indians*, 7 vols. (Washington, DC, 1946–59), II:184. It should be noted that the first major sixteenth-century epidemic in the Andean zone struck in the 1520s, *before* the European conquest in 1532.

68. On the importance of livestock herds as a kind of insurance resource in Huamanga and elsewhere, see Bandera, "Relación general," 177; Murra, *Formaciones*, 202–203.

69. See the "Relación de Amancebados, Hechiceros y Huacas" included in Luis Millones, ed., *Las informaciones de Cristóbal de Albornoz: Documentos para el estudio del Taki Onqoy* (Cuernavaca, 1971).

70. Noble David Cook, ed., *Tasa de la visita general de Francisco de Toledo (1570–1575)* (Lima, 1975), 261.

71. Hemming, *Conquest*, 386–387.

72. On the importance, in Andean culture, of "balanced" relationships with the gods for the material welfare and health of the living, see Stern, "The Challenge of Conquest," 30–35. For the tendency to interpret disease and misfortune as the work of offended deities, see Poma de Ayala, *Nueva corónica*, 109, 137, 158, 286; Francisco de Avila, *Dioses y hombres de Huarochirí*, translated by José María Argüedas (Lima, 1966), 47, 49, 149, 151.

73. Marqués de Cañete to various Corregidors, Lima, Nov. 9, 1556, HC, doc. 1012.

74. See Lockhart, *Spanish Peru*, 52–55.

75. Marqués de Cañete to various Corregidors, Lima, May 25, 1557, HC, doc. 1009; Bandera, "Relación general," 176; García de Castro to Priests of Huamanga, Lima, Dec. 16, 1564, HC, doc. 1008.

76. Marqués de Cañete to Corregidor of Huamanga, Lima, Feb. 21, 1556, HC, doc. 1017.

77. For examples from the 1560s, see Vargas, *Fray Domingo*, "Escritos" section, 59; "Autos . . . contra Juan Arias Maldonado . . . 1573," AGN, DI, leg. 2, cuad. 17, fol. 208r.

78. "Autos . . . contra Juan Arias Maldonado . . . 1573," AGN, DI, leg. 2, cuad. 17, fols. 194v, 209r; Montesinos, *Anales del Perú*, I:243, II:18.

79. See Polo, "Ordenanzas de las minas de Guamanga," 139–151.

80. Santo Tomás to Don Alonso Manuel de Anaya, Huamanga, Mar. 23, 1562, Santo Tomás to Council of Indies, Andahuaylas, Apr. 5, 1562, Santo Tomás to Royal Council of the Exchequer in Lima, Andahuaylas, Apr. 6, 1562, AGI, V, Lima, 313 (also available in Vargas, *Fray Domingo*, "Escritos" section, 55–62).

81. "Libro 50 del Cabildo . . . 1568," BNP, ms. A603, fol. 23v.

82. Archbishop Gerónimo de Loayza to King, Lima, Nov. 30, 1562, AGI, V, Lima 300; Santo Tomás to Anaya, Huamanga, Mar. 23, 1562, AGI, V, Lima, 313. See Hemming, *Conquest*, 385–390, for an overview of the encomienda perpetuity issue.

83. All the evidence cited above is from the period 1563 to 1571. "Libro de penas de cámara . . . 1559," BNP, ms. A336, entry for May 3, 1563; Viceroy Toledo to Judge of Huamanga's mines, Yucay Valley, June 10, 1571, HC, doc. 984; Lohmann, *Las minas*, 93 n.3; "Autos . . . contra Juan Arias Maldonado . . . 1573," AGN, DI, leg. 2, cuad. 17, fol. 196r; Lohmann, *El corregidor*, 28; Cristóbal de Molina, *Relación de las fábulas y ritos de los incas*, in Francisco A. Loayza, ed., *Las crónicas de los Molinas [sic]* (Lima, 1943), 79.

84. Molina, *Relación de las fábulas*, 82; Cristóbal de Albornoz, "Instrucción para descubrir todas las guacas del Pirú y sus camayos y haciendas," edited by Pierre Duviols, *Journal de la Société des Américanistes* 56–1 (1967), 36.

85. A detailed presentation of this movement's history in Huamanga lies beyond the scope of this article. For an extended discussion, see Stern, "The Challenge of Conquest," 101–143; see Juan M. Ossio, ed., *Ideología mesiánica del mundo andino* (Lima, 1973), especially the essays by Luis Millones and Nathan Wachtel on 85–142.

It should be noted that the crisis of the Indian-Spanish alliances did not lead to a *total* breakdown of native-white cooperation or alliance. The rupture was most severe on the issue of mine labor, and some evidence suggests ambivalent attitudes of *kurakas* in the 1560s. Nonetheless, events of the 1560s plunged earlier relations and expectations into crisis. See Guillermo Lohmann Villena, "Juan de Matienzo, autor del 'Gobierno del Perú' (su personalidad y su obra)," *Anuario de Estudios Americanos* 22 (1965), 767–886; Stern, "The Challenge of Conquest," 124–130, 140–145.

86. See, for example, Eric R. Wolf and Edward C. Hansen, *The Human Condition in Latin America* (New York, 1972), 29–30, 57–59. For a sixteenth-century version of this observation, see Cieza de León, *Parte primera*, chap. 13.

87. See, for example, James C. Scott, *The Moral Economy of the Peasant: Rebellion and Subsistence in Southeast Asia* (New Haven, 1976); Philip Wayne Powell, *Soldiers, Indians, and Silver: North America's First Frontier War* (Tempe, 1975; orig. pub. 1952), 32–54; R. C. Padden, "Cultural Change and Military Resistance in Araucanian Chile, 1550–1730," *Southwestern Journal of Anthropology* 13 (Spring 1957), 103–121.

88. For examples in Brazil, Paraguay, and North America, see Alexander Marchant, *From Barter to Slavery: The Economic Relations of Portuguese and Indians in the Settlement of Brazil, 1500–1580* (Baltimore, 1942); Stuart B. Schwartz, "Indian Labor and New World Plantations: European Demands and Indian Responses in Northeastern Brazil," *American Historical Review* 83 (Feb. 1978), 43–79; Elman R. Service, *Spanish-Guaraní Relations in Early Colonial Paraguay* (Ann Arbor, 1954), esp. 18–22, 33; Gary B. Nash, *Red, White, and Black: The Peoples of Early America* (Englewood Cliffs, NJ, 1974), passim.

3

Persistent Maya Resistance and Cultural Retention in Yucatán

Nancy M. Farriss

When the Spaniards encountered peoples such as the Maya, who practiced slash-and-burn agriculture, had no indigenous imperial structures, and lacked immediately marketable commodities (especially precious metals), they did not pursue systematic conquest with the same fervor as they did in central Mexico or in the Andes nor did they colonize in the same numbers. The trajectory of cultural change among the Maya, then, was completely different from that found in these two important central regions. The international market economy on the periphery did not penetrate as directly, and Spanish settlers were not able to install draft labor systems to draw indigenous workers into the colonial economy with the same success. The presence of the church was commensurately reduced, and the Christianization of the natives was understandably diminished in scope and character. The existence of a frontier enabled some natives to evade the colonial system and constituted a continuing threat and alternative to Spanish rule.

A case for the comparatively mild effects of Spanish colonization in Yucatán rests ultimately on the entire record of the colonial regime. Throughout most of the colonial period, Yucatán's position on the periphery of the Spanish empire preserved for the Maya a degree of isolation and autonomy that the Aztecs and other groups in the economic and political core had lost within decades of the conquest. But differences are apparent from the start, in the first confrontations between Indians and Spaniards in what is present-day Mexico. The conquest of Yucatán was a lengthy affair. The prolonged warfare produced much material devastation. Yet by the same token it represented a less abrupt and therefore a less traumatic break with the past than the rapid overthrow of the Aztec empire. Indeed, for large areas of Yucatán it is difficult to say exactly when the conquest ended and colonial rule began.

Yucatán was discovered in 1517 during a voyage of exploration out of Cuba. This first encounter with the more sophisticated Indians of the American mainland, who wore clothes, had stone buildings, and above all possessed gold, stimulated Spanish plans to colonize the new territory. But Yucatán itself was bypassed. A second voyage had received a friendlier reception and hints of more substantial wealth to the west. A third expedition, organized by Hernán Cortés in 1519, touched only briefly at Yucatán on the way to Veracruz and ultimately to Cortés's rendezvous with Moctezuma at Tenochtitlan.[1]

Only in 1527, after campaigns throughout the Mesoamerican highlands and into Honduras, did the Spanish turn their attention to Yucatán, under the leadership of one of Cortés's lieutenants, Francisco de Montejo. It took two full decades to conquer Yucatán, in contrast with a bare two years to subdue the Aztecs. The Maya had no overarching imperial structure that could be toppled with one swift blow to the center. Yucatán was divided into at least sixteen autonomous provinces with varying degrees of internal unity. Each of the provinces, and sometimes the subunits within them, had to be negotiated with and, failing that, conquered separately.

At times Yucatán must scarcely have seemed worth the trouble of conquest. Discontent with lack of gold thinned Montejo's ranks. The dense bush and potholed terrain of Yucatán proved difficult for horses and ill-suited to the pitched battles that favored Spanish weapons and tactics. Resistance was fierce in some areas; and, worst of all, the Maya refused to stay conquered.

The conquest of Yucatán is generally considered to have ended with the suppression in 1547 of the Great Revolt, a large-scale uprising by the Maya of the entire central and eastern regions. The Spanish hold over the peninsula was never again seriously challenged, but it was incomplete and remained so throughout the colonial period. In a low-key and sporadic way, the conquest was to continue for centuries.

The initial thrust had stopped at the southern borders of the provinces of Mani and Cochuah. Beyond them lay a vast, barely explored region stretching through the Montaña district and the Petén to the settled foothills of Guatemala and Chiapas, a region bypassed and largely ignored after Cortés's brief swing through the heart of the area on his march from central Mexico to Honduras in 1525.[2] An isolated missionary outpost was founded in the Montaña district but lasted only from 1604 to 1614. In the east along the Caribbean coast the Spanish had subdued the provinces of Ecab, Uaymil, and Chetumal but failed to occupy them permanently, except for the fortified settlement of Bacalar at the base of the peninsula. For the first century and a half after the colony was established, the Spanish actually lost ground, pulling back from territory that they still nominally claimed but lacked the means and the incentive to control.

The colonists had settled in the most hospitable part of the peninsula, the northwest, where the Indians were more numerous and the drier climate proved more attractive to Europeans. Spanish influence remained concentrated in this region for the same related combination of factors. The rain forests of the Montaña and the Petén, once the teeming heartland of Classic Maya civilization, had already suffered a severe population decline (although exactly how severe is still debated) long before the Spanish arrived. The depopulation of the eastern and southwestern coastal provinces was their unwitting handiwork. Except for Uaymil and Chetumal, these provinces had all submitted to Spanish rule with little or no resistance, so that losses through warfare and disruptions in food production were minimal in most areas. Climate and strategic location, which had been the basis of their prosperity, now contributed to their decline. The moist climate, with heavier rainfall and more surface water, produced good crop yields but was also particularly congenial to many of the Old World pathogens introduced by the Spanish and their African slaves.

Equally devastating in its effects, though perhaps more difficult to measure, was the collapse of the Maya economy, which had been based largely on long-distance trade. At the time of contact vigorous commercial centers nearly ringed the peninsula from Chauaca in the north, down through Cozumel and Tulum on the Caribbean to Nito on the Bay of Honduras, and across the base to the gulf coast. All were controlled by or affiliated with the "Putun," or Chontal Maya, in southwestern Campeche, who have been called the "Phoenicians of the New World."[3] Strategically located, they funneled goods between the peninsula and the highlands of Mexico and Central America. Even before the actual conquest of Yucatán, their traditional trade networks had been disrupted by the overthrow of the Aztec empire in central Mexico and of other trading partners in Guatemala and Honduras.[4]

By the time the Spanish turned their attention back from the northwestern part of the peninsula to these peripheral regions that had been so quickly and easily won (again, with the exception of Uaymil and Chetumal, which were virtually destroyed in a late, fierce campaign), they found them already in severe decline. What once had been flourishing zones were reduced to a few scattered settlements well before the end of the sixteenth century. By the latter part of the seventeenth century these regions had been officially abandoned. Their strategic location had contributed to their further decline, for they were exposed to attack by French, Dutch, and English pirates who had been attracted to the Caribbean by Spanish wealth and had already begun to harass ships and settlements along Yucatán's coasts by the 1560s. Faced with the impossibility of defending the peninsula's long, exposed shoreline, except for the major port of Campeche (itself sacked several times), the Spanish decided to move the remnant Maya populations well inland and abandon the coasts to the "Lutheran corsairs."[5]

In the mid-seventeenth century the colonial frontier had contracted to a line curving from below Champoton up to the Puuc hills, across to Peto and Tihosuco, and then angling northeast to the Caribbean along a line now marking the boundary between the states of Yucatán and Quintana Roo. The territory beyond that frontier was officially referred to as *despoblado*, or uninhabited. In fact, it became the home of large numbers of refugees who fled colonial rule to form independent settlements of their own or to join their unconquered cousins, who held out in small pockets in the east and controlled all the territory to the south. They were never left totally in peace. Every so often a wave of evangelistic fervor would sweep through the local Franciscans, and a missionary or two would be dispatched into the bush to make or renew contact with any unconverted or apostate Maya they could locate. The Indians generally received them peacefully. On occasion they became exasperated into discourtesy and even threats, but only three unescorted missionaries are on record as having won the "crown of martyrdom" in the entire unpacified area.[6] The Maya were aware that resistance would provoke armed reprisals and they found it more prudent to feign submission, and then relocate their settlements or simply revert to former habits once the friars had left.[7]

Military expeditions were also undertaken sporadically by the Spanish to round up fugitives by force and resettle them in the pacified areas, and these raids seem to have cleared out a large part of the eastern region.[8] The Spanish could not, however, mount guard along the entire frontier, and as long as the large and accessible territory to the south remained unsubdued, the conquest of the rest of the peninsula could not be considered complete.

The existence of totally independent Maya politics, the largest and most powerful of them the Itza kingdom centered at Lake Petén, blurred the boundary between pre-Columbian and colonial, pagan and Christian, unconquered and conquered. The effect was analogous in kind if not in degree to that of the Inca state in exile that held out on the borders of the kingdom of Peru for decades after the initial overthrow. In Yucatán as in Peru, there was no clean break with the past on either side of the frontier, which the Maya found highly permeable in both directions. Refugees, raiding parties, delegations from the Itzá and other groups, and, above all, traders moved back and forth in steady if often clandestine contact. We have no way of measuring the volume of the illicit trade, about which the Spanish had some notion but could not stop. Interregional commerce had been brisk in pre-Columbian times; it became reinforced by the new demand among both pagan and apostate Maya for the steel axes and other tools introduced by the Spanish. Trade in salt, which the west and north coasts of the peninsula had presumably long supplied to the interior, continued after conquest. It is more than likely that part of the honey and wax the Spanish collected in tribute from the pacified Maya for export to central Mexico came originally from the unconquered interior.[9]

The unconquered zones were an escape hatch for some of the colonized Maya; they were a cultural and political as well as an economic factor in the lives of all of them. Contact between separated kinsmen was not entirely broken, for news traveled rapidly with the trade goods. Even for the great majority of Maya who did not flee there, the zones of refuge were an ever-present and familiar (if only by hearsay) option rather than a frightening unknown. Masses of them chose this option during the latter part of the seventeenth century. They swelled the unconquered settlements in the south that seemed to be coalescing under a native "king." These groups became increasingly bold, raiding pacified border towns and making the not wholly bombastic claim of sovereignty over them.[10] Long at a standstill, the conquest now seemed to be going into reverse.

Despite some inconclusive forays into the Petén from Spanish settlements in Tabasco, Chiapas, and Yucatán, the interior remained largely outside Spanish control until 1697, when a combined expedition from Yucatán and Guatemala conquered the Itzá kingdom.[11] Another series of expeditions in the early 1700s finally expelled the English from the Laguna de Términos, where a military outpost was established to protect Spanish settlements along the gulf en route toward Tabasco.[12] A new mission was founded in the interior west of Bacalar, and thin archipelagos of pacified villages grew up along the trails linking Yucatán with Bacalar and a new outpost at Lake Petén. The much acclaimed conquest of the Petén did not, however, destroy the zones of refuge. The groups of fugitives and unpacified Maya merely moved further into the bush, harassed by occasional raids but never totally reduced to Spanish rule.[13] Deep in the interior, the Lacandon Maya, survivors of this population, have never, strictly speaking, been conquered to this day.

When did the conquest of Yucatán actually end? In 1547, with the suppression of the Great Revolt? In 1697, with the conquest of the Petén? Some might consider the nineteenth-century Caste War as the final fix. Drawn into the factional strife of postindependence Yucatán and regaining a long dormant taste for military victory, the Maya launched their own struggle in 1847 to rid themselves of what they still regarded as foreign domination. For a brief time it looked as if they might succeed. From the east around Valladolid, Tihosuco, and Sotuta (the same regions that had united in the Great Revolt three hundred years earlier), the rebellion spread south to Bacalar and, much more menacingly, began to close in on Mérida. The city and the whites who had taken refuge there were saved only by the "grace of God," the Maya term for maize. Reaching within attacking distance of Mérida just as the rainy season was approaching, the Maya troops—farmers all—retreated to their villages and their maize fields. First things first: the maize had to be planted, tended, and harvested, and only then could they return to finish the war. But they had lost their chance. The *dzuls* (foreigners) were not, after all, to be driven out of Yucatán. On the other hand, the Maya never admitted defeat, either. They only retreated east again and established a rebel state around a Maya-Christian cult of a Speaking Cross, acquiring the name of *cruzob* Maya from the *Santa Cruz* or Holy Cross they worshipped. They actually managed to push the old colonial frontier back to its mid-seventeenth-century position, where it was to remain, with minor advances and retreats, for the next fifty years.[14]

In 1901, Chan Santa Cruz, the *cruzob* capital, fell to federal troops from central Mexico. Does this defeat mark the end of the Caste War and, along with it, the conquest of Yucatán? Or did both the war and the conquest continue for another sixty years or so? During this time the *cruzob* Maya still controlled the district into which they had retreated and which encompassed a large portion of the present state of Quintana Roo in eastern Yucatán. But perhaps the conquest was not complete until 1969, with the death of the chief of the *cruzob* town of Chumpom and the last of the Caste War leaders. His successors decided after much deliberation not to carry out their threat to attack the highway crew that pushed its way into the formerly isolated territory. Federal troops had been sent to guard the crew, and the Maya had been unsuccessful in obtaining modern carbines to replace their antiquated firearms. The road was completed and the *cruzob* Maya, like it or not, are now being incorporated into the fabric of national society. Some of them hold jobs with the national archaeological institute as custodians of the pre-Columbian sites in their areas; others have already been tapped for military service in the army that their grandfathers held off for so long.

Maya Perceptions of the Conquest

The Yucatec Maya have left several accounts of the sixteenth-century Spanish conquest, accounts that differ markedly in tone and perspective from the Aztec versions. Their narratives of the arrival and military campaigns of the Spanish are spare and matter-of-fact.[15] And while there is a certain poignancy in the later chronicles that record the evil times ushered in by the conquest, they lack the immediacy and grief-stricken anguish of the Aztec elegies for a world that had been suddenly and irrevocably shattered.[16] The contrast reflects, in part, different experiences: swift and total military defeat with the leveling of a mighty city to a heap of rubble, as opposed to a drawn-out series of skirmishes and battles carried on for the most part outside the population centers. It also reflects different perceptions of the significance of defeat and foreign domination.

The Spanish conquest was a particularly rude shock to the Aztecs because of their own mystique of invincibility based on a long, virtually unbroken record of military success. Foreign domination was an unfamiliar experience in the central highlands, where the pattern was conquest from within. The Aztecs, and the Toltecs before them, were outsiders originally, but they had arrived as humble migrants who gradually assimilated into and then dominated the local scene before expanding outward.

If the Mexican highlands were the dynamic center of expansion within Mesoamerica, Yucatán was a favored target, and the Maya had a long history of conquest to prepare them psychologically and cognitively for the arrival of the Spanish. The well-known "Toltec" invasion, which brought the cult of the Feathered Serpent (Quetzalcoatl-Kukulcan) and other distinctively highland influences to the peninsula in the late tenth century, was once thought to be unique. It is now seen by scholars as simply one of a series of more or less warlike intrusions into the lowlands, ranging in time from at least the early centuries of the Christian era down to the Spanish conquest itself.[17] The Spanish invasion could take its place in that series with a little stretch of the imagination.

These intrusions were not always or necessarily full-scale invasions directly from the highlands. The lowland Maya engaged in much local warfare among themselves. Border conflicts and civil strife provided ideal opportunity for small groups of foreign adventurers, either Mexican or Mexicanized intermediaries, to gain a foothold. Rather than replace the local contenders entirely, the foreigners joined in the fray, jockeying for position by strategic alliances and eventually merging with the local rulers through intermarriage. The struggle for control of the late Postclassic center of Mayapán, abandoned in 1441, provides one of the better-known examples, involving at least three different foreign groups of varying antiquity in the peninsula. The Cocom lineage, identified with the former rulers of Chichén Itzá, was overthrown by the more recently established Xiu, despite the aid of Mexican troops, and these latest arrivals were then able to establish themselves as local rulers in the Ah Canul province.[18]

The record of these past invasions was well preserved in the Maya's written chronicles and oral traditions.[19] The memory was kept fresh by the expansionist activities of the Chontal Maya traders and by the continued presence of Mexican troops in their trading enclave at Xicalango on the shores of the Laguna de Términos (the source of the earlier Cocom allies). At the time of the Cortés expedition the Aztecs are reported to have assembled a large force in Xicalango under Moctezuma's brother for yet another major invasion, a plan that was thwarted only by the collapse of the Aztec empire at the center.[20]

Whether or not the Maya were expecting this particular invasion, Spanish actions followed patterns familiar enough to suggest that history was repeating itself. And since the Maya's entire view of time was based on the conviction that each of their twenty-year *katun* periods repeated itself with the same recurring events at 256-year intervals (with no doubt some ex post facto juggling to make the proper fit), the suggestion must have had compelling force. The Spanish arrived in small numbers, invading the peninsula both via the east coast into the interior around Chichén Itzá as the Itzá had done perhaps eight centuries before, and then via Tabasco into Campeche, the route of more recent penetrations. They quickly adopted the local stiffened cotton quilting for armor instead of steel cuirasses. In their second invasion they even brought central Mexican (Aztec and Tlaxcalan) troops, whose participation in the conquest meant in a sense that Moctezuma's original scheme was not totally aborted. These auxiliaries, like their predecessors, settled in Yucatán as conquerors. They retained throughout the colonial period the special privileges granted them by the Spanish for their services, and they followed precedent by merging genetically and culturally with the conquered Maya.[21] Thus it was not only due to the Maya's cyclical view of time, in which history and prophecy are intertwined in recurring patterns, that the major pre-Columbian invasions (called "descents" by the Maya) are often hard to distinguish from the Spanish in the native chronicles.

The Maya did not confuse the fair-skinned bearded Spaniards with Mexicans, whom they knew well as trading partners as well as potential conquerors. But neither did they take them for gods. The Spaniards must have been a strange and frightening sight with their "thunder sticks," their horses, and their fierce hunting dogs. But the Maya were not troubled by the same perceptual problems that initially paralyzed the Aztecs, who were at first unsure whether the newcomers were gods, emissaries of gods, or mere men and therefore vacillated in their reactions to them.[22] We find no supernatural overtones in the Maya's responses. They seem to have accepted the Spanish simply as some kind of human strangers and to have acted on purely pragmatic political grounds in dealing with them, according to how they calculated their best interests.[23]

In view of the fragmented political structure of the lowland Maya, it is not surprising that their interests were narrowly conceived, often in terms of possible advantages to be gained against neighboring groups. Interprovincial rivalries, sometimes based on centuries-old traditions of enmity, prevented the Maya from uniting against the intruders. Foreign conquerors throughout history have profited from this kind of provincialism that, with hindsight, seems so myopic. The Maya leaders, like many others in similar circumstances, sought to place the newcomers into the existing framework of the region's politics, without realizing that the new element would destroy the framework and thus render obsolete the basis of their calculations.

Some of the Maya lords chose a policy of active cooperation, joining the invaders in the conquest of neighboring provinces. Such alliances seem to have been a traditional expedient in local warfare. Many of the Maya lords were of foreign origin themselves and at least some had gained ascendancy through similar means. In theory, all the lowland Maya dynasties traced descent from one or another earlier group of conquerors as part of their claim to rulership, no matter how remote the ancestral ties. Some were, however, of more recent stock, and it is among these comparative newcomers, such as the Chontal Maya on the gulf and east coasts, the Pech, Chel, and Canul dynasties, and most notably the Xiu rulers of Mani province, that the Spanish found the friendliest receptions.[24]

In the interior of the peninsula, among the Cupul, the Cochuah, and the Cocom (of Sotuta), the Spanish met with unrelenting resistance from beginning to end—and beyond. For these same provinces joined forces again in the Great Revolt of 1546–47. The antecedents of the Cochuah have not been recorded, but it is perhaps no coincidence that the most unequivocal enemies of the Spanish were the Cupul and the Cocom, the two most ancient ruling lineages in Yucatán, who traced their ancestry back to the Itzá invaders who had established their capital at Chichén Itzá.[25] They were presumably more thoroughly Mayanized, certainly more isolated from foreign influences, and possibly for that reason more hostile to outsiders, especially Mexican outsiders.

Only in retrospect does the policy of resistance seem the more astute choice or at least the more farsighted one. We cannot credit Nachi Cocom, the lord of Sotuta, with any clearer insights into the consequences of Spanish victory than his neighbor and enemy, Tutul Xiu of Mani, who chose to ally himself with the Spaniards. All the Maya rulers drew on more or less the same historical traditions, and all of them must have been dealing in their calculations, based on the region's past experience, with questions of political power, not cultural survival. They merely reached different conclusions about how best to preserve or enhance their own power.

However unwelcome domination by foreigners had been in the past, leaving a legacy of resentment that can be detected in the later chronicles, it does not seem to have been coupled in the minds of the Maya with devastating culture shock. Mexicans, after all, were part of the larger Mesoamerican civilization that had come to share many basic features through centuries of interaction. Some of the influences trickled in through the peaceful vehicle of long-distance trade; some were imposed by force. Foreigners had left traces of their impact in the style of public monuments, in Nahuatl words incorporated into the vocabulary, in new deities added to the local pantheon, and in other innovations.[26] There is evidence that the old guard continued to find some of these innovations very distasteful.[27] But the Yucatec Maya had shown a capacity again and again to absorb alien influences without being overwhelmed by them.

Immediate impressions of the Spanish were in this context reassuring, giving the Maya little hint that anything drastically different was in store for them. Aside from bringing familiar Mexican auxiliaries with them, with their familiar central Mexican *atl-atls*, or spear throwers, and aside from following the usual invasion routes, the Montejos (father, son, and nephew all confusingly bearing the same name of Francisco) pursued prudent and—again—familiar policies in their dealings with the Maya lords. They always sought to negotiate a peaceful agreement first, often sending ahead native emissaries. They offered, and initially honored, highly reasonable terms that left the local power structure intact under Spanish overlordship.[28] None of the native rulers was deposed. Even the implacable Nachi Cocom retained his position, as did the other leaders of the Great Revolt, despite the fact that they, having once taken an oath of fealty to the crown, were all in Spanish eyes guilty of treason.

The terms of submission to Spanish authority included, along with the loss of autonomy and the exaction of tribute (a galling but predictable price of conquest), the acceptance of Christianity. It is unlikely that this acceptance implied for the Maya lords any radical break with the past. The introduction of new religious cults by a conquering group—cults that would coexist along with the old—was a Mesoamerican tradition. That Christianity was an exclusive religion, one that demanded the total extinction of the Maya's own beliefs and deities, would not have been immediately apparent. Montejo, though by all accounts a devout Christian, was no religious zealot. Neither he nor the chaplains who accompanied his forces were given to dramatic scenes of idol smashing of the sort indulged in by Cortés. This was in part because Maya idolatries, which did not involve human sacrifice on any large scale, outraged Spanish sensibilities considerably less than the gory spectacles of the Aztecs. But only in part, for Cortés had already started his iconoclastic activities on the Maya island of Cozumel.

Evangelization was a decidedly low-key affair in Yucatán during the initial stages of contact. Several local lords, we are told, sought baptism, although it is hard to say what significance they attached to this ceremony, since none of the few clergymen who accompanied the Spanish forces ever learned the Maya language, and all confined themselves almost exclusively to their duties as military chaplains.[29] The old cults persisted virtually unchallenged in practice. No churches were built for the Indians and no organized program of conversion was undertaken until a handful of Franciscan missionaries arrived at the end of 1544 or early in 1545.[30]

The conquest itself brought much suffering, as any protracted military struggle will do. Reprisals and systematic devastation were, however, limited to the Uaymil and Chetumal districts under the desperate and semi-independent campaign of the Pachecos, although other provinces also resisted as stubbornly. Montejo had rivals and enemies within his own ranks, and if he had countenanced or committed similar acts of cruelty and indiscriminate slaughter (which also characterized Spanish campaigns in the Caribbean islands, in Panama, and in Mexico under Cortés's successor, Nuño de Guzmán), his accusers would have mentioned them in the detailed inquiry into his conduct ordered by the crown. The one major accusation against him that involved the Indians, as opposed to acts deemed detrimental to the interests of the crown or his follow Spaniards, was the shipment of prisoners of war to central Mexico for sale as slaves.[31] Whether consciously or not, Montejo had merely followed local tradition. Slaves had been one of Yucatán's principal exports in pre-Columbian times, and slave taking a major incentive for the endemic border warfare in the region. Montejo's local allies were induced to aid in suppressing the Great Revolt (and most likely to aid in the original conquest) with the promise that they could continue their custom of enslaving the prisoners they captured.[32] Far more objectionable and portentous from the Maya rulers' point of view than Montejo's slave trading must have been the crown's subsequent order emancipating all slaves in the recently conquered territory, whether owned by Indians or Spaniards.

During the first decades of confrontation with the Spanish, then, the Maya had little cause to believe that this latest incursion would not take its place in the same recurrent pattern of earlier conquests. Logically, this small band of warriors, vastly outnumbered and far from their home base, would be assimilated into the local elite like their Mexican predecessors. A few adjustments would have to be made: some loss of autonomy, new gods added to the local pantheon, extra tribute. Disagreeable, perhaps, but hardly intolerable. If some of the Maya lords expected a replay of previous episodes of foreign hegemony, the prohibition against slavery, which represented an important source of their wealth, was simply one of the many unpleasant surprises in store for them as the new overlords set about turning the conquered territory into a colony organized according to entirely alien principles.

Perhaps the Maya never perceived or acknowledged the full significance of the Spanish conquest. Along with the sense of grievance and loss, their later accounts of the conquest reveal that they retained from the pre-Columbian past their cyclical view of time, which under the circumstances must have been a great source of comfort. According to this view, all human history repeats itself in the same orderly fashion as the recurrent movement of the heavenly bodies. All things good and bad have their appointed time to end and to be repeated in an endless cycle, in which past is prophecy and prophecy is the past.[33] The persistence of this sustaining cosmology (when it was lost, if ever, is uncertain) is symptomatic of the resilience of Maya culture.[34] Some of the resilience rested on a history of accommodation already sketched out. Much, however, was due to the circumstances of colonial rule itself. Conquest, which was less immediately catastrophic for the Maya than for the Aztecs—less literally world shattering as an event—was also to prove less destructive in its long-term implications.

Notes

Abbreviations for works frequently cited:

AA	Archivo del Arzobispado (Secretaría), Mérida.
AGI	Archivo General de las Indias, Seville.
AGN	Archivo General de la Nación, México, D.F.
BN	Biblioteca Nacional, México, D.F.
DHY	*Documentos para la historia de Yucatán.* 3 vols. France V. Scholes et al., eds. Mérida: 1936–1938.
RY	"Relaciones de Yucatán." In *Colección de documentos inéditos relativos al descubrimiento, conquista y organización de las antiguas posesiones de Ultramar.* 25 vols. Madrid: 1885–1932, vols. 11, 13.

1. Robert S. Chamberlain, *The Conquest and Colonization of Yucatán, 1517–1550* (Washington, 1948), provides an impeccably documented summary of the main events from discovery to the establishment of royal government in 1551.

2. The journey, which actually lasted from October 1524 to April 1526, is recounted in Hernán Cortés, *Cartas de relación* (1522–1525), edited by Manuel Alcalá (Mexico, 1963), (fifth letter), 185–208; and Bernal Díaz del Castillo, *Verdadera historia de la conquista de la Nueva España* (1554?–1568), edited by Joaquín Ramiro Cabañas, 2 vols. (Mexico, 1968), 2:188–217.

3. J. Eric S. Thompson, *Maya History and Religion* (Norman, 1970), 7. The basic study of the late Postclassic "Putun" and their commercial and political networks is France V. Scholes and Ralph L. Roys, *The Maya Chontal Indians of Acalan-Tixchel: A Contribution to the History and Ethnography of the Yucatán Peninsula* (1948), 2d ed. (Norman, 1968), 15–87. See also Anne Chapman, "Port of Trade Enclaves in Aztec and Maya Civilizations," in *Trade and Market in Early Empires*, edited by Karl Polanyi, C. M. Arensberg, and H. W. Pearson (New York, 1957), 114–153; Thompson, *Maya History*, 3–47, 124–158; Jeremy A. Sabloff and William L. Rathje, "The Rise of a Maya Merchant Class," *Scientific American* 233 (1975), 72–82; and Arthur G. Miller, *On the Edge of the Sea: Mural Painting at Tancah-Tulum, Quintana Roo, Mexico* (Washington, 1982), chap. 4.

4. Cortés, *Cartas*, 185–186, 206.

5. On the postconquest decline and eventual abandonment of the east coast, see Ralph L. Roys, France V. Scholes, and Eleanor B. Adams, "Report and Census of the Indians of Cozumel, 1570," *Contributions to American Anthropology and History* (Washington, 1940), 6:1–30; and Arthur G. Miller and Nancy M. Farriss, "Religious Syncretism in Colonial Yucatán: The Archaeological and Ethnohistorical Evidence from Tancah, Quintana Roo," in *Maya Archaeology and Ethnohistory*, edited by Norman Hammond and Gordon R. Willey (Austin, 1979), 224–229. On southwestern Campeche, see Scholes and Roys, *Maya Chontal*, 159–167, 229–315. On the effects of pirate raids, see, for example, AGI, Justicia 1029, Probanza sobre los daños . . . corsarios luteranos, 1565; Patronato 75, no. 1, ramo 1, Probanza Diego Sarmiento de Figueroa, April 4, 1578; Mexico 359, Governor to Crown, Nov. 28, 1565, April 2, 1579, and Nov. 15, 1600; Mexico 360, Governor to Crown, July 10, 1638; and a number of *expedientes* from the 1670s and 1680s in AGI, Escribanía de cámara 307-A and 307-B.

6. Two Dominicans in the southern Petén in 1555 (Juan de Villagutierre Sotomayor, *Historia de la conquista de la provincia de el Itzá* [1701] [Guatemala, 1933], 49–54) and a Franciscan in Tayasal in 1628 (Diego López de Cogolludo, *Historia de Yucatán* [1654] [hereafter cited as Cogolludo] [Madrid, 1688], Lib. 10, cap. 2). Five others were killed while they were accompanying Spanish military expeditions, which appear to have supplied the provocation: one in Saclum in 1624 (Cogolludo, Lib. 10, cap. 3) and four in or near Tayasal in 1696 (Villagutierre Sotomayor, 284–294, 314–315, 352, 375). An unverified martyrdom is reported by Pedro Sánchez de Aguilar, *Informe contra idolorum cultores del obispado de Yucatán dirigido al Rey N. Señor en su Real Consejo de las Indias* (c. 1613), 3d ed. (Mérida, 1937), 120–121, who alleged that the Indians of Cozumel had deliberately drowned their curate in a boating "accident."

7. AGI, Mexico 359, 367, 369, and 3048, and Indiferente 1387 contain many letters and reports, 1564–1585, referring to the sporadic missionary activity on Cozumel and the east coast, some of them published or summarized in Roys, Scholes, and Adams, "Report and Census"; Miller and Farriss, "Religious Syncretism"; France V. Scholes and Eleanor B. Adams, *Don Diego Quijada, Alcalde Mayor de Yucatán, 1561–1565*, 2 vols. (Mexico 1938), 2:79–83; and *DHY*, 2:70–

94. See, especially, Mexico 369, Relación del viaje de Fray Gregorio de Fuente-Ovejuna y Fray Hernando de Sopuerta, Aug. 15, 1573. Missionary activity, sometimes in conjunction with military *entradas*, was more intense along the southern frontier. France V. Scholes and J. Eric S. Thompson, "The Francisco Pérez 'Probanza,' of 1654–1656, and the 'Matrícula' of Tipu (Belize)," in *Anthropology and History in Yucatán*, edited by Grant D. Jones (Austin, 1977), 43–68, summarizes information on the Bacalar-Tipu region, 1618–1655. See also Cogolludo, Lib. 8, caps. 5–10, 12–13 (including Tayasal), Lib. 11, caps. 12–17; AGI, Mexico 360, Governor to Crown, July 10 and Nov. 30, 1638; and Mexico 369, Bishop to Crown, June 1, 1606, and Memorial Bishop of Yucatán, 1643. Scholes and Roys, *Maya-Chontal*, 251–290, contains material on the Montaña and Tichel-Popola-Sahcabchen regions to the 1660s. Villagutierre, *Historia*, 119–128, 156–158, 200–208, 233–243, 252–257, 262–264, 303–311, summarizes activities converging on Tayasal, 1575–1700. On the Montaña region, 1604–1624, see also Cogolludo, Lib. 8, cap. 9, Lib. 10, caps. 2–3 (including Tayasal); Francisco de Cárdenas Valencia, *Relación historial eclesiástica de la provincia de Yucatán de la Nueva España escrita en el año de 1639* (Mexico, 1937), 74; AGI, Mexico 359, Cuaderno de documentos, 1604, Governor to Crown, June 21 and Sept. 19, 1608, and Certificate Francisco de Sanabria, June 22, 1608; Mexico 369, Governor to Crown, Dec. 22, 1604, Bishop to Crown, Sept. 29, 1604 and Dec. 12, 1605; Mexico 294, Testimonio del requerimiento, 1604, and testimonio de varias cartas, 1604–1605; Escribanía de cámara 308-A, no. 1, pieza 3, Probanza Fray Gerónimo de Porraz, 1624.

8. For raids into the *despoblado* of the east coast, see Cogolludo, Lib. 7, caps. 13 and 15 (1592 and 1596), and Lib. 8, cap. 8 (1602); AGI, Patronato 56, no. 2, ramo 4, Probanza Juan de Contreras, 1596; Mexico 294, Probanzas Andrés Fernández de Castro, n.d. (1601), and Antonio de Arroyo, 1604; Mexico 130, Información . . . Br. Juan Alonso de Lara, 1611; Mexico 140, Probanza Capt. D. Juan Chan, 1622; and Escribanía de cámara 308-A, no. 1, pieza 6, Testimonio de información a favor de la religión franciscana, 1644.

9. Cogolludo, Lib. 8, cap. 9. See also Grant D. Jones, "Agriculture and Trade in the Colonial Period Central Maya Lowlands," *Maya Subsistence: Studies in Memory of Dennis E. Puleston*, edited by Kent V. Flannery (New York, 1982), 275–293, and, among the many references in the contemporary documents to the "comercio oculto," AGI, Mexico 359, Franciscan Provincial to Audiencia of Mexico, May 5, 1606.

10. On *sublevaciones* in the central Montaña region in the period 1614 to 1624 (including the Saclum massacre of 1624), see Cogolludo, Lib. 10, cap. 3; AGI, Escribanía de cámara 305-B, ramo 6, Antonio de Salas to Governor, Oct. 16, 1624, and ramo 7, Méritos y servicios Diego de Vargas Mayorga, Nov. 12, 1624; Mexico 359, Royal cédula to Governor, Nov. 18, 1624; and Escribanía de cámara 308-A, no. 1, pieza 3, Probanza Fr. Gerónimo de Porraz, 1624. Documentation on the heightened unrest in the 1660s and 1670s is voluminous, most of it contained in the *residencia* of Governor Rodrigo Flores de Aldana: see especially AGI, Escribanía de cámara 317-A, cuad. 4, Autos contra Antonio González, 1670; Escribanía de cámara 317-5. cuad. 8, Autos hechos por Pedro García Ricalde, 1668; and Escribanía de cámara 317-C, Papeles y recaudos presentados por . . . Flores de Aldana, 1664–1674. Franciscan reports are in AGI, Escribanía de cámara 308-A, no. 1, piezas 13–15, 1664–1680; and BN, Archivo Franciscano 55, nos. 1142 and 1143, letters from Fray Cristóbal Sánchez to the Provincial, 1672–1673.

11. The actual battle for the Itzá stronghold in Tayasal, recounted in Villagutierre, *Historia*, 366–373, was brief, culminating a two-year campaign of encirclement and intense diplomatic pressure.

12. See María Angeles Eugenio Martínez, *La defensa de Tabasco, 1600–1717* (Seville, 1971), 72–158, on expeditions against the English, 1680–1717. On the construction of the fort, 1718–1765, see AGN, Real caja 54, Informe Antonio Bonilla, April 29, 1772.

13. Raids by and against both pagan and apostate Maya were reported into the nineteenth century: AGI, Mexico 1018, Sobre conversiones del Itzá y Petén, 1703–1704; Mexico 898, Josef de Zaldívar to Crown, Dec. 14, 1742; AGN, Historia 534, no. 4, Sobre aprehensión de indios caribes en los ríos de Usumacinta, 1784; AA, Asuntos pendientes 2, Expedte. sobre . . . la misión de Chichanha, 1782; Oficios y decretos 3, Franciscan Provincial to Bishop, Sept. 9, 1786; Oficios y decretos 4, Joseph Nicolás de Lara to Bishop Feb. 19, 1782, and Juan José Arias Roxo to Bishop, April 10, 1785; Documentos del Petén Itzá. Exp. sobre residencia de un religioso en el pueblo de San Antonio, 1799; Domingo Faxardo to Provisor, Oct. 21, 1800, and Faxardo to Bishop, May 14, 1813.

14. Nelson Reed, *The Caste War of Yucatán* (Stanford, 1964), is an excellent summary account of the war and the *cruzob* Maya up to 1915. Moisés González Navarro, *Raza y tierra: La guerra de castas y el henequén* (Mexico, 1970), links the war to the socioeconomic background of nineteenth-century Yucatán.

15. The earliest extant accounts are probably two almost parallel texts written by members of the Pech lineage of Ceh Pech province in the mid-sixteenth century: "Chronicle of Chac-Xuleb-Chen [Chicxulub]," Maya text and English translation, in Daniel G. Brinton, *The Maya Chronicles* (1882, reprint, New York, 1969), 187–259, and Juan Martínez Hernández, ed. *Crónica de Yaxkukul* (Mérida, 1926), Maya text and Spanish translation. Alfredo Barrera Vázquez, ed., *Códice de Calkini* (Campeche, 1957), Maya facsimile and Spanish translation, written in the latter part of the century, is a history of the Ah Canul province, including an account of the conquest period, 25–31, 41–57. Gaspar Antonio Chi, of the Xiu lineage of Mani province, has accounts of the conquest in RY 1:42–45, and AGI, Mexico 104, Probanza de Gaspar Antonio Chi, 1580. See also AGI, Guatemala 111, Probanza de don Francisco, cacique of Xicalango, 1552; and the Acalan Chontal account, composed c. 1610 from oral traditions or earlier documents, in Scholes and Roys, *Maya Chontal*, 367–382. It should be noted that all these accounts were written by Maya lords (or their descendants) who had allied themselves early with the Montejos and were concerned to record (and sometimes exaggerate) the friendly reception they gave the Spanish in contrast with the Chilam Balam books, cited below, which were intended solely for a Maya audience and reflect purely Maya concerns.

16. From internal evidence the extant texts of the Chilam Balam books seem to date from the seventeenth century. They were copied and recopied later but without major modification. They thus represent midcolonial perceptions of the pre-Columbian and the conquest pasts. In addition to the straightforward historical accounts of the conquest, in, for example, Ralph L. Roys, *The Book of Chilam Balam of Chumayel*, 2d ed. (Norman, 1967), 119–120, 145–146, the sections known as *katun* prophecies contain many references, some of them explicit, more commonly veiled in the characteristically metaphorical language of Maya sacred texts, to the conquest and the afflictions and miseries that followed: Roys, *Chumayel*, 144–163; Eugene R. Craine and Reginald C. Reindorp, eds., *The*

Codex Pérez and the Book of Chilam Balam of Mani (Norman, 1979), 157–171. Ralph L. Roys, ed., "The Maya Katun Prophecies of the Books of Chilam Balam. Series I," *Contributions to American Anthropology and History* (Washington, 1960), 12:1–60, contains a composite translation of the Series I prophecies from the Chilam Balam books of Tizimin, Mani, Chumayel, and Kaua, with notes and commentary; Miguel León-Portilla, ed., *Visión de los vencidos: Relaciones indígenas de la conquista* (Mexico, 1959), contains Spanish translations from a variety of Nahuatl sources, prose and verse, many of them previously unpublished. Not surprisingly, the Tlaxcalan version, excerpted here, is closer in its pragmatic tone and self-serving interpretations to the accounts produced by the Spaniards' Maya allies, cited in note 15. Nathan Wachtel, *The Vision of the Vanquished: The Spanish Conquest of Peru through Indian Eyes* (New York, 1977), 13–32, compares Maya, highland Mexican, and Andean perceptions of the Spaniards and the conquest, based on these same texts. It may not be fortuitous that the Peruvian and highland Mesoamerican "Dances of the Conquest" (analyzed in Wachtel, 33–58) have no counterpart among the lowland Maya. Perhaps, having assimilated the fact of conquest into their cyclical conception of time, the lowland Maya have had no need to reenact it in search of psychic resolution.

17. Gordon R. Willey, "External Influences on Lowland Maya: 1940 and 1975 Perspectives," *Social Process in Maya Prehistory*, edited by Norman Hammond (London, 1977), 57–75, summarizes the archaeological literature on the entire Maya lowlands from 1940 to 1975. Many references to foreign intrusions (usually lumped together under the label "Itzá") into the northern lowlands are contained in the oral traditions recorded in Landa, *Relación*, 16–17, 20–26, 32–35; RY, for example, 1:121–122, 161, 213, 254–255, and 2:159–161; Sánchez de Aguilar, *Informe*, 140; and a fragment from the "Valladolid Lawsuit" (1618), in Brinton, *Maya Chronicles*, 114–116, in addition to the chronicles and *katun* prophecies of the books of Chilam Balam. For recent attempts to sort out the obscure chronology of these references and correlate them with archaeological evidence, see J. Eric Thompson, *Maya History*, 5–25; Joseph W. Ball, "A Coordinate Approach to Northern Maya Prehistory: A.D. 700–1200," *American Antiquity* 39 (1974), 85–93; Arthur G. Miller, "Captains of the Itzá: Unpublished Mural Evidence from Chichén Itzá," *Social Process in Maya Prehistory*, edited by Norman Hammond (London, 1977), 197–225; and "The Little Descent: Manifest Destiny from the East," *Actes du XLII Congrès des Américanistes, Paris 1976* (Paris, 1979), 8:221–236.

18. Barrera Vázquez, *Códice de Calkiní*, and Diego de Landa, *Landa's Relación de las cosas de Yucatán*, translated and edited by Alfred M. Tozzer (Cambridge, 1941), 32–39. See also Ralph L. Roys, "Literary Sources for the History of Mayapán," *Mayapán, Yucatán, Mexico*, by Harry E. D. Pollock et al. (Washington, 1962), 24–86.

19. See the chronicles and oral traditions (recorded by the Spanish) cited in notes 16 and 17.

20. RY 2:221–222, Relación of Giraldo Díaz del Alpuche, who married doña Isabel, daughter of an unnamed brother of Moctezuma in charge of the invading force. The Mexican garrison apparently remained at Xicalango (RY 1:352, 364), where Díaz del Alpuche presumably learned the story and teamed up with doña Isabel in 1537 en route to Campeche from Tabasco on Montejo's second *entrada*.

21. Antonio de Ciudad Real, *Relación de las cosas que sucedieron al R. P. Comisario General Fray Alonso Ponce . . .* (1588), *Colección de documentos*

inéditos para la historia de España, vols. 57 and 58 (Madrid, 1872), 2:400–401, 413. A 1605 document mentions that there were "criollos mexicanos" in Mérida who could still speak Nahuatl (AGI, Mexico 369, Memoriales de los indios de los pueblos de Usumacinta), but by the eighteenth century only the patents of *hidalguía* distinguished them from the Maya: AGI, Mexico 898, Diego de Anguas to Crown, July 12, 1735. See also the parish censuses, 1784–85, in AA, Visitas pastorales 5, for Sisal de Valladolid, and Vistas pastorales 6, from Chunhuhub.

22. In addition to the native chronicles of the conquest already cited, Spanish accounts of the initial contact with both groups also attest to the differing reactions. See Henry R. Wagner, *Discovery of Yucatán, by Francisco Hernández de Córdoba* (Berkeley, 1942), and *The Discovery of New Spain in 1518, by Juan de Grijalva*, edited by Henry R. Wagner (Berkeley, 1942), for texts (in translation) relating the early voyages of exploration. For a comparative view, see Díaz del Castillo, *Verdadera Historia*, who participated in all the voyages (except the Grijalva voyage of 1518, according to Wagner) as well as the conquest of Mexico. On Maya reactions to the first Montejo *entrada* in 1527, see Gonzalo Fernández de Oviedo y Valdés, *Historia general y natural de las Indias* (1535–1547), 4 vols. (Madrid, 1851–1855) Lib. 32, caps. 2–3; and, among the various conquerors' accounts, the Probanza of Blas González, 1567, in AGI, Patronato 68, no. 1, ramo 2.

23. The Xiu later claimed (RY 1:44–45) that they had submitted to the Spanish because of prophecies of their arrival (without any suggestion that the Spaniards themselves might be gods), but their cooperation seems rather to have been stimulated by the recent flare-up of their old conflict with the Cocom of Sotuta province: RY 1:288–289; Landa, *Relación*, 54; AGI, Mexico 104, Probanza Gaspar Antonio Chi, 1580, all recounting the Cocom massacre of Xiu nobles on a pilgrimage to Chichén Itzá. A later, more self-serving Xiu version of the incident, with the victims portrayed as peace emissaries of the Spanish, is given in *Codex Pérez*, 187–188; Cárdenas Valencia, *Relación*, 100–101; and Diego López de Cogolludo, *Historia de Yucatán* (1654), Lib. 3, cap. 6 (Madrid, 1688).

24. See Scholes and Roys, *Maya Chontal*, 88–128, on the Acalan Chontal. For the east coast, see Oviedo y Valdés, *Historia*, Lib. 32, cap. 2; AGI, Patronato 68, no. 1, ramo 2, Probanza Blas González, 1567; RY 2:110–111. Ralph L. Roys, *The Political Geography of the Yucatán Maya* (Washington, 1957), summarizes the background of the Canul (11–13), the Pech (41), the Xiu (61–64), and the Chel (81) dynasties.

25. "Valladolid Lawsuit," in Brinton, *Maya Chronicles*, 114–116; and Landa, *Relación*, 23, n. 126 (quoting from Torquemada on the Cocom). Corroborative evidence is equivocal but the Cupul are elsewhere identified with early invaders from the east (RY 2:161–162), and the Cocom claimed to be a more ancient lineage than the Xiu "foreigners": RY 1:161, 288; Landa, *Relación*, 26, 31, 40.

26. Alfred M. Tozzer, *Chichén Itzá and Its Cenote of Sacrifice: A Comparative Study of Contemporaneous Maya and Toltec*, 2 vols. (Cambridge, 1957), is a detailed treatment of "Toltec" influence at Chichén Itzá. For other discussions of "Mexican" cultic influences, see E. Wyllys Andrews IV, *Balankanche: Throne of the Jaguar Priest* (New Orleans, 1970); Miller, *On the Edge of the Sea*; and Harry E. D. Pollock, Ralph L. Roys, Tatiana Proskouriakoff, and A. Ledyard Smith, *Mayapán, Yucatán, Mexico* (Washington, 1962), especially 136–139, 428–431. The frequent assertions that idolatry and human sacrifice were unknown in Yucatán until introduced by Kukulcan (RY 1:52, 78–79, 121–122, 215, 225–226, 242–

243, 270–271) presumably refer to new cults and a greater emphasis on human sacrifice.

27. The Chilam Balam books contain many expressions of disapproval directed against the Itzá ("insolent," "impudent," "rogues," "rascals," "vulgar foreigners," "lewd," and "dissolute"), who were held responsible for the decline in Maya learning and religion. See the *tun* prophecies in Roys, "The Prophecies for the Maya Tuns," especially 173; and *Codex Pérez*, 98–116, especially 104–105, 108. A major complaint was the introduction of sexual license—a cult of eroticism that may have included homosexuality (*crimen nefando*); Roys, *Chumayel*, 151; RY 1:149, 216, 256.

28. AGI, Patronato 80, no. 1, ramo 1, Instrucción dada por el Adelantado n.d. (1543), in Probanza of Alonso Sánchez de Aguilar. See also AGI, Justicia 300, Residencia Adelantado Francisco Montejo, 1549, for much detailed testimony on the Montejos' policies.

29. Juan de Caraveo (probanza in AGI, Indiferente 1294, no. 11, 1533) accompanied the first *entrada*. Francisco Hernández, who accompanied the second, distinguished himself principally for his role in supervising the branding of slaves, for which services he was awarded an encomienda by Montejo (AGI, Justicia 300, Residencia Montejo, 1549; Mexico 364, Cabildo Merida to Crown, July 14, 1543). A third cleric, Francisco Niño de Villagómez (probanza in Indiferente 1209, 1547), did not arrive until the very end of the conquest.

30. Cogolludo, Lib. 2, cap. 5, Lib. 5, caps. 1 and 5, Lib. 8. As a Franciscan, Cogolludo was hardly an unbiased source, but he was generally favorable to Montejo. The evidence for the dating of this and an earlier abortive mission to Champoton in c. 1534 is analyzed in Gómez Canedo, "Fray Lorenzo de Bienvenida."

31. AGI, Justicia 300, Residencia Montejo, 1549. Justicia 244, no. 3, contains a summary of the twenty-nine charges brought in the *residencia*. See also AGI, Justicia 126, Juan Ote Durán con el Adelantado, 1537. The colonists' main grievance was in fact the suppression of the slave trade: AGI, Mexico 364, Cabildo Merida to Crown, June 14, 1543; RY 1:229, 234.

32. *Cartas de Indias* (Madrid, 1877), 70–80, Fray Lorenzo de Bienvenida to Crown, Feb. 10, 1548, quoting Montejo, "No querrán ir los amigos, si no les damos licencia de hacer esclavos."

33. See Miguel León-Portilla, *Tiempo y realidad en el pensamiento maya* (Mexico, 1968), for a discussion of the ancient Maya's conception of time.

34. Although the ancient *tzolkin*, or ritual calendar of 260 days, may have died out among the Yucatec Maya (see Robert Redfield and Alfonso Villa Rojas, *Chan Kom: A Maya Village* [Washington, 1934], 367) awareness of the prophecies of Chilam Balam, with the notion of recurring events, was still widespread in the mid-nineteenth century: Justo Sierra O'Reilly, *Los indios de Yucatán* (1848–1851), edited by Carlos R. Menéndez, 2 vols. (Merida, 1954–1957), 1:87.

4

Cultural Adaptation and Militant Autonomy among the Araucanians of Chile

Robert Charles Padden

Some indigenous peoples stopped Spanish colonial expansion in its tracks. The most acclaimed and best studied of these cases of successful resistance is that of the Araucanians of Chile. The Araucanians maintained control over the southern third of this territory until the last quarter of the nineteenth century, as often as not taking the offensive against the Spaniards and even seizing parts of southern Argentina during the colonial period.

To continue as a politically autonomous people, however, the Araucanians had to make profound changes in their way of life, even in their diet and in their settlement patterns, as Robert Padden illustrates in his examination of this phenomenon. A number of Spanish deserters, including clerics, lived among the natives, and there was continuous contact between the Spaniards and the Araucanians during this entire period.

The term "Araucanian culture" suggests a definition and unity which are more applicable to present-day aborigines of Chile than to the culture which the Spaniards encountered in the sixteenth century. While the great majority of Chilean Indians were closely related in race, language, and culture, there were minor variations among them.[1] Those differences, however, were infrequently heeded by the Spanish invaders. Thinking in geographical rather than ethnological terms, and measuring culture with reference to military proficiency, the Spanish chroniclers postulated three spatial bands of culture, the first extending from the Aconcagua to the Nuble River; the second from the Nuble to the Imperial River; the third from there to the Gulf of Reloncavi.[2] Within these regions the Indians were of a single Mapuche culture, as they so identified themselves. Peoples living to the north of any given Mapuche group, although still within it, were identified as Picunche, those to the south as Huilliche.[3] The Spaniards applied these denominations to their conception of cultural distribution, thus making them appear to be raciocultural entities, which, of course, they were not.[4]

The only outstanding difference among these three groups, as the Spaniards saw them, was the ability of the central band to resist effective Spanish settlement, not only through the sixteenth century, but, as it developed, into the late decades of the nineteenth century. The Araucanian culture in which the present paper is interested is limited to the widest Spanish designation, that is, those Indians between the Nuble and Imperial rivers, and more precisely, the area which today comprises the province of Arauco. This tiny province, some sixty miles long and twenty wide, was the focal point of Araucanian resistance.

The Spanish conquest of Araucanian Chile began in 1550 when Pedro de Valdivia and his followers built a fort and founded the town of Concepción on the northern bank of the Biobío River. From this point they moved south, inflicting military defeats on the Araucanians and dividing them in encomienda. Within three years the Spaniards had ranged below the Calle-Calle River, founding towns and reducing most of the Indians to servitude. The Indians were restive under this imposition of Spanish dominion, but offered no openly unified resistance. On the heels of this initial pacification Valdivia brought in experienced prospectors and miners from Santiago to search out the gold deposits that were believed to exist. The gold seekers enjoyed incredible success: several strikes were made which yielded nuggets the size of almonds. "*Desde agora*," quoth Valdivia, "*comienzo a ser señor.*"[5]

But the Araucanians were not of like mind. Rapid development of the mines and discoveries of new ones portended undisguised slavery. Under such apprehension the Indians of Tucapel contrived a cunning trap for Valdivia into which he fell, and he was then killed and eaten.[6] This signal event inspired a general uprising which lasted for four years, ending with the death of the Indian leader Lautaro in the battle of Peteroa in 1557.[7] Although the general rebellion was ended at this time, the War of Arauco was begun. The Indians of Arauco, Tucapel, Catiray, and Purén (the present province of Arauco and its peripheries) stubbornly resisted effective Spanish settlement. This phase of the struggle lasted until 1598, when the Indians captured and ate Governor Martín García de Loyola.[8] There followed a spontaneous rebellion of subjugated Indians from the Maule River to Osorno in the south: every Spanish town worthy of the designation was wiped out below the Biobío, with the exception of Castro on the Isle of Chiloé.[9] Thus by 1600 the Spaniards, in spite of heavy expenditures of blood and treasure, faced a triumphant foe across the Biobío.

This impasse which marked the turn of the century suggests the central problem in understanding Araucanian culture. What faculty or genius did the Araucanians possess which enabled them to succeed so brilliantly where other indigenous American cultures had failed? How was it possible for the Araucanian warriors to boast rightfully, after some fifty years of warfare, that the Spaniards knew almost as much about the military art as they did?[10] Historians have been prone to avail themselves of superficially reasonable explanations: most cite the numerical superiority of the Indians; some blame the forest because it hampered the functions of the Spanish cavalry; others stress the overly long lines of supply from Peru, coupled with a chronic lack of viceregal interest. These factors are joined to a common belief that the Araucanians simply adopted the Spanish forms and techniques of war, making up in numbers what they lacked in skill. Chilean historians, especially since the nineteenth century when their homeland fought for independence from Spain, have quite happily viewed the historical record as a proof of Araucanian, hence mestizo, thence Chilean, bravery and love of freedom. The point is that it is not merely a question of military science, topography, relative numerical strength, or racial declension. These may be significant particulars, but a war of survival between two ethnic groups implies a conflict of total cultures.

At once we are at a serious disadvantage because we have no such conception of early Araucanian culture, however well we may feel that we know the Spanish. By means of archaeological evidence and brief narratives of exploration we are able to piece together a rather crude notion of what Araucanian culture was like before the Spaniards came, but nothing more. Largely because the area under discussion became almost at once a zone of perpetual conflict, the work of the religious orders did not develop as it did elsewhere in the Indies, and we keenly feel the lack of Mendicant chronicles. Consequently, most of our information concerning Araucanian life during the first century of conquest is derived from chronicles and histories of the war in which brief glimpses of Indian life all too infrequently appear. There are added limitations. Wherein the Indians were concerned, the chroniclers were seldom efficient observers. In matters of simple fact they tend to be trustworthy, but when the fact becomes interpretive they almost invariably fail to grasp the human thought and action that lay behind it. Rather than as men, they thought of the Indians as wild savages who blindly resisted the sweet yoke of Christianity and Spanish dominion. For this reason they seldom inquired into the possibility of Indian method; rather, Indian resistance was madness. Another weakness inherent in the chronicles is the factor of cultural change. At any given moment the chroniclers made their notations in the belief that what they saw was and had been thus from the beginning of time.

Only when contemporaries gave information which contradicted their own observations did they give evidence of change, but without attempting to explain it.

It is seldom wise to take an interpretive fact, as disclosed by one of the chroniclers, at its face value. When we are told, for instance, that the Spaniards lost a given battle because the Indians outnumbered them it is entirely unlikely that the chronicler is telling us the whole truth. We have every reason to doubt him because we already know that the Spaniards, with or without Indian allies, had an enormous talent for winning military victories with inferior numbers. At no time was it normal for Spanish forces to outnumber the enemy anywhere in the Indies. Why, then, did the Indians win not only the battle in question, but a majority of the engagements? The suggestions are several: perhaps the Indians, in their own right, had become superior strategists; perhaps they had improved their own weapons to a point which offset the Spanish advantages of gunpowder and horse; perhaps they had developed a creed for life which made resistance both possible and meaningful. Our questioning of an apparently reliable fact leads us to recognition of a neglected factor, the potentiality of early Araucanian culture. By following these suggestions through and corroborating them with associated evidence, we may well come to an understanding of that particular battle which is far superior to that entertained by the chronicler. More importantly, when the battle is multiplied by 1,000 and the conditions of Spanish defeat remain relatively constant, significant conclusions concerning Araucanian culture are inescapable.

By the passing of the first generation of conquistadores the war had become institutionalized, and observers began to think and write about it historically. In the seventeenth and eighteenth centuries several histories of Chile and its Araucanian War were written which contained a relative abundance of passages describing Indian life. These writers, like their predecessors in the sixteenth century, did not take into account the factor of cultural change, and their judgments were almost entirely based upon the present in which they observed and wrote. Nor did they, with few exceptions, have the opportunity of consulting the major chronicles of the sixteenth century. Most of those manuscripts were sent to Spain for publication, but a good many of them were intentionally or innocently shuttled off to a dark repository to await the dawn of modern historiography on Chilean historians.

There are thus three categories of documentary materials from which to draw an image of Araucanian culture: the chronicles of first contact, the chronicles and documents of the first century of conquest, and the histories of the later colonial period. In past reconstructions scholars have tended to assign cultural forms found in later and better documented periods to earlier periods wherein documentation is not generously provided. With disregard for the depth of time, elements have been taken from documentary sources of the entire colonial period and placed side by side in a synchronic mosaic. At best, this type of reconstruction is an abstraction of culture, and like any abstraction, it is essentially unreal. Nowhere does it give a hint of the potentiality of Araucanian culture: on the contrary, such description lends itself to demonstration of a culture which, by the lessons of historical anthropology, should never have survived the first Spanish onslaught. Such reconstruction follows from a basic assumption of cultural constancy. In some phases of material culture this technique is doubtless warranted and valid, especially in the presence of sufficient archaeological documentation. However this may be, the idea of constancy stands in opposition to the idea of change, and from what can be made of the documents, the strength with which the Araucanians resisted Spanish domination was derived not from a constancy of their cultural forms but from the ability to change them. It seems valid, therefore, to view the sources of the later colonial period as indications of what Araucanian culture *became* under the stress of the long Spanish war rather than as evidence of what it was before the conquest.

The chronicles of the first century of conflict, when viewed from this position and subjected to critical analysis, provide considerable insight into the design of change. The term "culture" in the present case does not refer to fine art and letters and the numerous connotations usually associated with the term. Such development was not a concomitant of war, nor, it seems clear, did the Araucanians tend in the direction of refined sensibility. Araucanian cultural development occurred only in those arts which had a survival value, and was canalized by the hostile forces which threatened the total culture. Spanish pressure was exerted in three areas—military, political, and religious. The Araucanians, under the stimulus of this external pressure, turned inward upon themselves and developed their own corresponding forms to a point of equal resistive strength. The Spanish challenge in terms of relative force of impact was first military, secondly political, and lastly religious. Araucanian reaction and response to the challenge followed the same gradient.

The founding of Concepción by Valdivia in 1550 marked the real beginning of Araucanian resistance. Located just across the Biobío, out of Araucanian territory proper, it served as a strategic base of operations and key position of Spanish strength. Before its foundation the Spaniards posed a transient threat, but after it began to serve as a springboard for trans-Biobío conquest and settlement, the Indians better understood the consequences involved. With alarming speed the Spanish moved southward, through the provinces of Arauco, Catiray, Tucapel, Purén, and

Marigueño, coming to a temporary halt at the Calle-Calle River. This entire area, bordered on the west by the sea and on the east by the Camino Real (the easiest passage through the central valley), was divided in encomienda, Arauco, Tucapel, and Purén being retained by Valdivia as the basis of a princely estate.[11] These provinces, especially Arauco, were highly prized by the Spaniards as the most heavily populated of the whole kingdom, and as possessing an abundance of foodstuffs, fine lands, and a most provident climate.[12]

Within this area the Indians lived in small, decentralized kinship groups, with no apparent intergroup relationship of an institutional nature. The sources of the sixteenth century are so meager as to preclude the possibility of clear understanding of the sociopolitical divisions within the individual group. The local clusters of dwellings, in early chronicles called *levos*, in later ones *reguas*, composed a larger unit known as the *allaregua* (or *aillarewe*). Each *allaregua* was composed of nine or less *levos*. [Miguel de] Olaverría, writing in 1594, describes this area as consisting of only five *allareguas*, but the context in which he mentions them suggests that this semicentralization was of relatively recent origin.[13] There is no factual basis for postulating anything but a crude kinship relationship, markedly particularized by geographical isolation, at the time of the Spanish arrival.

These people, albeit ready warriors, were soundly defeated by Spanish arms and remained so for almost four years. Subsequent events, the revolt against Governor Valdivia in December 1553, and the continuing War of Arauco, indicate quite clearly that this short peace was a period of Araucanian maturation. Through military action, service in encomienda, and free intercourse in the Spanish towns (Concepción, Imperial, Valdivia, and Villa Rica) they observed and learned much about Spanish military organization and strategy, government, social custom, mores, and religious concepts. The lessons they learned were adequately demonstrated in subsequent resistance against the invaders.

This initial period of communication with Spanish culture was constantly amplified throughout the following century. Military action was usually confined to the summer months. During harvest time and winter both Indians and Spaniards tended to refrain from active combat, holding what had been gained and preparing for summer campaigns. Through peaceful Indians, those serving the Spanish, the rebels kept themselves fully informed of all Spanish activity. Never lacking information, the Indians always had a precise idea of Spanish strength or weakness. There was seldom a rigid military perimeter; in those areas where the invader could maintain a fort and military supremacy the Indians were reduced to servitude. With a weakening of Spanish strength, rebellion inevitably occurred, so that the distinction as a peaceful or warlike Indian depended largely upon the state of affairs of the moment. Because the Indians so frequently changed roles, they were never out of personal contact with the Spanish.

The Indians received some aid and encouragement from Spanish deserters. There is no telling how many deserted to enemy ranks in the course of the sixteenth century, but in the year 1600 alone it is known that there were over sixty desertions.[14] A good many of these renegades were still living among the Indians in 1607.[15] In fear of peace and subsequent retribution, the traitors taught the Indians many things that would have been difficult for them to learn themselves, such as the proper use of firearms, the building of forges and ironmongering, and even the techniques of political administration. The Spaniards were greatly perturbed when a mestizo powder maker went over to the other side. With volcanic sulphur, saltpeter, and charcoal in abundance, the Indians could make deadly use of the large stores of field pieces and firearms which they had captured. As luck would have it, the deserter repented and returned to the Spanish fold, whereupon he was forgiven and permitted to return to Peru. There were also clerical renegades who apostatized and urged the Indians on in their own religious beliefs and practices.[16]

It is most important to understand that the motive for Araucanian observation of Spanish cultural forms was not to emulate them and thereby raise the level of their own, but to discover Spanish weaknesses and to mobilize Araucanian strength for forceful opposition. A fundamental weakness of Spanish occupation was its dire need of peace. Exploitation of this weakness became a cornerstone of Araucanian strategy throughout the sixteenth century and beyond. Spanish forces, both civilian and military, were too few and too widely dispersed, and the line of supply from Peru was much too long. Effective occupation and permanent settlement depended upon a guaranteed supply of Indian labor. This, of course, was in turn dependent upon total pacification, which would allow the colonists to concentrate on development of mining and agriculture rather than military defense. As experience in Mexico and Peru had shown, a mere handful of soldiers, colonists, and friars could work great wonders if the Indians would but submit. When they first settled Santiago the Spaniards proved that they could provide their living with their own hands, but full barns and producing mines were impossible to realize without Indian labor.[17] Because of this, the Spaniards always hungered for peace, and through past experience in the Indies, expected it to follow each victory over the Indians.[18] This was the great error of the Spaniards in the sixteenth century. Whenever the Indians found it advantageous to themselves to live in peace—whether because of famine or disease or military weakness—they willingly surrendered themselves to service in the encomienda, there to repair their fortunes and to watch. The Spaniards, hopeful that this was indeed the dawn of a new day, almost invariably sought immediate expansion of their mining and agricultural activities. With a quickening of economic activity, military vigilance declined to a point which invited rebellion. The Araucanians honored such invitations without fail.[19]

Spanish military strategy was also based upon the gnawing hunger for peace. From past experience the invaders knew that peace would follow the defeat and usurpation of a central authority. In the absence of a central Araucanian authority the only alternative was to instill fear by demonstration of military supremacy, and so the Spaniards constantly sought a definitive battle which, when won, would convince the Araucanians of the futility of resistance. Some civilians differed, advising an Indian policy founded upon kind treatment and remission of personal service, but their voices were seldom heard. Recognizing the Spaniards' willingness to do battle, the Araucanians always chose their own battle sites where the terrain could be used to advantage, where the horse, as a military instrument, could be rendered less effective, and where their own strategies could be best effected. With monotonous regularity the Spaniards, always seeking the big victory, sent an army to defeat a rumored gathering of Indians, which rumor was usually broadcast by the Indians themselves. Upon arrival the Spaniards found themselves outmanned and outmaneuvered, and so were frequently forced to flee for their lives, leaving baggage trains in the hands of the enemy.[20]

It was military planning of this kind that led to the capture and death of Valdivia. Historians generally recognize the death trap into which he fell as the handiwork of Lautaro, the most famous former groom in all history. Lautaro has since become one of Chile's great national heroes, symbolizing all that was best in Araucanian culture. Be that as it may, there is considerable reason to believe that Lautaro hailed from the vicinity of Santiago, and was therefore an Araucanian by nothing more than association.[21] His relations with Araucanians are not clear historically beyond the fact that he led their resistance, aided by other chiefs, until his death in 1557. He was extremely well versed in military strategy, and his deployment of squadrons in place of mass attack and the use of encirclement were valued contributions to Araucanian knowledge, but the fact that many other military techniques were developed after he had passed from the scene would indicate that there were countless Araucanians of equal ability.

Generally speaking, the Araucanians retained their own weapons in the war against the Spanish. Bows and arrows, long lances, spears, long clubs with weighted heads, and slings were the weapons most often used.[22] Strategy was much more important than weapons. As noted above, the Indians never fought in a place that was not of their own choosing if they could avoid it. The horse was their greatest problem and one around which their strategy revolved. They chose battle sites wherein the horse would be difficult to manage; they made use of snares on long poles with which to pull the rider from his horse; they dug pitfalls and trenches, placing sharp stakes upon which rider and mount would be impaled; in all of this their chief aim was to get the Spaniard off his mount.[23]

Through the spoils of war and peacetime thievery the Indians acquired a vast supply of horses. By 1594 it was not uncommon for them to put several hundred horsemen in the field. It is to be noted, however, that they used the horse as an auxiliary rather than as an instrument of war. Riding as far as thirty miles a night, they raided settlements and ranches under the cover of darkness, leaving death and destruction in their wake.[24] But acquisition of this new mobility did not alter their basic strategy for fighting Spanish forces. Throughout the sixteenth century they continued to lure Spanish troops into carefully prepared ambuscades, themselves remaining on foot. To have done otherwise would have undone their whole strategy. As the Spanish horsemen approached the main Indian force, their lines of retreat were closed by concentric rings of warriors. If the Spanish were fortunate enough to defeat the enemy, they found no difficulty in retracing their steps. If, on the other hand, the Indians proved too strong for them, they could retreat only with great difficulty. Once having forced the Spaniards into retreat, the Indians followed them on foot. When the horses tired sufficiently, their riders could be struck down. A Spanish horseman afoot, because of the weight and bulk of his equipment and his inability to dodge through the forest undergrowth, did not have a chance for his life.[25]

The idea of Indians running down horses is not as incredible as it at first seems. In the heat of summer, when most of the fighting took place, the Spanish mounts tired quickly, especially after the long trip to the Indian ambuscade. Besides this, the Araucanians were accustomed to hunting wild game by literally chasing it to death. This required a tireless trot, at which they were proficient. Profiting by the lessons of their own strategy, the Araucanians devised an extremely light saddle in order to increase the endurance of their mounts on long rides. When they used captured Spanish saddles they first cut them down so as to make them considerably lighter.[26]

Shortly after the turn of the century, by 1611 to be exact, the Indians developed a cavalry that in terms of mobility was superior to the Spanish. They likewise possessed the best horses in the whole of Chile. These advantages were demonstrated in more daring raids on Spanish towns and a willingness to meet the Spanish cavalry on its own ground.[27] From this time forward the war passed into a new phase in which Araucanian offensive power became an increasingly significant factor. The source of that power, of course, lay in mastery of the horse. In little more than a generation the animal from which the Indians had once fled in terror had been incorporated into their culture, transforming it into a factor of defiant military power, dedicated to the eradication of Spanish culture. The Spaniards were not only dismayed to recognize this development of Araucanian military strength, but were piqued as well at the sight of barbarous savages riding horses with an air of equality. In answer to Spanish resentment the Indians pledged never to quit their war for freedom and their horses to enter serfdom on foot.[28]

The existence of a skilled and effective military force bespeaks the presence of a comparable political organization under whose genius it is formed and directed. In the development of Araucanian political organization the chronicles indicate two major forces at work: the geographical particularism in which the Araucanians traditionally lived and a counterforce provoked by the presence of the enemy and inclining towards Araucanian unity. Throughout the first century of conquest ancient localism clashed with incipient nationalism. This conflict produced a political ambivalence which in itself contributed heavily to the cause of Araucanian independence. Centralization of politico-military authority was achieved to a point where successful resistance was possible, but did not develop to a state where the Spaniards could defeat and usurp it.

The center of anti-Spanish unity was founded in what the Spanish termed *"el estado."* This was a geographical expression signifying the area that Valdivia held in personal encomienda.[29] It was these Indians, particularly those of Arauco, Tucapel, and Purén, who planned and carried out the revolt of 1553, and who assumed leadership of the resistance movement. After the first few years of bitter warfare the Spaniards began to imbue the term "estado" with political connotations, hence Don Alonso de Ercilla's image of *"el estado indómito"* was much more than a flight of poetic fancy.[30]

It is virtually certain that the Indians, in pre-Hispanic days, were in the habit of seeking transient familial and friendship alliances in the conduct of war between localities. Upon their first major defeat by Valdivia, following which he recrossed the Biobío and founded Concepción, the more intelligent Indian leaders voiced a wide call to arms.[31] The resulting alliance was effective in that it led to the downfall of Valdivia, but it had no permanent character. With each new Spanish thrust the caciques of the *estado* had to re-form alliances and seek wider support for their efforts.

In 1556, for example, Lautaro and the chiefs established relations with the Indians of Santiago, attempting to incite them to rebellion.[32] Temporary alliances were both frequent and effective. In search of allies the chiefs used glass beads, dogs, and various types of Spanish plunder to effect negotiations.[33] There also developed a type of Indian mercenary who supplied his own weapons and served for a specified length of time at a prearranged scale of pay.[34]

It seems quite clear that there was no pan-Araucanian sentiment to which the *estado* could appeal. When local chiefs were asked for troops they not uncommonly rejected the request. If they acceded to the demand, they chose the bravest man for a leader and dispatched the force under his command. Service was performed in the *estado*'s forces for no more consideration than lodging and hospitable treatment. In the event of mortality the close relatives of the fallen warrior were compensated by the residents of the province in whose defense he had died.[35]

Some of the localities simply did not want to fight the Spaniards, preferring to make the best of conditions under Spanish rule. The Indians around Angol, for instance, joined the Spaniards in war against the *estado* for a number of years. While the *estado* leaders accused them of subverting the general Indian cause, the Angol tribes retaliated with accusations of plunder and theft.[36] The *estado*, with its own crops destroyed by warfare, never hesitated to raid the stores of those who were not immediately allied to the cause. Araucanians who refused to fight were subjected to violent reprisal.[37] Even in the province of Arauco all was not unanimity. An old chief was forced to flee with his family and take refuge in the Spanish fort in Arauco because he would not support the war, thereby giving evidence of pro-Spanish sympathies.[38] It is difficult to guess how many others there might have been.

By 1594, according to Olaverría, the *estado* claimed suzerainty over all of the *allareguas* from the Biobío to the Imperial River, and was held in dread by all of the Indians as far south as Osorno. The *estado* was so feared and respected, he said, that Indians in the extreme south would break the peace when the chiefs of the *estado* so desired.[39] Nevertheless, the chiefs never succeeded in gaining effective suzerainty, even for purposes of war. Authority continued to be local, rather than central, and cooperation was most often found in the realm of diplomacy.

With the turn of the century a more precise political and military division was created by the Araucanians. The region between the Biobío and Toltén rivers was divided into three longitudinal strips called *butanmapos*: they were the sub-Andean range, the central valley, and the coastal strip (including the *estado*). Each *butanmapo* had clearly defined limits and jurisdictions; each had, at least in time of war, a principal chief, or *toque*. It was customary for the chiefs to debate plans for war in a parliamentary junta in which the three territories were represented. Strategy was agreed upon by common consent.[40] The relationship between the local chiefs and territorial *toques* is not clear, but it seems likely that military power was held both to qualify and to assure authority. When disagreement occurred between *toques*, war between territories could and did sometimes develop.[41]

Gerónimo Pietas, writing around 1729, describes a further development of this general schema. At this time the territorial strips had been increased to four in number. These provinces were still called *butanmapos*, but they extended farther north and south than did the older territories. This extension of Araucania is mute testimony to the growth of Araucanian strength and confidence. In Pietas's description each *butanmapo* had a hierarchy of three superior chiefs: a *toqui-guilmen* (commander), a *guinca-guilmen* (field commander), and a *pelqui-guilmen* (diplomatic courier). While these officers assumed absolute authority in their positions within the province, they were inferior to a *toque-general* who apparently wielded a measure of authority over the whole of Araucania. He further describes a conventionalization of diplomacy involving three forms for the calling of war. A general war could be called for only by the *toque-general*, and at his discretion. When he desired to begin hostilities word was passed to all chiefs through a group of subchiefs called *cones*. Only the *toque-general* could dispatch the *cones*, and in the event of hostilities between the provinces, the fact of being called to council by a *con* was a guarantee of safe conduct. All chiefs attended the councils, wherein strategy was planned and forces drawn up.

War could also be called for by a regional *toque*. As messenger he sent his *pelqui-guilmen* to the other *butanmapos*, asking their aid and support, which they might or might not give. In the third instance war could be initiated simply by attacking the Spaniards. In this event the warring chieftain used force of arms to enlist the support of the local Indians for his designs.[42] As incomplete as this description is, it does give evidence of a relatively sophisticated politico-military organization which stands in sharp contrast against that of the first generation of *estado* caciques.

Development of religious beliefs among the Araucanians is a most difficult postulation because we know so very little about their pre-Hispanic religious ideas. The chroniclers generally agree that the spirits of Araucanian ancestors formed an important cult, each kinship group having an ultimate progenitor whose spirit was called *Pillán*. This spirit was believed to be immanent, and so could be propitiated. Before going into battle the Indians sometimes sought divination from oracles, and once having gained a victory in a given locality through the intercession of supernatural forces, they believed that they could not lose a subsequent battle in that particular place.[43] Given the immediate religious background of the chroniclers of the sixteenth century, one in which religious and nationalistic sentiment were perfectly united, and the omnipresent tradition of the *reconquista*, one must always wonder if the early chroniclers reported what the Indians actually believed, or if they instead reflected the paths of their own cognition.

As the Spaniards made war in the name of an omnipotent God, the Araucanians appear to have rationalized a deity for their own defense. There were innumerable *Pillàns* hovering over every locality, and in the absence of concerted missionary effort they doubtless remained. In describing an Araucanian ceremonial that he witnessed in 1629, [Francisco Nuñez de Pineda y] Bascuñan depicts an interesting bit of symbolism which suggests the evolution of a super-*Pillán*. The occasion of ceremony was the execution of a Spanish captive. Involved in the execution was a lance with three knives fixed to its end, representing the three *butanmapos*. After the captive's brains had been dashed out, his captor took from the lance that knife which represented his personal region of Araucania and used it to cut out the victim's heart. He sucked its blood, took tobacco smoke and blew it to the heavens, then passed the heart around to the other chiefs for similar usage, after which it was divided and eaten.[44] The three knives symbolized Araucania, and the sucking of blood was a form of thanksgiving to the *Pillán* for victory. This ceremony closely approaches the abstraction of Home, Country, and God.

Later in his captivity Bascuñan had occasion to spend several days in the company of one of the small sons of a chief. One afternoon he asked the child if he would like to learn how to pray. The boy answered affirmatively; he had already learned something of prayers from a Spanish captive. With little instruction the child recited the Pater Noster in Spanish, but without understanding what it was he was reciting. Bascuñan, speaking Araucanian fluently, decided to teach him in the Araucanian tongue. The child was delighted to understand the recitation. The trenchant Bascuñan then asked him if he understood the idea behind the prayer. Yes indeed, was the reply. God could be none other than a great *Pillán*, superior to other *Pilláns*.[45] Bascuñan registered satisfied delight. The question is, should he have been so delighted?

In order to maintain a spirit of unqualified resistance the leaders of the *estado*, who manipulated majority opinion, instituted indoctrinational forms for boys and youths. Beginning at six years of age boys were taught the use of military weapons. By observing him the boy's tutors would decide which weapon he was most proficient with, and then he would be trained as a specialist in the use of that weapon. At the same time he was arduously trained in running and swimming.⁴⁶ Another type of training begun at this early age was the torture of Spanish captives. The boys were given knives and living Spaniards, then instructed in the arts of slow dissection, roasting, and eating.⁴⁷ They were further required to memorize certain verses which recounted Spanish offenses since the beginning of the war, and were made to recite them at the command of their elders. In this way a boy became a man with a clearly fixed purpose in life. As a youth the Araucanian would speak thus of his lance: "This is my master: it does not order me to dig for gold, or to carry food or firewood, or to herd cattle, or to follow it about. And since the master sustains my liberty, it is with him that I wish to pass."⁴⁸

There was seldom talk of peace in the *estado*. Even a chief, if he dared speak of peace in war council, could be cut down on the spot by the nearest soldier. Apparently it was quite common for the warriors to kill any Indian who spoke of peace, or who was suspected of having the word in his mouth. [Alonso González de] Nájera describes a rigorous "inquisition" by the warriors to suppress the minority who wanted to farm rather than fight. Christianity was also forbidden. In the course of time many Indians were introduced to its tenets through close contact with the Spanish, especially the Indians who lived around the Spanish settlements. After the disaster of 1598, of course, the towns were no more. Many of the Indians had become reconciled to Spanish occupation and were genuinely converted to Christianity. Now they were exposed to the mercy of the *estado*'s inquisitors. From what we know, it did not go well with them.⁴⁹ Standing in opposition to Christianity was an apparently well-defined Araucanian concept, to wit: the Indian way of life is the only one; those who die in war against the Spanish go to another land where they enjoy more women and luxuries than they ever had in this life; there is nothing to fear in death.⁵⁰

Araucanian opposition to Spanish intrusion was not confined to the field of battle. At all times they waged psychological warfare with consummate skill. While they always celebrated a victory over the Spaniards, and let the settlers know of their celebration, they never disclosed the identity of the fort or community that had fallen.⁵¹ With great finesse they obstructed Spanish intelligence, keeping the enemy in a state of worried ignorance. It is relatively certain that human flesh was not eaten by the Araucanians in pre-Hispanic times except in times of dire necessity.⁵² With the advent of the Spanish invasion, however, the eating of Spaniards became institutionalized. Time and time again the chroniclers tell of Spaniards being eaten, in whole and in part, and sometimes, their horses with them. Since there does not appear to have been a tradition to support this practice, nor any magical or superstitious belief connected with the act, it seems reasonable to assume that it was developed for its propaganda value. This would represent an intended clash of values. Discovering the abhorrence with which the Christians viewed cannibalism, the Araucanians appear to have developed it as a cultural opposite, a symbol of resistance. The great chief of Arauco, Caupolican, in hurling a challenge at Governor García Hurtado de Mendoza, boasted that he had eaten the previous governor (Valdivia) and would do the same with him.[53] In some cases, even the well-picked bones of Spaniards were consumed in wine after being burned and powdered, the idea being that no memory of the Spaniards should remain.[54]

Another Araucanian device was the making of flutes from Spanish shinbones, most often extracted while the victim was still alive. On occasion the victim was forced to play his threnody on his own shinbone.[55] After the Indians developed their own cavalry they used the shinbones in lieu of trumpets. Nájera describes the sound they made as one which was doleful and morose, producing depression in those who heard it.[56] One can but imagine the effect on the settlers produced by a night-riding horde, sweeping over the countryside, accompanied by its unearthly music.

The Araucanians had still other ways to indicate their scorn for Spanish culture. On occasion they cut [tree] limbs and made crosses upon which to crucify their captives before roasting and eating them.[57] In their treatment of captive Spanish women the Indians made calculated mockery of the enemy's institutions. The conquerors' ladies were highly prized by the chiefs, who used them as concubinary slaves. In 1605 a new Spanish governor, Don Alonso García, came down from Lima with one thousand troops. With this show of force he opened negotiations with the caciques of the *estado* for return of female captives, offering Indian hostages in exchange. The chiefs of Arauco decided to part with some of their prizes, and at the appointed time produced the prisoners. Before waiting husbands and fathers the women appeared, calloused, lousy, naked below the waist, and, more often than not, visibly pregnant.[58] Now we know that the Araucanians had the same ideas of physical propriety as did the Spaniards. Both made the same distinction as to public and private parts of the anatomy.[59] It was by intention alone that the chiefs of Arauco forced their unfortunate victims to appear thus before their menfolk. The chiefs of Purén, although they liked the Spanish no better, provided coverings with which their captives could hide their shame.[60]

The foregoing brief review of Araucanian culture in its history has embraced the outward manifestations of change rather than its internal mutations. Two principal aims have directed the study: one intended to restore the chronology which is so basic to cultural history; the other to divert study of the problem of Araucanian resistance from narrow analysis of Spanish strength and weakness. It is apparent that understanding is to be found in the sphere of Araucanian cultural experience. In plowing the furrow it is inevitable that questions tentatively answered should suggest a multitude of new ones lying deeper beneath the surface.[61] With more intensified study, surface appearances which now seem to be certainties will doubtless be proved to be more apparent than real. Even so, we can better understand why an observation made by an historian in the middle of the eighteenth century could, with small exception, have been made in the sixteenth:

> In a short time the Spanish conquered the three powerful empires of the American hemisphere, those of Peru, Mexico, and Bogotá, but the hundred and ninety years that have elapsed since the beginning of this conquest have not sufficed to end it with the subjugation of the Araucanians. Nor has the vast expenditure of fifty million pesos and more than 25,000 recruits, nor the effusion of blood that has been spilled done so, even though in the past century the King declared this war to be equal to those of Spain, Flanders, and Italy. Today the Araucanians possess the fairest portion of Chile, from the Biobío River to the Straits of Chiloé, a hundred and fifty leagues stretching between the Cordillera and the sea. In the whole of this area the Spanish hold nothing but the fortified towns of Arauco and Valdivia: the Indians live in independence and enjoyment of their coveted liberty.[62]

Notes

1. For discussion of Chilean prehistory see Francisco Antonio Encina, *Historia de Chile desde la prehistoria hasta 1891* (19 vols., Santiago, 1940–51), vol. I, chaps. 2, 3; Ricardo E. Latcham, *La prehistoria chilena* (Santiago, 1928), 147–154, passim.
2. Miguel de Olaverría, "Informe de don Miguel de Olaverría sobre el reyno de Chile, sus indios y sus guerras" (in Claudio Gay, *Historia física y política de Chile*, Paris, Santiago, 1844–71). This work comprises twenty-eight volumes, two of which are document collections, numbered I and II, hence, Gay, II:19–20. Olaverría was an old soldier in Chile when he wrote his chronicle in 1594. His work is both dependable and readable. Also see "Viaje de García Hurtado de Mendoza al sur de Valdivia y fundación de Osorno" (Gay, I:224–225).
3. Encina, I:72–74; cf. Latcham, *La prehistoria*, 152–154.
4. The term *Picunche* did not come into vogue until the seventeenth century. Writers of the eighteenth and nineteenth centuries accepted and compounded these delineations. In addition to these three areas the Spaniards further differentiated between the Picunche, who extended somewhat south of the Maule River, and the Promaucaes, who lived between the Ñuble River and the Biobío, including the site of Concepción. The Promaucaes were extremely warlike, but since they lived north of the Biobío they were not Araucanians in the proper sense, nor did they make up any part of the *estado* (see note 29).
5. Alonso de Góngora Marmolejo, "Historia de Chile desde su descubrimiento hasta el año de 1575" (in *Colección de historiadores de Chile y documentos*

relativos a la historia nacional, 49 vols., Santiago, 1861–1942), II:33–34 (this collection will hereafter be cited as CHC). Marmolejo came to Chile with Valdivia in 1549, hence he wrote with considerable experience and authority. His work is fundamental to the study of Araucanian culture.

6. Idem, 37–39. Marmolejo's account of Valdivia's death is based on an eye-witness account, hence it is more acceptable than are the many others that are based on rumors and hearsay.

7. For a survey of the first general uprising see Encina, vol. I, chaps. 8 and 9.

8. Idem, vol. II, chap. 23; also see Gregorio Serrano, "Relación de lo subcedido en Chile desde veinte de diciembre de noventa y ocho hasta primero de mayo de noventa y nueve" (CHC, XLV:227–233).

9. Alonso González de Nájera, "Desengaño y reparo de la guerra de Chile" (CHC, XVI:10–14, 63–65, passim). The author was in Chile from 1601 to 1607. Experienced in military science, he made a brave attempt to analyze Araucanian resistance. His work is invaluable for Araucanian study.

10. Idem, 93–94.

11. Olaverría, 20.

12. Marmolejo, 25; Pedro de Valdivia to King, Sept. 25, 1551 (Gay, I:139–142).

13. Olaverría, 21.

14. Encina, II:306.

15. Nájera, 117.

16. Idem, 69, 73–75, 117–122, 143–148. In spite of Spanish fears, firearms did not play a significant role in Indian strategy until late in the seventeenth century.

17. It should be kept in mind that conquest and settlement were private financial ventures, and very expensive ones. See Governor García Hurtado de Mendoza's complaint in Marmolejo, 90.

18. This was Valdivia's experience in Santiago; the Indians tired of "running like beasts" and submitted to reduction (Valdivia to King, Sept. 4, 1545, Gay, I:61).

19. This technique of dissembling was practiced widely, both in Spanish towns and on the frontiers. The Indians were so skilled that the Spanish were never able to tell whether they really meant to keep the peace or not. Either way, there was nothing the Spanish could do but accept, driven as they were by the economic imperative of their way of life. The Indians seem to have understood this perfectly. The granting of terminal peace in critical areas as a part of wider strategy became common. Revolts were well planned: the chiefs had the white women divided among themselves in advance; the gold that had been dug for the whites during peace was thrown into the nearest river, or used to ransom Indian hostages; bloody revenge was visited upon the erstwhile masters. See Marmolejo, 58–59, 125; Nájera, 46–47, 65.

20. For typical accounts see Marmolejo, 35ff., 85, 101, 171–176, 186–187. In the matter of Indian strategy and resistance the Spaniards could not see the forest for the trees. They laid responsibility for their failures on everything but the Indians. A widely prevalent idea, as expressed by Martín Ruiz de Gamboa (Gay, II:123), held that more polished *peninsular* gentlemen were needed to fight the Indians, ignorant Creoles being unfit for the task. Discrimination against Creoles was a constant source of dissension in Spanish ranks. In 1557, García Hurtado de Mendoza arrived in Chile as governor with many *peninsulares* in his train. The abandon with which he handed out encomiendas to his *peninsular* friends

enraged the luckless Creoles. In his reply to their complaints he suggested that no more than a handful of the Chileans knew the identity of their fathers, and then insultingly inquired, "En qué se andan aquí estos hijos de putas?" (Marmolejo, 80). Nájera (36–37) took a more realistic view. He stated that Creoles were born in war and carried the brunt of the fighting, and did it well. Because the chroniclers ignored their deeds, he added, they were unappreciated in Spain. He considered the disparity between Creole and *peninsular* to be utterly inane.

21. Marmolejo simply states that among those who plotted Valdivia's downfall was a yanacona named Alonso, who had been Valdivia's servant (36). This brief notice is the only valid evidence of Lautaro's origin. Among the chroniclers in Chile the term *yanacona* invariably meant a friendly and allied Indian from the north. Chilean historians are prone to begin with the premise that he was an Araucanian, but have difficulty in explaining how he could have become so *españolado* in the brief period between Valdivia's first contact with the Araucanians and his death. It seems much more likely that Lautaro was taken by Valdivia in Santiago when he was a boy. See Benjamin Vicuña Mackenna, *Lautaro* (Santiago, 1876), for the standard nationalistic version.

22. Olavarría, 33–34; Nájera, 95–98. For a plausible account of Araucanian reaction to the Spanish danger after 1550 see Ricardo Latcham, "La capacidad guerrera de los Araucanos: Sus armas y métodos militares" (*Revista Chilena de Historia y Geografía*, vol. 15, no. 19, 1915, 122–193). While this study is valuable for purely military affairs, it does not attempt to explore or interpret the force behind Araucanian military organization beyond the factor of Indian bravery. Another weakness is the author's uncritical use of Pedro Mariño de Lovera's *Crónica del reino de Chile* (CHC, vol. VI). Lovera was another soldier who came to Chile in 1551, served there for a number of years, and then retired to Lima to write a history of Chile. Ostensibly because it was not well written, the manuscript was turned over to a Jesuit, Bartolomé de Escobar, for rewriting. As a true courtier, he shifted emphasis to flatter his patron, García Hurtado de Mendoza, and otherwise took liberties which rendered the history worthless. After his revision it was probably revised by Hurtado himself. A copy was subsequently disseminated in Spain by Hurtado in suit for royal reward for services rendered. In like vein, Hurtado was irked at publication of Ercilla's *La Araucana*, which he felt slighted his person. In retaliation he commissioned Pedro de Oña to write his dull *Arauco Domado*, an epic in which Hurtado emerged as the conqueror of Arauco. As Nájera remarked, Oña merely made himself a fool in describing Arauco as subdued when in fact Arauco was more victorious and impregnable than ever before (36–37). See Diego Barros Arana, *Historia jeneral de Chile* (16 vols., Santiago, 1884–1902, II:282–288).

23. Marmolejo, 44–49, 85, 62–63. John M. Cooper, "The Araucanians" (in *Handbook of South American Indians*, Julian H. Steward, ed., Bulletin, Bureau of American Ethnology, no. 143, 1946, II:697), is in error when he concludes that the Indians mastered European military tactics and strategy, making them their own.

24. Olaverría, 34.

25. Marmolejo, 40–43, 47–49. These are but representative of many such descriptions.

26. Nájera, 42, 110–116. Cooper (II:704) gives the impression that Indian saddles and riding gear were nothing more than crude imitations of Spanish models.

27. Nájera, 107–110; "Informe de Juan de Xaraquemada," May 1, 1611 (Gay, II:239); Xaraquemada to King, Jan. 29, 1611, and Jan. 28, 1612 (idem, 247, 255–257); Alonso García Ramón to King, 1613 (idem, 267).

28. Nájera, 116. Whenever the Indians found it necessary or advisable to grant a temporary peace, the Spaniards first insisted that they turn in their horses and move about on foot, as subject persons were expected to do. The Indians invariably turned in their *rocinantes*, keeping their good stock hidden for use after the next rebellion (idem, 128).

29. Olaverría, 20. The area included the Indian localities of Talcamavida, Laucamilla, Catiray, Marigueño, Angol, Arauco, Andalicán, Tucapel, and Purén. After the *estado* had been recognized as a political entity the term was applied to all or part of it. In essence, the term *estado* came to mean the center of Indian resistance, whether it embraced all of the above-named provinces or merely one of them.

30. Alonso de Ercilla y Zúñiga, ed., José Toribio Medina, *La Araucana* (5 vols., Santiago, 1910). Historians and anthropologists seem to be under a strange compulsion to use this poem as a prime documentary source. This is not to say that in select instances the practice is not warranted, but the wide use to which it has been put must certainly be held in question. Everyone knows that there is much truth in it, although seldom is it possible to determine precisely where it resides.

31. Marmolejo, 22–23. It took nearly three years to organize the first rebellion. It is sometimes implied that the Araucanians were introduced to cooperative military effort on a large scale through attempted invasions by the Incas. This seems most unlikely because the Incas were held at the Maule River, and the Indians occupying this area, as nearly as can be ascertained, were the warlike Promaucaes, who were not Araucanians. Nor could the Inca invasions have had anything to do with the formation of the *estado* since, as we have seen, it was created by the imposition of Spanish dominion, without which it could have had no meaning.

32. Idem, 61–62.

33. Idem, 105, 133.

34. Juan de Herrera, "Relación de las cosas de Chile" (CHC, II:251).

35. Olaverría, 23.

36. Marmolejo, 126–127.

37. Idem, 83. The Indians around the settlements who were friendly toward the Spanish were sorely vexed by the depredations of the *estado*'s warriors. Crops were burned or stolen, and women and children were carried off to be used as drudges. See Alonso García Ramón to the King, 1613 (Gay, II:270, 279); "Informe de Juan de Xaraquemada" (idem, 241–242; Nájera, 60). Through acts of terror the *estado* sometimes forced friendly Indians to rebel against the Spanish. Through maladministration the Spanish sometimes achieved the same end. Plundering of Indian stores and raping of their women brought alienation and revolt. See Francisco Nuñez de Pineda y Bascuñan, *Cautiverio felíz* (CHC, III:51–52).

38. Marmolejo, 110–113.

39. Olaverría, 22.

40. Bascuñan, 39–41. Latcham (*La prehistoria chilena*, 153–154) considers this to be an ancient Mapuche military organization, even though it is first reported almost a century after the Spaniards arrived. From what we know of the ancient Mapuche, this would appear to be an unduly sophisticated organization.

41. Idem, 94–99, 144–148; "Relación de Luis de Valdivia," 1611 (Gay, II:281–282).

42. Gerónimo Pietas, "Noticias sobre las costumbres de los Araucanos" (Gay, II:489–493).

43. Marmolejo, 172; Nájera, 48; also see Latcham, *La prehistoria chilena*, 193–194. Cooper (742–752) makes a noble attempt to unravel the confused threads of early Araucanian religious belief.

44. Bascuñan, 39–43. The author was a captain in the Spanish infantry and the son of Alvaro Núñez de Pineda, *maestro de campo general*, one of Chile's distinguished soldiers. In 1629 the Araucanians crossed the Biobío and fell on Chillán. They captured Bascuñan and took him back to their stronghold. His captivity was one of those storybook affairs, almost too romantic and dramatic to be real. He was befriended by Maulican, a powerful chieftain of the *estado*, and likewise the son of a famous warrior. When the other chiefs learned of Bascuñan's identity they demanded his head to use as a trophy to incite peaceful Indians to war. By chicanery and ruse Maulican saved him and, after some months of comfortable captivity, returned him to his own people. His account of the adventure is invaluable, although it is somewhat tiresome to read. He was a creole and educated in Chile. He apparently felt compelled to show that a creole scholar could hold his own with a *peninsular*, hence his excessive quotation from and reference to classical authors.

45. Bascuñan, 155–156. Also see Córdoba y Figueroa, *Historia de Chile* (CHC, II:26).

46. Olaverría, 23.

47. Nájera, 60.

48. Idem, 61, 105.

49. Idem, 60, 70, 100, 119, 163; "Tratado de la importancia y utilidad que ay en dar por esclavos a los indios rebelados de Chile," 1599 (in José Toribio Medina, *Biblioteca hispano-chilena, 1523–1817*, 3 vols., Santiago, 1897–99), II:13.

50. Oliverría, 40.

51. Nájera, 75–76, 98, 100.

52. See Cooper, 732, and José Toribio Medina, *Las aborígines de Chile* (Santiago, 1952), 220–221. Marmolejo (57) states that in the spring of 1556 the Indians were visited by a terrible plague (called *chavalongo*). In the aftermath of famine the Indians turned to cannibalism as a means of survival.

53. García Hurtado de Mendoza, "Relación" (Gay, I:183–184).

54. Nájera, 54.

55. Idem, 53–54, 54–57.

56. Idem, 115.

57. Idem, 58.

58. Nájera, 67–71, 118. The author also stated that over five hundred Spanish women had been taken captive and at the time of writing some two hundred remained in captivity (37–38).

59. Idem, pp. 46–47.

60. Idem, p. 69.

61. One such problem is suggested by the sources. In pre-Hispanic days the Araucarians were sedentary farmers of predominantly vegetarian habits. Frequent mention is made in the documents of a growing cattle economy, especially in Spanish sheep and goats. Inasmuch as warfare disrupted agricultural planting in the valleys, the Araucanians moved their fields to impenetrable sierras. It may be

that lower yields in the mountains created a greater need for animal foodstuffs to supplement lowered agricultural production. See, for example, Julián de Bastida to Don García Hurtado de Mendoza, Nov. 15, 1563 (CHC, XXIX:498); Olaverría, 36–38; Marmolejo, 76–77; Nájera, 23. The implications suggested in a shift of basic economy are highly significant and require further investigation.

62. Córdoba y Figueroa, *Historia de Chile* (CHC, II:29). His statistics seem to be far from the mark. In 1664 the casualty figures, as Latcham reports them, were twenty-nine thousand Spaniards and sixty thousand Indian allies ("La capacidad guerrera de los Araucanos," 58).

5

Coping in Cuernavaca with the Cultural Conquest

Robert Haskett

The natives of Cuernavaca, the head town of the valley of the same name just south of the Valley of Mexico, avoided the devastation of the Spanish conquest. No true military campaigns were conducted there, as was typical of much of Mexico. The people accepted Spanish rule rather readily and saw many aspects of European culture that were compatible with their established way of life. Spanish clothing and animals were quickly adopted. The native people also incorporated important aspects of Catholicism into their belief systems and ritual practices, often without the active supervision of Spanish priests. Further, many soon adjusted to the European emphasis on commercially oriented, privately owned estates as central units in the local economy. Such patterns of ownership and trade were not unknown in precontact Mesoamerica.

The Hispanization of the indigenous elites' material culture has often been seen as a negative force, gradually removing them from contact with the Indian world and making them aliens in their own communities. At the same time, it has been thought that those who failed to reconcile themselves with the intrusive culture became indistinguishable from the commoners they once dominated, leading to the simplification of indigenous society.[1] But as far as the Cuernavaca jurisdiction is concerned, the political and social history of its indigenous ruling group is already putting these older scholarly notions in doubt.[2] It is true that active members of the ruling group owned an extensive array of Iberian goods. A fair number owned good-sized, Spanish-like landed estates. None of this stopped them from being dominant actors in local indigenous society, not even in the later eighteenth century. From the beginning, the essentially conservative native elites mediated the intrusion of alien goods and strategies. Consciously or otherwise, they protected themselves and their culture from total disruption.

Material Culture

As in many societies, the accumulation of material possessions was an important mechanism used to display social status. Despite legal prohibitions, elite Indian men and women eagerly adopted items of Spanish dress in the years following the conquest. Men wore swords and rode horses, both marks of rank in mainstream colonial society.[3] The records are full of requests for the special licenses that would allow them to array themselves in this way. For instance, in 1594 a *principal* of Xiuhtepéc, don Gaspar de Aquino, obtained a license to wear Spanish clothing and carry a sword and dagger, while in 1618 a *cacique y principal* of Tepoztlán, don Bartolomé López, received the same kind of permission for the "ornament and defense of his person."[4]

Others never bothered with legal channels, but whether or not they had proper licenses, *caciques* and town officers rode horses, carried arms, and dressed as Spaniards. Spanish authorities granted permission or looked the other way in an effort to co-opt influential local Indian nobility and to cement their loyalty as intermediaries. Those lacking permission only did so if for some reason they needed to legalize already well-established practices.[5] No better example of this can be found than that offered by the governor-class mestizo Hinojosa family of Cuernavaca. The mid-seventeenth-century governors don Juan and don Agustín de Hinojosa dressed and comported themselves as closely as possible to the Spanish ideal. Don Antonio de Hinojosa (don Agustín's son) dressed and even looked like a Spaniard, a fact remembered well after his death. He also kept and rode horses and possessed a variety of European weapons. His wife and daughters not only dressed like Spanish ladies, but were also said to look like *españolas*. His son, don Melchor de Hinojosa, who also served the *villa* as governor, resembled a Spaniard, dressed like a Spaniard down to a pair of leather shoes with shiny buckles, and carried a knife, sword, and musket. None of the Hinojosas ever bothered to obtain the necessary licenses for such practices; because of their status (and perhaps their ethnicity) the adoption of such outward manifestations of Spanish culture were as necessary as they were expected.

When challenged, members of the ruling group were quick to defend their sartorial habits. In 1732 don Juan Rojas, *cacique* and former governor of Tepoztlán, complained that he, his nephew don Nicolás de Rojas (the governor at the time), another relative, don Francisco de Rojas (a *cacique* and past governor), and don Antonio de Rojas were being forced to wear their hair and clothing in the Indian fashion. Don Juan, claiming that this made them figures of public ridicule, swore that they would "rather be dead" than dress as commoners.[6] In 1714 don Melchor de Hinojosa had been confronted with a similar situation when a rival political faction contested his tenure as governor. Though the authorities ignored this particular charge, don Melchor felt compelled to offer an explanation anyway. He informed his listeners that he wore fine woolens (*paños finos*), which were much better than the apparel of the common people, because they would identify him as an important and influential individual, facilitating his essential political services to the Marqués and king. Moreover, the weapons were necessary to protect the tribute he collected from nearby estates and subject towns. According to don Melchor, the black and mulatto workers on these estates "run away . . . and become nothing but fugitives and thieves," posing a real threat to the money as well as to his own person.[7]

Over time, the same desire to mimic the Spanish upper class prompted members of the Indian ruling group to surround themselves with intrusive goods in their homes.[8] Among the possessions listed in the 1579 Nahuatl testament of the Cuernavacan *tecuhtli* (lesser ruler) and governor don Juan Jiménez were such Spanish items as tables, a horse, tackle, and eight saddles. But listed prominently alongside these things were many cherished symbols of indigenous rank, including four feathered headdresses (*yhuitzoncalli*), three little shields for dancing (*chimaltotontin nehtotiloni*), a *teponaztli,* a *huehuetl,* and a *tlalpam huehuetl* (drums of various types and sizes), and four big parrots (*alome)*.[9] This was a common theme in the testaments of New Spain's sixteenth-century Indian elites. A *teuctli* (titled head of a lordly family) of mid-sixteenth-century Tlaxcala still owned some insignia and feathered garments associated with pre-Hispanic nobility.[10] For such people, traditional symbols of rank were still as important as innovative ones.

Things began to change in succeeding generations. The early seventeenth-century will of don Juan's daughter and sole heir listed none of the preconquest-style goods so esteemed by her father. By the time of don Juan's great-grandson, don Antonio de Hinojosa, the triumph of intrusive goods apparently was complete. An inventory of don Antonio's possessions made in 1694 shows his house (which had been passed down from don Juan Jiménez) to have been filled with a variety of tables, chairs, and an assortment of carved *cajas* (chests) from Michoacán of various sizes (the latter were probably of indigenous manufacture, though Spanish in type). The house was crowded with religious images such as crucifixes, Madonnas, and paintings of various saints. Don Antonio also kept his weaponry, such as an *arcabus*, in the building. Doña Felipa de Haro Bravo y San Roman, don Antonio's wife, brought a dowry with her that was made up of two hundred pesos' worth of clothes and jewelry, much of it imported from Europe.

The trend toward Hispanization had been solidified and was maintained in the possessions of eighteenth-century officers. A governor of Tepoztlán, don Juan Diego, owned many items of Spanish clothing, at least seventeen religious paintings and sculptures of various types and sizes, many pieces of wooden furniture, a silver serving spoon, assorted balls of yarn, several storage boxes, and paper.[11] Yet it would be a mistake to assume that the dominance of intrusive goods marked the disappearance of older ways. It is true that precontact furnishings such as sleeping mats, low seats known as *icpalli*, and ceremonial drums were gone; but native items which retained their usefulness, such as *metates* (grinding stones) and clay pots, could still be found in the kitchens of people like don Juan Diego. Even the Spanish-style wooden chests mentioned in so many testaments served the same purpose as the woven *petlacalli* (wicker chest) of pre-Hispanic times.[12]

By the early seventeenth century, the preference of the jurisdiction's ruling elite for Hispanic material goods had become a deeply ingrained cultural trait, even a psychological necessity. It served to set them apart from the ruled in the same way that in most of the world's societies social ascendancy continues to be displayed through stunning dress and showy possessions. Even in the eighteenth century, members of the ruling groups were extremely sensitive about their habits, hence their exaggerated concern to defend them. For this same reason, they reacted swiftly and sometimes violently when the ruled sought, for instance, to array themselves in the same fashion. On several occasions, don Melchor de Hinojosa forcibly cut the hair of commoners wearing it in the Spanish style. Others confiscated Spanish clothing from hapless commoners.[13]

There was nothing really new in all of this, since the pre-Hispanic ruling class had garbed themselves traditionally in ostentatious finery. They jealously guarded this privilege, forbidding even the wealthy commoner *pochteca* (long-distance traders) from public displays of their wealth, fine clothing, and costly household furnishings. In an effort to strengthen differences in social rank, Mexica rulers beginning with Moctezuma I issued a series of sumptuary edicts which stated that only the nobility could wear fine decorated cloaks, elaborate headdresses, and showy jewelry. Commoners were barred from wearing anything but the coarsest fibers and plainest accessories.[14] Miscreants, in fact, were often "shamefully punished" by the forced shearing of their hair, which represented public degradation.[15]

At least one recent study has concluded that the elaborate sumptuary laws of the Aztecs may not have been as effective in reality as they seem in intent, but they did enshrine the belief that the nobility must set itself above the ruled through the outward display of status.[16] Heirs to this tradition, the men and women of the Cuernavaca jurisdiction's indigenous ruling group, asserted their social and political status by imitating the true power holders in the colonial world, the Spanish elite. The European symbols of rank adopted by those who were full members of indigenous society served to maintain and not to destroy or compress its internal stratification.

Livestock Ownership

The introduction of European domesticated animals into New Spain had a profound effect on the indigenous population, not the least because it increased the variety of food types available to them. Chickens, pigs, goats, and sheep are said to have become "an inseparable part of the indigenous household" by the late sixteenth century. Because chickens were cheaper than the indigenous turkey, by the late sixteenth century they actually became more common than the native fowl.[17] Moreover, horses, mules, donkeys, and oxen were eagerly adopted as useful and heretofore unknown beasts of burden despite colonial legislation to the contrary.

As intermediaries, the ruling elites probably were best positioned to acquire these animals. Their enthusiasm for horses has already been mentioned, as has their ability to gain at least tacit permission from the authorities to own them. In 1597 the authorities loosened the obviously moribund prohibitions against Indian equine ownership to the extent that Indian traders were allowed to keep a maximum of six horses.[18] Characteristically, this regulation seems to have been very loosely applied, and made it even easier for elites to acquire the animals. Few members of the jurisdiction's ruling group owned more than six horses, but it is doubtful that the 1597 ordinance had much to do with this. Rather, realities such as the cost and upkeep of horses were the cause.[19] Very wealthy individuals, such as the *cacica* doña Inés Cortés of Yecapixtla, could afford more; in 1632 she had fifteen mares grazing on her large *hacienda de labor* (agricultural estate, in this case growing maize).[20]

Doña Inés also owned thirty-five plow oxen; and though her herd was larger than most, from the early seventeenth century it was not unusual to find elites raising cattle, oxen, and other beasts of burden.[21] By the eighteenth century it was even more widespread, with mules joining oxen and horses in ever larger numbers. A former governor of Tecpantzingo owned five oxen, as well as a horse and a mare, in 1743, and about a decade later the wealthy Tepoztecan noble don Juan Diego is known to have kept fifteen plow oxen and eight mules. At the same time, ten other members of Tepoztlan's ruling group owned a total of thirty-four mules, twenty-eight plow oxen, and four horses.[22]

Ownership of *ganado mayor* (large animals) was an indication of wealth and status within the indigenous community. Moreover, livestock raising was attractive to the indigenous nobility because it was not labor intensive and was also a typical activity of the Spanish nobility, a fact that their Indian counterparts were not slow in perceiving. But members of the jurisdiction's ruling group who owned oxen and mules were just as interested in profit as in prestige. As in other regions of New Spain, their superficially Hispanic livestock enterprises probably serviced the Indian market.[23] Even when livestock was not raised for sale, the use of plow oxen or mules on agricultural lands must have increased productivity and profit. And since not everyone in the community owned work animals, it is likely that those who did rented their oxen or mules to local indigenous agriculturalists.[24]

Elite owners of horses and mules used them as beasts of burden in other commercial activities as well. Some of the jurisdiction's ruling group earned a living through trade in nonagricultural goods, at first glance an occupation completely out of keeping with *principal* status and traditional social teaching (of which, see more below). Yet activity in trade, usually at the level of *tratante* (petty trader of locally produced goods), was common among the officer class of New Spain, and had been so from the beginning of the colonial period.[25] The Spanish authorities finally got around to codifying this by-now traditional practice in 1597, prohibiting Indians from dealing in Spanish arms and imported silks but permitting commerce in all other items already being traded.[26]

The more prosperous *principal*-class traders of the Cuernavaca jurisdiction not unnaturally also tended to be mule-train operators. In 1640 a noble *tratante* (peddler) and mule-train owner of Tepoztlán, which was something of a center for Indian traders, reported that he sold "all kinds of provisions and locally produced merchandise (*mercaderias de la tierra*)," mainly to Indian consumers.[27] In the eighteenth century, Tepoztlán continued to be a center for elite traders, and there are reports of several members of the highest elite, among them at least one frequent governor, who sold *ropa de la tierra* (locally produced goods) in the surrounding region.[28]

An important and attractive market for officers who sold native goods was the mineworkers of Taxco. Again, Tepoztlán emerges as a principal center of such trade, with several officers selling clothing, capes, blankets, and cloth to the Indians of the mines.[29] Mexico City, a traditional magnet for the Cuernavaca jurisdiction's trade, remained the focus of much mercantile traffic after the conquest. The son of Cuernavaca's governor don Josef Gaspar Díaz traveled to Mexico City to sell *guacomote* (manioc), perhaps a crop grown by the governor himself.[30] Similarly, an *alcalde* (mayor) of Tepoztlán reported that he bought and sold various foodstuffs, an activity that often took him to Mexico City. If business warranted, he would sometimes push on from the viceregal capital to Toluca. This *alcalde* was a leader of one of Tepoztlán's several political factions. During the course of litigation he often traveled to the capital, an activity that may have facilitated his commercial dealings in the area, or vice versa.[31]

Some of the elite mule-train operators carted goods for others but did not sell themselves. They ranged from relatively well-off *arrieros*—pack train owners, a profession found among the indigenous elite elsewhere in New Spain—to owners of one or two mules. The size of the mule train seems to have been directly linked to social and political status; in Tepoztlán it was people of the *alcalde* level or above who owned large strings of mules, with lesser officers tending to own only a few pack animals. Once again, wealth and social and political status were very closely related.[32] The possession of a large pack train may have imparted a certain amount of prestige to members of the indigenous elite who were otherwise cut off from the higher levels of colonial commerce. And at least as important as prestige to the jurisdiction's colonial elite traders was the profit motive, shared by large and small operators alike.

Houses

One way the Iberian elite displayed their wealth and status was through the ownership of a substantial house located as close to the center of town as possible. This tradition, transferred to the New World with the conquest, was absorbed by the surviving Indian ruling class, whose forebears had similar customs. It has been thought that the colonial indigenous elite built their dwellings in conscious imitation of Spanish styles, and even in the *Florentine Codex* pictures of supposedly pre-Hispanic dwellings have such Spanish embellishments as tile floors.[33] Seventeenth-century descriptions of the homes of two members of Cuernavaca's early sixteenth-century ruling group mention such features as round arches, second stories, and even a patio large enough to accommodate gatherings of officials and dances associated with public fiestas.[34]

This last attribute sounds more thoroughly indigenous than the others, and, in fact, houses belonging to the Cuernavaca jurisdiction's ruling group preserved a characteristically mixed architectural style that betrayed a strong continuity with the past. According to a description in his 1579 Nahuatl testament, the home of the Cuernavacan *teuctli* don Juan Jiménez was located near the center of town in the Tecpan district at a site called Tepepan. The house was described as a *calli* (house) on a *calmilli* ("house field," equivalent to the Spanish *solar* [urban house lot]).[35] In Nahuatl usage, *calli* could mean either "room" or "dwelling complex"; and, in fact, the houses of the more substantial social levels were usually made up of several of these individual *calli,* each with its own entrance and arranged around a central court. Any gaps in the enclosure were filled by a wall.[36] While this might be taken to be a fair description of a Spanish house centered on its patio, early colonial Nahuatl documents from the Cuernavaca region suggest that this scheme had been standard before the conquest.[37]

The *calli* house complex was long lived in central New Spain, as is evident in a house plan appended to a will dated 1645 from Tulancingo in the Valley of Mexico.[38] A tendency for seventeenth- and eighteenth-century Spanish-language documents to refer to Indian houses in the plural as *casas, casas de morada,* or *piezas* when speaking of a single location also suggests the longevity of this sort of physical plant.[39]

Following this convention, the former residence of don Juan Jiménez, now in the hands of his great-grandson the governor don Antonio de Hinojosa, was called *unas casas* (some houses) in the 1690s. The *sala principal* (main hall) was a substantial affair built of stone and covered with a beamed roof made of material called *tajamanil* (wooden shingles).[40] It was located on a rather irregular patio enclosed by five other main structures, including four *aposentos* (lodgings), which served as living quarters, and a *cocinilla* (literally, little kitchen). All of these structures had windows and lockable doors, and one of the *aposentos* was divided into two chambers. The sixth *casa* was a stone oratory with a large, lockable door recessed in a portal of stone and mortar. This portal had nine stone steps and seems to have been a rather grand affair. Across from the oratory were a small adobe pantry roofed with *zacate* (straw or grass) and a *colgadizo* (lean-to) of *tajamanil*. The property also boasted a preconquest-style *cuexcomate* (grain bin) filled with thirty-five *cargas* of maize (3,700 liters), as well as a chicken coop. The entire *calmilli* was said to measure fifty-five and one-half *varas* (approximately 152 feet), which probably refers to the length of the longest side. The unnamed side could have been a standardized measure, perhaps twenty *varas* if the indigenous vigesimal system was still in use.[41] In general, the exact size and shape of lots in Cuernavaca and in other towns would have been dictated by population density, the need to distribute holdings among multiple heirs, and the growth of a resident non-Indian community hungry for town *solares*.

The Hinojosas, in fact, had been able to use their well-developed ties to the Spanish and indigenous communities to marry into, purchase, or improve a large urban estate. The origins of the houses of two of don Antonio's daughters in the San Pedro district show this very plainly. Doña Petronila's house had been a gift in 1685 from a childless maternal uncle (the dwelling had originally been purchased from Spaniards in 1631), while doña Antonia's residence was built by her husband in 1683 on a lot purchased from a Spanish *vecino* of the villa. Architecturally, the homes were similar to their father's house complex. Both were situated on lots across from the *calvario* (cemetery) that still stands on one of the main roads leading out of town and, like most *calmilli* in Cuernavaca and elsewhere, had stables, orchards, and small garden plots; this, in fact, had been a preconquest norm.[42] Both dwellings were substantial *tajamanil*-roofed adobe structures with stone foundations and wooden floors. One of them even had a second story and had a *tienda* (store) on the ground floor run by the husband, the *cacique* Luís Bermúdez. In fact, though in Spanish culture shopkeeping was considered a plebeian occupation, it was not unknown for members of the jurisdiction's ruling group to maintain retail outlets or artisan shops in their residences. A representative of Tepoztlán's eighteenth-century governor-level Eslava family ran a *tienda de pulpería* (general store) and sold mules and bulls from around 1775 until his death in 1811.[43] Don Hipólito Méndez, who served both as *juez* and *gobernador* in early eighteenth-century Cuernavaca, was a *velero* (candlemaker) as well as a maize farmer.[44] Here, it would be well to remember that in the pre-Hispanic era it was expected that members of the nobility would learn craft skills, and in the Cuernavaca jurisdiction some remnant of this attitude seems to have persisted long after the conquest.[45]

Whether or not they included shops, all of the *calli* described here had been modified over the years to mimic various Iberian architectural conventions. In some ways, don Antonio de Hinojosa's complex, with its decorated stone oratory and solid main *sala*, seems to have resembled an elaborate two-story, arcaded stone house known as El Hospital (it was next door to the village hospital), located directly across from the Franciscan monastery.[46] Accordingly, these *calli* were worth a substantial amount of money, from one hundred pesos to the very considerable sum of five hundred pesos in the case of don Antonio de Hinojosa's dwelling.[47]

Prices in places such as Cuernavaca may have been high because they were centers of Spanish population and retained significant indigenous populations throughout the colonial period. But houses belonging to the lesser elite of Cuernavaca or of towns in its hinterland were not quite as elaborate. Though most were embellished with wooden doors and private chapels, they seem to have been built of adobe only. The homes of the ruling group of impoverished *pueblos,* such as seventeenth-century Tezoyuca, which had been devastated by demographic losses, were really quite humble and perhaps only marginally better than those of the commoners. In 1644 the home of the Tezoyucan *cacique* and former governor don Juan García was described as a group of three cane and adobe *jacales* (huts), a term also used to describe the dwellings of the rest of the town's officers.[48]

In sum, the typical physical plant belonging to the Cuernavaca jurisdiction's elite would include a walled compound of several individual structures, the most important of them constructed of stone or adobe, arranged around a central patio. The *calli* complex would be located on a larger lot which could be used to graze animals or perhaps to grow some kind of crop. Since the owners of these house compounds were members of the local elite, they were usually located as near to the center of town as possible, as "good" an address in colonial New Spain as it had been in pre-Hispanic times.[49] While it is true that the houses of the highest elite displayed many elements of Hispanic architecture, these clearly had been superimposed on much older forms; even the Catholic oratories were no innovation, for religious shrines were a typical feature of elite houses before the conquest.[50] The more rustic, windowless structures owned by the humbler members of the ruling group suggest this continuity more strongly. Typically, in the houses of the Indian elite a fusion of Iberian and Indian elements was solidified by the early seventeenth century at the latest.

Rural Landholding

In the Spanish system, possession of wealth and property went hand in hand with elevated social status and access to political power. It is no wonder that the jurisdiction's colonial indigenous ruling group sought to construct and maintain what at first sight appear to have been European-style landed estates. But this socioeconomic strategy was not without precontact precedent. It has even been suggested that the successful increase of an estate may have replaced warfare as an avenue of social mobility after the conquest.[51] It is known that before the arrival of Cortés the higher nobility controlled substantial amounts of land, usually in a dispersed pattern, with a similar though more restricted tendency displayed by the lesser elites.[52] Some of these estates, or at least parts of them, survived the dislocations of conquest; a Tepoztecan *tlatoani,* for example, retained a large amount of rural property in 1530.[53]

The Spanish policy of favoring elite collaborators fostered this land-holding continuity, since properties of hereditary *tlatoque* were often granted the status of entailed *cacicazgos* in grants known as *mercedes de cacicazgo.*[54] Yet extensive *cacicazgo* records are rare for the Cuernavaca jurisdiction, with only the large estates belonging to don Hernando, the conquest-era *tlatoani* of Cuernavaca, and to don Toribio de San Martín Cortés, the powerful sixteenth-century governor of the *villa,* obviously fitting this description.[55]

Nonetheless, in the sixteenth century and later, land ownership remained both common and important among the jurisdiction's ruling group, who among Indians tended to own the largest and best holdings.[56] Estates were attained and maintained in a variety of ways. As in the case of Spanish grantees, lesser indigenous nobles could obtain *mercedes* (grants) as a reward for some "great service to the king" (such a common criterion that it was a standard assertion in the jurisdiction's primordial titles); similar grants, of course, were not unheard of before the conquest.[57] The definition of "service" was apparently quite broad, for the *merced* was actually one more mechanism used to co-opt the native nobility. Typical were grants of ownership recognition made in 1552 by the Marquesado in favor of three *principales* (two of them women) of Oaxtepec to *tepillalli* (noble land) in an area called Xochimilcatzingo.[58]

Those failing to win a grant or award early took up an apparent colonial innovation, the ability to lease or rent land from Indian communities, the Marquesado, or Spaniards.[59] One of the more spectacular cases of this sort revolved around the efforts of don Hilario de la Cruz, a wealthy *cacique y principal* of the *pueblo* Mazatepéc, to renegotiate his rental of a *rancho de ganado mayor* (cattle ranch, which included a half *caballería* of arable land).[60] In 1705 don Hilario requested that the Marquesado take over the lease, which had been obtained originally from the *pueblo* of Ahuehuetzinco in 1700 for six pesos per year. Hoping to arrange a more secure *censo perpetuo* (perpetual lease) in the process, he claimed that Ahuehuetzinco was both a great distance from the *rancho* and that its citizens were no longer cultivating any land in the area. A survey of the broken and irregular property by Cuernavaca's *alcalde mayor* determined that the *rancho* was indeed *tierras baldías* (unclaimed lands) and that the *pueblo* had sufficient lands elsewhere. The property was said to measure an astounding *tres leguas en redonda* (three leagues around), but was good only for livestock since it was rocky and dry. In essence, the Marquesado used this process to usurp the "vacant" land from the *pueblo* and added it to its portfolio of income sources by leasing it to don Hilario for twenty pesos per year. The *cacique y principal* received stronger title to the *rancho* than the tenuous and poorly documented arrangement with Ahuehuetzinco. Rental (which, in this instance, amounted to little more than legalized theft) helped make the jurisdiction's land-tenure situation more flexible than it otherwise might have been by giving those with enough money access to land that was otherwise unobtainable.[61]

Grants, and in many cases formal leases, were externally sanctioned mechanisms of estate building, since to obtain them the jurisdiction's ruling group depended on the goodwill of the authorities. Other internal and far more traditional methods were just as important. Judicious marital alliances were as crucial for land tenure as they were in the forging of political alliances. Together with inheritance, marriage often resulted in the increase or improvement of a family's landholdings. The core of the extensive seventeenth-century estate of Cuernavaca's Hinojosas came to them by way of marriage into the governor-class Jiménez family. Don Juan Jiménez's 1579 testament listed thirteen properties held at scattered locations in the greater Cuernavaca area. Some were described by using pre-Hispanic terminology.[62] One piece was glossed as an *amiltzintli* (irrigated field), while two others were called *tlacpactlalli*, literally "land on top," which probably meant that they were located at a higher elevation than the rest. One of the *tlacpactlalli* was described as a *calpolpa pillalli*, or privately held noble's land located within a *calpulli* (or perhaps at a place called Calpolpa).[63]

The largest property, known as Teocuauhco, was glossed as *tlatocatlalli* (combining forms of *tlatoani* and *tlalli*, or land), translated as *patrimonio* by an interpreter. Pre-Hispanic *tlatocatlalli* are generally believed to have been lands attached to the office of *tlatoani* but not private property.[64] But in don Juan's will, the parcel was being treated as private property, suggesting that members of the elite had been able to claim exclusive ownership of such plots at the expense of their communities in the fluid years following the conquest.[65] This practice clearly was the norm by the early seventeenth century, for in the 1607 will of don Juan's daughter and heir, Teocuauhco was once again passed on, this time labeled *tlatocamilli*, a rough equivalent of *tlatocatlalli*. Even though the meaning of these terms had been altered by the colonial experience, they still connoted high social status.

In the early part of the seventeenth century, when don Agustín de Hinojosa became a property owner by marrying the heiress doña Juana Jiménez, the physical composition of the estate had begun to evolve (see Table 1). Some of the original Jiménez properties were still held, but others had been replaced with new parcels. A number of the additions were acquired through legal means, and don Agustín is known to have bid on land at auction on several occasions.[66] Other parcels may have been usurped from the community, since one of his holdings was described as *calpullalli* (corporate land).[67] The colonial indigenous elite, often with the aid of obliging Spaniards, were notorious for their absorption of *calpullalli*, which was normally land from which usufruct plots were distributed to commoners.[68]

Table 1. The Evolution of the Hinojosa Estate, 1579–1695

Don Juan Jiménez, 1579	*Doña María Jiménez, 1607*	*Don Antonio de Hinojosa, 1695*
Atlinepilohuayan	Atlinepilohuayan Quaquauhtzontlan	Atlinepilohuayan
		San Pedro
Santa Barbara		
Teocuauhco	Teocuauhco	Teocuauhco
Tlatzalán	Tlatzalán	
Xochtlán Atlauhtzinco		
		Zacamolpán
Tepepán	Tepepán	Tepepán (house lot)
Tlalli	Tlalli	
Ahuacaquauhyo	Ahuacaquauhyo	
Coatepéc		
Olactzinco	Olactzinco	Olactzinco
Quauhchiltonco	Quauhchiltonco	
Tlechialco	Tlechialco	Tlechialco
Tepetitlán		Tepetitlán*
Tzacualpán	Tzacualpán	
Tzacualpán amilli	Tzacualpán amilli	
Yauhtlica	Yauhtlica	Autlica (*sic*)

*Tepetitlán (next to or among the hills) is a very common and descriptive place name. Therefore, there is no compelling reason to think that these two plots, held at two points over a century apart, were the same.

By 1695, in the time of don Antonio de Hinojosa, don Agustín's eldest son, the estate still consisted of a collection of scattered plots of various sizes. Teocuauhco, now also known as San Nicolás, was still the largest plot, measuring 668 by 150 *varas* and worth the substantial sum of five hundred pesos (value was based on the richness of the soil, the terrain, the size, and the going prices in the area).[69] It was worth so much because it was prime sugarcane land, actually being rented at the time by the Cortés *ingenio* of Atlacomulco. Nine smaller parcels, measuring anywhere from 250 to 410 *varas* on their longest sides, were held in several of Cuernavaca's *sujetos*. They, too, were either rented to Atlacomulco, to local residents, or to district councils.[70] Though by 1695 the estate was not made up of as many individual properties as in the late sixteenth century, its total size of 3,000 *varas* (2,400 meters) was probably as great or greater than it had been before. The combined properties were several times larger than the traditional 500-*vara* townsite that was then considered the minimum necessary for a viable townsite.

Indian land in the jurisdiction was measured with a variety of methods. Purely indigenous measures persisted, such as the *quahuitl* (literally, a rod or stick; that is, a standard measure), which was said to equal a *braza de indios* (variable, but around three meters).[71] The *mecatl*, named after a cord used to measure land, was also employed into the early eighteenth century.[72] A Nahuatl Cuernavacan land document equated the *mecatl* with twenty *varas* (*yn sesen mecatl quipia senpoalli vara . . .* ; "each mecatl has twenty *varas*"), but it was sometimes given as twenty-one *varas*, probably depending on the exact size of the cord being used in a particular place at a particular time.[73]

Purely Spanish measures, such as the *vara,* were in use by the seventeenth century, though there were seemingly many local variations of length. By the late eighteenth century, the repertoire of intrusive measures had increased to include such things as the *cuartillo de sembradura de maíz* (at the time equated with one-quarter *almud*, or around a liter in modern usage, an *almud* being approximately equal to four and one-half liters). The *cuartillo* referred to the measure of maize that could be sown on a given piece of land. A plot of land belonging to a don Juan Marcos of Zacatepéc measuring, or rather, that could be sown with, eighteen *cuartillos* needed three yokes of oxen (or perhaps three days of labor from a single yoke) for cultivation, suggesting a large plot. However, the difficulty of the terrain involved may have affected the measure, since another plot of one *cuartillo* needed the labor of two yokes of oxen for cultivation.[74] Unfortunately, the dimensions of the ruling group's lands are rarely given, so precise definitions for most of these measures must await the accumulation of more as well as better evidence. The persistent use of traditional measures into the eighteenth century is significant, however, in that it is one more indication of the tenacity of indigenous culture.

By the seventeenth century the owners of some of these properties had mimicked their Spanish counterparts, who over time had been constructing large unitary estates. In 1632 the maize estate of an unmarried Yecapixtlan *cacica* named doña Inés Cortés, for example, amounted to three *caballerías* (315 acres) and had a resident work force of ten *gañanes* and an *indio capitán* (foreman). In the 1530s the estate of another wealthy Hinojosa family, *caciques* of the *pueblo* of Tlayacac, totaled twenty-seven and one-half *caballerías* and was made up of from twenty-three to twenty-six scattered parcels (one of which, called *tierras de señorio,* was still being worked by resident tributaries). By 1691 their property had been transformed into a contiguous estate of twenty-four *caballerías*.[75] More typical, however, was the persistence of traditional indigenous landholding strategies. In a pattern that repeated itself over and over again, members of the jurisdiction's ruling group maintained estates that were really collections of scattered parcels of varying size and type. This was true not only of the Cuernavacan Hinojosa and Díaz families, who held scattered but extensive lands in and around the *villa* and its *sujetos* into the eighteenth century, but also of many noble officers of the late eighteenth and early nineteenth centuries.[76]

The persistence of this ancient pattern could be laid at the door of emerging colonial realities, since by the seventeenth century a majority of the jurisdiction's ruling group may have been unable to follow the lead of their Spanish neighbors simply because the latter had come to control large segments of arable land. But there is also compelling evidence that older strategies persisted. A reading of many Nahuatl documents suggests that the proximity of one parcel to another was not the primary concern of many Indian landowners. Rather, just as in pre-Hispanic times, land was selected primarily with an eye to fertility and location. The scattered Díaz estate included certain plots glossed as *tlalhuactli*, or nonirrigated; and in 1647 the widowed doña Francisca Gerónima of San Gaspar Coatlán held lands designated *amilli* (irrigated field) and *xalmilli* (dry or nonirrigated field), which probably represented a variety of soil and land types.[77] Typically, doña Francisca held her lands in twelve different places. She, the Díazes, the Hinojosas, and others like them seem to have selected land for its suitability as crop land, as pasturage, or as a source of firewood or other nonagricultural products; they sought to build up a complementary set of holdings, not necessarily a monolithic estate.[78]

Land as an Income Source

There was more than a drive for power and status in the anxiety of members of the jurisdiction's ruling group to amass and maintain as much agricultural property as possible. Most of them depended on their agricultural holdings for a certain part of their incomes. Though the coming of Spaniards may have contributed to the specific shape that most of these operations assumed, land and landed estates worked by resident laborers had always provided support for the elite of central Mexico and may have been used to produce surpluses sold in markets.[79] Pre-Hispanic social thought, embodied in the *huehuetlatolli* (sayings of the ancients), stressed among other things the fact that nobles should be knowledgeable in matters of what amounted to agronomy.[80] Nobles were not expected to do manual labor, and not always to manage their holdings themselves. Instead, the day-to-day operation would be in the hands of professionals known as *calpixque* (in this case, something like hacienda *mayordomos*) by the time of the conquest. Yet it is clear that estate management and a working knowledge of crops and cultivation were not contradictory to elite status in pre-Hispanic central Mexico.[81]

Maize, tomatoes, chiles, amaranth, maguey, honey, and other food crops, and especially cotton, were the most important specialty crops grown in the orbit of pre-Hispanic Cuauhnahuac.[82] The precise role of the local elite in the cultivation of these crops, surpluses of which were sold in Tenochtitlan-Tlatelolco, is not known, but it would be surprising if elite agriculturalists were not involved. The conquest of Mexico must have disrupted the operation of the region's economic system, but there is compelling evidence that the surviving indigenous nobility in many areas of New Spain began to participate directly in the Spanish economy, generally in whatever activity was paramount among Iberians living in a given area. Though most of these indigenous enterprises were run nearly or completely by the Indians themselves, many had adopted European techniques—including the use of plows and plow oxen—in the sixteenth century, a trait they had in common with similar people in other parts of New Spain and even of central Peru. Typically, whatever surpluses were produced by these operations, which grew maize, beans, chiles, and other winter crops, were destined for Indian markets.[83]

Maize retained its importance in the scheme of the jurisdiction's postconquest agriculture. Typically, many of the jurisdiction's ruling group adopted European-style agriculture, which by the seventeenth century had become so important to some of them that active town officers would refer to themselves as *labradores*, a term connoting land ownership and mainly applied to Spaniards.[84] The seventeenth-century *hacienda de labor* owned by the *principala* doña Inés Cortés near Yecapixtla epitomized the jurisdiction's large profit-oriented indigenous maize estates. Doña Inés was, in fact, one of a number of elite women who owned and managed estates on a par with or more extensive than elite men in the area.[85]

Precise information about the size of a specific individual's maize crop is available in a few cases. In 1710 a past *alcalde* of the *pueblo* Ayoxochiapa reported that he owned a field that could be planted with 1.5 *fanegas* of maize.[86] Maize yields varied from place to place and from year to year, but could range from a ratio of 70 to 1 to as much as 150 to 1. Using an average yield of 80 to 1 suggested by a study of the Mexican Bajío, the past *alcalde* could have expected to reap 120 *fanegas* (6,000 liters) from his 1.5 *fanegas* of seed maize. This would have been considerably above the subsistence level, which has been placed at from 550 to

1,100 liters (10 to 20 *fanegas*) for an average Indian family of the colonial Valley of Mexico.[87]

The exact productivity of most maize holdings owned by members of the ruling group is usually not stated so forthrightly, but information preserved in inventories of noble possessions can help. Don Antonio de Hinojosa of Cuernavaca, for example, had approximately eighty *cargas* (one *carga* equals two *fanegas*, or around 110 liters) of maize stored in a *cuexcomatl* in late 1694.[88] The total, therefore, would have been somewhere around 8,800 liters of maize. The governor's stock represented a large surplus that must have been earmarked for outside sale. For tribute purposes, at least, maize was usually valued at 9 reales per *fanega*, suggesting that don Antonio's maize was worth 180 pesos. Similar examples summarized in Table 2 can help determine the size of elite-owned maize agriculture. Not all town officers produced a surplus crop, and some of them even seem to have failed to reach the subsistence level. Not surprisingly, there was also some correlation between relative official and social status and the amount of maize possessed.[89]

Table 2. Maize Held in Storage by Town Officers, 1743–1761

Year	Officer	Location	Amount of Maize	Amount over Subsistence
1743	*vocal*	Tecpantzinco	68 *fanegas*	48–58 *fanegas*
1743	*vocal*	same	8 *fanegas*	none
1743	governor	same	6 *fanegas*	none
1758	governor	Tepoztlán	262 *fanegas*	242–252 *fanegas*
1759	same gov.	same	60 *fanegas*	40–50 *fanegas*
1759	*alcalde*	same	200 *fanegas*	180–190 *fanegas*
1759	*vocal*	same	60 *fanegas*	40–50 *fanegas*
1759	*vocal*	same	40 *fanegas*	20–30 *fanegas*
1759	*vocal*	same	30 *fanegas*	10–20 *fanegas*
1759	*alcalde*	same	8 *fanegas*	none
1759	*alcalde*	same	5 *fanegas*	none
1759	*vocal*	same	4 *fanegas*	none
1759	*vocal*	same	3 *fanegas*	none
1761	*alcalde*	Xochitlán	14 *fanegas*	4 *fanegas*

Officers who were not producing much maize were probably mainly involved in some other agricultural endeavor. For example, on Table 2 the Tepoztecan officer possessing only five *fanegas* of maize in 1759 also grew maguey (a cactus whose products could be sold), which was likely his major source of income. In fact, the jurisdiction's elite agriculturalists commonly augmented maize with other crops. Don Agustín de Hinojosa, and later his son don Antonio de Hinojosa, who either grew or dealt in a considerable amount of maize, also sold *cacahuates* (peanuts) in the period between the 1640s and 1690s. Neither cultivated this product themselves, instead receiving it as rent from Indians of the *pueblo* of Acapantzinco who were working the land. In 1645 don Agustín received eight *fanegas* (440 liters) from his renters, and then sold the crop to a master blacksmith of the *ingenio* of Cuautecaco for a total of thirty-six pesos (four pesos, four reales per *fanega*).[90] Orchards, usually containing European fruit trees, were another common element of the ruling group's agricultural endeavors. Others grew other indigenous food crops such as chiles, melons, tomatoes, and even anise.[91] Some of the jurisdiction's elite agriculturalists may have worked the fields themselves—a wealthy maize grower of Tecpantzinco claimed that he personally tended his chile plantings, for example—but most of those with larger holdings undoubtedly relied on the labor of local Indian citizens.

Cotton, once the principal export of the Cuauhnahuac region, retained its importance as a specialty crop for some time after the conquest, and Indians continued to control its production. But by the latter half of the sixteenth century cotton had been more or less replaced by several other crops; in the area of Chalcatzinco, for example, wheat agriculture replaced cotton cultivation. But the real demise of cotton as a commercial crop, and of probable elite involvement in its production, was the rise of the local sugar industry, which came into its own by the early seventeenth century.[92] Members of the jurisdiction's elite were able to make the transition and become sugarcane growers themselves. Most sold their cane to Spanish sugar-mill owners.[93] Most Indian growers seem to have supplied the local Indian market. In 1684, for instance, a *principal* of the *pueblo* of Temimiltzinco reported that he grew cane on a small plot of land, selling the product raw and in small pieces to Indians in the *plazas y tianquez* (squares and markets) of New Spain. Soon he petitioned the Estado for a license to erect a *trapichillo* (little *trapiche*, or animal-powered sugar mill) so he could more easily pay tribute and support himself, as the standard litany went. The mill would be used to produce *panocha o chancaca usual*— raw, unrefined sugar "which the *naturales* [Indians] and others like."[94]

This indigenous cane grower was at pains to stress the small-scale nature of his operation because not only were licenses required to erect and operate a *trapiche*, but special regulations also were attached to permits issued to Indians. Neither refined sugar nor *mieles* (molasses) could be produced or sold to other Indians. Furthermore, such mills could not be rented or sold to mulattoes, blacks, or mestizos.[95] In fact, many members of the jurisdiction's ruling group operated *trapiches*, and most of them did so without the appropriate licenses. Typically, they would only apply for permission if the existence of their mills became an issue.[96]

Licenses for *trapiche* construction and operation were still necessary in the last years of Spanish rule. In 1808 the *principal* José Bacilio Roque of San Francisco Tetecala applied for permission to build a *trapiche*. He argued that the mill was to be not only for his own benefit (for he grew cane on various pieces of land in the region), but also to service the local indigenous community, since many of its inhabitants grew cane. José alleged that the Spanish mill owners charged the Indian growers ruinous prices to grind their crop or bought it outright at well below the market rate. Indian cane also had to wait until the *ingenio*'s own harvest was processed, and the resulting delay was often disastrous to the indigenous product. After due consideration, the Estado issued the license, charging José a yearly five-peso operational fee. The *trapiche* continued to operate until at least 1820, at which time the now rundown mill was sold to a Spaniard.[97]

Members of the ruling group who grew cane were concerned with turning a profit and not merely with whatever prestige would be attached to their endeavors. Since few cane growers could have financed and operated larger-scale refineries in competition with Spaniards, they produced for the local market even when they adopted a Hispanic crop and Iberian production methods. The same could be said of other elite agriculturalists who produced a surplus for sale. The ubiquitous statement that crops were grown for the "support of the family" could have various shades of meaning. There was a world of difference between the large maize operations of a wealthy governor and those belonging to humble officers. The profit earned from the sale of maize in the former case could help support the life-style of the highest indigenous elite, while in the latter instance the maize itself provided the sustenance necessary for familial well-being.

Some of the officers who grew maguey used it to produce *pulque*, an important pre-Hispanic product whose consumption by Indian men and women tended to increase after the conquest even when the population was on the decline.[98] *Mezcal*, an alcoholic drink made from the baked hearts of another variety of maguey, was also produced by some of the Cuernavaca jurisdiction's ruling group, but *pulque* (an alcoholic drink made from fermented maguey sap) seems to have been far more important.[99] Though *pulque* entered the colonial economy at an early date, with some exceptions production of *pulque* remained in most places an indigenous cottage industry until the end of Spanish rule. Only in Mexico City, and even then not until the eighteenth century, did a large concentration

of *pulque* consumers conducive to full-scale commercialization exist, and
there Spanish hacienda owners virtually monopolized production at the
expense of the indigenous manufacturers.[100]

One study has concluded that only residents of the *pueblo* Huichilac
in the Cuernavaca jurisdiction were engaged in large-scale production of
pulque for sale, but this is an understatement.[101] *Pulque* was actually produced all over the jurisdiction from an early date. In 1609, Chalcatzinco
had at least four families specializing in the manufacture of *pulque*, and
in 1645 production was reported to be widespread in the *pueblo* of
Xochitepéc. In that same year, Indian witnesses stated that the *trato y
cosecha* (trade and harvest) of the *pueblo* of Atlacholoaya was *pulque*. In
1694 an *alcalde mayor* complained that the *naturales* (natives) of Santa
María, a *sujeto* of Cuernavaca, were spending most of their time in *pulque*
production to the neglect of food crops such as maize.[102] In communities
involved in the trade, a given producer might plant a field with from 70 to
120 maguey plants. At any one time, a crop of this size would provide
from 15 to 20 productive plants.[103]

An excellent example of an elite-class *pulque* producer is the
Tepoztecan governor don Juan Diego. A 1749 inventory of his estate shows
that don Juan, with the help of at least one *gañán* (permanent estate
worker), raised maguey on three different plots, which held a total of 250
plants averaging a *vara* and one-half in height. Productive plants, at the
time around 15 percent of the total, were valued at six reales each, while
nonproductive ones were worth only one real each, giving a total value at
the time of fifty-five pesos, five reales.[104] It is not clear how long or how
often a given maguey could be tapped for juice in the area, nor how much
pulque could be produced from one plant during the course of a year.

Aside from social and private uses in the home, indigenous witnesses
reported that *pulque* was important in ritual, essential to replace water
during the dry season, and useful in the fields where it was drunk by
workers to revive themselves from the heat of the day.[105] Almost everyone
making the beverage in the region seems to have sold at least some of it to
others. There were few formal taverns in most *pueblos de indios*, and local producers in the Cuernavaca jurisdiction (as in other areas of New
Spain) habitually supplied their customers informally and without paying
official fees.[106] This kind of sale was supposed to be taxed; but when the
Spanish *cobradores de pulque* arrived to collect their fees, the indigenous
producers steadfastly claimed to be making the brew only for their own
use.

All of these commercial activities—growing crops for sale, producing low-grade sugar, raising livestock, selling and carting goods, and
manufacturing alcoholic drink—were essentially entrepreneurial in na-

ture, requiring time, money, and some sort of specialized knowledge. Members of the jurisdiction's ruling group used their resources to make money in more passive ways as well. If they were wealthy enough, they were likely to become moneylenders, though it is not known if they charged interest.[107] Money was loaned to help people buy goods and property or to finance economic ventures which were otherwise beyond their reach.[108] Another typical and important purpose of personal loans was to help fellow officers make up tribute shortfalls, since those charged with collection could lose their estates if they failed to deliver the required amount. The 1651 will of don Agustín de Hinojosa of Cuernavaca, governor of the *villa* in the 1640s, shows that he loaned 126 pesos to four of Cuernavaca's *mayordomos* and a notary who had had trouble collecting the entire tribute amount assigned to them. He had loaned the same group 20 pesos to help them pay for a *capellanía* (chaplaincy) originally endowed by a local *principal*. On another occasion, the governor loaned 221 pesos, 2 reales to another group of *mayordomos* and a notary and 90 pesos to a third notary because of tribute shortfalls. Finally, don Agustín had lent a total of 52 pesos to a pair of governors from nearby *pueblos* who had not been able to deliver the entire assessed amount of their town's tribute.[109]

If moneylending proves to have led to few tangible material rewards, it still would have represented a kind of sociopolitical income. If his wealth enabled him to do so, it was in a governor's best interest to help other officers make up for tribute shortfalls by loaning them the necessary money, since he was ultimately responsible for the tribute owed by the citizens of his municipality. Loans of this nature not only created goodwill but also kept town officers solvent, their economic enterprises intact, and the whole financial structure of the town operating smoothly. Many of these loans were not called in for many years, often only upon the death of the elite creditor. The lax collection with the resulting obligations of long duration were one more mechanism tying together the ruling group of a town or even a region.

Tangible material rewards did accrue from another common passive economic activity of the jurisdiction's elite, however. They, like Indian nobles elsewhere in New Spain, began to lease out their urban and rural properties in the years immediately following the conquest.[110] The standard length of such rental agreements was nine years, and some of the jurisdiction's *principales* arranged *censos perpetuos* (perpetual quitrents) along the lines of those issued by the Marquesado.[111] A typical arrangement was one made in 1581 between don Toribio de San Martín Cortés, a governor and *cacique* of Cuernavaca, and the Cortés sugar mill of Atlacomulco. Don Toribio rented several pieces of sugarcane land to the *ingenio* in a *censo perpetuo*, and by 1590 the *cacique* was receiving a yearly rent of eighty pesos for a total of 420 acres of land, about half of all property rented by the estate.[112] Don Toribio also rented at least one of his houses in Cuernavaca to a Spaniard, and in general these sorts of transactions had become quite common by the end of the sixteenth century.[113]

In the seventeenth century, private rental agreements between members of the ruling group and others were as common as the rental of municipal properties. A Nahuatl rental agreement dated May 24, 1642, drawn up for the *cacique*, former governor, and current *fiscal* (attorney) of the *pueblo* of Tezoyuca, don Martín García, recorded the nine-year lease of some *cacicazgo* land to a Spanish *labrador* at the rate of ten pesos per annum. Don Martín stressed that no one was forcing him to rent this *pillalli* (private land), and in reality the population of Tezoyuca in the 1640s was at its lowest ebb. As in the case of surplus municipal properties in this period, there were few obvious demographic constraints on the leasing of private property.[114]

Again closely paralleling patterns of municipal leasing, members of the jurisdiction's ruling group continued to rent plots of rural and urban property to others, chiefly non-Indians, in the later seventeenth- and eighteenth-century era of demographic recovery. Those who possessed significant amounts of land and urban property could still turn a good profit from rentals and did not hesitate to enter into such agreements. Cuernavaca's Hinojosa family leased two large plots of prime cane land to the *ingenio* of Atlacomulco during much of the seventeenth century. Moreover, in the 1680s and 1690s the governor don Antonio de Hinojosa rented a total of eight small parcels to several of Cuernavaca's *sujetos*, within whose corporate limits the property was located. He also rented two houses in the *sujeto* of Xochitlán, one to a Spaniard and the other to a mulatto. In total, the governor received well over one hundred pesos per year from the rental of his properties.[115]

Members of the ruling group who had surplus property also sold it outright for profit.[116] Sometime before 1607, for example, the noblewoman doña María Mendoza of Cuernavaca sold a lot complete with house and corral to a local tailor (*tlatzonqui*) of unknown ethnicity.[117] In 1685 the chance for profit also led two *principales* of Cuernavaca to request the right to sell some *pillalli* inherited from their mother to a Spanish merchant of the *villa* who was buying up large quantities of land in the same area.[118] Voluntary alienations in the late sixteenth and seventeenth centuries had taken place in a period of population decline and a concomitant lessening of pressure on the land. But land was still sold in the eighteenth century, when the situation had reversed itself, if conditions warranted such an action. Around 1730, the houses which had belonged to doña Antonia and doña Petronila de Hinojosa were profitably sold to Spaniards, though in 1732 doña Petronila's former dwelling was still known as "the house that belonged to doña Petronila de Hinojosa."[119]

Rental and sale of land was an attractive source of income to town officers heavily involved in local politics and government, since it freed them from time-consuming property management and crop maintenance. Those officers who gave most of their energy to corporate officeholding, such as don Toribio de San Martín Cortés and don Antonio de Hinojosa of Cuernavaca, may have received the bulk of their legal yearly income as landlords rather than as active agriculturalists. Land-rich ambitious officers could also avoid equally time-consuming and potentially demeaning trades in this manner.

Land Disputes and the Loss of Estates

The same methods used to maintain, enlarge, or profit from landholding could get unwary members of the ruling group into trouble. Land disputes among individuals, between Indian elites and Indian municipalities, and pitting members of the ruling group against non-Indians were at least as common in the Cuernavaca jurisdiction as they were all over central New Spain.[120] The latter type is the most notorious and for this reason is the best to study. The indigenous elite of New Spain began losing land to Spaniards in the early colonial period, sometimes voluntarily, sometimes not. Among the first victims in the Cuernavaca region were the *villa*'s conquest-era *tlatoani*, Yaotzin, and his son don Hernando. Cortés usurped the *tlatoani*'s tribute and property rights around 1523. When don Hernando reached his majority at the end of the decade he was given only a portion of the preconquest estate. The rest formed the nucleus of the Marqués's Cuernavacan empire.[121]

The period of drastic population loss and congregation of Indian towns into more compact units lasting from the conquest period into the seventeenth century was an era when land changed hands rapidly, benefitting Spaniard and Indian alike. A complaint brought by the *cacique y principal* don Juan Bautista of Xochitepéc in 1624 is perhaps symptomatic. He alleged that one-quarter *caballería* of his land at the site of a depopulated *pueblo* known as Chiconcoac was included in a parcel being "denounced" by a Spaniard. (A *denuncia* was a legal process whereby land could be condemned and seized if it was declared "vacant.") Those initiating the process, or their agents, were usually able to gain possession. This was "a procedure which encouraged additional usurpation of Indian lands," at least in the Valley of Mexico.[122] Since don Juan could easily prove that he had been in possession for eighteen years, the authorities upheld his tenure. On the other hand, possession of the remaining land in Chiconcoac was given to the Spaniard, since no owners had come forward to pro-test.[123] Don Juan was lucky, for it was during two major *composición* (legal settlement of land claims) programs in the region during the 1620s and 1640s that many "vacant" lands that were actually the properties of Indian communities or individuals found their way into Spanish hands.[124] As in the case of municipal lands, pressure on individual holdings belonging to the ruling group increased in the next century. In the process, some were able to retain their land rights while others lost them.

Far from a majority of the indigenous elite feared loss of land to Spaniards, as evidenced by the tendency to rent or sell property to such outsiders. Yet despite the monetary rewards involved, which among other things allowed the elite to purchase high-status material goods or to spend more time in politics and less in agriculture, rental or sale of land to outsiders was indeed dangerous, especially when demographic increase began to put more pressure on the existing land base in the eighteenth century. Outright alienation, of course, meant that the land was lost to the Spanish world forever. Ideally, this would not have been true of leases, but all too often land entering Spanish hands tended to stay there.[125]

Moreover, the *composición* process, a creature of the Marquesado and royal governments' unending quest to maintain their treasuries, offered many non-Indian land renters a chance to become landowners. There are many recorded instances in which the Marquesado assumed ownership of land once rented by Spaniards from the Indian nobles during the *composición* programs of the seventeenth and early eighteenth centuries; as in the case of the *cacique y principal* don Hilario de la Cruz described above, these Spaniards convinced the receptive authorities that the land involved was *tierra baldía*. Some particularly aggressive claimants presented Spanish officers with Nahuatl rental agreements, claimed that the Indian owner had given up his or her claim to tenure, and got away with it![126]

Yet as infamous as Spanish encroachments have become, they were not the only threat to the integrity of an Indian landholding. The property of those dying intestate or without designated heirs normally was taken over by their former municipalities, which sometimes sold or rented it to outsiders.[127] When estates were divided among multiple heirs, as was often the case, new pressures could be created if there was little land involved or if one or more of the inheritors aspired to exclusive control of the property.[128] A well-documented struggle of this nature took place in 1708 and involved two daughters of Cuernavaca's long-time governor, don Antonio de Hinojosa. Because their father had lost much of his estate to tribute debts, his children were left with no more than the property they had acquired as adults. This meant that doña María Hinojosa, a minor at the time of the family's disaster, had received no inheritance. This self-described "poor orphan with no place to live" brought suit against her sister, doña Antonia, over the ownership of the house built by doña Antonia's husband in the 1680s. Doña María's claim that she had been awarded ownership of the residence by an executor of the husband's will was based on very slender evidence, however, and her two key witnesses were dead by the time of the suit. In the end, doña Antonia's known tenure prevailed.[129]

Land disputes between elites and commoners, as ubiquitous as inheritance disputes, were another internal threat to the ruling group's land tenure. This was mainly because of the propensity of the ruling group to usurp corporate holdings during the sixteenth- and seventeenth-century eras of demographic decline. Once population began to recover and pressure on the existing land base increased, however, conflict between communities and alleged noble usurpers inevitably expanded.[130] A three-sided conflict of this sort between two sides of a deceased *cacique*'s family and the town of Zacatepéc flared in 1783 and focused on the ownership of a plot of *tierra de repartimiento* (land to be distributed to individuals). Any claim that Zacatepéc's council might have had to this former municipal property was ignored, and even the Marquesado judges accepted the notables' right to hold and inherit this kind of property.[131] Indeed, members of the ruling group were more likely to prevail in this kind of dispute than when their opponents were Spaniards; even in the late colonial period the authorities tended to favor the interests of elite intermediaries over those of Indian corporations.

On rare occasions, town officers might give up some of their property out of altruistic motives. This seems to have been the case in seventeenth-century Tlayacac, when don Pedro Jorge de Hinojosa gave some property to his community because it lacked sufficient land of its own. When in 1732 the municipality faced the loss of this parcel through encroachment, a family member came forward to defend Tlayacac's legal tenure.[132] The exact date of this occurrence, as well as the precise reasons for it, have not been found, but by giving up a little of their land the Tlayacac Hinojosas at least must have won the loyalty and admiration of their community.

Other forms of voluntary philanthropy, such as bequests of land to the church, were actually a very real threat to the integrity of elite estates in the Cuernavaca region and elsewhere in New Spain.[133] Donations to the church, made in life or as part of a last will and testament, became so expected and traditional that they were even described in primordial titles; nine of the thirty-three *principales* of Cuernavaca mentioned in the *Municipal Codex* supposedly had designated some of their land for the support of the church.[134] Endowments often were in the form of *capellanías*, in which income from a certain piece of property would be used to finance a certain number of Masses or to help support a favorite saint's altar. Typical was the bequest of Cuernavaca's don Toribio de San Martín Cortés, who upon his death in the late sixteenth century ordered that a *capellanía* for the benefit of his soul was to be financed from the rent of some of his land to the *ingenio* of Atlacomulco.[135] Of European origin, *capellanías* were favored by the indigenous elite for the prestige that they gave to the endowing family. However, similar "endowments" to religious groups had not been unknown before the conquest, a fact that helps explain the rapidity with which the intrusive form was adopted after the conquest.[136]

Theoretically, the property from which the income for the endowment was derived remained a family possession. But the story of a large bequest made in 1632 by the Yecapixtlan noble doña Inés Cortés shows that this did not always turn out to be true.[137] In her testament, doña Inés donated profits raised from the sale of a house to purchase an ornament for the monastery of Yecapixtla. In addition, she directed her two immediate heirs and their descendants to pay fifteen pesos per year to the father prior for a *capellanía* of three Masses, dedicated to Saint Nicholas and the Virgin, which were to be said for her soul and for the souls in purgatory. The money was to be raised from the sale of maize grown on a *caballería* of land belonging to her hacienda.

Under normal circumstances the land would have remained in the family. But doña Inés had also stipulated that her entire estate was to devolve on the monastery if her heirs died without issue. In fact, the monastery did come to own the property, though not precisely because of this provision. In 1636 the two heirs voluntarily (or perhaps under pressure from the friars; it was a fairly valuable estate) ceded their entire inheritance to the religious, stating that they were unmarried, childless, and unable to run the hacienda or support the *capellanía*. It was not until 1774 that a presumed descendant contested this transfer, most likely without success.[138]

Since the unintended result of an endowment could be the loss of some or all of a family estate, it is not surprising that potential heirs sometimes brought suit to block such bequests. In 1696 the *india principala* doña María Ramírez, of the *pueblo* of San Gaspar Coatlán, gave the income from an agricultural plot known as Tlacomulco to the Mazatepecan *cofradía* of Santisimo Sacramento so that the sodality could buy oil, wax, "and whatever else is needed" for its religious activities.[139] After her death, she intended to endow a Mass for her and her late husband's souls with income from Tlacomulco and five other small properties. The possibility that ownership of the property might be lost irrevocably to outsiders prompted other family members to contest her actions. Displaying typical elite awareness that documentary evidence was essential to prove ownership, the litigants submitted a 1647 Nahuatl will which they claimed was a legitimate title for all six properties, which seemed to have been left to their side of the family. When it was discovered that the family held several parcels with the same names, the counterclaim fell apart (no definitive conclusion of the case has survived).

Authentic written evidence of property ownership, such as records of *mercedes*, testaments, rental agreements, or records that the proper license has been obtained for a land sale, were all considered in law to be legitimate "titles." Those members of the jurisdiction's indigenous ruling group who had such documentary evidence stood a far greater chance of protecting their estates than those who lacked such proof.[140] Unfortunately, few elite families possessed records of conquest-era grants. Nahuatl testaments were often ambiguously worded, and legal procedures for rent and sale were not always followed.

So officer-class litigants who found themselves with a shaky or nonexistent title to their land used the same strategies they employed when defending corporate property, including the fabrication of authentic-seeming *títulos*.[141] This explains the inclusion of noble properties in primordial titles such as the so-called *Municipal Codex of Cuernavaca*, a companion piece entitled *Reedificación de la villa de Cuernavaca*, and a lengthy Nahuatl document conveniently discovered in 1732 by the Cuernavacan notable don Josef Gaspar Díaz.[142] Its "discovery" was so convenient because it just happened to coincide with don Josef's effort to regain ownership of ancestral lands that had been usurped from the family sometime in the past. Here was the written proof necessary to establish the legitimacy of don Josef's claim, for the title, describing the properties at some length, recorded that the land had been granted to the family in the early conquest period. Unfortunately for don Josef, the document was soon declared a fake (however, because of his connections in the Marquesado, don Josef finally gained access to the disputed land anyway).

Less spectacular forgeries, often in Nahuatl, were probably more common and perhaps less apt to be discovered. Town officers were uniquely placed to have spurious deeds or receipts drawn up in their favor by obliging notaries.[143] Members of the powerful and corrupt Rojas clan of Tepoztlán were skillful practitioners of this art. They were able to use their networks of allies in both the Indian and Spanish worlds to usurp land from their community or their rivals and then defend their "ownership" in court.[144] One of them, don Francisco de Rojas, had altered the will of a political ally (or perhaps had prevailed on his ailing friend to change his will) in 1746 to show that a certain property had been left to a *cofradía* rather than to an under-age male heir. The *cofradía* had then obligingly rented the plot in question to don Francisco for a very modest sum. Don Francisco's fraud was only discovered in 1769, when the now adult heir brought suit.[145]

Political power, connections, and outright fraud could sometimes protect threatened properties. But the ruling group ultimately had little recourse if faced with perhaps the most deadly threat of all to their holdings. Service in town government, especially at the higher levels, carried many responsibilities. Failure to fulfill these obligations sometimes resulted in the sequestration of entire estates. The Marquesado seized and auctioned the homes, moveables, livestock, and even the lands of officers convicted of tribute fraud or indebtedness. If the debt were too large to be satisfied by the sale of the governor's property, then goods of lesser council members suffered a similar fate; this happened to twenty-eight of Tepoztlán's *vocales* (electors) and council members in 1759, implicated along with their governor, don Juan Diego, in the creation of a tribute debt of 1,193 pesos.[146] It seemed to make no difference to the authorities that population fluctuations or poor harvests were as likely causes of tribute indebtedness as personal ineptitude or dishonesty. The remedy was always the same: the forced loss of an estate which had been built up over the course of many years.

A final examination of the career of Cuernavaca's don Antonio de Hinojosa is in order here, since it well illustrates the economic pitfalls of corporate politics.[147] On Friday, December 17, 1694, don Antonio de Hinojosa took sanctuary in the *villa*'s Franciscan monastery because as governor of Cuernavaca he owed nearly 4,000 pesos in unpaid tribute assessments. The debt was broken down as follows: 2,388 pesos for the money tribute, 1,194 pesos for the maize tribute (both owed to the Marquesado), and 394 pesos from the royal *medio real de ministros* (199 pesos) and *medio real de fábrica material* (195 pesos). The size of this debt becomes clear if one considers that a real (one-eighth of a peso), or at most a real and one-half, was the standard daily wage of an agricultural worker. Thus began a long series of maneuvers by the governor to stall the authorities and, perhaps, to gain the time necessary to save as much of his estate as possible. He first denied that he knew how much was owed, and then wavered between cooperation and obstinacy as events proceeded.

In the days following his flight to the monastery, Indian town officials were sent out to inspect don Antonio's properties. Following this, the *alcalde mayor*, a Spanish *alguacil mayor* (constable), and other witnesses made their way to don Antonio's house, where they compiled an inventory of his goods as his wife, doña Felipa de Haro Bravo, looked on. Doña Felipa assured the Spanish officers that her husband had no other possessions in or around the residence, despite the fact that the chest said to have held money collected as tribute was empty (one of the *mayordomos*, however, recalled having seen don Antonio place ninety pesos in this depository not long before). Inventories were also made of houses belonging to don Antonio's daughters in another part of the *villa*.

The moveables found in all three houses were sequestered and put on deposit with trustworthy indigenous council members. Following a break for Christmas, the *alcalde mayor* extracted a list of the rural properties owned by don Antonio and sequestered these as well. On January 21, 1695, the first in a series of proclamations was made in which don Antonio's goods were offered for sale. Up to this point, the ex-governor had been able to do little to save his property, but in the middle of January his daughters attempted to salvage at least some of their own possessions. The forceful doña Petronila de Hinojosa y Haro, widow of the *cacique* [don] Antonio del Castillo, along with her sister, doña Antonia, claimed that their houses should not have been attached since they were not their father's property. The two women went on to relate the histories of the acquisitions of these houses (as discussed earlier).

Soon another stumbling block was thrown into the path of justice. Doña Felipa, don Antonio's wife, claimed that 802 pesos was hers by right of a dowry (*dote*) and bride gift (*arras*) made by her brother and husband, respectively, some four years after her marriage. The dowry had consisted of 302 pesos in cash plus 200 pesos' worth of clothing and jewelry, much of it imported from Europe. The bride gift, provided by don Antonio out of respect for her "honor, virginity, and purity," was an additional cash amount of 300 pesos. At the time this agreement was made, doña Felipe had followed the legal procedure which protected her gifts from any possible attachments in the future.

Initially, the *alcalde mayor* dismissed these pretensions, but the Hinojosa daughters retained an attorney (*procurador*) to act on their behalf in the matter. Thanks to their persistence as well as to an overwhelming amount of evidence skillfully presented in their favor by the *procurador*, in August the Estado finally confirmed the two women's possession of their houses; only an addition to doña Petronila's house financed by don Antonio would still be sold (it would presumably be torn down and the materials auctioned). In addition, the two would receive, from the proceeds of the coming auctions, the dowry and bride gift as the heirs of their now deceased mother, who had died unexpectedly in May.

During the course of the auctions, the family was able to save more of their property. Doña Petronila, for example, bought back thirty-five *cargas* of maize for 122 pesos. The *alcalde mayor* accused her of using part of an alleged "secret horde" of the missing tribute money to do so, but this was never proved, and the sale was upheld. Don Antonio took a hand in matters in September, when he complained that the sums offered for his household goods were not high enough. The ex-governor probably hoped that if enough money was raised from such things, the Estado would not need to auction off his entire estate. Doña Petronila also bid for don Antonio's house, offering the same amount as a local Spanish resident. Her *procurador* claimed that her offer predated the other, but late documents which speak of doña Petronila's possessions do not mention this house, and the Spaniard probably prevailed.

In the eleventh hour of the case, doña Josefa de Hinojosa, the ex-governor's sister, claimed that she was coheir to that part of the estate that had been inherited from her mother. As such, she was entitled to nearly half of all monies realized from the sales, since her goods could not be attached to pay off her brother's debts. This problem was not settled until January 2, 1697, during the administration of a new *alcalde mayor*, when it was discovered that doña Josefa had made a legal donation of her share of the inheritance to don Antonio some years before. The timing of this attempt to reclaim half of the property, or at least the money raised from it, is suggestive. It may have been a last-ditch effort by the cloistered don Antonio to save some of his wealth by using his sister as a front. If such was the case, the donation was too well known for the trick to succeed.

Don Antonio died in the monastery sometime during 1697 or 1698. His tribute debt was not completely erased by the sale of his estate, and later Cuernavaca governors fell heir to the obligation. Don Antonio may have well hidden some of the tribute money and an alleged forty-five *cargas* of maize to save it from seizure, since these goods and monies were never located by the Spaniards. It is possible, of course, that the money really had been used to buy back some of the possessions put up for auction, and they may also have paid for the services of the *procurador*.

Don Antonio's vague and at times misleading information about his debts and properties was a form of civil disobedience intended to slow the advance of the case. But in the end it was all to no avail. His final years saw the destruction of an estate carefully built up by his ancestors through marriage, inheritance, purchase, and perhaps usurpation. Prime agricultural land that had been rented to Atlacomulco, the Cortés sugar *ingenio*, became the Marqués's property when it was placed on the auction block. Don Antonio had obviously mismanaged or misappropriated the tribute that it had been his duty to collect. Caught in his misdeed, he had been made to pay the ultimate price. This was a risk shared by all town officers, including those not directly involved in the creation of the debt. Just as power and government service could aid a member of the ruling group in the formation of an estate, it could also lead to the destruction of that estate.

The estates built and sometimes lost by members of the jurisdiction's ruling group, as well as other aspects of their material culture, were rarely completely Hispanic in conception or physical reality. They may have seemed so by the end of the sixteenth century, but beneath an often imperfect facade of Europeanization older traditions survived. The material culture of the Cuernavaca jurisdiction's ruling group represented the adoption, modification, or rejection of certain aspects of Iberian culture, a process which was based firmly on indigenous perceptions of society. Those aspects of traditional material culture, of residence patterns, and of landholding strategies which remained useful or which were compatible with Spanish ways were retained. Intrusive items and significant landholdings might help establish their owners as members of an elite in colonial terms, but the motivation behind the adoption of such goods and construction of such estates—to express rank and social status and to distance oneself from the common people—had always animated the indigenous ruling class.

In the same way, the concern for profit in the colonial economy (more often than not within the indigenous sector), whether related to landholding or to some other profession, was only one dimension of the ruling group's commercial endeavors. Income earned from such activities helped support the kind of life-style that differentiated the elite from the rest of Indian society. Solvency allowed town officers to loan money to others, thus forging important networks of obligation that helped give the ruling group cohesion. Moreover, there was some pre-Hispanic precedent for members of the elite to hold large productive estates, to perhaps run them for "profit," to be knowledgeable estate managers, and even to have various craft skills. The cultural strategies of the jurisdiction's colonial ruling group were an important part of their struggle to cope with the colonial system. Some lost out in the scramble to survive, though not for lack of trying, but other members of this group successfully grafted their preconquest heritage onto the new culture of the conquerors. These were resilient, resourceful people; they were not simply demoralized or culturally bankrupt imitators of their conquerors' society.

Notes

1. See Charles Gibson, *The Aztecs under Spanish Rule* (Stanford, 1964), 153; and Woodrow Borah, "Population Decline and the Social and Institutional Changes of New Spain in the Middle Decades of the Sixteenth Century," *Aktern des 34.*

Internationalen Amerikanistenkongress, Wien (July 18–25, 1960), 173–78, for discussions of this point of view.

2. These studies include S. L. Cline, *Colonial Culhuacan, 1580–1600: A Social History of an Aztec Town* (Albuquerque, 1986); James Lockhart et al., *The Tlaxcalan Actas: A Compendium of the Records of the Cabildo of Tlaxcala, 1545–1627* (Salt Lake City, 1986); Susan Parry Schroeder, "Chalco and Sociopolitical Concepts in Chimalpahin: Analysis of a Seventeenth-Century Nahuatl Historian of Mexico," Ph.D. diss., University of California, Los Angeles, 1984; Stephanie Wood, "Corporate Adjustments in Colonial Mexican Indian Towns: Toluca Region, 1550–1810," Ph.D. diss., University of California, Los Angeles, 1984; and for comparison with colonial Mayan Mesoamerica see Nancy M. Farriss, *Maya Society under Colonial Rule: The Collective Enterprise of Survival* (Princeton, 1984); W. George Lovell, *Conquest and Survival in Colonial Guatemala: A Historical Geography of the Cuchumatan Highlands, 1500–1821* (Kingston, 1985); and Sandra Orellana, *The Tzutujil Mayas: Continuity and Change, 1250–1630* (Norman, 1984).

3. The relevant regulations can be found in the *Recopilación de leyes*, law 33, book 6, title 1 (1568), and in an earlier *cédula* of 1528. For more information, see Gonzalo Aguirre Beltrán, *Formas de gobierno indígena* (Mexico, 1953), 35–36; Gibson, "The Aztec Aristocracy in Colonial Mexico," *Comparative Studies in Society and History, 2* (1960), 181, and *Aztecs*, 155; Delfina López Sarrelangue, *La nobleza indígena del Pàtzcuaro en la época colonial* (Mexico, 1965), 119; and William B. Taylor, *Landlord and Peasant in Colonial Oaxaca* (Stanford, 1972), 38.

4. Archivo General de la Nación, Mexico (hereinafter cited as AGN), Indios, vol. 6 (first part), exp. 787 (don Gaspar de Aquino of Xiuhtepéc, 1594); AGN, Indios, vol. 9, exp. 307 (governor don Diego de Mendoza of Cuernavaca is granted a license to carry a sword and dagger as long as he holds public office), and AGN, Indios, vol. 4, exp. 396, fol. 127v and exp. 715, fol. 200v (a *principal* and a governor of Tepoztlán both receive licenses to ride horses anywhere in New Spain without restriction, 1590).

5. See AGN, Civil, vol. 1823, exp 13; and vol. 2175, exp. 5; Don Nicolás de Rojas is said to wear Spanish-style shoes rather than sandals and carry a knife illegally, but is never penalized for this offense.

6. AGN, Hospital de Jesús, leg. 208, exps. 190, 191, and 203 (Petitions of don Juan de Rojas of Tepoztlán, 1732).

7. AGN, Criminal, vol. 39, exp. 26 (don Melchor de Hinojosa to the Marquesado, 1714). Don Melchor's reasoning was similar to that of Cuauxintlán's governor of 1634, who stated that a mount was essential when tribute delivery compelled him to travel from his town to Cuernavaca, and the firearm was needed to protect the money he carried (AGN, Indios, vol. 12, exp. 107). Information about the material culture of don Melchor and other Hinojosas can be found in another form in Robert Haskett, "Living in Two Worlds: Cultural Continuity and Change among Cuernavaca's Colonial Indigenous Elite," *Ethnohistory*, 35:1 (Winter 1988), 34–59.

8. Charles Gibson, "The Transformation of the Indian Community in New Spain, 1500–1810," *Journal of World History, 2* (1955), 589, and *Aztecs*, 156. See also Cline, *Colonial Culhuacan*, 102–5.

9. AGN, Tributos, vol. 52, exp. 17 (hereinafter cited in text).

10. Arthur J. O. Anderson, Frances Berdan, and James Lockhart, *Beyond the Codices* (Berkeley, 1976), 44–53 (will of don Julian de la Rosa, 1566). Similar

mixtures of Spanish and indigenous goods can be seen in other testaments in this book, 44–83, and in Guido Munch G., *El cacicazgo de San Juan Teotihuacan durante la colonia, 1521–1821* (Mexico, 1976), 44–46. For comparison with another region, see Farriss, *Maya Society*, 178–79.

11. AGN, Hospital de Jesús, leg. 78, exp. 15 (possessions of don Juan Diego, Tepoztlán 1759). Members of the ruling group tended to own large numbers of religious imagery; in 1783 an oratory belonging to don Juan Marcos of Zacatepec held two crucifixes, several religious paintings featuring the Baby Jesus and various saints, and a statue of San Miguel (AGN, Tierras, vol. 1939, exp. 3).

12. See Francisco Xavier Clavijero, *Historia antigua de México* (Mexico, 1979), 255; Francisco López de Gómara, *Historia general de las Indias, vol. II* (Barcelona, 1966), 406; and Jacques Soustelle, *Daily Life of the Aztecs on the Eve of Spanish Conquest* (Stanford, 1961), 121–22.

13. AGN, Hospital de Jesús, vol. 85, exps. 20 and 26 (don Melchor de Hinojosa, 1716); AGN, Civil, vol. 2175, exp. 5 (officers of Tepoztlán confiscate clothing from commoners and forcibly cut their hair, 1720).

14. Patricia Anawalt, "Costume and Control: Aztec Sumptuary Laws," *Archaeology* (January/February 1980), 33–35, 42. See also Frances Berdan, *The Aztecs of Central Mexico: An Imperial Society* (New York, 1982), 47; Fray Diego Durán, *Historia de las Indias de Nueva España* (Mexico, 1967), 211–14; Clavijero, *Historia antigua*, 212–13; and Brigitta Leander, *Herencia cultural del mundo Náhuatl a través de la Lengua* (Mexico, 1980), 101–21. Jonathan I. Israel, *Race, Class, and Politics in Colonial Mexico, 1610–1670* (Oxford, 1975), 42, discusses the retention of some preconquest apparel among the elite for a time after conquest.

15. Berdan, *Aztecs of Central Mexico*, 97; and Jerome Offner, *Law and Politics in Aztec Texcoco* (Cambridge, 1983), 254.

16. Anawalt, "Costume and Control," 43.

17. Alejandra Moreno Toscano, *Geografía económica de México (siglo XVI)* (Mexico, 1968), 64. Charles Gibson, *Tlaxcala in the Sixteenth Century* (Stanford, 1952), 151, discusses small animal raising. Perhaps because of their low monetary value, chickens are rarely mentioned in the testaments of estate inventories of the jurisdiction's ruling group. The dominance of the sugar industry seems to have meant that neither Spaniards nor Indians raised pigs, goats, or sheep on a significant scale.

18. Gibson, *Aztecs*, 359.

19. See Cline, *Colonial Culhuacan*, 93–96.

20. AGN, Tierras, vol. 1935, exp. 4 (hacienda de labor of doña Inés Cortés, 1632).

21. AGN, Indios, vol. 12, exp. 107 (1634, a governor of Guaxintlan, don Diego Gerónimo, reportedly owns twenty head of cattle and one bull); AGN, Civil, vol. 1608, exp. 10 (don Nicolás Rojas of Tepoztlán raises cattle and employs a young Spanish cowhand to look after them); AGN, Hospital de Jesús, vol. 51, exp. 27, and vol. 84, exp. 15 (don Hilario de la Cruz of Mazatepéc rents a *rancho de ganado mayor* measuring three leagues in circumference). For comparison, see Farriss, *Maya Society*, 178–79.

22. AGN, Hospital de Jesús, leg. 80, exp. 80 (Tecpantzinco, 1743); AGN, Hospital de Jesús, leg. 78, exp. 15 (possessions of don Juan Diego, Tepoztlán, 1759). See also AGN, Hospital de Jesús, leg. 323, exp. 1 (Xalostóc, 1733; ownership of oxen by a governor and two alcaldes).

23. Taylor, *Landlord and Peasant*, 47, found that most of the indigenous markets of Oaxaca sold meat raised on native *estancias*, many owned by *principales*. For comparison, see Farriss, *Maya Society*, 180–82; Gibson, *Aztecs*, 156, 342–46; Lockhart, "Capital and Province, Spaniard and Indian: The Example of Late Sixteenth-Century Toluca," in Ida Altman and James Lockhart, eds., *Provinces of Early Mexico* (Los Angeles, 1976), 114; Ronald Spores, *The Mixtecs in Ancient and Colonial Times* (Norman, 1984), 124–25; and Judith Zeitlin, "Ranchers and Indians on the Southern Isthmus of Tehuantepec: Economic Change and Indigenous Survival in Colonial Mexico," *Hispanic American Historical Review,* 69:1 (February 1989), 47–48.

24. For officers raising and selling oxen for a profit, see AGN, Hospital de Jesús, leg. 323, exp. 1 (governor and several town officers of Xalostoc are said to raise oxen for profit, 1733); AGN, Hospital de Jesús, vol. 76, exp. 4 (past *alcalde* of Tlaquiltenango selling oxen to other Indians, 1749). For oxen raised as beasts of burden, see AGN, Tierras, vol. 1935, exp. 4 (estate of doña Inés Cortés, 1632); AGN, Hospital de Jesús, leg. 80, exp. 80 (officers of Tecpantzinco raising oxen as beasts of burden, 1743); AGN, Tributos, vol. 21, exp. 2 (the same for Tepoztlán, 1758); AGN, Tierras, vol. 1939, exp. 3 (the same for Zacatepéc, 1783). Most officers raising horses and mules seem to have done so for their personal use. See AGN, Hospital de Jesús, leg. 55, exp. 1 (Tepoztlán, 1807) and AGN, Criminal, vol. 38, exp. 6 (Tepoztlán, 1811) for possible small-time mule raisers.

25. For example, Cline, *Colonial Culhuacan*, 95–96, mentions a town notary who was a trader in late sixteenth-century Culhuacan. There had been regional merchants in preconquest times known as *tlanecuiloque*; see Frances F. Berdan, "Enterprise and Empire in Aztec and Early Colonial Mexico" (unpublished paper, author's files), and *Aztecs of Central Mexico*, 31–35, for more general information on pre-Hispanic traders. Another excellent source for such information is Ross Hassig, *Trade, Tribute, and Transportation: The Sixteenth-Century Political Economy of the Valley of Mexico* (Norman, 1985).

26. Leslie Lewis, "In Mexico City's Shadow: Some Aspects of Economic Activity and Social Processes in Texcoco, 1570–1620," in *Provinces of Early Mexico*, 134, mentions the 1597 ruling (obviously hard to enforce), which allowed only six mules per Indian trader. See also Berdan, "Enterprise and Empire," for the persistence of Indian traders in sixteenth-century Xochimilco, Cholula, and Coyoacán; and David M. Szewczyk, "New Elements in the Society of Tlaxcala," in *Provinces of Early Mexico*, 142, for the same type of information.

27. AGN, Indios, vol. 12 (2d part), exp. 20 (noble *tratante* of Tepoztlán, 1640). Hassig, *Trade, Tribute, and Transportation*, 200, mentions the tendency of Indians to run cargo mules, some of the regulations required, and the fact that by the later sixteenth century Tepoztlán had become a center for Indians engaged in local and longer-distance trade. His study includes many relevant details on both preconquest and sixteenth-century trade, information which is far beyond the scope of the present work. Evidence for officer-class *arrieros* outside of Tepoztlán is slim, but they did exist, such as a ninety-five-year-old *mestizo principal* of Santa María (a *sujeto* of Cuernavaca) who by 1714 had been an *arriero* for many years; AGN, Criminal, vol. 39, exp. 26.

28. AGN, Hospital de Jesús, vol. 76, exp. 31; and leg. 74, exp. 72 (activities of Tepoztlán's elite-class Eslava family in trade, 1740s and 1750s; descendants of this family continued to follow the same pursuits later in the century).

29. AGN, Civil, vol. 1608, exp. 10 (five *alcaldes* of Tepoztlán are involved in trade with Taxco; from boyhood the *alcalde* Cristobal Marcial travels to the mines to sell cloth *mantas*—sometimes blankets or capes, sometimes simply lengths of cotton cloth). They were often manufactured by the same family that marketed them; the *alcalde* Juan Francisco sold *calzones blancos de manta* (some sort of long white pants) made by his wife to the mineworkers of Taxco. Berdan, "Enterprise and Empire," says that New Spain's mines were a new market for Indian traders and that producers-sellers dominated.

30. AGN, Hospital de Jesús, leg. 447, exp. 7 (commercial activities of the Díaz family, early eighteenth century).

31. AGN, Civil, vol. 1608, exp. 10 (trade between Tepoztlán and Mexico City, late seventeenth and early eighteenth centuries).

32. AGN, Hospital de Jesús, leg. 78, exp. 15, and AGN, Criminal, vol. 38, exp. 6 (1759–1811, *alcaldes* of Tepoztlán own many cargo mules; in 1759 one has at least ten cargo mules and another, Juan de Santiago, Tlapango, runs a string of twenty-four pack mules—but there are individuals from the lower ranks of the ruling group who only own one cargo mule). See also Farriss, *Maya Society*, 182; Gibson, *Aztecs*, 359 (Indian muleteers in Zacualpan, Cuautla Amilpas and the Valley of Mexico respectively); Israel, *Race, Class, and Politics*, 42, who mentions a *cacique arriero* of Tehuacan employing black and mulatto muleteers in 1620; Spores, *Mixtecs*, 126; Eric Van Young, "Conflict and Solidarity in Indian Village Life: The Guadalajara Region in the Late Colonial Period," *Hispanic American Historical Review*, 64:1 (February 1984), 71, discusses a *principal* as *arriero* in Tlajomulco, Guadalajara, in 1789; and Zeitlin, "Ranchers and Indians," 47.

33. Donald Robertson, "The Treatment of Architecture in the Florentine Codex of Sahagún," in Munro S. Edmonson, ed., *Sixteenth-Century Mexico: The Work of Sahagún* (Albuquerque, 1974), 161–63.

34. "Códice municipal de Cuernavaca," Bibliothèque Nationale de Paris (hereinafter cited as BNP), 291/292 (house compounds of the *cacique* and governor don Lucas de San Martín y Sandoval and another *principal*).

35. This is typical: see John M. Tutino, "Creole Mexico: Spanish Elites, Haciendas, and Indian Towns, 1750–1810," Ph.D. diss., University of Texas at Austin, 1976, 279, who indicates that houses and their lots were a typical part of indigenous elite patrimony in Acolman. Wills included in Arthur J. O. Anderson, Frances Berdan, and James Lockhart, *Beyond the Codices*, mention house-lot units.

36. The home of the powerful sixteenth-century *cacique* and governor don Toribio de San Martín Cortés also answers this description; AGN, Hospital de Jesús, leg. 312, exp. 20. See also Cline, *Colonial Culhuacan*, 97–101; S. L. Cline and Miguel León-Portilla, eds., *The Testaments of Culhuacan* (Los Angeles, 1984), various testaments.

37. Pedro Carrasco, "La casa y la hacienda de un Señor Tlalhuica," *Estudios de Cultura Náhuatl*, 10 (1972), 240 (referring to a census of 1540).

38. James Lockhart, "Some Samples from the Tulancingo Collection" (manuscript, author's files).

39. AGN, Tierras, vol. 1935, exp. 4 (Yecapixtla, 1632); AGN, Hospital de Jesús, leg. 345, exp. 50 (home of a governor of Tecpantzingo, 1745); leg. 78, exp. 15 (house of don Juan Diego, Tepoztlán, 1759, which included a large main hall, two other buildings serving as living quarters, a kitchen, and a granary).

40. Frances Karttunen, *An Analytical Dictionary of Nahuatl* (Austin, 1983), 302. "Tajamanil" is a corruption of *tlaxamanilli*, literally "something cracked, splintered, or split." The use of spruce or fir wood was common. The term used to describe the beams was *morillos*, which were rafters typical of "rustic" house construction in central and northern Mexico; Francisco J. Santamaría, *Diccionario de Mejicanismos* (Mexico, 1979), 739 and 996.

41. It is difficult to determine whether single measures refer to length or area. In this case, the former is most likely, since in the eighteenth century lots belonging to the rival Díaz family measured thirty by fifteen *varas* and fifty by twenty *varas*, with the twenty suggesting the survival of a vigesimal system; AGN, Hospital de Jesús, leg. 447, exp. 7 (Nahuatl document, c. 1732). Pedro Carrasco, "Las clases social en el México antiguo," *Verhandlungen des XXXVIII Internationalen Amerikanistenkongress, Stuttgart-Munchen, 1968* (1970), 373, gives dimensions of property belonging to members of Yautepec's elite in 1540. These were much larger than holdings of commoners.

42. For comparison, see AGN, Tierras, vol. 1751, exp. 6, fols. 4r-5v (three-structure *calli* of a noble widow of San Gaspar Coatlán, doña Francisca Gerónima, is located on a *milli*, Nahuatl testament, 1647); AGN, Hospital de Jesús, leg. 75, exp. 72 (urban property of don Bartolomé de los Angeles of Tepoztlán); and AGN, Tierras, vol. 1939, exp. 10 (the same of the *cacicazgo* of don Miguel Gerónimo, Tepoztlán's governor, of 1769). See Clavijero, *Historia antigua*, 255, for information about pre-Hispanic orchards. See also Farriss, *Maya Society*, 178–79.

43. AGN, Hospital de Jesús, leg. 55, exp. 1 (don Juan de Eslava, shopkeeper of Tepoztlán, 1775–1811). See also AGN, Civil, vol. 1062, exp. 16 (past governor of Temimiltzingo buys melons from local Indian growers and resells them to a mulatto *frutero* [fruiterer], 1795). For comparison, see Lewis, "In Mexico City's Shadow," 134 (Indian shopkeepers in Texcoco); and Van Young, "Conflict and Solidarity," 70–71 (the same in *pueblos* of the Guadalajara region, including *principales* and a *cacique*).

44. AGN, Criminal, vol. 39, exp. 26, and AGN, Hospital de Jesús, vol. 50, exp. 6 (don Hipólito Méndez of Cuernavaca is a *velero*, early eighteenth century); AGN, Civil, vol. 1118, exp. 5 (Tepoztecan *regidor* runs an *horno de cal* [lime kiln], same period). See also AGN, Hospital de Jesús, leg. 344, exp. 79 (former *mayordomo* of Cuernavaca reports he is an *albañil* [mason]). For comparison see Spores, *Mixtecs*, 127 (a *principal* blacksmith in Mixtecan Oaxaca).

45. Works such as the *huehuetlatolli* and the *Florentine Codex* exalt knowledge of various high-level crafts, notably those in which precious materials were involved.

46. AGN, Hospital de Jesús, leg. 93, exp. 32 (the house "El Hospital" of Cuernavaca, 1690s).

47. AGN, Hospital de Jesús, vol. 52, exp. 9 (two *casas* on one lot listed in the will of the widow Magdalena Juárez of Cuernavaca are worth 100 pesos, 1602); AGN, Tierras, vol. 1935, exp. 4 (will of doña Inés Cortés of Yecapixtla shows her residence to be worth 200 pesos, 1632); AGN, Hospital de Jesús, vol. 73, exp. 33, fol. 21 (house of doña Petronila de Hinojosa, widowed daughter of don Antonio de Hinojosa, is worth 120 pesos, 1694, having been purchased in 1631 for 100 pesos).

48. AGN, Hospital de Jesús, vol. 52, exp. 17 (1644 *padrón* of Tezoyuca, hereinafter cited in text). *Jacal* is derived from the Nahuatl *xacalli*, and usually con-

notes a humble, impermanent building of small size, most often constructed of thatch or sticks, with few openings beyond a door, an immemorial Mesoamerican style. For houses in other areas, see Cline, *Colonial Culhuacan*, 97–102; and Moreno Toscano, *Geografía económica*, 63.

49. Soustelle, *Daily Life*, 11, comments on the pre-Hispanic relationship of house location and social status. Spores, *Mixtecs*, 113, finds that the homes of the Mixtecan nobility tended to be in the center of town during the colonial period.

50. Carrasco, "La casa y la hacienda," 240, describes pre-Hispanic house forms in the Cuauhnahuac region. See also Clavijero, *Historia antigua*, 254–55; Gómara, *Historia general*, 43; and Alonso de Zorita, *Breve y sumaria relación de los señores de la Nueva España* (Mexico, 1963), 34.

51. Spores, *The Mixtec Kings and Their People* (Norman, 1967), 125. Van Young, "Conflict and Solidarity," 68, 73, and Spores *Mixtecs*, 109, discuss the acquisition of property in the Guadalajara region and Mixtecan Oaxaca, respectively.

52. Gibson, *Aztecs*, 263. See also John K. Chance, *Race and Class in Colonial Oaxaca* (Stanford, 1978), 24; and Hans Prem, "La propiedad rural como indicador de estratificación social," in Pedro Carrasco and Johanna Broda, eds., *Estratificación social en la Mesoamérica prehispánica* (Mexico, 1976), 178.

53. Carrasco, "Political Economy," 34. See Luis Reyes García, *Documentos sobre tierras y señorío en Cuauhtinchán* (Mexico, 1978), various Nahuatl documents, for evidence of this kind of retention in other parts of central New Spain.

54. Carrasco, "Political Economy," 34; Spores, *Mixtec Kings*, 114–18.

55. Pedro Carrasco, "Las tierras de dos indios nobles de Tepeaca en el siglo XVI," *Tlalocan*, 4 (1963), 97–119, and "Los señores de Xochimilco en 1548," *Tlalocan*, 7 (1977), 229–64, presents *cacicazgo* records.

56. This was true of other areas; see Farriss, *Maya Society*, 180; and Spores, *Mixtecs*, 131.

57. Nine of the thirty-three nobles listed in the Cuernavacan Municipal Codex (BNP Manuscrit Mexicaine 291/292) supposedly had obtained *tierras de merced* from the crown, and it was also asserted in the Díaz title that some of the family's holdings came by way of grants from "the Marqués and the king" (AGN, Hospital de Jesús, leg. 447, exp. 7). A similar grant was made to don Juan de San Pedro of Tlayacac by the first Marqués, as reported by a descendant of don Pedro de Hinojosa in 1723 (AGN, Hospital de Jesús, leg. 208, exp. 211).

58. Viceregal and Ecclesiastical Mexican Collection, Latin American Library, Tulane University, leg. 77, exps. 29–31 (Marquesado recognizes *tepillalli* ownership of *principales* María Texeda, Cristobal Tlilancalqui, and Magdalena Teacapan; original investigator was the Indian *principal* Miguel Sánchez, of Ahuehuepan). And see François Chevalier, *Land and Society in Colonial Mexico* (Berkeley, 1972), 195; Gibson, *Aztecs*, 265; Taylor, *Landlord and Peasant*, 40.

59. See AGN, Hospital de Jesús, leg. 447, exp. 7 (Cuernavaca's don Josef Gaspar Díaz rents land from the Marquesado, early eighteenth century); vol. 84, exp. 16, fols. 32r-33r (the *principal* Baltasar de Tapia of Tepoztlán pays a yearly *censo* to the Marquesado for some land, 1719); vol. 79, exp. 3 (Tepoztecan *cacique* Bartolomé Domingo pays a Spaniard one *carga de maíz de sembradura* a year for a plot of land, 1749); vol. 82, exp. 17 (a man named don Pablo Oaxtepéc rents the *rancho de Jaral* from Oaxtepéc for thirty pesos a year, 1804). See also Cline, "Culhuacan, 1572–1599: An Investigation Through Mexican Indian Testaments,"

Ph.D. diss., University of California, Los Angeles, 1981, 283, and "Land Tenure and Land Inheritance in Late Sixteenth-Century Culhuacan," in H. R. Harvey and Hans J. Prem, eds., *Explorations in Ethnohistory* (Albuquerque, 1984), 293–94.

60. Details of the don Hilario de la Cruz case can be found in AGN, Hospital de Jesús, vol. 51, exp. 27 (early eighteenth century); vol. 67, exp. 4 (1728); vol. 84, exps. 15 and 16 (1705–1719); and leg. 339, exp. 1 (1708).

61. Similar strategies were followed by Spanish renters in the jurisdiction; see AGN, Hospital de Jesús, vol. 52 and leg. 96 for extensive seventeenth-century records of such transactions; and Haskett, "A Social History of Indian Town Government in the Colonial Cuernavaca Jurisdiction, Mexico," Ph.D. diss., University of California, Los Angeles, 1985, 504–7.

62. Cline, *Colonial Culhuacan*, 135–49, presents a detailed analysis of surviving pre-Hispanic land terminology. For the importance of marriage and inheritance to Indian land tenure, see Farriss, *Maya Society*, 251–52; and Spores, *Mixtecs*, 131.

63. See Cline, *Colonial Culhuacan*, 146–47, and Haskett, "Colonial Cuernavaca," 494, for discussions of *pillalli*. Some believe that prior to conquest, *pillalli* was a form of *mayorazgo*, inherited property or land received as an inalienable grant from the monarch (see Clavijero, *Historia antigua*, 214; and Fernandó de Alva Ixlilxochitl, *Obras históricas, vol. II* [Mexico, 1977], 91). Others believe this land was held by right of status and public service and was not private property (see Pedro Carrasco, "Social Organization of Ancient Mexico," in *Handbook of Middle American Indians: Archaeology of Northern Mesoamerica, Part I* [Austin, 1971], 359–60; and Victor M. Castillo F., *Estructura económica de la sociedad Méxica* [Mexico, 1972], 79–84). There is no doubt that after the conquest, *pillalli* was private property of the elite in the Cuernavaca jurisdiction.

64. Alva Ixtlilxochitl, op. cit., 90; Castillo F., op. cit., 78.

65. For comparison, see Berdan, *The Aztecs of Central Mexico*, 50; Cline, *Colonial Culhuacan*, 140–41; Gibson, *Aztecs*, 257–61.

66. See, for example, AGN, Hospital de Jesús, vol. 48, 1st part, exp. 1, 643–44.

67. This plot had originally been listed in the 1607 Nahuatl testament of doña María Jiménez, who claimed that she had obtained legal title to it from the Marquesado (AGN, Tributos, vol. 52, exp. 17). The usage in the following sources makes it clear that *calpulli* and *calpullalli* referred to the subdivisions of corporate entities and their properties. A more detailed discussion can be found in Haskett, "Colonial Cuernavaca," 495–99. AGN, Civil, vol. 1103, exp. 8 (Nahuatl land sale document, Cuernavaca, 1608); AGN, Hospital de Jesús, vol. 48 (1st part), exp. 1 (Nahuatl petition, Cuernavaca, 1685); AGN, Hospital de Jesús, leg. 210, exps. 23, 25, and 43 (Nahuatl petitions, Cuernavaca, 1607); AGN, Tierras, vol. 1501, exp. 2 (Nahuatl petition, Cuernavaca, 1722); vol. 1962, exp. 8, fol. 23r (Nahuatl document, 1582). For another view see Luis Reyes García, "El término calpulli en los documentos del centro de México" (unpublished paper), 21–22; and "El término calpulli en documentos del siglo XVI" (unpublished paper), 27–28.

68. Gibson, *Aztecs*, 265; and Taylor, *Landlord and Peasant*, 43. For additional, comparative information, see AGN, Tierras, vol. 2535, exp. 13 (governor of Calimaya, Toluca, don Francisco Antonio, acquires corporate land, 1733–34).

69. The "total size" given for Teocuauhco was nineteen hundred *varas ordinarios* (Spanish, as opposed to the larger Indian *vara*). As is often the case, the exact

meaning of the latter dimension is not clear; but if the plot was sufficiently irregular, perhaps it approximates the circumference.

70. For more detailed discussion of these parcels and their values, see Haskett, "Colonial Cuernavaca," 472–73, 477.

71. See examples in AGN, Tierras, vol. 1962, exp. 8 (Nahuatl document showing two plots, land belonging to a Cuernavacan noble measuring 15 by 18 *quahuitl* and 5 1/2 by 4 1/2 *quahuitl*, respectively, c. 1570). Juan López y Magaña, "Texcocan Land Map Documents" (unpublished paper, author's files), finds that a *tlalquahuitl* in sixteenth-century Texcoco equaled 2.5 meters and was likened to the Spanish *braza*. For *quahuitl* and the *braza* in other areas, see Anderson, Berdan, and Lockhart, *Beyond the Codices*, 26 (*quahuitl*); Victor M. Castillo f., "Unidades Náhuas de medida," *Estudios de Cultura Náhuatl,* 10 (1972), 210–11 (*brazas*), and 223 (*quahuitl*); and Gibson, *Aztecs*, 257 (*braza*).

72. AGN, Hospital de Jesús, 495:55, ff.14r-v (land of don Juan Andrés Peralta of Mazatepéc measures six *mecatl*, or approximately 120 *varas*, 1704).

73. AGN, Hospital de Jesús, vol. 48, 2d part, exp. 9, cuaderno 3, fols. 545r-v, 552r-v (Nahuatl documents of Cuernavaca, 1697 and 1704). The c. 1580 *relación geográfica* of Tepoztlán equates a *mecatl* with twenty *brazas* (Paso y Troncoso, *Relaciones geográficas,* 246–47). Manuel de Olaguibel, *Onomatología del Estado de México* (Mexico, 1975), 41; and Luís Cabrera, *Diccionario de aztecquismos* (Mexico, 1978), 90, referring to other areas in central New Spain, give the *mecatl* as anywhere from five to fifty *varas*, and state that it could also be an areal measure of four hundred square *varas*. The *mecatl* is also found in the so-called Techialoyan manuscripts.

74. A 9-*cuartillo* plot was said to require one and one-half days of labor for a yoke of oxen. This usage is found in the will of doña María Catalina, widow of Zacatepec's don Juan Marcos, 1783, AGN, Tierras, vol. 1939, exp. 3, and is used interchangeably with the more familiar *cuartilla*, in modern times considered a measure of volume equal to around 25 liters. For definitions of *cuartillo*, see Gibson, *Aztecs*, 357; and Herman W. Konrad, *A Jesuit Hacienda in Colonial Mexico: Santa Lucía, 1576–1767* (Stanford, 1980), 421; and for *cuartilla,* Santamaría, *Diccionario de Mejicanismos*, 320.

75. A *caballería* is generally considered to be 105 acres. AGN, Tierras, vol. 1935, exp. 4 (estate of doña Inés Cortés, 1632); AGN, Tierras, vol. 1661, exp. 1, fols. 34r-37v, 44v-48r, 73v-81r (evolution of the estate of the Tlayacac Hinojosas, 1530s–1691; the owner in the later year, doña Magdalena de Hinojosa, possessed 350 cattle, 20 horses, and several mules). For Spanish norms see Ward Barrett, *The Sugar Hacienda of the Marqueses del Valle* (Minneapolis, 1970), 39; and Martin, *Rural Society in Colonial Morelos* (Albuquerque, 1985), 35 and 38.

76. For other examples of dispersed landholding, see AGN, Tierras, vol. 1826, exp. 4 (don Diego Martín de Mendoza of San Francisco Tetecala holds ten distinct *pedazos de tierra*, 1701–1702); AGN, Tierras, vol. 1939, exp. 3, fols. 8 (estate of don Juan Marcos of Zacatepéc is made up of five distinct properties, 1783); and AGN, Hospital de Jesús, leg. 358, exp. 1 (estate of don Pablo Antonio López, governor of Oaxtepéc, has nine distinct properties, 1814). Martin, *Colonial Morelos*, 26–27, discusses a seventeen-parcel estate owned by the indigenous noblewoman doña Isabel Cortés of Oaxtepéc (1599). Others have identified the same pattern elsewhere; see Cline, *Colonial Culhuacan*, 125.

77. AGN, Tierras, vol. 1751, exp. 6 (Nahuatl will of doña Francisca Gerónima, San Gaspar Coatlán, 1647).

78. For similar customs in the neighboring Toluca Valley, see Lockhart, "Capital and Province," 119. Cline, *Colonial Culhuacan,* 135–38, discusses land and soil types.

79. See Edward Calnek, "Tenochtitlan in the Early Colonial Period," *Proceedings of the XLII International Congress of Americanists, Paris, 1976,* 18 (1979), 37; Pedro Carrasco, "La económia del México prehispánico," in Pedro Carrasco and Johanna Broda, eds., *Economía política e ideología en el México prehispánico* (Mexico, 1978), 47; and Fredric Hicks, "Land Tenure and the Supply of Food to the Tenochtitlan Market" (unpublished paper, author's files).

80. MS. M-M 458, Bancroft Library, University of California, Berkeley. Agricultural knowledge appears to have been ranked behind war, government, rites, and honorable crafts as far as importance was concerned. Noble girls were said to have been taught a variety of domestic skills only.

81. Soustelle, *Daily Life,* 140–41.

82. See Paso y Troncoso, "Relación de la villa de Tepuztlán," 247–48.

83. Gibson, *Tlaxcala,* 50, and *Aztecs,* 310, 323; and Martin, "Haciendas and Villages in Late Colonial Morelos," *Hispanic American Historical Review,* 62:3 (August 1982), 413. Calnek, "Tenochtitlan in the Early Colonial Period," 37–38, states that Tenochtitlan's nobility lost most economic resources save those derived from privately owned agricultural estates. See also Lockhart, "Introduction," 21; and John M. Tutino, "Creole Mexico: Spanish Elites, Haciendas, and Indian Towns, 1750–1810," Ph.D. diss., University of Texas at Austin, 1976, 280.

84. John K. Chance and William B. Taylor, "Estate and Class in a Colonial City," *Comparative Studies in Society and History,* 19 (1977), 469, state that *labrador* could be applied to holders of entailed estates, large and small landowners, and sharecroppers. For use of *labrador* by members of the Indian elite, see AGN, Civil, 1608, exp. 10 and AGN, Hospital de Jesús, vol. 76, exp. 20 (members of Tepoztlán's Rojas family, early to mid-eighteenth century); AGN, Hospital de Jesús, leg. 80, exp. 80 (same type of information for nobles of Tecpantzinco, 1743); and AGN, Hospital de Jesús, leg. 73, exp. 15 (same for Tepoztlán, 1759).

85. AGN, Tierras, vol. 1836, exp. 4 (estate of doña Inés Cortés, seventeenth century).

86. AGN, Hospital de Jesús, vol. 86, exp. 46 (maize field of the past *alcalde* of Ayoxochiapa, 1710).

87. Similarly, a *cacique* of Tepoztlán who planted one-half *fanega* of maize on some land in the 1740s could have produced a crop amounting to around forty *fanegas* (2,200 liters), and a don Juan Marcos produced at least seventy-three *fanegas* (4,015 liters) that same year; see AGN, Hospital de Jesús, leg. 74, exp 72. John M. Tutino, "Provincial Spaniards, Indian Towns, and Haciendas: Interrelated Agrarian Sectors in the Valleys of Mexico and Toluca, 1750–1810," in *Provinces of Early Mexico,* 183, gives ten *fanegas* as the minimum subsistence requirement for late eighteenth-century Acolman. D. A. Brading, *Haciendas and Ranchos in the Mexican Bajío: León, 1700–1860* (Cambridge, 1978), 65, gives measure equivalents. For related information see Gibson, *Aztecs,* 122, 130–11; and Hicks, "Land Tenure and the Supply of Food," 5.

88. AGN, Tributos, vol. 52, exp. 17 (maize of don Antonio de Hinojosa, 1694). For the size of the *carga,* see Brading, *Haciendas and Ranchos,* 66; and Gibson, *Aztecs,* 600–601.

89. Some caution must be exercised when analyzing such figures. Those listed in Table 2 with small amounts of maize could have sold most of their crop before

the inventory was undertaken, or, conversely, the investigation may have taken place before a crop had been harvested. And since many of these inventories were made as personal property was seized to pay off tribute debts arising through public service, maize could have been hidden or liquidated quickly to avoid its loss.

90. AGN, Tributos, vol. 52, exp. 17 (*cacahuate* crop of don Agustín and don Antonio de Hinojosa, middle-to-late seventeenth century).

91. AGN, Hospital de Jesús, leg. 80, exp. 80 (don Pedro Antonio, a past governor of Tecpantzinco, grows chiles as well as maize, 1743); AGN, Hospital de Jesús, leg. 78, exp. 15 and AGN, Tributos, vol. 21, exp. 2 (Tepoztlán's governor don Juan Diego augments maize with anise, 1758–59); AGN, Hospital de Jesús, leg. 74, exp. 83 (governor of the *pueblo* San Esteban Tetelpán grows melons, raises livestock, and sometimes catches and sells fish, 1760). Martin, "Haciendas and Villages," 413, says melons and fish were typical indigenous products of colonial Morelos. Cline, *Colonial Culhuacan*, 139, and Spores, *The Mixtecs*, 123, note the incorporation of European seed and fruit crops by Indians. Farriss, *Maya Society*, 180–81, finds that Yucatecan indigenous elites often grew cacao for commercial purposes.

92. Martin, "Haciendas and Villages," 409; and G. Micheal Riley, *Fernando Cortés and the Marquesado in Morelos* (Albuquerque, 1973), 80.

93. AGN, Hospital de Jesús, leg. 312, exp. 53 (*cacique y principal* of S. F. Tetcala sells cane crop to Spaniard for 180 pesos, 1697); AGN, Hospital de Jesús, vol. 86, exp. 38 (governor of San Francisco Tetecala grows sugarcane to support family, pay tribute, 1715).

94. Barrett, *Sugar Hacienda*, 50.

95. AGN, Indios, vol. 29, exp. 22 (licensing laws for Indian-owned *trapiches*).

96. AGN, Indios, vol. 29, exp. 205 (don Esteban Gabriel Cortés, a frequent governor of the *pueblo* San Gaspar Coatlán, runs a mill used to process cane, grown on land belonging to his *patrimonio*, into *panocha*, 1675; applies for license when an *alcalde mayor* threatens to shut down the mill); AGN, Indios, vol. 29, exp. 119 (a *principal* of the *pueblo* San Lucas Mazatepéc finds his well-established *trapiche* threatened with closure and only then applies for a license, 1686).

97. AGN, Hospital de Jesús, leg. 304, exp. 71 and leg. 426, exp. 25 (mill of José Bacilio Roque of San Francisco Tetecala, 1808–1820).

98. See AGN, Hospital de Jesús, vol. 86, exp. 42 (*principal* of Xochitlán and his sister manufacture *pulque* in their homes and sell it to others, 1701); AGN, Criminal, vol. 39, exp. 26 (*alcalde* of Santa María produces *pulque*, 1714). Cline, *Colonial Culhuacan*, 138–39, discusses maguey and its uses. Good sources of information for Indian involvement in the production of *pulque* include John E. Kicza, "The Pulque Trade of Late Colonial Mexico City," *The Americas*, 37:2 (1980), 193–221; and Taylor, *Drinking, Homicide, and Rebellion*, 28–34.

99. AGN, Hospital de Jesús, vol. 76, exp. 20; and leg. 323, exp. 1 (don Juan de Rojas and son don Hipolito are *mezcal* producers, Tepoztlán, first half of the eighteenth century). Taylor, *Drinking, Homicide, and Rebellion*, mentions production in the Bajío, in central Mexico, and in Oaxaca.

100. See Chance and Taylor, "Estate and Class," 471; Gibson, *Aztecs*, 318; Kicza, "Pulque Trade," 194–95; Lockhart, "Capital and Province," 115–16; and Taylor, *Drinking, Homicide, and Rebellion*, 36.

101. Taylor, *Drinking, Homicide, and Rebellion*, 36.

102. AGN, Hospital de Jesús, vol. 49, exp. 14 (Chalcatzinco, 1609); leg. 312, exp. 34 (Xochitepéc and Atlacholoaya, 1645); AGN, Tributos, vol. 45, exp. 7 (Santa María, 1694).
103. Taylor, *Drinking, Homicide, and Rebellion*, 52.
104. AGN, Tributos, vol. 21, exp. 2. Figuring worth: 39 plants, or 15.5%, at 6 reales each = 29 pesos, 2 reales; 211 plants, or 74.5%, at 1 real = 26 pesos, 3 reales. In the eighteenth-century valley of Toluca, a productive plant's value ran from eight to twelve reales, a figure based on the price received for *pulque* minus various production and marketing expenses. The ratio of don Juan's productive to nonproductive plants was similar to those found for other parts of New Spain. See Wood, "Corporate Adjustments," 169.
105. AGN, Criminal, vol. 39, exp. 26 (uses of *pulque*, Cuernavaca, 1714).
106. See Gibson, *Aztecs*, 318; Kicza, "Pulque Trade"; and Taylor, *Drinking, Homicide, and Rebellion*, 34–54.
107. Typical is the eighteenth-century Tepoztecan governor don Juan de Tapia, who in the 1740s loaned money to several fellow officers, including forty pesos to another past governor. See AGN, Hospital de Jesús, vol. 76, exp. 3.
108. Nahuatl wills are a good source of such information. See Cline, "Culhuacan, 1572–1599," 194–96 (testator of Culhuacan loaning the purchase price of a horse to a member of a nearby *pueblo*'s nobility); and Anderson, Berdan, and Lockhart, *Beyond the Codices*, 58–83 (Nahuatl wills containing debt and loan information).
109. AGN, Tributos, vol. 52, exp. 17 (moneylending activities of don Agustín de Hinojosa). See also AGN, Hospital de Jesús, leg. 74, exp. 88 (Yautepéc, 1760s; Spanish-language will shows that the *principal* Bonifacio Severino loans a total of 126 pesos to three of the *villa*'s town officers, 100 of which went to the governor to help him pay overdue tribute. He makes loans to several other local residents for various private ends).
110. See Archivo General de Indias, Seville (hereinafter cited as AGI), Justicia, leg. 177, no. 1, fol. 119r (two *principales* of Cuernavaca, don Juan Sánchez and Francisco Vázquez, rent land to the Marquesado, 1751). See also Spores, *Mixtecs*, 131, 134.
111. For comparison, see Cline, "Culhuacan, 1572–1599," 283; Lewis, "In Mexico City's Shadow," 134; Taylor, *Landlord and Peasant*, 48; and Tutino, "Provincial Spaniards," 183.
112. About one-third of all cane land used by the *ingenio* was rented at this time. See Barrett, *Sugar Hacienda*, 29–30.
113. AGN, Hospital de Jesús, leg. 312, exp. 20 (house rental by don Toribio de San Martín Cortés, later sixteenth century). See also AGN, Civil, vol. 1103, exp. 8, fol. 67r (Nahuatl petition of 1586 showing don Diego de San Lucas of Cuernavaca renting an urban *solar* to a commoner for four *tomines* a year). A *tomín* equalled one real, which was one-eighth of a peso.
114. AGN, Hospital de Jesús, vol. 52, exp. 17, fols. 2r-2v (Nahuatl land rental document of don Martín García, 1642; agreement is witnessed by one Indian and two *castilteca* [Spaniards]).
115. AGN, Tributos, vol. 52, exp. 17 and AGN, Hospital de Jesús, vol. 80, exp. 1, fol. 3r (receipt for yearly payment of 16 pesos for Teocuauhco, 1624, issued by Atlacomulco to doña María Jiménez, grandmother of the governor don Antonio de Hinojosa). Later, Teocuauhco, the largest piece rented to Atlacomulco, had been leased since very early in the century. In the 1690s the rent was 25 pesos a

year. Three parcels known collectively as Olactzinco and a fourth called Zacamolpa were rented to Chiamilpa, three other small plots were rented to Ocotepéc, and one peanut field (part of the crop was the rent) was held by the *pueblo* of Acapantzinco. Money rents on the smaller rural properties were from 2 to 5 pesos a year. House rents totaled 5.5 pesos. See AGN, Hospital de Jesús, leg. 208, exp. 198 (governor of Jonacatepec rents a small house to a Spaniard, 1730s). For comparison see López Sarrelangue, *La nobleza indígena de Pátzcuaro,* 40.

116. See AGN, Hospital de Jesús, vol. 52. exp. 8 (executors sell two of don Toribio de San Martín Cortés's Cuernavaca houses to the Spaniard Diego de Benavides, 1620). Martin, *Colonial Morelos,* 27, 36, notes that members of the elite sold land to outsiders, usually Spaniards, a trend which accelerated during the *congregación* program of 1603–1605. Barrett, *The Sugar Hacienda,* 133–34; and Anderson, Berdan, and Lockhart, *Beyond the Codices,* 98–109, include information about such sales. Chevalier, *Land and Society,* 212–13 considers these sales "heedless" in that they were made without regard to future need for the land.

117. AGN, Hospital de Jesús, leg. 210, exp. 25, fol. 1r (Nahuatl petition concerning sale of house lot and corral, Cuernavaca, c. 1607).

118. AGN, Hospital de Jesús, vol. 48 (first part), exp. 1, fol. 43r (Nahuatl petition; two *principales* of Cuernavaca sell *pillalli* to a Spaniard named Pedro López de Solis; see same *expediente* for other examples of López's activities).

119. AGN, Hospital de Jesús, leg. 411, exp. 1 (Cuernavaca, 1730–1732). Doña Petronila was without heirs, and a possible heir of doña Antonia, Juan Josef Bermúdez, voluntarily sold her house. The purchasers were don Josef de Cano (doña Antonia's house) and doña Rosa López de Riofrio (doña Petronila's house).

120. Woodrow Borah, *Justice by Insurance: The General Indian Court of Colonial Mexico and the Legal Aides of the Half Real* (Berkeley, 1983), 128–48, gives many samples of such cases.

121. Riley, *Marquesado in Morelos,* 236–39.

122. Charles Gibson, *Spain in America* (New York, 1966), 154.

123. AGN, Hospital de Jesús, leg. 96, libro 4 (complaint of don Juan Bautista of Xochitepéc, 1624). See AGN, Indios, vol. 12, exp. 162, for a similar case in which, in 1634, a *cacica* of Ahuehuetzinco was granted possession of land that had formed part of her husband's patrimony.

124. See various *expedientes* in AGN, Hospital de Jesús, leg. 96 for examples.

125. Barrett, *The Sugar Hacienda,* 133–34, discusses the 1620 purchase by the Cortés sugar estate of Atlacomulco of four *caballerías* of cane land from the executors of Cuernavaca's don Toribio de San Martín Cortés. The land originally had been rented from the *cacique.*

126. See AGN, Hospital de Jesús, vol. 52, exp. 17 (Tezoyuca, 1643: land once leased by a Spaniard from a Tezoyucan noble absorbed by the Marquesado as *baldía;* the Spaniard had presented his Nahuatl rental agreement, but claimed this proved his and not the owner's tenure on the property); leg. 208, exp. 198 (Jonacatepéc, 1732: governor is renting a house to a Spaniard, but the renter claims the house as his property and moves to get ownership confirmed). Similar reviews were taking place in other parts of the Marquesado. See Wood, "Corporate Adjustments," for the process in the Toluca Valley.

127. AGN, Hospital de Jesús, leg. 210, exp. 23 (Nahuatl petition: *huehuetque* of Cuernavaca's Xallan district intend to rent some *pillalli* that had come into their possession upon the death of a childless widow); AGN, Civil, vol. 1103,

exp. 8, fols. 67v-68r (Nahuatl petition: elders of Cuernavaca's Tianquiztenco district acquire *pillalli* from intestate heirless *principal*; the land was sold to a Spaniard to liquidate the *principal*'s debts, 1608).

128. AGN, Hospital de Jesús, leg. 210, exp. 39 (Nahuatl petition of Juan Cortés and sister Antonia Salomé of Cuernavaca, who complain that their stepmother is trying to usurp a *calmilli* and five other plots left to them by their real mother, 1607); leg. 210, exp. 63 (Nahuatl petition from the two daughters of doña Magdalena Cortés of Cuernavaca, accusing her of usurping land left to them by their grandmother).

129. AGN, Tierras, vol. 1806, exp. 1 (Hinojosa property dispute, Cuernavaca, 1708).

130. For representative cases, see AGN, Hospital de Jesús, leg. 210, exp. 38 (Nahuatl petition [1607] of the *principal* Pedro de Molina of Cuernavaca, who asserts that land granted to his grandfather by the king [1528] is being wrongfully claimed by commoners); AGN, Tierras, vol. 1826, exp. 4 (San Francisco Tetecala's *cabildo* attempts to force a *cacique* off lands allegedly usurped from the town years before, 1701); AGN, Hospital de Jesús, leg. 495, exp. 55 (*cacique* don Hilario de la Cruz vs. his cousin, the *alcalde* don Juan Andrés de Peralta, and the *cabildo* of San Lucas Mazatepec over allegedly expropriated property, 1704–1723); and AGN, Hospital de Jesús, leg. 358, exp. 1 (the council of Oaxtepéc vs. nine-time governor Don Pablo Antonio López over allegedly expropriated land, 1814).

131. AGN, Tierras, vol. 1939, exp. 3 (elite vs. community land dispute in Zacatepéc, 1783).

132. AGN, Hospital de Jesús, leg. 208, exp. 211 (don Pedro Jorge de Hinojosa donates land to Tlayacac, seventeenth century to 1732); AGN, Tierras, vol. 1960, exp. 1, fol. 137 (Antonio de Torres Hinojosa, *cacique* of Tlayacac, helps defend town land from encroachment by a Dominican monastery, Tlayacac, 1730s).

133. Anderson, Berdan, and Lockhart, *Beyond the Codices*, 110–17, includes several Nahuatl documents in which bequests to the church are made.

134. BNP Manuscrit Mexicain 291/292: One of the nine, the *cacique* don Juan Piltzintli, endowed a yearly Mass to be said in honor of the "Nino Jesús," whose *hermita* (chapel) was near don Juan's *cacicazgo*. This Mass was to be supported by the income of one of his pieces of land, and the obligation would be inherited by his descendants.

135. AGN, Hospital de Jesús, vol. 48, second part, exp. 9, fols. 1r-5r (*capellanía* of don Toribio de San Martín Cortés; in 1743 the obligation had been inherited by the community, which complained that it was having difficulty collecting the rent from the *ingenio*). For comparison, see AGN, Hospital de Jesús, vol. 52, exp. 9 (1602 testament of Cuernavacan *cacica* stipulates that some houses are to be sold to finance a *capellanía* for Masses for the souls of her four deceased husbands); and Martin, *Colonial Morelos*, 26, who describes a *capellanía* established in 1599 by a noblewoman of Oaxtepéc.

136. Cline, *Colonial Culhuacan*, 26.

137. AGN, Tierras, vol. 1935, exp. 4 (bequest of doña Inés Cortés, Yecapixtla, 1632).

138. For a similar case, see 46. Biblioteca Nacional de México, Fondo Reservado (hereinafter cited as BNM/FR), Fondo Franciscano Caja 92:1393, no. 3, Caja 108:1481, no. 5, and Caja 108:1483, no. 5 (Cuernavacan *principal* don Toribio de Santiago had left twenty pesos raised from "many pieces of [his] land" to

support a *capellanía* of seven Masses at the local Franciscan monastery, 1692; through an unknown process, the land became the property of the municipality, which continued to pay for the *capellanía* through at least 1755).

139. AGN, Tierras, vol. 1751, exp. 6 (doña María Ramírez of San Gaspar Coatlán vs. the *cofradía* of Santisimo Sacramento over land, 1696—the *cofradía*'s membership included both Indians and Spaniards).

140. *Recopilación de leyes*, law 27, book 6, title 1; aside from licenses, all sales had to be announced in public for thirty days prior to their closure. The resulting legal records could serve as land titles.

141. For important discussions of primordial titles, see James Lockhart, "Views of the Corporate Self and History in Some Valley of Mexico Towns," in George A. Collier et al., eds, *The Inca and Aztec States* (New York, 1982); and Wood, "Corporate Adjustments," 300–362. A published example of such a document can be found in Byron McAfee and Robert H. Barlow, "The Titles of Tetzcotzinco," *Tlalocan*, 2:2 (1946), 111–27.

142. These three Cuernavacan primordial titles have already been discussed. See also Robert Barlow, "Unos títulos de Cuernavaca," *Tlalocan*, 2:3 (1946), 213–22, for a Nahuatl fragment that may be closely related to the *Municipal Codex*.

143. For an example, see AGN, Hospital de Jesús, leg. 345, exp. 50, a case from 1745 in which a governor of Tecpantzinco presented a forged Nahuatl document purportedly showing the bequest of an urban residence to him by two uncles. At one point in the document, the uncles were made to state that "you are to settle here in this house, where you are to serve San Pedro and the Virgin of the Conception. No one is there yet; you will be there. No one is to evict you, for this is the home of your mother."

144. See, for example, from the 1720s, AGN, Hospital de Jesús, vol. 52, exp. 5, in which Tepoztlán's don Francisco de Rojas claimed that a Nahuatl will of 1707 proved his ownership of some land which others claim is *tierra de repartimiento*. It was subsequently determined that the land mentioned in the will was not the same as that involved in the litigation.

145. AGN, Tierras, vol. 1939, exp. 19 (don Francisco de Rojas of Tepoztlán attempts to usurp property by altering a will, 1746–1769).

146. AGN, Hospital de Jesús, leg. 73, exp. 15 (don Juan Diego and others are tribute debtors, Tepoztlán, 1759). See also a similar case from Tecpantzinco in 1743, AGN, Hospital de Jesús, leg. 80, exp. 80. The governor don Pedro Antonio and several other officers lost some of their property in the same case. Don Pedro, a *diputado mayor* of a *cofradía*, was also accused of stealing some of the brotherhood's silver ornaments.

147. AGN, Tributos, vol. 52, exp. 17 (the Marquesado vs. don Antonio de Hinojosa concerning tribute debts).

6

Negotiating Roots: Indian Migrants in the Lima Valley during the Colonial Period

Paul Charney

In colonial Latin America native peoples did not reside exclusively in traditional communities in the countryside. Even Lima, a city founded by Spanish settlers in 1535, soon possessed a substantial, diverse Indian population. Some natives were abducted to Lima by Spaniards who wanted to use their labor, others were recruited, and still others migrated to the city because of deteriorating circumstances in their home communities and the allure of greater promise in an urban setting. While most of the natives in Lima came from nearby areas, some traveled long distances, even migrating from other colonies. Once in Lima, a number, but far from all, lost their affiliation with their place of origin.

L atin American colonialists generally agree that the Spanish conquest stimulated a great deal of movement among the conquered Indian peoples. This Indian migration was important in shaping the colonial society and economy, and it changed village life in countless ways. Some studies on Indian migrants in colonial Peru have emphasized their rootlessness, depicting their migration as leading to the breakdown of family and communal life. They imply that Indians who migrated to avoid paying tribute neither returned to nor remained in touch with their home communities. Consequently, many of them either became integrated into the Spanish world or were considered unwelcome strangers in their newly adopted Indian communities.[1] Other studies have also found that not all migrants abandoned their homes, nor were all Indian communities depopulated as a result of emigration. While some villages experienced a loss of manpower and the breakup of numerous families, others benefited from the influx of *forasteros*, or outsiders, who were slowly integrated into the receiving village through marriage with the locals and participation in its communal institutions. These studies emphasize the adaptability of *forasteros* to their new homes, although the original inhabitants, or *originarios*, did not always accept them. They further show that, with the exception of Indians forced to move great distances to work in the mines, most Peruvian Indians either migrated for relatively short distances or proceeded from rural areas to nearby Spanish urban centers, which implies that Indians were perhaps seeking temporary employment and had every intention of returning home.[2] A complex picture has thus emerged of geographically mobile Indians in colonial Peru.

Indian migration to the city of Lima and its hinterland was no less complex, but this study does not intend to trace its geographical extent. Neither does it focus on the economic activities of Lima's Indians, nor on those who identified with their own kind and reestablished familial or communal ties in the valley, thereby severing any association with their original communities. These topics have been sufficiently investigated elsewhere.[3] This study, therefore, intends to focus on the circumstances of such migration, to reveal new aspects of the Spanish colonizers' exploitation of the Indians, and to examine the Indians' ability to control their individual or collective destiny. The colonizers' actions and policies did create a substantial number of Indians with little memory of or desire to see their homeland; other migrants maintained ties to their birthplace, which certainly reflects their capacity to negotiate the circumstances of migration as well as the inner strength of the Indian community and family. These contrasting experiences characterized the subgroups of Indian migrants that this article will discuss and who were in Lima on either a short-term or long-term basis: *yanaconas* (native retainers), abducted children and adolescents, forced and free wage laborers, members of the Indian elite, and the enslaved. Indian migration as a result of the Spanish intrusion, then, was a complex phenomenon that wrought many contradictions in indigenous lives.

The Lima valley was home to thousands of Indians before the onslaught of epidemic diseases took its toll. Nonetheless, Indian migrants populated Lima soon after its founding in 1535, providing a readily available labor force for the Spanish colonizers.[4] The surviving pre-contact population that once made up the *curacasgo*, or ethno-political territory, of Lima occupied a barrio of the city and cultivated suburban agricultural plots for its subsistence. Their neighbors in the barrio were *yanaconas* in the service of Don Francisco Pizarro. The *yanaconas*, identified as Cañares from Ecuador, served Pizarro as military auxiliaries, couriers, and guides during the conquest and defeat of the Incan armies, and he subsequently brought them to Lima in 1536. Their travels with Pizarro signified an early form of migration in Peru and presaged more extensive movements of Indians. Rewarding them for their services, the conqueror of Peru distributed to the *yanaconas* fourteen *solares* (urban plots) in a city barrio and some *chacras* (small farms) on the banks of the Rimac River that flowed only two blocks away from the main plaza.[5] *Encomienda* Indians also inhabited Lima, though generally on a temporary basis. The *cabildo* had set aside areas in Lima for these Indians to deliver tribute to the city, some remaining for a while to serve their Spanish *encomenderos* in *servicio personal*. (This unpaid forced labor was outlawed in 1549.) Indians migrating on their own to seek temporary or permanent work also formed part of Lima's native residents.[6] *Yanaconas*, wage laborers, tributaries, and locals, then, comprised the Indian population and workforce of early colonial Lima.

The pre-contact origin and political leadership of Lima's Cañares differentiated them from individual Indians who acquired *yanacona* status after the Spanish conquest. The Cañares maintained themselves as a separate group; they had their own chieftains and cultivated their own lands.[7] The 1613 census of Lima's Indian population noted a number of these Cañares and their "captain," which indicates that they continued to exist.[8] In pre-contact Peru, *yanaconas* generally served the Inca and the Indian nobility for lifelong duty. Their duties varied: some had specialized tasks, while others held high political office, as in the case of Gonzalo Taulichusco's family, who governed the *curacasgo* of Lima and who were most likely installed there by the Inca. Furthermore, *yanaconas* inherited their specialization or political office generationally. Without indigenous precedent, and by coercion or choice, numerous Indians in colonial Peru became *yanaconas* permanently attached to a Spanish master by a semi-legal bond.

Although they were only one or two percent of the pre-contact population, the number of *yanaconas* dramatically increased during the early stages of conquest. Spaniards added to the *yanacona* group by seizing many Indians and exploiting them as servants and farm workers; they then considered these uprooted Indians to be *yanaconas*. Their numbers also increased when Indians broke away from their communities and designated themselves *yanaconas* in order to avoid paying tribute.

The legal status of a colonial *yanacona* hardly differed from that of a domestic servant, apprentice, or manual laborer, none of whom had much freedom to leave their masters.[9] Lima's *yanaconas*, like others surviving after the conquest, drew on indigenous tradition by retaining their political leadership, economic function, and group identity. But many Indians designated *yanaconas* after 1532 had left their villages as individuals, the victims of Spanish conquest. Whether of pre- or post-contact origin, the *yanaconas* in Lima represent part of a wider movement of Indians, some of whom found themselves in Lima against their will.

Enslaved Indians brought to the city by Spaniards came primarily from Central America until the 1540s and subsequently were brought from Chile. Other enslaved peoples, generically called *indios* but actually Asians, had been imported by the colonizers from the Spanish and Portuguese dominions in the East Indies. The peripheral areas of the Spanish Empire were generally the main source of Indian slaves, resulting from the Spanish policy of enslaving Indians who resisted conquest.[10] Of the eighty Indians from Chile listed in the 1613 census, some were children and adolescents taken as captives in the war against the Araucanian Indians and subsequently raised by Spaniards, while others were brought to Lima to be sold on the auction block.[11] One hundred and fourteen "Indians" came to Lima from East Asia in the company of Spaniards, the census either defining them as slaves or implying that they had some bond to their Spanish masters.[12] How long such slavery was practiced remains unknown.

Another coercive means of procuring Indian labor for Lima's residents was the state-sanctioned *mita de plaza*. This *mita* furnished needed labor in the city and the countryside, a labor assignment intended to accustom Indians to work for wages. By drawing able-bodied Indians from the surrounding rural provinces, the *mita* established Lima's link to an outside Indian labor force. As early as the mid-1500s, Viceroy Conde de Ñieva (1561–1564) issued an order to implement the *mita de plaza*, and Viceroy Francisco de Toledo (1569–1580) subsequently codified this arrangement. The order required a designated number of Indian males (around 200, expanding under Toledo to 1,200) from the nearby provinces, both coastal and highland, to come to Lima periodically and assemble daily in the central plaza. There, the city's *alcalde ordinario* (city ward magistrate) assigned the *mitayos* to various Spanish residents who required their labor in the city or the countryside. Most became temporary residents in Santiago del Cercado, a barrio built in 1570 and located on the eastern outskirts of Lima proper. After fulfilling their work assignments in two or three months, many *mitayos* chose to remain longer in Lima, tempted by the higher wages (one or two reales more than forced labor) paid to freely contracted labor.[13] Perhaps Indians considered that with the extra income they could help their families and communities back home. The *mita* thus contributed much to maintaining the indigenous presence in the Lima area, and it also introduced Indians to a wage labor system.

The *mita*, however, did not evolve into an enduring institution, which helps account for not only the continuing use of Indian slavery but also the rise of other forms of labor. By the early seventeenth century, widespread epidemic diseases hit the Indian population hard and reduced their involvement in the *mita*. This, coupled with the complaints voiced by Spanish landowners in the latter half of that century that they could not keep *mitayos* on the job, and the rise of a free wage and African slave-labor pool, made such a public requisitioning system obsolete and unreliable.[14]

The increasing unreliability and ephemeral nature of state-sponsored labor drafts perhaps compelled Spaniards to resort to illegal means of obtaining Indians for permanent service in Spanish urban households and artisan shops. In large measure, this illegal requisitioning involved orphaned or abandoned Indian children and adolescents. Spanish *corregidores* (Indian affairs officers) and priests shamelessly abducted Indian minors from their rural communities to work as servants for Spanish residents in Lima and in smaller urban centers. The Indians of Canta, a province just north of Lima, vehemently protested in 1575 against the *corregidor*'s abduction of orphaned boys and girls, aged six to eight years old, who had then settled among several Spanish residents of Canete, a Spanish coastal town seventy-five miles south of Lima.[15] Despite such complaints, the abduction of Indian minors apparently went unabated. The eighteenth-century viceroy, Conde de Superunda, observed that members of the Spanish bureaucracy and priesthood frequently took Indian children from rural villages on the pretext that the children willingly left the village, undoubtedly misleading some of these children and their parents with promises of a better life in the city. Many of these uprooted minors, according to the viceroy, subsequently served in the artisan shops of tailors and shoemakers in Lima.[16] A late seventeenth-century census of the Indians of the parish of San Marcelo reveals the extent of orphanhood and the consequent breakdown of the Indian family and communal structure: of the 173 Indians of all ages, fourteen of the thirty-five boys and twenty-two of the thirty-five girls were orphaned or did not know one of their parents.[17] Indian children and adolescents, forced or persuaded to move to Spanish cities, became part of the urban workforce. Many may have had little desire to return to their own communities; some may have even lost their memories of home.

Indian minors who were victims of kidnapping primarily grew up in Spanish households and were therefore disassociated from rural indigenous society. As such, they became acculturated into the Hispanic urban world. The 1613 census indicates that Spaniards did act as surrogate parents to young Indians, some even involving themselves in their upbringing. Of course, such uprooted children were still expected to serve. For example, a Spanish mistress noted to the census taker that she had an eighteen-year-old orphan girl "in her service because she had raised her,"[18] perhaps implying that the girl was paying her back for fulfilling her duties as surrogate mother. This ransom-like arrangement apparently justified slaving and the cover-up of illegal ways of obtaining Indian labor.[19] In the census, fifty-two native males and forty females claimed to have been raised or born in Spanish households in Lima and elsewhere in Peru. But the males were not mere servants, as more than half claimed to be journeymen or apprentices. Indian boys growing up in the households of Spanish artisans often had an opportunity to acquire a trade, and the census listed several Indian orphans apprenticed to Spanish artisans.[20] Thus, the Indians' induction into the Hispanic urban world did not always mean, especially for most of the males, a lifetime of domestic service, but it did indicate that generations of young Indians had been torn from their communities in order to serve Spanish masters.

These generations of uprooted Indian minors made up a captive labor pool, culturally and economically dependent upon the colonizers. Work contracts merely gave legal guise to the coercive circumstances under which these minors had been brought to Lima to live and work in Spanish homes. Spaniards thus viewed the many children orphaned by Indian depopulation as a potential labor resource. Those Spaniards willing to exploit Indian minors, however, also had to assume some responsibility for their upbringing. A 1602 work contract, for instance, specified that the seven-year-old Alonso Indio, "brought stolen to Lima," could not yet serve his master, Pedro Gamboa, because of the child's tender age. The contract obliged Gamboa to feed and clothe Indio and to provide him with a Christian education. It further added that between the ages of ten and eighteen (i.e., until reaching tributary age), Indio would act as Gamboa's servant. During those eight years, Gamboa had to pay the child twelve pesos each year.[21] Alonso Indio's abduction, which led to his placement in Gamboa's urban residence, was a common experience for many Indian children in Lima. This is another example of "ransoming," whereby in return for Christianization and provisioning, the captive works for his benefactor. Moreover, Indio's contract considered ten years of age and older as the proper working age, or at least as an age at which he could begin collecting wages. The 1613 census makes clear that many Indian youngsters over the age of ten were working for Spaniards as apprentices or servants.[22]

Such proximity to Spaniards created a population of Indian *ladinos*, those familiar with Spanish ways and probably with the language. Once again, contracts can be used as an indicator of acculturation. Those examined here from the second half of the sixteenth century and early eighteenth century identified the Indian apprentice or servant as a *muchacho(a)*, that is, an adolescent or younger person. These young Indians, all employed by Spaniards, undoubtedly learned their employers' language. Several of the contracts also describe the Indian in question as a *ladino*, suggesting that he had sufficient contact with Spaniards as a child, perhaps even before the contract was made, which enabled him to learn Castilian.[23] Work contracts involving Indian minors essentially gave legality to a de facto situation: Indians became dependents in Spanish households long before they established any contractual arrangements; once the Indian reached a productive age, the Spanish master legally contracted him to work for a wage. For example, in a three-year contract, the Spanish widow, Ana Salgada, was to pay María Salgada, a *ladina* (note the same surname), eighteen pesos and provide her with food and clothing. Ana claimed to have raised María since birth, and her statement in the contract, "la crio desde que nació," suggests that María had lived in Salgada's household for a number of years prior to being put under a formal contract. Of course, some Spaniards did not even bother with wages or contracts, especially for Indians who were in Lima against their will.[24] María de la Cruz, another *ladina*, stated in her 1623 will that she had entered Lima, "stolen away" from the northern coastal city of Trujillo, and that her Spanish mistress owed her sixteen years of back wages.[25] Indians thus removed from their homelands formed a captive workforce tied to the colonizers' world. Work contracts legally recognized only what had been for the Indian youths many years of service and habitation in Spanish homes.

Not all Indian youths in Lima, however, were orphans or victims of kidnapping. Some Indians acknowledged that their parents had brought them to Lima when they were young, or that they were born in the capital of migrant parents.[26] With the concurrence of parents and relatives, Indian children also traveled to Lima to learn an artisan trade or to obtain an education. Undoubtedly, becoming a *ladino* facilitated the individual's upward mobility, if not entrance, into the Hispanic world. Miguel Jaramillo has also examined this process of ladinization and found that 40 percent (274) of the 685 Indians under a work contract in the first decade of the seventeenth century indicated their degree of *ladinidad*; of that number, 92 percent (270) claimed to be *ladinos*. Many became so while in Lima, and those who made no *ladino* claim in their first contract often stated, after signing a contract for an additional year, that they had learned some Spanish. Since Spaniards did most of the hiring, the Indians had an economic motive for Hispanization and thus eased their adaptation to an urban environment.[27] Nevertheless, such acculturation did not necessarily mean the Indians' permanent break from their homelands.

Acculturation also came about in more formal ways. Political leaders, or *curacas* (Quechua for chieftain), of the Indian communities often sent their sons and younger relatives to Lima for an education. This young generation of future Indian leaders and professionals often learned to read and write Castilian under a Spanish mentor. One ten-year-old student, for instance, the brother of an Indian *principal* (subaltern), was learning the profession of notary public.[28] The Jesuit-run Colegio de Cacique in the Cercado educated sons of the native nobility according to European curricula and standards. Established in 1619, the Colegio intended to create a loyal following among the designated heirs of the *curacasgos*, attracting young students from the highland and coastal provinces near Lima.[29] If they returned to their communities, these Spanish-educated members of the Indian elite undoubtedly served as agents of acculturation for their people.

Indian commoners also encouraged the younger generation to educate themselves, primarily by learning the artisan trades. Several eighteenth-century contracts indicate what might have been a continuing trend: Indian boys were placed by members of their families—by one or both parents, or older brothers—in apprenticeships with Spanish artisans in Lima.[30] The contract terms bound the young apprentice to his employer, who usually provided him with room and board, a clothing allowance, medical care, and sometimes a yearly salary (from twelve to eighteen pesos). Placing their sons in a trade may have reflected a strategy used by Indian families to obtain an additional source of income when the sons finally acquired journeyman status. In the sixteenth and early seventeenth centuries, the contracts of journeymen were much like those of apprentices, but the former generally earned a greater annual income.[31] The fact that most contracts were only for one or two years suggests that no long-term debt was involved, thereby making available more of the artisans' wages to help support families and/or relatives back home or pay tribute to the *curaca*.[32] The communal or family strategies behind the migration to Lima in order to obtain such contracts characterized other migratory patterns.[33] Some children might have been used in this fashion, especially if they were in Lima with the permission of their families. And they did not necessarily forget their roots or whether they had parents. An eight-year-old Indian girl from Huánuco (nearly 140 miles northeast of Lima) "working" in a *pulpería* (general store), for example, acknowledged that her parents still lived in her village, even though a Spaniard had taken her to Lima.[34] Some Indian families, then, may have consented to the removal of minors from the home communities to Lima without considering this a loss of manpower. Instead, the community and family viewed these Indian youths as future wage earners who might later benefit their people.

Of course, many adult male migrants of tribute-paying age (eighteen to fifty years old) in colonial Lima did not necessarily lose their links to family and community. They willingly, or perhaps because the *curacas* or tribute collectors insisted, paid for their share of the tribute which helped cover what was owed to the colonial state, the expenses associated with community affairs, the upkeep of the church, and the salaries of Indian officials. Half of the 103 Indian migrants in the 1613 census who referred to tribute indicated that they continued paying it to their community of origin. The rest admitted that they had not. Such continued payments indicate not only that the migration itself had a communal sanction,[35] but also that the migrant wanted to uphold his communal ties and loyalty. For some, long-term residency and distance did not matter. According to that same census, a tailor from Quito, a resident in Lima for some twenty years, claimed that "he pays his tribute to those coming from his land to collect it."[36] Regardless of the severe disruptions brought on by conquest and the imposition of the European market economy, which permeated the indigenous culture, numerous Indian migrants were simply unwilling or unable to break ties with their homeland.

The tribute collectors undoubtedly performed a vital function by sustaining links between the migrants and their communities. To promote these links, the collectors had to reside in Lima while maintaining contacts back home. Tribute collector Juan Alonso Mosquera, a *ladino* resident of Lima, stated in his 1617 will that he collected tribute in the form of wheat and corn from several Indians of his homeland. He then delivered the tribute to the *curaca* at Chancay. Yet Juan Alonso had an additional link between Lima and his birthplace. He held land in his village of San Juan de Huaral (about forty miles north of Lima and ten miles east of Chancay), and he had a brother-in-law living in the village and a godparent in Lima, both of whom he appointed executors of his will.[37]

The collectors' effectiveness depended on the *curacas*' support and the use of Hispanic legal devices which compelled errant Indians to pay their share of the tribute. A 1600 *concierto y obligación* initiated by the Indian governor of Huaylas (150 miles due north of Lima) obligated Francisco Chavca, a *ladino*, to work on a Spaniard's *chacra* in Luringacho (about five miles northeast of Lima) for four months in order to pay his tribute debt to the Indian collector.[38] Although the *corregidores* also used their authority to procure tribute payments, the *curacas* were ultimately responsible for ensuring their people's payments to the community and to the Spanish state. The *corregidor* of Chancay ordered the *ladino curaca* of Huaura (sixty-five miles north of Lima on the coast), Don Juan Solac, to collect tribute from Gaspar Huayac, a *ladino* then living in Lima's port of Callao. In another 1600 *concierto y obligación*, Huayac agreed to work for a Spanish fisherman and to pay Don Juan out of his wages the tribute debt of twenty-four pesos.[39] Despite the *corregidor*'s intervention, he implicitly recognized the *curaca*'s role as intermediary in obtaining the tribute owed by Huayac to the colonial state. In this instance, Don Juan's use of Hispanic legal instruments—the contract and the promissory note— actually bolstered his traditional authority and control over his subjects. Spanish legal and economic notions thus favored efforts to collect tribute well beyond the boundaries of the Indian village. These attempts, when successfully carried out, underscored Indian adaptability in times when emigration threatened communities with the loss of tribute-paying members. For some migrants, leaving the community did not always guarantee an evasion of tribute nor did it indicate that the migrant had forsworn his tribute and communal obligations.

Evidence of their continuing ties to their communities suggests that Indian migrants did not always intend to evade tribute. Wills and other documents manifest the migrants' desire to retain their landholding rights or, at the very least, to remain in touch with families back home. Seventeenth-century Indian highlanders who had settled with their families in the valley of Late, about seven miles east of Lima proper, sometimes visited relatives in the homeland. After visiting several days, Late's settlers "returned to live in the valley as they have been always accustomed to."[40] More often than not, Indian migrants from nearby highland areas maintained contact with the home community; their short-term residency in Lima further indicates their intention of returning to their birthplace. The 1613 census data on the length of residency for Lima's male migrants reveal that roughly 30 percent (325 of 1,083 in the fifteen to fifty-plus age category) had resided in the viceregal capital less than two years.[41] Perhaps these migrants were temporarily in the capital to earn extra income for families or relatives left behind; many would eventually return to their original communities. An Indian carder, for instance, had been in the city two or three months but said he intended to return to his village in Canta, a province east of Lima, where he had a wife and child.[42] Migrants who did not stay in Lima for long periods probably soon returned home. Others who maintained permanent residencies in Lima may have continued to communicate with relatives in the home community, as in the case of the Indian shoemaker from highland Huamanga (almost 200 miles southeast of Lima) who, though living in Lima for eleven years, "sometimes" visited his village.[43]

The wills of migrants from the seventeenth and eighteenth centuries provide additional evidence of the migrants' strong connections with their provincial families. These thirty-one wills,[44] belonging to seventeen male and fourteen female residents of Lima and the Indian barrio of the Cercado, listed land or other property items they possessed in their home villages which they bequeathed to surviving relatives or even to their preferred *cofradía* (religious confraternity). Some claimed urban or rural property in the Lima area, and two even stated that individuals from back home owed them money. Relatively close proximity probably contributed to such continuing links. Twenty-two came from villages that were within the present-day province of Lima (at least eleven of the total from Huarochirí, a province less than fifty miles east of Lima), and the remainder originated in places not much farther away.

Two cases illustrate the extent of this group's close attachments. In his 1621 will, Alonso Taco, a *ladino* resident of Lima, possessed a house occupied by his son and nephew in his village in the province of Jauja (about eighty miles east of Lima) in addition to several plots of land. Taco named his six-year-old son, then under the custodianship of the village's *curaca*, as heir. He also left land in the home community to the *cofradía*.[45] The other case also reveals that some migrants did not forget their roots. María Villalta was a resident in the Cercado and originally from the village of San Juan de Visca in the province of Yauyos (around seventy-five miles southeast of Lima). Her 1759 will instructed that the land she had inherited from her father be left to a *cofradía* back home, thereby obligating it to pay for the saying of two High Masses for the souls of her father and mother.[46] Indians used will-making to uphold their land claims, which in turn helped support relatives or religious institutions in the home community. This partially assured Indian migrants of their perennial membership in the community, and their kinsmen, Indian leaders, and institutions back home provided some continuity in the migrants' social and economic indigenous life.

Besides his payment of tribute, an Indian's uninterrupted attachment to his birthplace depended much on his family and the community leadership. His relatives who remained in the community could and probably did act as keepers of his property. The community's leaders, such as the *curaca* or Indian officials of the *cabildo*, could also protect and uphold the mobile Indian's landholding rights so long as he continued to meet tribute payments.

At times, however, conflict arose over the legitimacy of the links between a migrant and his community. The community's leaders treated a member's absence or failure to fulfill tribute obligations as justification enough to redistribute the absentee's landed property. An 1800 litigation case suggests that Indian migrants had legal recourse to dispute the loss of their land to members of the community. It also suggests that traditional functions, such as the *curacas'* administering of the community's holdings, had by this late date fallen under the control of individuals who were most likely commoners and who held Spanish-imposed offices like the *alcaldes* and *regidores* of the *cabildo*.[47]

Silverio Durán, from San Pedro de Paya (sixty-five miles northeast of Lima) in the province of Canta, spent four years in Lima working as a buttonmaker. He subsequently discovered that during his absence the Indian *alcaldes* of his village had dispossessed him of a land parcel which his "kinsmen" held in his name and reassigned it to "other Indians," presumably of the same community. In order to dispute this dispossession, Durán petitioned the Spanish sub-intendant (the eighteenth-century version of the *corregidor*) to force the *alcaldes* to restore the land to his kinsmen based on his birth in San Pedro de Paya and his continuing payment of tribute. As proof of his tribute status, Durán produced a 1787 document in which the Spanish *alcalde ordinario* of Canta certified him as a tribute-payer and original inhabitant (*tributario y originario*) of the community. Yet the Spanish authorities reviewing the case found that the Indian *alcaldes* repeatedly complained about Durán's delinquency in meeting tribute payments, which could have justified the reassigning of the migrant's property.[48] Unfortunately, the case left unresolved whether Durán retained his land or if any truth existed in the accusation that he "delayed" his tribute payments.

Land reassignment itself involved a traditional function performed by the *curaca* or his subalterns. In pre-contact times, the *curacas* were responsible for protecting the land of the *ayllu* or of the community member from encroachment or alienation by Indians of a different *ayllu* or even by members of the same community.[49] In fact, the Indian leaders mediated disputes over land arising between "brothers" or kinsmen of an *ayllu* member under terms of reciprocity as long as he and his family worked the land or had need of it. But when the family died out or its land became vacant, the *curaca* commonly reassigned the property to another family.[50] In Durán's case, the *alcaldes*, regardless of the Spanish term and its non-hereditary status, were thus still drawing upon a pre-contact tradition of land assignment. They perhaps considered other Indians of the community in greater need of Durán's land, which they may have viewed as vacant or unworked. Although his kinsmen held the land in Durán's name, they probably did not work it, which could also justify the redistribution of the land belonging to the absent emigrant. Like the *alcaldes*, Durán also drew on Andean custom by relying on his community membership, his kinsmen, and the indigenous leaders to retain and protect his landholdings. When made aware of this dispossession, however, Durán appealed to the colonial bureaucracy to uphold his *tributario* status and his land claim. By soliciting the help of the Spanish authorities, Durán sidestepped the native leadership's traditional role as mediator of land disputes and manager of land assignments in the community. In sum, Durán argued for returning the land to his kinsmen based on his community affiliation which, as for all Indians, resided in the continuing payment of tribute.

Historian Ann Zulawski finds similar concerns among the *forasteros* working and living in the city of Oruro in seventeenth-century Upper Peru. Many also sustained connections with their home communities because they were not at a great distance. In a 1683 census of Oruro, she found that most *forasteros* were paying tribute to their village leaders and correctly suggested that the communities had not lost track of these migrants and that such payments ensured the continuation of their communal rights.[51] A *forastero*'s proximity to his home community generally correlated with his ability to retain homeland ties, and perhaps these were sustained in many cases by the emigrant's family and/or the village leaders.

Evidently, Indians were in Lima either because of circumstances over which they had little control or because their migration reflected an individual or collective strategy that was intended to bolster village life. Ann Wightman, a student of migration in colonial Spanish America, discusses the gradual incorporation of Indian migrants into a class-based system and how over time they relied less on traditional authority figures, like the *curaca*, and more on their class or fellow workers.[52] Of course, *yanaconas* almost immediately fell into an exploitable or proletariat class, as did those in Upper Peru (Bolivia),[53] though in Lima some *yanaconas* had pre-contact origins and even a political leadership. Also, a number of Lima's migrants who might have been inducted into a class-like structure did not necessarily sever their connections with village life. The making of wills, a legal device drawn from Spanish society, indicates that relatives left behind in the community acted as keepers of the migrants' traditional rights to land. In fact, the migrants often named these very relatives as beneficiaries in their wills, which acted to sustain the connections between migrant and homeland.

Certainly, rootlessness characterized numerous Indian migrants in Lima. The emerging sixteenth-century capitalist economy did reach into many corners of the world, exerting its power to change forever the lives of powerless, non-Western peoples. Sixteenth-century Western Europe— the center—availed itself predominantly of free labor, while the New World—the margin—was unfree. Enslaved and kidnapped Indians brought to Lima, or those obligated to go there by the *mita*, were the prevailing kind of labor found on the periphery; even so-called free wage labor, brought about by the use of a capitalistic device—the work contract— was actually the recycling of the Spanish Christian-Moorish practice of ransoming.[54] This telling example reveals the trans-Atlantic migration of Spanish values and practices and how a pre-modern world-system device, essentially non-capitalistic, was harnessed to European capitalism. Many Indians were caught in this cruel economic paradox.

This study has also focused on those Indians who tried to retain ties to their home villages even while participating in the world market economy—similar to the actions of slave-raiding Spaniards who themselves drew on a rich cultural memory. To be sure, their move to Lima was related to tribute demands and the imposition of capitalist relations of production, but these migrants were not above borrowing from the dominant culture in order to empower themselves. Indians in this context were thus able to negotiate some control over the circumstances of their migrations, which approximated a communal or individual strategy intended to prevent losing themselves forever to the Hispanic world, and thereby retained part of their pre-conquest heritage.

Notes

1. Noble David Cook, *Demographic Collapse: Indian Peru, 1520–1620* (Cambridge, Eng., 1981), 251; Rolando Mellafe, "Consideraciones históricas sobre la visita," in John V. Murra, ed., *Visita de la Provincia de León de Huánuco en 1562. Inigo Ortíz de Zúñiga, visitador, I* (Huánuco, 1967), 340–42; Rolando Mellafe, "The Importance of Migration in the Viceroyalty of Peru," in Paul Deprez, ed., *Population and Economics: Proceedings of Section V (Historical Demography Section) of the Fourth Congress of the International Economic History Association, 1968* (Winnipeg, 1970), 303–15.

2. Elinor Burkett, "Early Colonial Peru: The Urban Female Experience," Ph.D. diss., University of Pittsburgh, 1975, 212; Nicolás Sánchez Albornoz, "Mita, migraciones y pueblos: variaciones en el espacio y en el tiempo, Alto Perú, 1573–1692," *Historia Boliviana*, 3 (1983), 38–39; Steve J. Stern, *Peru's Indian Peoples and the Challenge of Spanish Conquest: Huamanga to 1640* (Madison, 1984), 154, 174.

3. Paul Charney, "The Destruction and Reorganization of Indian Society in the Lima Valley, Peru, 1532–1824," Ph.D. diss., University of Texas at Austin, 1989, 172–203; Noble David Cook, "Les Indiens immigrés à Lima au début du XVIIe siècle," *Cahiers des Amériques Latines*, 13–14 (1976), 33–50; Miguel Jaramillo, "Migraciones y formación de mercados laborales: la fuerza de trabajo indígena de Lima a comienzos del siglo XVII," *Economía*, 15: 29 & 30 (1992), 265–320.

4. The valley of Lima's pre-contact population numbered around 200,000, which drastically declined to 2,000 by 1575, increasing to 5,488 by the end of the colonial period; those estimates may include both the Indian population in the city of Lima and the valley's Indian communities. According to the 1613 census of the city's Indian population, 95 percent, or 1,732 of the total numbering 1,930, were migrants. See Charney, "The Destruction and Reorganization," 38, Table 1.1 and 178, Table 4.1. Marriage records of the Cercado, an Indian barrio on the eastern outskirts of Lima, indicated a slight increase in the number of Indians born in the valley from 1575–1610 to 1650–1686. The vast majority in the latter period, how-

ever, continued to be migrants: 75 percent, or fifty-four of seventy-two marrying men, and 78 percent, or fifty-six of seventy-two marrying women. See Charney, "The Destruction and Reorganization," 351, Table 6.3. Throughout the colonial period, Lima probably continued to attract Indians in substantial numbers from the coastal and highland provinces. Meanwhile, in the city of Lima and its hinterland, Spaniards, blacks, and mixed bloods numbered nearly 23,000 in 1614 and 46,000 in 1792. The Indians were always a minority of the total population. For 1614, see Buenaventura Salinas y Córdova, *Memorial de las historias del Nuevo Mundo, Perú, [1630]* (Lima, 1957), 245. For 1792, see "Dirigiendo el adjunto papel en que se explica la población que contiene el reyno del Perú en su estado actual," 1792, Archivo General de Indias, Seville (hereinafter cited as AGI), Estado 75, f. 33.

5. "Probanzas de los yanaconas de marqués don Francisco Pizarro contra don Gonzalo Taulichusco, cacique de Lima y sus indios sobre las solares y tierras . . . ," 1550, Biblioteca Nacional de Perú, Lima (hereinafter cited as BNP), A15, ff. 10–13; "Expediente de la causa judicial que siguen don Francisco de la Torres, en nombre de los yanaconas del marqués don Francisco Pizarro y don Gonzalo Taulichusco, sobre la propiedad de unas tierras y solares . . . ," 1560, BNP, f. 150; James Lockhart, *Spanish Peru, 1532–1560: A Colonial Society* (Madison, 1968), 207–8.

6. Lockhart, *Spanish Peru*, 199, 207–8.

7. "Probanzas de los yanaconas . . . ," 1550, BNP, A15, ff. 1–2.

8. Miguel de Contreras, *Padrón de los indios de Lima en 1613*, with an introduction by Noble David Cook (Lima, 1968), 336, 344–45, 507.

9. Lockhart, *Spanish Peru*, 218–19; Stern, *Peru's Indian Peoples*, 144–45; John V. Murra, "Nueva información sobre las poblaciones yana," in idem, *Formaciones económicas y políticas del mundo andino* (Lima, 1975), 227–40; Keith A. Davies, *Landowners in Colonial Peru* (Austin, 1984), 35.

10. Lockhart, *Spanish Peru*, 200–203. Many Spaniards during the early "colonization" of Panama indulged in the thriving trade of Indian slaves. See Mario Góngora, *Los grupos de conquistadores en tierra firme, 1509–1530* (Santiago, 1962).

11. Contreras, *Padrón*, 106–7, 138, 270, 276–77, 279, 282, 285–87.

12. A separate count of these Asians is in Contreras, *Padrón*, 526–46.

13. John Howland Rowe, "The Incas under Spanish Colonial Institutions," *Hispanic American Historical Review*, 37:2 (May 1957), 171; Bernabé Cobo, *Historia de la fundación de Lima [1650]* (Lima, 1882), 74–76; Lockhart, *Spanish Peru*, 207–8.

14. "Informe de los hacendados," AGI, Escribanía 519-A, ff. 19,79,107; Jaramillo, "Migraciones y formación," 307–8; Marcel Manuel Haitín, "Late Colonial Lima: Economy and Society in an Era of Reform and Revolution," Ph.D. diss., University of California, Berkeley, 1983, 159–62. That so few *mita* workers were counted in the 1624 labor draft is indicative of significant Indian depopulation in the coastal Lima area. See Don Diego de Ayala y Contreras, " . . . le diesse testimonio de la cantidad de yndios que deben reunir a las mittas . . . ," 1624, Archivo General de la Nación, Lima (hereinafter cited as AGN), uncatalogued and without folio numbers.

15. "Expediente sobre el juicio de residencia . . . de Hernán Vásquez . . . ," 1580, BNP, A537, ff. 103–4.

16. Manuel Atanasio Fuentes, *Memorias de virreyes que han governado el Perú durante el tiempo del coloniaje español*, 4 (Lima, 1852), 94–95.

17. Lyn Lowry, "Forging an Indian Nation: Urban Indians under Spanish Colonial Control (Lima, Peru, 1535–1765)," Ph.D. diss., University of California, Berkeley, 1991, 321–22, Appendix II.

18. Contreras, *Padrón*, 406–7.

19. Despite laws against enslavement, Spaniards in colonial New Mexico were allowed to "ransom" Apache captives in order to Christianize them, and, in return for their use of Apache labor, the Spaniards were obligated to feed and clothe them. This sort of practice, then, seemed to have few geographical limitations. See Cheryl J. Foote and Sandra K. Schackel, "Indian Women of New Mexico, 1535–1680," in Joan M. Jensen and Darlis A. Miller, eds., *New Mexico Women: Intercultural Perspectives* (Albuquerque, 1986), 25.

20. Contreras, *Padrón*, 62, 298, 305.

21. Rodrigo Alonso Castillejo, 1599–1602, AGN, Protocolos Notariales, f. 1583.

22. Paul Charney, "El indio urbano: un análisis económico y social de la población india de Lima en 1613," *Histórica*, 12:1 (1988), 11–13.

23. In this study, thirteen servants' contracts (1575 to 1602) and a dozen apprentices' contracts (1591 to 1601 and 1731 to 1732) were examined in the AGN, Protocolos Notariales. See the servants' work contracts in Diego de Alvarez, 1559–1563, registro #8, ff. 69, 87, 92; Francisco Marcos Esquival, 1578–1581, f. 468; Juan García Torrico, 1552, 1551–1589, f. 1229; Castillejo, 1591–1595, f. 555; Castillejo, 1599–1602, ff. 84, 665, 1341, 1583. See also the apprentices' work contracts in Diego de Cordoba Maqueda, 1590–1595, f. 75; Castillejo, 1591, f. 597; Castillejo, 1597–1598, f. 1373; Castillejo, 1599–1602, ff. 34, 774; Francisco Cayetano de Arrendondo, 1731–1732, ff. 618, 640, 645, 650, 694, 804.

24. Castillejo, 1599–1602, AGN, Protocolos Notariales, f. 665.

25. Cristóbal de Piñeda, 1620–1623, AGN, Protocolos Notariales, ff. 6–7.

26. Contreras, *Padrón*, 174, 353, 383, 472; Francisco Roldán, 1734–1742, AGN, Protocolos Notariales, f. 23.

27. Jaramillo, "Migraciones y formación," 276–77, 283–84, 292.

28. Castillejo, 1599–1602, AGN, Protocolos Notariales, f. 446. For other examples of Spaniards educating the relatives of native rulers, see Contreras, *Padrón*, 164, 340.

29. Mario Cárdenas, "La reducción indígena del Cercado," Tesis bachiller, Universidad Nacional Mayor de San Carlos, Lima, 1972, 102–12.

30. Arrendondo, 1731–1741, AGN, Protocolos Notariales, 355, 588; Roldán, 1734–1742, AGN, Protocolos Notariales, f. 331; Francisco Humac Minoyulle, 1732, AGN, Protocolos Notariales, ff. 200, 829.

31. The following citations refer to journeymen's contracts: García Torrico, 1551–1589, AGN, Protocolos Notariales (registros sueltos), f. 1358; Castillejo, 1599–1602, AGN, Protocolos Notariales, ff. 384, 427, 525, 803, 849, 1148, 1159, 1211; Piñeda, 1612–1613 and 1617–1618, AGN, Protocolos Notariales, f. 286. See also Jaramillo, "Migraciones y formación," 296–98.

32. Jaramillo, "Migraciones y formación," 292–93. His examination of eighty-six contracts reveals that 90 percent of them had a limited time period.

33. Ann Zulawski, "Wages, Ore Sharing, and Peasant Agriculture: Labor in Oruro's Silver Mines, 1607–1720," *Hispanic American Historical Review*, 67:3 (August 1987), 425–30.

34. Contreras, *Padrón*, 405–6.

35. Miguel Jaramillo, "Una aproximación al problema de la fuerza de trabajo indígena 'libre': La formación del mercado laboral urbano, Lima a comienzos del siglo XVII," (personal correspondence, Lima, photocopy, 1985), 14–17.

36. Contreras, *Padrón*, 403–4.

37. Piñeda, 1612–1613 and 1617–1618, AGN, Protocolos Notariales, ff. 90–92.

38. Castillejo, 1599–1602, AGN, Protocolos Notariales, f. 786. A *concierto y obligación* contract had a second purpose: a promise to pay the debt (*obligación*) out of the wages earned in the contracted job (*concierto*).

39. Castillejo, 1599–1602, f. 497.

40. Visita de Ate (Late) . . . , 1654, Archivo Arzobispal, Lima, Perú, expediente XXXII, ff. 7, 11–12.

41. Paul Charney, "El indio urbano," 13–14, cuadros 3 and 4. Excluded from consideration are Indians in the adolescent category (ten to fourteen years old) under the assumption that most were acting less independently than older males.

42. Contreras, *Padrón*, 50.

43. Contreras, *Padrón*, 511.

44. Testamentos de indios, AGN. It included the wills of Domingo Quispe (1608), Lucas Hatoc (1608), Catalina Carguay Chumbi (1608), María Allacaxa (1611), Juan Cullacay (1613), Jilia Pasna (1617), Francisca Isabel (1622), Isabel Chumbicarua (1628), Martín Quispi (1632), Diego Samuna (1632), Pedro Chaplla (1643), Agustín Aguilar (1643), Andrés Manco (1643), Doña María Pasquala (1664), Juana María (1678), Lucas Martín (1684), Don Julio Tanta (1687), Pedro Toledo (1714), Andrés de Ortega (1741), Antonio Avento (1745), María Theodora (1748), Gabriel Jaguario (1751), María Villalta (1759), María de la Puenlanon (1759), María de la Roca (1763), Feliciana del Sacramento Armas (1770), María Gabriela de los Reyes (1770), María de la Encarnación (1770). And three wills— Juan Alonso, Don Pedro Lazana, Alonso Taco—were found in Piñeda, 1612–1613 and 1617–1618, AGN, Protocolos Notariales, ff. 90–92, 344–60, 351–53. In sum, there were twenty wills written in the 1600s and eleven in the 1700s.

45. Piñeda, 1620–1623, AGN, Protocolos Notariales, ff. 351–53.

46. María Villalta, 1759, AGN, Testamentos de indios.

47. See note 48.

48. "Autos promovidos por Silverio Durán, natural de doctrina de San Pedro de Paya, provincia de Canta, indio tributario y soldado de la primeria companía de naturales . . . ," 1800, AGN, Superior Gobierno, cuaderno 869, 6 ff.

49. The *ayllu* is generally understood to mean a group of related households that identify with a common ancestor.

50. John V. Murra, "Derechos a las tierras en el Tawantinsuyu," *Revista de la Universidad Complutense*, 28:17 (1980), 273–79; Karen Spalding, *Huarochirí: An Andean Society Under Inca and Spanish Rule* (Stanford, 1984), 25–32.

51. Zulawski, "Wages, Ore Sharing, and Peasant Agriculture," 424–26.

52. Ann Wightman, " '. . . residente en esa ciudad . . . .': Urban Migrants in Colonial Cuzco," in David J. Robinson, ed., *Migration in Colonial Spanish America* (Cambridge, Eng., 1990), 86–111.

53. Ann Zulawski, "Frontier Workers and Social Change: Pilaya y Paspaya (Bolivia) in the Early Eighteenth Century," in Robinson, ed., *Migration in Colonial Spanish America*, 116–17, 124–26.

54. Immanuel Wallerstein, *The Modern World System: Capitalist Agriculture and the Origins of the European World-Economy in the Sixteenth Century* (New

York, 1976), passim. Hispano-Christian capture and enslavement of Hispano-Muslims and vice versa during the Middle Ages, and their continuation into the early modern era, established a practice of abducting peoples of different and oftentimes hostile cultures. See Ellen G. Friedman, *Spanish Captives in North Africa in the Early Modern Age* (Madison, 1983), and James W. Brodman, *Ransoming Captives in Crusader Spain: The Order of Merced on the Christian-Islamic Frontier* (Philadelphia, 1986). The Spaniards undoubtedly transplanted this long-standing practice of abduction to the New World and justified using it on particularly belligerent Indians. And, of course, the Spaniards would have few misgivings as they facilitated, expanded, and abused the indigenous practice found in some parts of the New World of enslavement for the purpose of obtaining laborers or sacrificial victims.

7

Patterns and Variety in Mexican Village Uprisings

William B. Taylor

In recent years, scholars have become increasingly aware of the commonality of local uprisings in the rural zones of Mesoamerica and the Andes. Contradicting the long-prevailing view of stolid Indian acquiescence to European domination, numerous studies now demonstrate that recurrent resistance to attempts to modify their accepted patterns characterized many native communities throughout Latin America. In certain cases, these local resistance efforts even took the offensive, seeking to regain lands previously alienated or uniting in regional revolts.

In this selection, William Taylor examines both the recurrent patterns in and the internal dynamics of a number of revolts that took place in important regions in late colonial Mexico. His analysis of these uprisings tells us a great deal about the composition of and relationships within the rural villages that participated.

Uprisings have been a popular topic in the study of lower-class life and change in the Latin American countryside. Modern historiography of rural uprisings goes back to the works of nineteenth-century local historians, who used examples of rural violence to inform a literate urban readership of the barbarousness of peasants and vagabonds, and to warn of the horrors awaiting Latin America's pockets of "civilized" city life. The 1920s brought a new surge of interest in the history of rural revolts in Mexico. Studies undertaken then were designed to document a tradition of peasant uprising against injustice that could presage and give added meaning to the great upheaval in Mexico from 1910 to 1920. More recently, Latin American and foreign scholars have been much interested in the study of such major insurrections as the Tupac Amaru rebellion in late-eighteenth-century Peru, the Tzeltal revolt in Chiapas in 1712, the Indian wars of northern Mexico in the eighteenth and nineteenth centuries, and the participation of rural people in national upheavals such as the independence wars of the early nineteenth century. Sociologists and anthropologists as well as historians have shown increasing interest in the history of rural violence as a touchstone to demonstrate and explain the revolutionary potential of the rural segment of modern Latin American countries.[1]

Despite obvious differences, the forebodings of nineteenth-century local historians, the teleologically inspired studies of the 1920s, and the more analytical, detached research of modern social scientists share a common focus: insurrections or regional revolts, in which whole zones of rural people band together in a violent assault on state authority and privileged classes. In setting out to discuss rural uprisings in colonial Oaxaca and central Mexico, I am not primarily concerned with major insurrections of this sort for the good reason that there were precious few of them. To be sure, plans for insurrection were rumored in both areas, and a few short-lived regional uprisings occurred in the jurisdictions of Tulancingo, Actopan, and Metepec, along with a number of simultaneous uprisings in villages within the same region. But there was nothing comparable to the eighteenth-century Andean insurrections or, closer to home, the regional movements in Chiapas in 1712, in the Sierra Zapoteca of Oaxaca in 1660 and 1696, and in Yucatán during the 1840s and 1850s.

That regional revolts were isolated and infrequent in Oaxaca and central Mexico does not mean that the countryside was at peace with the demands and abuses of Spanish rule, "the peace of the grave" as José Vasconcelos once put it. Nor does it mean that colonial villagers were fatalistic, long-suffering people who were content to leave their fate to God ("sea por Dios") or the *patrón*, rarely taking the law into their own hands. In fact, a great deal of collective violence erupted at the community level.

The numerous violent village outbursts, or local rebellions, are the main subject of this chapter. The distinction between "rebellion" and "insurrection" is crucial to understanding the kind of collective acts described here. Both are violent political acts, but rebellions are localized mass attacks, generally limited to restoring a customary equilibrium. They do not offer new ideas or a vision of a new society. Insurrections, on the other hand, are regional in scope, constitute part of a broader political struggle between various segments of society, and aim at a reorganization of relationships between communities and powerful outsiders.[2] This distinction between rebellion and insurrection may not always be so clear in practice—simultaneous rebellions in a number of villages could have the same consequences as an insurrection—but nearly all of the examples located in my search for rural uprisings qualify as rebellions.

The evidence is a series of 142 judicial investigations of communities in revolt between 1680 and 1811. Of these cases, 91 are from the districts of central Mexico used in this study, 19 from the Mixteca Alta, and the remaining 32 from the Valley of Oaxaca. Rebellions and insurrections of earlier periods and in areas on the fringes of our central and southern Mexican regions are included only when they suggest new developments or shed light on main points. I have grouped my questions about these uprisings into two main sections. First, speaking generally, what happened? How did the movements begin, who participated in them, what did the rebels do and say, how long did the uprisings last, and how did they end? Second, what were the causes and the results of these village rebellions? I should emphasize that I am interested primarily in identifying general patterns. Individual uprisings are discussed when they illustrate a general point especially well or provide a striking exception. Most of the evidence and specific illustrations, however, will be found in the notes.

Peasants in Revolt: General Characteristics

Eighteenth-century rebellions were not random or limitless in variety. They reveal quite a definite structure and sequence of development. Most of the village uprisings in central Mexico, the Mixteca Alta, and the Valley of Oaxaca were alike in repertory of actions, instruments, and dramatis personae. Some features are especially striking. Nearly all were spontaneous, short-lived armed outbursts by members of a single community in reaction to threats from outside; they were "popular" uprisings in which virtually the entire community acted collectively and usually without identifiable leadership. The rebellions were highly aggressive but significantly patterned acts, punctuated by open insults, threat, attacks, and a general release of high emotion; most were directed against agents of the state and local buildings that symbolized outside authority. The rebellious behavior was controlled in the sense that there were few examples of general destruction and pillaging.

The spontaneous, collective quality of these village uprisings is repeated time and again throughout the eighteenth century. At a commonly understood signal, usually the ringing of the church bells or the sounding of a trumpet or drum, the townspeople assembled with whatever weapons were at hand.[3] The weapons—household tools, farm implements, sticks, and rocks—generally confirm the spontaneous eruption of the violence. These humble tools provided variety enough: pickaxes, hatchets, machetes, cattle bones, hoes, iron bars, clubs, cudgels, chains, sharp-tipped spindles, knives, burning sticks of pitch pine, lances, and a unique indigenous weapon, powdered chile peppers, used to blind and immobilize the enemy temporarily. Uprisings that lasted for more than a few hours usually brought into play more specialized weapons, such as bows and arrows, sabers, spears, javelins, and horses. Infrequently, eyewitnesses mention firearms. Only three cases of an old blunderbuss or flintlock pistol being used by villagers are recorded among the 142 risings. This would suggest that firearms were rarely to be found in rural villages, whether because the colonial prohibitions against Indian ownership were rigorously enforced or because villagers could rarely afford to acquire them. Rocks, thrown by hand or hurled with slings, usually were the most damaging weapon used by villagers in revolt. In cases of serious harm to persons and property, the victims frequently spoke of "a deluge of stones" or "a shower of rocks" descending upon them.

Virtually the entire community turned out for local rebellions.[4] Militiamen called in by the Spanish authorities were likely to encounter nasty mobs of hundreds of women brandishing spears and kitchen knives or cradling rocks in their skirts, and young children and old people carrying or throwing whatever they could manage, as well as better-armed groups of adult men. "The whole community" and "multitudes" of armed villagers of all ages are descriptions constantly repeated in the reports and testimony. The place of women is especially striking. Perhaps because men were more often traveling outside the community or working fields several miles from town, more women than men usually took part. In at least one-fourth of the cases, women led the attacks and were visibly more aggressive, insulting, and rebellious in their behavior toward outside authorities.

In 1719, Mariana, a tall scar-faced Indian of Santa Lucía near the city of Oaxaca, led a mob of men and women against a group of royal officials, priests, and militiamen who had come to mark the town's boundaries. After cutting the measuring rope, she took on one of the Spaniards in a hand-to-hand struggle, held up a bleeding arm to spur on her compatriots, and led the rock-throwing barrage that drove the outsiders back to the city.[5] Scenes like this have been repeated often, not just in the eighteenth century, but well into contemporary times. This open, sometimes leading role of women in the Oaxaca and central Mexico rebellions contrasts with the accounts of uprisings and Indian wars in northern Mexico, which consistently refer to adult men doing the fighting. Perhaps the difference stems from clearly defined male specialization in hunting and the use of weapons in the less sedentary native societies of the borderlands and the more active participation of women in the complex social relationships of sedentary peasant villages in central and southern Mexico.

The question of leadership in village uprisings is difficult to document. Colonial authorities were inclined to assume premeditation and leadership by a few local troublemakers, but the evidence from trials and investigations does not lend strong support to this assumption. Alcaldes mayores and higher judges usually were determined to find *cabecillas*, people who led or incited others and who were singled out for punishment as examples to the rest of the community. This was a convenient way of demonstrating the firm hand of Spanish justice without encouraging the whole community to desert for fear of punishment, but I suspect that colonial Spaniards, whether Creoles or *peninsulares*, could not conceive of a political movement that did not have a leader who planned and directed it.

In spite of the assumption that movements require leaders and of the political advantages of exemplary punishment, surprisingly few of the trial records for community uprisings provide clear evidence of planned leadership. In the formal trials village rebels, in order to escape punishment themselves, sometimes willingly testified against a few of their compatriots in response to leading questions from the prosecutor. Still, of the 142 cases, only 20 offer clear evidence against one or a small group of peasant leaders (usually the village governor and other members of the hereditary nobility). Parish priests led five attacks; five more—all from central Mexico—were inspired by resident non-Indians; and in another twenty cases prosecutors alleged individual leadership but were consistently contradicted by peasant witnesses who insisted that the violence was not organized ahead of time by local leaders. The choice of everyday objects for weapons, the timing of uprisings when some adult men were away, and a lack of clustering by season, festive calendar, or days of the week lend additional weight to the conclusion that these outbursts were generally unplanned.[6]

The behavior of villagers in revolt belies the image widely held by scholars of docile, or *encogido*, Indian peasants who were too attached to servitude and too alienated from society at any level to take up arms for social reasons. Thunderous shouts, whistles, obscene mocking insults, and impudent gestures, often accompanied by the beat of a drum or the sour notes of an old trumpet, were standard accompaniments to the rebellions. Role reversal was another distinguishing mark. Village rebels could assume the arrogant manners of their colonial masters. Especially in central Mexico, peasant rebels insulted district officials in the same terms that Spaniards had heaped upon them—"dog," "nigger," and "pig." Priests and alcaldes mayores were forced to humble themselves before the village elders. Outside our regions there are examples of peasants forcing local Spaniards to hear pagan services and making Spanish women marry

Indian men with the blessing of native priests.[7] Generally, such changes in roles parallel Octavio Paz's description of Mexican fiestas—an explosive suspension of everyday rules and privileges when the poor could dress like the rich and men like women, without fear of censure. The fiesta, according to Paz, is a kind of symbolic revolution, but as a symbolic act it replaces or exhausts the commitment to overturn the social circumstances that resume at the end of the fiesta. The rebellion is not identical in its result, for it is a political action more than a therapeutic expression of conflict that usually did not return the community to exactly the same position afterward. On the other hand, community rebellions usually did exhaust themselves without spreading their feelings of outrage to other communities and without creating an unflinching opposition to colonial rule. After initial success in driving out the enemy, the rebellions occasionally turned into festive celebrations with music, dancing, singing, and general *alegría* replacing the howls of anger.

Although the rebellions seem to have been unplanned and accompanied by a spontaneous and noisy release of emotions, there is pattern and direction in the way the outbursts were played out. Certain landmarks in the village were starting points for organized violence; other places were the usual targets at which the violence was aimed. The village church was usually at the heart of the action. The townspeople often gathered in the churchyard cemetery to hear the news before moving on the enemy. Since rebellions were directed against outside authority including the priesthood, it seems paradoxical that the church, the religious arm of the colonial state, should provide a symbolic dwelling place, a home base from which to assert the community's power. The answer, I think, is that Christianity occupied an ambiguous but very important place in the adjustment of Indian villages to Spanish rule. The church, in pursuing its own purposes—conversion, enrichment, and ministry to the souls of Indian neophytes—nurtured communal responsibilities through *cofradías* and new rituals.[8] Although not always displacing local popular beliefs, Christianity reinforced an Indian inclination to communal organization. The parish priest might be hated and ridiculed by villagers, but the church and its grounds were sacred places, connecting the past to the present and future.[9] Colonial parish churches often were built on the holy places of pre-Hispanic gods, sometimes with the very stones of ancient temples. Village churches were impressive in size and by the eighteenth century venerable in age, many of those in our two regions having been constructed in the sixteenth century. Their grounds often enclosed the cemetery, which further connected the community to its past. The atrium, or courtyard, facing the church (usually walled) was a sanctuary of trees and shade and a meeting place for community business, public ceremonies, and *cofradía* activities—a living arena of community decision making and collective activity.

Few of the rebellions turned into general looting and burning. On the contrary, the violence was almost always focused on a particular person or place. The object of attack typically was a colonial official or a building identified with outside authority, usually the *casas reales* (government offices) or the jail. The jail was the most frequent inanimate victim of the people's wrath, villagers descending upon it to release a native son or daughter and then set it aflame. It was the most concrete and hated symbol of the rule of alien law. As one thoughtful Oaxacan priest tells us, "Because the Indians grow up in the open fields, they view imprisonment as a fate worse than death."[10] Human objects of community violence were local agents of the state: usually the alcalde mayor or his deputy assigned to the town (26 percent); sometimes the parish priest (22 percent) or officials who attempted to collect an unpopular or increased duty (20 percent); and occasionally the schoolmaster (3 percent). If the victims were not state officials, they were likely to be citizens from a rural town, or from the political head town or a subject town, and sometimes abusive native officials or local rivals in a factional dispute.

Restriction of violent action to specific targets was not accompanied by restraints on the intensity of the violence itself. Although most of the armed uprisings were short-lived they were more than just symbolic gestures. Weapons were used to expel the offending parties. Killings and serious injuries were often the result. In at least eighteen cases colonial officials, militiamen, and other outsiders were killed.[11] In many other cases the enemies were seriously injured or fled just in time to escape alive. In one case an alcalde mayor saved his own life by hiding in a roll-up mat in a dark corner of the *casas reales*.[12] Priests seem to have been the one group that was attacked but rarely injured. Unlike their martyred brothers in the northern borderlands or Chiapas and Yucatán during the regional insurrection, priests in central Mexico and Oaxaca were menaced and sometimes injured by flying rocks, but none was killed.

The violence was not often sustained for long. Unless militia forces were sent in, the attacks usually ended in a day or two, although short bursts of collective violence seem to have occurred sporadically in some villages over long periods of time.[13] Occasionally, the local priest or the alcalde mayor persuaded the villagers to lay down their arms, identify the *cabecillas*, and negotiate a settlement. Since priests are often considered to have had great moral suasion in their parishes, it should be noted that the voices of spiritual reason and moral authority counted for little in subduing these village outbursts. There are many more cases of priests shoved aside with cross in hand and words rebuffed than cases of priests swaying the angry mob in the heat of battle. A few rebellions were quelled in midcourse when the crowds were dispersed with firearms, and in one case an alert militiaman halted a rising by cutting the bell ropes.[14] But most village rebellions simply burned themselves out without much interference from the colonial authorities. The violence usually ended with the villagers achieving their immediate goal of driving off the intruders, releasing their fellow townsmen from jail, or extracting a promise from the colonial authorities that their grievances would be acted upon. Especially if the rebellion had resulted in killings or serious injuries, the attackers, and sometimes the entire community, abandoned the town site for refuge in the mountains. Depending on the season, the town might be vacated for several months, but such an exodus rarely led to permanent desertion. Village representatives were usually quick to complain to judicial authorities in the provincial capital and enter into litigation for a formal settlement.

The Spanish response to community uprisings in central and southern Mexico, a calculated blend of punishment and mercy, generally followed the principle of "pacification without destroying the Indians." Since the colonial militias were small and often ill equipped to subdue peasants in revolt, and since the surplus produced by villagers in the form of taxes and labor drafts was an important source of revenue for the crown, or as an Oaxacan priest put it, "La tilma del indio a todos cubre" (the Indian's cloak covers us all), colonial leaders were anxious to end revolts by negotiation and especially to prevent them from spreading. The Spaniards' fear of regional insurrection was apparently quite real. It was common for officials to think of rural uprisings in terms of dread diseases such as epidemic "contagion," "cancer," and festering wounds that would spread and consume the body politic. Such fear was strong in the minds of Mexican officials after the widespread uprisings in southern Peru and Bolivia in the early 1780s. A 1781 rebellion at Izúcar de Matamoros evoked fear of another Tupac Amaru uprising; and late colonial rebellions north of Mexico City made royal officials take precautions against spread to the "wild" Chichimec and Huaxtec Indians.[15] As long as the violence had not spread to neighboring communities, colonial magistrates were inclined to conciliatory verdicts in which village loyalty to the Crown was reaffirmed. Generally, a few local rebels were singled out by the judge as leading troublemakers subject to exemplary punishment (whippings, labor service, exile, and occasionally execution), whereas the community at large received a pardon, tempered with a threat of harsh punishment for future violence.

Sentences for presumed leaders of village revolts in central and southern Mexico ranged from the indignity and pain of the lash to fines, exile from the district (usually for two to six years), and penal servitude. The last, which was quite common in eighteenth-century sentences, took the form of service in an *obraje* for one to six years, in a presidio for up to ten years, or on public works projects for shorter periods. In one extraordinary case the judge ingeniously combined penal service with the improvement of local security by sentencing the leaders to construct a sturdy jail and to clear one league of land surrounding the town in order to destroy the rebels' easy refuge.[16] Fines had the same effect as a sentence to hard labor. Since peasants were rarely able to pay in cash, their fines were often paid by employers who were allowed to claim the labor of the convict up to the value of the fine. The harshest sentences were reserved for individuals who had escaped arrest and were sentenced in absentia. In most cases of conviction the leaders were released before the sentence to service had been completed or were pardoned with a threat of severe punishment if they were involved in an uprising again.[17] Capital punishment or long periods of penal servitude were more common in the rare eighteenth-century regional insurrections, such as the Tzeltal revolt of 1712. Captives taken by the Spaniards in the chronic warfare with Indians in the northern borderlands were most likely to be executed or shipped south as slaves.[18]

Except for an occasional fine and a stern warning, the community as a whole was unlikely to be punished, even in cases where death or serious injuries were inflicted. The murder of a hacienda overseer by the people of Macuilxóchitl (Valley of Oaxaca) in the 1740s can serve as an example. Macuilxóchitl's bitter land dispute with a hacienda of the Bethlemite order had escalated into regular raids against the estate and retaliatory whippings by the overseer. The overseer eventually blundered into the village to vent his anger and was immediately seized by a large group of townspeople and taken to the *casa de comunidad* for trial. With the entire community vociferously present, the elders pronounced the death sentence, and the unfortunate Spaniard was hurried off to the town plaza and hanged. Several elders were arrested, but in the course of the gathering evidence it became clear to the Audiencia that the entire community had passed judgment and carried out the sentence. Without individual culprits the court was at a loss. It exacted a pledge of loyalty from the town and ordered a stone gallows to be erected in the plaza as a permanent symbol of the punishment the community deserved for its crime.[19]

One major exception to this flexible, almost lenient pattern of sentencing was the verdicts handed down by Visitador José de Gálvez following the local rebellions in Michoacán and San Luis Potosí during 1767 to 1769. In the 1767 rebellions, which coincided with the expulsion of the Jesuits from New Spain, the colonial authority's response was swift and severe: in San Nicolás (jurisdiction of San Luis Potosí), eleven Indians were executed, the town secretary's right hand was cut off, and the village was deprived of its political rights; in El Venado (jurisdiction of San Luis Potosí), twelve Indians were executed, seven received two hundred lashes, seventy-two were exiled, and the community lost its usufruct rights to public lands; in San Francisco (jurisdiction of San Luis Potosí), eight were executed, two were whipped, seven were sentenced to life imprisonment, and twenty-six received limited prison sentences; in Pátzcuaro (jurisdiction of Michoacán), two Indians were executed, twenty received life sentences, twenty-four were subjected to two hundred lashes, and twenty-nine were exiled. In uniquely cruel fashion, these sentences amounted to punishment for the sake of punishment as the unbending response of a leading *peninsular* reformer who had little understanding of the delicate divide-and-rule policies that had governed the Mexican countryside for two centuries. Two years later, when a major uprising occurred at San Sebastián Agua del Venado in the jurisdiction of San Luis Potosí, the sentence was again exceptionally severe, but it followed the standard pattern of penal servitude: all three hundred Indian men arrested were sent to presidios for varying periods of service, and eleven received heavy fines —fifty pesos for ten of them, and five hundred pesos for the principal leader, which effectively meant that he would spend the rest of his life in servitude.[20]

Although the Spanish reaction to communities in revolt was usually restrained, it did not mean that the colonial authorities sympathized with or respected the peasants' reasons for resorting to arms. Little of the utopian good will that was an important strand of Spanish motivation in the sixteenth century was evident in these eighteenth-century investigations, even among the clergymen who appeared as witnesses. Occasionally, a hostile outburst was forgiven as overexuberance on a festive occasion or the product of a legitimate grievance, but official explanations of the risings usually seized on solemn abstractions and innate personality traits of Indian peasants, such as their lazy, ignorant, uncouth, vice-ridden, insolent, rebellious nature or their uncivilized way of life, "lacking God, Law, and King."[21] When the colonial officials got down to specifics, they condemned especially the village traditions of government "in which everyone rules." In trying to discover the cause of a major rebellion in Zimatlán (Valley of Oaxaca) in 1772, the parish priest concluded that it resulted from the Indians' "wicked" style of government. Drawing a parallel to Spain's archrival England, he warned that continual uprisings could be expected in Indian villages because "everyone rules," including women and children.[22] Consensus decision making in peasant villages received little sympathy from Spaniards, imbued with the idea of a natural order based on highly stratified hierarchies. Occasionally, colonial authorities saw the root of rebellion in the bad example of a neighboring town or in excessive drinking. In one case we can look beyond the rather restrained language of the Spanish magistrates and find a local Spaniard's feelings about Indian villagers in the wake of a rebellion. The evidence comes in the form of an anonymous note tacked to the door of the magistrate of Tlamatlán, who was investigating the uprising of two small villages against the parish priest. The note read: "The monkey, even dressed in silk, is still a monkey. Whoever speaks of Indians speaks of shit because the Indian is like the monkey. It's as simple as that, because the Indian, like the monkey, utters a thousand stupidities which have neither beginning nor end. This is the truth and no lie. They are also very malicious and devilish."

This is not a very coherent statement of opinion, but it is nevertheless a rare glimpse of feelings that are usually masked from the historian's view, of the hatred and fear of a Spaniard living close to villagers but sharing with them few if any affirmative beliefs.[23] Underlying this anonymous author's hatred and fear is the knowledge that the Indian villagers were certainly capable of mob violence if they sensed an overt threat to their lands or to the psychic territory of their daily and seasonal routine.

For their part, villagers usually acquiesced in the conciliatory spirit of colonial judges, tentatively returning to the village from their mountain refuges. In the end, both villagers and colonial authorities wanted rapid resolution and return to settled village life. The villagers had land to farm, families to feed, and a sense of community that was not easily destroyed at one blow; they were also aware of the costs of lengthy litigation. The crown had taxes to collect and a political system to preserve. Considering the slow pace of much colonial administration in the eighteenth century, the judicial system dealt with most *tumultos* with remarkable speed, completing most investigations in a matter of weeks. The old leader of the little village of Coamelco in the jurisdiction of Meztitlán, which had risen up against the parish priest in 1777, knew from experience when he wrote with obvious resignation that "a poor settlement now is better than a long lawsuit that eventually turns out well."[24]

Few of the eighteenth-century uprisings in central and southern Mexico developed into regional movements with peasant villages banding together in common cause. Those exceptional movements that did submerge purely local interests in an abortive or temporarily successful regional union followed patterns familiar to peasant insurrections at other places and times. They developed as millenarian movements or formed around nonvillage leaders with whom the peasant shared a common enemy. In both cases, they were fragile movements centered on loyalty to particular leaders rather than to principles based on an identity of conditions and desires.

One impressive regional uprising of peasants occurred in the jurisdiction of Tulancingo (state of Hidalgo) in 1769, with several thousand Indian villagers from as far away as Meztitlán and Tenango joining a "New Savior" in the mountain fastnesses of Tututepec. Millenarian appeal—a retreat from the burdens of colonial life into a new theocratic utopia— seems to have been the source of regional support. The New Savior, a charismatic native messiah, was an old Indian who was accompanied by a woman venerated as the Virgin of Guadalupe. Together, they worshipped an idol-studded cross, proclaimed death to the Spaniards, and ruled above a newly created Indian priesthood that was to replace the Catholic hierarchy and end the hated clerical and state taxes. According to these spiritual leaders, the Catholic priests were true devils who should not be obeyed. The One True God of the movement was dedicated to the cornfields and chile fields, clearly an appeal to the popular fertility cults at the heart of peasant religion.[25] By calling for an end to all colonial taxes, for sparing the lives of only those Spaniards who would pay tribute to the Indians, and envisioning a world in which bishops and parish priests would line up to kiss the New Savior's hand, the movement hinted at a classlike war of poor against rich and sanctioned bloody attacks on colonial officials and nonbelievers who blundered into the believers' path.

A second short-lived regional revolt flared in the jurisdiction of Actopan, not far from Tulancingo, in 1756. The immediate cause of this uprising is clearer than the inspiration of the one at Tulancingo, and it followed a rather different, nonmillenarian course. The occasion for violence was a new labor draft in the jurisdiction for the purpose of draining the mines at Pachuca. Villagers complained that the mine labor was dangerous and that they were just beginning to harvest their corn crop. The revolt began on a Wednesday market day in the provincial center of Actopan, with as many as two thousand Indian men and women from nearby towns joined by non-Indians who were also subject to the labor draft. They converged on the plaza, brandishing knives, rocks, and banners, closing off the roads into town, shouting "Death to the Governors," and threatening to destroy the place. In the ensuing three days, eight Spaniards were killed or wounded and there was considerable destruction of property. Priests, some of whom had supported the Indian complaints prior to the uprising, negotiated a settlement: a half-caste *lobo* was singled out for punishment as the leader, the excesses of the common people were pardoned, and the towns agreed to a reduced labor service.[26] This insurrection is more like the sort of working alliance between villagers and lower-class townspeople who shared a common grievance that might be expected to produce strong feelings and violence against Spaniards in general. In this case, the movement joined Indian villagers chafing under new mine labor levies with vagrants and mestizos and mulattoes from the head town of Actopan, who also were being forced into the mines.

A local uprising in 1762 in the town of San Andrés, jurisdiction of Tenango (state of Mexico), exposed plans for another regional movement. The incident for the local revolt was the district lieutenant's search for contraband liquor on the evening of the patron saint's fiesta. In one house he found many men and women getting drunk around a large pot of *tepache*. As he tried to make arrests, the church bells were rung and "a multitude" of people descended on the house. The lieutenant and his militiamen barely escaped with their lives. In the course of the investigation into these events, witnesses testified to the long history of community revolts in Tenango and the neighboring jurisdiction of Metepec: a history of colonial officials driven out of town, of villagers refusing to obey written orders, and of several unsuccessful attempts at regional movements against Spanish authority.[27] Spanish fears of regional revolts, however, were rarely justified when the movement depended upon simultaneous uprisings by villages without a millenarian leader who could connect them to other groups outside the villages.

In Oaxaca, stirrings of regional unrest in the eighteenth century did not reach such proportions, but the revival of the cochineal trade, with coercive methods used to force production in villages of the Mixteca and the Sierra Zapoteca, did give rise to several brief regional uprisings. Townspeople of San Felipe, San Mateo, and San Francisco in the jurisdiction of Teozacualco rebelled simultaneously in 1774 against the district lieutenant for interfering in local affairs, demanding cochineal, and attempting to collect tax on liquor produced for local consumption. Rebellion planned in Achiutla (Mixteca Alta) during 1785 nearly became a regional uprising. Messengers from Achiutla carried the call to arms to surrounding villages. Again, the common enemy was the district lieutenant, who was hated for harsh treatment and abuse in the collection of the tribute tax and cochineal.* In general, however, peasants in eighteenth-century central

---

*Additional light might be cast on the low incidence of regional revolts in the settled highlands of Mexico in the eighteenth century by comparison to the other great highland peasant societies in Peru and Bolivia, where regional revolts were more frequent. A cycle of three periods of major uprisings have been identified in eighteenth-century Peru: 1737–1740, 1750, and 1780–1782. These widespread uprisings seem to have been touched off by similar changes in tax levies and land encroachments and the *reparto de efectos* that we have noted in the Mexican regions. One distinctive feature of the three periods of insurrection in Peru and Bolivia absent in the rural unrest in Mexico was messianic leadership by

Mexico and Oaxaca were not engaged in new economic activities that could lead to new perceptions about deprivation.

No one village rebellion typifies the structure discussed here, but the events at Tlapanoya (tributary to Atotonilco in the jurisdiction of Atitalaquia, modern state of Hidalgo) in July 1690 and at Amanalco (jurisdiction of Metepec, state of Mexico) in February 1792 bring a number of characteristics into play.[28] A brief description of these two uprisings can make our composite picture more vivid.

The Tlapanoya *tumulto* began on a Sunday afternoon when the Indian *gobernador* and two nobles of Atotonilco arrived in the village with an order signed by the alcalde mayor. They were to be given custody of two citizens of Atotonilco who recently had settled in Tlapanoya to avoid the personal services exacted by the *gobernador* and the alcalde mayor. The Tlapanoyans who encountered the messengers refused to obey the order and, after muttering to themselves, declared that they no longer accepted the alcalde mayor as their judge. They began to whistle and call for the villagers—men and women—who assembled in a menacing crowd with clubs, rocks, plows, and other weapons to attack the Atotonilco *gobernador*, who fled for his life. When word of the *tumulto* reached the alcalde mayor, he sent the militia to arrest the officials of Tlapanoya. The townspeople fled to the mountains, but two sons of the *gobernador* of Tlapanoya were captured. The *gobernador* himself was in Mexico City at the time to register a complaint with the Audiencia against the forced labor and cash extortions demanded by the alcalde mayor. During the investigation of the *tumulto* ordered by the Audiencia, the alcalde mayor asserted that the Tlapanoyans were insolent people who refused to perform labor service for the king and who were his enemies because he had

---

hereditary native nobles who proclaimed a return to the rule of the Incas, with themselves as the legitimate heirs. The bases for such a series of messianic movements would appear to be the survival of a Hispanicized native elite and ethnic ties among Indian peasants reinforced by rivalries among different regions, more movement of peasants outside the villages, and weaker village units. There is some disagreement about the nature of the Tupac Amaru revolt in Cuzco province in 1780. Oscar Cornblit emphasizes the role of local Creoles in launching the revolt and the participation of *forasteros* (uprooted Indians from other regions). Magnus Mörner's careful new work on the rebellion in Cuzco province returns to the importance of the community nobles, who were fighting among themselves for the control of bridges as well as against the abuse of power by local colonial officials. *Forasteros*, according to Mörner, played a minor role in the uprising. It was basically fought by groups of villages attached to a mutually acceptable *curaca*. By contrast, we have noted the general decline of ethnolinguistic units in Mexico and the rarity of collective action by Indian linguistic groups in the late colonial period (AGN *Criminal* 306 exp.1).

arrested seventeen men and twenty-three women of the village for producing illegal alcoholic beverages. The Audiencia was not impressed. It ordered that the village be protected against arbitrary demands of the alcalde mayor and released the arrested Tlapanoyans with a stern warning not to take up arms against the king's representative.

The occasion for the uprising in the Amanalco jurisdiction was an attempt by the parish priest, with the aid of three Indians, to take a census for tax purposes. Three of the villages in the parish refused to allow the census takers in, saying that the priest and his assistants could not be trusted to make a proper accounting. When the priest tried to take the census in San Lucas, the villagers, joined by knife-wielding, rock-throwing men and women from Amanalco and San Miguel, chased the census takers back to the priest's lodgings in Amanalco. Amidst a peal of church bells, shouts and whistles, and general *alegría*, a "numberless" mob (consisting mainly of women) broke into the church, stormed the jail, and released three of their own number. Waving his blunderbuss, the priest fought off what amounted to a halfhearted assault on his person by the women. *Gente de razón* in the district quickly came to his aid, and in the ensuing hours of confusion one Indian died and three were seriously injured. The rebellion died down only after the peasants seized and battered Isidro Hernández, one of the three Indians who were in league with the priest. A few peasants were arrested, but most escaped to the mountains; and the priest was relieved of his duties. In his attempt to investigate the uprising, the *subdelegado* of Metepec was frustrated by the welter of name-calling, complaints, and counterclaims lodged by the peasants and the *gente de razón*. He did determine that the priest had overcharged the peasants for his services, obstructed their travel to Mexico City, whipped local people without sufficient reason, and allowed his three assistants, particularly Hernández, to usurp community lands. Hernández was also hated for supposedly perpetrating several deaths by witchcraft. In September, having noted that the peasants had returned in peace and were paying their taxes, the *subdelegado* released the rebels who were still in prison.

In what circumstances were the personal representatives of outside authority attacked? Perhaps the most common occasion for attacks on the royal or divine representative was the collection of new or higher taxes, an apparently universal reason for peasant unrest.[29] An uprising by the villagers of Pozontepec in September 1758, for example, was touched off by the parish priest's attempt to collect a new schedule of higher clerical fees authorized by the crown (subsequent investigation revealed other, perhaps more fundamental, peasant grievances against the priest's behavior in this parish and earlier rumors of rebellion). An argument between the priest and some of the peasants escalated to insults and shoves. That night a general *tumulto* broke out, the priest's house was set on fire, and the priest himself narrowly escaped the flames in his underwear.[30] Of the more than thirty uprisings against parish priests, all but eight were touched off by new clerical fees, with villagers complaining of raised charges for baptism, marriage, burial, and celebration of the Mass, or of withholding of priestly services because the villagers were not performing exceptional services for the cleric.

The collection of secular taxes was an equally important occasion for touching off community violence against tax collectors and local judges. Changes in the tribute schedule frequently ignited community violence, and some state taxes, no matter what the rate, had explosive potential. Particularly galling to villagers in central Mexico were the taxes on pulque commerce and salt production. Late colonial schoolmasters who tried to supplement their incomes as tax collectors on monopoly goods, such as tobacco, also invited violence.[31] In both central Mexico and Oaxaca, the *reparto de efectos*—the alcalde mayor's monopoly on the sale of certain goods within his district, such as horses and mules, which were often forced upon village buyers—touched off still other rebellions.[32]

Rejection of new or unexpected taxes is part of a larger set of circumstances of economic deprivation and economic incursion. Tax increases meant the allocation of additional family and community resources to nonproducers and outsiders, principally the state and the church. As a new demand, however, the tax increase had a greater impact on the local economy than merely that of extracting another increment of the community's production. Since taxes normally were collected in cash in the eighteenth century, higher charges usually forced villagers to look outside their community for additional sources of cash, through the sale of village produce, rental of lands, or wage labor. The effect of a tax increase was to make the village more dependent on cash-bearing employers, buyers, and trading partners, in addition to reducing the community's share of its production. In spite of these unsettling effects of taxation, it is important to note once again that eighteenth-century peasants in revolt rarely were challenging the structure of colonial relationships between themselves and the Spanish state. They were protesting *new* taxes or new levels of old taxes, not the right of the state to tax and the Indian subjects' obligation to pay tribute and other traditional levies.

Other economic threats also occasioned collective violence in peasant villages. Labor demands by local officials, the priest, or neighboring hacendados; forced sale of community stores of an essential product, such as corn, salt, or lime; and government orders to allow traders from a rival town to sell in the local market all led to mass uprisings at the village level in central Mexico and Oaxaca.[33] The most important economic incursion after the changing tax burden and labor demands was boundary encroachments. Like tax rebellions, mass invasions or occupations of land are familiar events to students of peasant uprisings in other areas of the world. Land disputes between villages or between a private landowner and a village are not especially numerous in this sample of village rebellions (30 of 142 cases), but my earlier work on land tenure in the Valley of Oaxaca suggests that control of land was a particularly tender matter because such a close relationship endured between village identity and a specific territory. As the judge in the Santa Lucía case realized, every official boundary inspection involving the borders of a peasant village was provocation enough for a collective outburst. Comprehending this potential rarely enabled the authorities to prevent an uprising. In the case of Santa Lucía, the judge was careful to prepare himself with all the trappings of royal authority—a large retinue of high church and secular officials, militiamen, and public criers who announced the official orders for the survey. Nevertheless, the mere attempt to execute a formal measurement aroused the villagers to take matters into their own hands and send the officials running for their lives with a shower of rocks and curses. New pressures on the land in the eighteenth century—resulting from population growth and the expansion of private estates producing for urban markets—suggest that boundary questions were a chronic occasion for violence in both of our regions, but it is noteworthy that the Oaxaca examples (both from the Mixteca Alta and the Valley of Oaxaca) of boundary wars and attacks on public officials in *vistas de ojos* were especially prolonged and acrimonious. Although their fears were not always justified, valley peasants assumed that a survey would mean a loss of land. As one sympathetic alcalde mayor understood, "What they fear most is losing the peace and tranquillity in which they live, and the lands that each individual and his community peacefully possess."[34] Menacing crowds of Indian peasants usually turned out for these inspections. Occasionally, they would throw rocks at the officials, steal the measuring rope, and mass in front of the inspectors, refusing to let them proceed with the measurement. A frightened alcalde mayor of the Cuatro Villas jurisdiction reported the following scene at a boundary survey east of the city of Oaxaca in 1720:

> When we reached the boundary of a plot of land belonging to Gabriel Martín, a native of the pueblo of Santa Cruz . . . , many Indians from Santa Cruz appeared, joining others who had assembled there. Massing together in a crowd, they sought, in disobedience of the Royal Order and Royal justice, to stop the proceedings, shouting that we would not be allowed to go beyond the said boundary. At the same time, the

Indians picked up stones and threw three; they aimed one at Your representative, but it struck one of the Indian officials instead.[35]

There surely were many more cases of specific economic incursions of this type (new taxes, labor drafts, boundary troubles) than there were *tumultos*. One additional ingredient in a number of our examples of rebellion that seems to have been a final—if not always indispensable—precipitating factor was the arrest or corporal punishment of village officers for failing to enforce the decisions of colonial officials. Many uprisings began with the storming of the local jail where the officers were being held, with an attack on the militia detachment that was removing an arrested official to the head town for trial, or with an attack at the scene of an exemplary punishment—usually a whipping—of village leaders for objecting to the new exaction. Whippings were a special form of humiliation to Indians because . . . by law Spaniards could not be whipped.

A second major category of occasions for village uprisings has apparently little to do with material conditions or new economic incursions, but much to do with villagers' sense of autonomy and community. In these cases, of which there are thirty-four examples, villagers testified that they rose up in defense of their liberty or their way of life. Revolts against parish priests provide some well-documented examples of such symbolic affronts. In 1799 the people of Atlautla staged a violent uprising when they learned that the parish priest had sold their prized altarpiece to a nearby rival town; in a similar incident the priest of Cuauhtitlán provoked violence in 1785 by attempting to refurbish an Indian chapel without consulting the parishioners; other priests courted trouble by repairing village churches with stones from ancient ceremonial structures. In Zimatlán in 1773 the townspeople protested violently against a priest who tried to keep them from speaking their native language, Zapotec; another town, Almoloya (1787), protested the priest's refusal to preach in their language by not attending Mass and, finally, by driving him out of town. Another priest aroused the people of Chacatongo to revolt in 1674 by moving his place of residence to another town within the parish; the priest of Almoloya created a similar complaint among the subject towns in his parish in 1792 by removing their baptismal fonts and requiring them to attend the principal church to receive the sacraments. Other priests angered peasant parishioners by interrupting local celebrations, forbidding processions, and meddling in the selection of village officials.*

---

*In the Papantla revolt of 1768, the alcalde mayor's plan to cut down trees in the community combined material and ideological threats to the local people: "The trees gave the people shade and helped them to persevere; also, they served for tying up their animals and protected their houses from fire; also, the twigs

Attempts to quarantine villagers in order to prevent the spread of epidemic disease also represented the kind of violation of local independence that could provoke a violent response. Teotitlán del Valle, a peasant community in the Valley of Oaxaca especially hard hit by the smallpox epidemic of late 1792, was singled out for special attention by the Board of Physicians in the city of Oaxaca. At the board's request, the intendant ordered the entire community quarantined and a makeshift infirmary constructed on the outskirts of the town to separate the afflicted from the healthy. Residents of Teotitlán were not permitted to leave the village, even to tend their crops, nor could families visit or send food to their isolated relatives in the infirmary huts. To *teotitleños* this forced community isolation and separation of family members was an intolerable intervention. Their first response, conditioned by three centuries of colonial experience, was to hire a lawyer in the city to petition the viceroy for relief. The leisurely legal process was not, however, a satisfactory means of coping with this kind of real emergency. The peasants soon took the issue into their own hands, storming the infirmary, retrieving sick relatives, and burying the dead in the churchyard. The attack was apparently spontaneous, beginning with a mother attempting to recover her child from the infirmary.[36] It ended, like so many rebellions, with a plan for appeasement designed to avoid permanent confrontation with communities in the region. The intendant in Antequera first ordered the urban militia to patrol the outskirts of Teotitlán (an assignment that lasted more than two weeks) but did not attempt a punitive expedition against the town or dare to punish the townspeople beyond the brief imprisonment of fifteen men and women. Colonial authorities hit upon making a scapegoat of the lawyer as a way out of direct confrontation with the peasants. In spite of the fact that the *teotitleños* had come to him for advice in opposing the quarantine, the lawyer was charged with stirring up innocent Indians and condemned to a stiff prison sentence and a heavy fine. The *teotitleños* emerged from the affair as "extremely peaceful people" who had never been rebellious until they met this city lawyer—a convenient case of Spanish amnesia, judging by the violent land disputes involving Teotitlán with Macuilxóchitl and Tlacolula throughout the eighteenth century.[37]

A third category of conditions leading to collective violence is political relationships, both within individual villages and among villages in the same political jurisdiction. The growth of the rural population in the

---

and leaves provided fodder" (AGI *Audiencia de Mexico* 1934). Sentiments of village liberty were also aroused by official attempts to force villagers to move to a new town site or, in one case, by efforts to make them stay where they were (AGN *Civil* 1599 exp. 9, 2166 exp. 5).

eighteenth century contributed to new conflict between subject towns and head towns in our regions. Agitation by *sujetos* to acquire cabecera status—and thereby separate themselves from nominal political subordination to another town and the consequent irritating service obligations—was a common occurrence. Attempts to transfer villages from one district to another were also common. These jurisdictional tensions sometimes touched off village uprisings.[38] The Los Reyes–Xocotitlán (jurisdiction of Ixtlahuaca) *tumulto* of October 1767 and the Zozoquiapan (jurisdiction of Meztitlán) *tumulto* of May 1805 provide good examples. The *sujeto* village of Los Reyes rose up against the *gobernador* of the cabecera, Xocotitlán, after he arrested the leading citizen of Los Reyes and his wife for "lack of respect" and failure to turn over all the tribute owed by the village. This incident brought to the surface the villagers' fears that the *gobernador* served only the interests of the cabecera and of the parish priest, who resided in Xocotitlán. The Zozoquiapan *tumulto* occurred when Indian villagers, led by a local noblewoman, Felipa Escudero, refused to accept an order from the Audiencia transferring their community out of the jurisdiction of Meztitlán. The militia was sent in to arrest members of the local cabildo, and the townspeople drove them out. Members of the village who testified in the alcalde mayor's investigation said they were afraid that the transfer would mean the loss of their lands and the disruption of local elections.[39]

Another kind of political problem leading to uprisings was internal factionalism, which seems to have been less directly connected to population growth than were intercommunity disputes. Armed uprisings of commoners against the local nobles and officeholders, especially after a disputed election, and attacks by one barrio on another bring us back to Georg Simmel's premise of the tensions inherent in the relationships between dominant and subordinate groups. What is important to us in a historical study of peasant life is that major violence related to factionalism does not seem to have been more prevalent in the eighteenth century than in the seventeenth. On the other hand, factionalism and the weakening of community bonds is more apparent in the mid-nineteenth century. (We will take up this change briefly in later pages.)

Crowd behavior was also an indicator of the occasions for rebellion. We have already considered the kinds of people who participated in the uprisings, the places and people attacked, and the ambiguous end to most outbursts of this sort. Another aspect of crowd behavior—the words exchanged with royal officials and the shouts that accompanied the attacks—is especially important for a consideration of precipitating causes. In sifting through the evidence, I found that the noise of village rebellions consisted of more than the terrific din of war whoops, profanity, ear-splitting whistles, church bells, horns, and drums. There were also choruses of shouts articulate enough to find their way into the testimony of two or more eyewitnesses. These spontaneous utterances are as close as we can probably come to identifying the conscious goals of the villagers' actions. Unlike the testimony in formal investigations—which can be useful in other ways—chants and shouts are unguarded direct declarations of feelings that are rarely expressed at other times or documented in other kinds of written records.

Many of the shouts were scornful insults and threats to the representatives who abused colonial authority, or to other outsiders who posed a threat to the community's peace, such as the owner or administrator of a neighboring estate: "We're going to kill you and drink your blood"; "Kill these dogs"; "Kill these niggers"; "Dirty pig"; "Nigger"; "Cuckold robbers"; "Now you'll see, you devil-dog alcalde mayor and your thieving cronies"; "We'll not leave a Spaniard alive in this town"; "You'll pay for this, you dog-governor"; "Now you'll see, you lying, thieving dog"; "Death to them all"; "The governor has ordered us to kill the Riveras"; "To hell with you, Rivera, you have stolen our lands and we're going to kill you"; "War, war."[40] Righteous indignation directed against outsiders who maligned the villagers, attempted to seize their lands, or imposed new taxes are contained in all of these heated words. But there is more here. "Pig," "dog," "devil-dog," and "nigger" were standard Spanish expletives, often applied to Indians.[41] In calling a *peninsular subdelegado* a "nigger" or the parish priest a "dog," the central Mexico villagers turned the tables on their political masters, repaying them in kind. In two of these examples, Ixmiquilpan in 1642 and Actopan in 1756—both in areas of Hidalgo where peasants were forced into service in the mines of Pachuca and Real del Monte—the sense of outrage against an individual Spaniard spilled over into a general call of "Death to them all"; "We'll not leave a Spaniard alive in this town."[42] This would seem to be a groping toward class war, but both rebellions burned themselves out in a few days, without spreading and without any mass killing of Spaniards. Nevertheless, they are early and interesting examples of a latent potential for insurrection and liberation.

A second type of common exclamation reveals what seem to be vague democratic aspirations and an instinct for self-preservation. They were not directed at anyone in particular; they were declarations of local rights and imperatives, and of strong opposition to any new infringement on local habits: "We alone are sovereign in this town"; "Now we're the masters of this land"; "We have no master"; "This boundary measurement should not be made; the King has no business here"; "We refuse to obey the alcalde mayor or to consider him our judge." One Indian alcalde

declared that his staff of authority was equal to that of the king's representative, after which the villagers shouted the same.[43] Villagers regarded
themselves as "free" people, but the kind of liberty that seems to have
animated the rebellions was confined to the small world of the local village. It did not readily translate into a notion of shared or equal rights
with other villages that could serve as the basis for regional revolts.

Community rebellions in central Mexico, the Mixteca Alta, and the
Valley of Oaxaca provide little evidence that accommodation was breaking down in the eighteenth century because of new peasant perspectives
on legitimacy, elite intransigence, or a significant gain in power by the
subordinate villages (all in spite of the major administrative reforms made
by the Bourbons at the provincial level). Real or imagined abuse of power
by district officials and loss of vitality of the ruling group seem to be the
political developments most closely related to village uprisings.

The new economic demands and the cultural conditions we have identified as the two types of occasions of collective violence share a common element. Both were actions taken by the state—by local judges or
priests acting either in compliance with colonial orders or on their own
initiative. They are the external events that explain the timing, if not the
underlying causes, of the rebellions. In Simmel's terms, the legitimacy of
the priests or alcaldes mayores suffered a temporary collapse because of
what the villagers perceived as an abuse of their power in making new
demands on the community. In a few cases it is also possible to speak of
the ruling group's loss of vitality as a factor in the descent into violence.
Rivalries between the parish priest and the local Spanish judge damaged
the unity of state control, confused the existing structure of accommodation, and raised village sensitivity to the abuse of state power. In five
cases we find parish priests intervening directly to lead village rebellions
against new laws on the administration of *cofradía* finances or against the
arbitrary acts of the alcalde mayor or his lieutenant. The growing reliance
of alcaldes mayores on lieutenants (appointed deputies who bear a resem-
blance to the corrupt political bosses of rural Mexico today) to oversee
public affairs at the local level also weakened the lines of loyalty between
peasant villages and royal officials in the late colonial period.

The vitality of the rural church was also in decline. The parish priest's
ability to guide his congregation was no longer as great as we might imagine from early church history in Spanish America. Many dedicated parish
priests still commanded the blind faith of their flocks in the last colonial
decades, but even more of their brethren had lost the sense of utopian
mission and personal sacrifice that had animated the "spiritual conquest"
in the sixteenth century and had won the neophytes' loyalty. In spite of
their numbers, eighteenth-century *curas* were usually more remote from

their peasant parishioners, weakening the ties between religious authority and village life.

Some priests complained that a rural assignment was like living in exile from the civilized world they had known as students.[44] Many others became permanent residents of the parish seat, where most non-Indians resided, making only infrequent visits to remote villages to administer the sacraments. At an urgent summons to the deathbed of a peasant in a village several hours' walk from his home church, one indifferent Oaxacan *cura* declined to go, sending a message that the dying man be given a sprinkling of holy water and a hot brick for his stomach.[45] Many quibbled with their parishioners over church finances, clerical fees, and the provision of food and lodging. All parish priests lost a measure of local prestige and wealth as a result of the Bourbon confiscation of *obras pías* and control of *cofradía* finances in the last decades of Spanish rule. Under these circumstances, it is not surprising that rural priests and peasant villages came into conflict, and that the moral authority of priests eroded— or that both developments could translate into collective violence.

The importance of actions by colonial authorities as occasions for local rebellions exposes the peasants' primary conscious motive for collective violence: the *defense* of relationships that were threatened. The structure of relationships showed geographic variation. Some regions— even in central Mexico—had not allowed a priest or alcalde mayor into their communities for years and paid the tribute tax grudgingly. Others paid existing tax assessments without complaint and served the priest and magistrate regularly. Defensive uprisings against state actions that were perceived as *new* encroachments were common to both kinds of villages, even though the degree of real deprivation caused by the demands of the colonial authorities was relative.

Rebellions often were set off by what appear to be minor changes, but to the rebels more than only a nominal tax increase or the arrest of a common criminal was at stake. Peasant villages were reacting to what they considered an immediate threat to their way of life. As one alcalde mayor put it, they feared "losing the peace and tranquillity in which they have lived," or being "deprived of [their] liberty," or "losing [their] lands and houses."[46] Peasants' beliefs about themselves and their communities also contributed to this climate of distrust and of resistance to change from outside. As the crowd behavior suggests, new colonial rules and restraints on customary behavior were commonly seen by villagers in revolt as threats to the ideal of the independent landholding community. Eighteenth-century peasant rebels who were later called to account and whose testimony was recorded in the formal records of investigation frequently proclaimed their "natural liberty" and inveighed against "the yoke of subjection."⁴⁷ Spanish witnesses spoke of the "false pride" of the villagers and their resistance to anything the crown's local representatives attempted to correct. Resistance to change in dealing with colonial officials represented an understandable distrust of powerful outsiders serving their own interests and an affirmation of the community's solidarity and belief in its separateness.

The considerable number of community uprisings in central Mexico and Oaxaca during the eighteenth century shows quite clearly that local villages were capable of popular spontaneous violence. As we have seen, this violence did not develop in a mindless way but had structure and coherence—even if the peasants did not fully control the situation. As a collective response to collective experience, it expressed community solidarity and hope. The spontaneous massing of armed villagers in the two regions bears witness to a long history of community violence and collective action in landholding villages under certain predictable conditions: specific changes in the economic demands of powerful outsiders and other direct encroachments on the community's rights. Defense of village integrity gave these uprisings the appearance of sacred struggles against violators of the community's visible and invisible boundaries. The community's perception of its independent rights was a relative matter, but it is noteworthy that nearly all of the 142 rebellions examined here took place in communities that possessed subsistence landholdings of their own and enjoyed a measure of separation and independence from the demands of colonial authorities through relative isolation, production of a significant surplus, or militant resistance.

The ability of our peasant communities to translate disaffection into political unrest rather than to retreat or fall into masochism is evidence of the strength of localized village identity. On the other hand, the rebels' goals were usually limited to correcting particular abuses; and the strength of *village* rather than regional resistance suggests very little identity of conditions and desires among villages that might bring them together in regional uprisings. Villagers in our two regions did not see themselves as a deprived class able to unite against a common oppressor. For most, the enemies were the neighboring villages as well as the abusive local magistrate or priest, not the higher authorities who were ultimately responsible for the burden of taxes and service. This local political unity and militant myopia made villagers good rebels but poor revolutionaries.⁴⁸ Individually, they defended their community borders with some success, but, in doing so, they failed to comprehend the larger forces that threatened their independence. They did not want to take power outside the local district, and, if they had, I suspect that they would not have known what to do with it. Without question villagers accepted the existence of neighboring haciendas and plantations; certain taxes and service; the formalities of a higher system of justice in certain kinds of crimes and disputes; the legitimacy of colonial priests and magistrates until they personally betrayed village trust; and the sanctity of that most remote figure, the king of Spain, and his personal representative in Mexico, the viceroy.

In late-colonial Mexico little village unrest was transformed into war on the rich or on the colonial system. A few of the longer lived village rebellions came close to spilling over into class wars with shouts of "death to the Spaniards" and "Death to the *gente de razón*." Some priests and colonial representatives died in the bloody outbursts, but the exalted threats to annihilate outsiders were never accomplished. There *were* regional uprisings in Chiapas (1712), Yucatán (1761), and the Petén (1775), which became limited race and anticolonial wars. For our regions, only the Tulancingo (Hidalgo) regional revolt of some two thousand peasants in 1769 might qualify as an uprising against the colonial system.

Our examination of peasant uprisings ends rather abruptly with the beginning of Mexico's wars of independence in 1810. Are changing conditions after independence reflected in new patterns of rural collective violence? To answer this question, we need to know much more than we now do about the last 150 years of Mexico's rural history. The secondary works on socioeconomic conditions and rural violence in nineteenth-century Mexico do, however, provide us with enough material to hazard a few guesses about changing conditions and responses that highlight our evidence on the eighteenth century. The postindependence period brought massive impersonal changes to peasant life, comparable in scale to the sixteenth-century political revolution, epidemics, resettlement programs, religious conversion, and labor and tax systems that resulted from Spanish colonization. These new challenges were in part conscious programs of the state and federal governments; in part, they were the product of Mexico's expanding population and growing role in the world economy as a neocolonial exporter of primary products.

The Indian peasant's legal status in independent Mexico was altered to make him a citizen equal before the law to other Mexicans. Paternalistic colonial laws for the protection of Indian communities were abolished. Non-Indians were no longer forbidden to reside in Indian communities, special Indian courts such as the Juzgado de Indios were disbanded, and the special protection of community property afforded by the colonial judicial system and the Indians' right to legal counsel fell into disuse. We know that these colonial laws were often honored in the breach and that the institutions created to protect Indians as wards of the Crown had serious shortcomings, but the colonial state did assume moral and legal responsibility for the survival of Christian tax-paying rural communities.

The weight of moral and legal authority in the colonial period did not sanction the dismemberment of rural communities and the seizure of their lands. This moral commitment was cold comfort to communities that lost their lands and their means of subsistence, but the survival of peasant villages was placed in greater jeopardy when the state became a moral enemy.

Equality of individual Mexicans before the law in independent Mexico would lead to careful scrutiny of the church and other groups that had had special rights and held corporate property under colonial law. As early as 1833 the state of Mexico, a new political jurisdiction that included most of our central Mexico region, enacted a law against communal property that opened the way to alienation of village lands.[49] The process of dismemberment began in the late 1820s and reached its peak during the reform period, from 1854 to 1876, when the Liberals attempted to integrate Indians into national society by dissolving their communal life. The national laws of the reform period against corporate property were not uniformly enforced, but illegal seizures as well as sale of village lands became more common. Village lands that were set aside for the support of the church or that were rented out were especially vulnerable to sale by the state. Finally, during the Porfirian dictatorship of the late nineteenth century, land survey laws allowed the alienation of more lands for which the peasant occupants could not produce formal titles. This final assault on village integrity affected our regions much less than it did the northern states of Sonora and San Luis Potosí and the semitropical areas of Veracruz and Yucatán.

At the same time that state and federal governments were expropriating corporate property, other pressures were being exerted on village lands: an expanding rural population throughout central and southern Mexico, and the growth of commercial farming in such lucrative export crops as sugarcane, henequen, and coffee. Commercial farming of sugarcane expanded dramatically in Yucatán and Morelos in the nineteenth century, henequen plantations opened in Yucatán, coffee fincas developed in Veracruz, and ranching expanded in the Bajío. These expanding enterprises competed for the peasants' means of livelihood—their farm land, water sources, common pasture lands, woodlands, salt deposits, and equally important, their labor. Whole zones of rural communities that had previously enjoyed a measure of local control and placed a high value on village independence were threatened with displacement and the total subservience of unorganized landless wage laborers. The assault on peasant lands was one of a variety of incursions against rural villages that intensified in the nineteenth century: peasant labor was the object of an expanding system of debt peonage and captive labor on the plantations;

and the value placed on modernization by Mexico's ruling Liberals and positivists led to a view of peasant villages as hard lumps of backwardness that had to be separated from their traditional ways if they were to become Mexican.

Central Mexico and Oaxaca were less affected by the changes in land tenure than many other regions because neither had great potential for producing the new export crops, and capital investment in the countryside of both regions was relatively weak. The central valleys of Oaxaca continued in the old pattern of strong landholding villages. Valley peasants were increasingly integrated into the regional economy and the urban marketplace of Oaxaca city, but largely on a voluntary, part-time basis. Other parts of Oaxaca were experiencing competition among peasants, politicians, and entrepreneurs for salt, farmland, grazing land, and the labor needed for weaving cotton textiles, but these new conditions did not resemble the engulfing commercial economies of Yucatán, Morelos, and Chiapas.

In the central Mexico region, pressure on village lands in the nineteenth century usually reinforced the colonial land and labor system rather than transforming land tenure and land use by new kinds of commercial agriculture. Demand for central Mexico's lumber increased in the late nineteenth century (especially for construction materials in the mines and railroad ties) and some commercial crops, such as *zacatón* (a native plant whose root is processed for broomstraw and brushes), blossomed; but the expansion of private lands happened more gradually, was mainly fostered by the Liberal politics of free enterprise, and pitted villages against their old foes, the pulque, ranching, and grain-producing haciendas that had their beginnings in the colonial period.* An estimated 40 percent of the central Mexican villages retained their lands throughout the nineteenth century.[50] Other politically unsettling circumstances of the nineteenth century were the weakness of the national government and the periodic foreign invasions that threw local politics into turmoil and destroyed the legitimacy of central authority enjoyed during the colonial period by the Spanish monarchy.

Accompanying these economic and political changes, which threatened the semi-independent position of rural villages, were more regional revolts and leagues of peasant communities, or community factionalism and resort to political homicide, which were barely evident in the eigh-

---

*In the eighteenth century some haciendas in the future state of Mexico had added textile workshops to process estate wool. If these weaving activities had been expanded in the nineteenth century, the expansion would have increased competition for local labor and perhaps fueled more land pressure.

teenth century. Nineteenth-century regional peasant movements were especially impressive in places that had waged earlier major insurrections, such as Chiapas (1712 and 1869), Yucatán (1761 and 1847–1855), and Papantla (1743, 1767, 1847–48, and 1891). In each case, however, the level of resistance was greater and the reasons for armed resistance more radical. The Caste War of Yucatán in the late 1840s was, for a time, a war to the death between Indians and whites; the Papantla rebels in 1848 spoke of the traditional grievances of heavy taxes, forced labor, and abuse of community freedoms, but they also called for the abolition of debt peonage and the destruction of haciendas and distribution of their lands to the villages.[51] Regional uprisings over land control were also occurring sporadically in central Mexico and the mountains of Oaxaca. The concentration of these insurrections in the late 1840s, 1860s, and early 1870s is illuminated by the weakness of elites, which was noted by Simmel as one of several changes in elite behavior that can bring on political violence. The Mexican-American War of 1846 to 1848 not only took the federal government's attention away from internal affairs, but also exposed the weakness of the government in defending Mexican territory. During this period, rural insurrections were mounted in Yucatán, the Isthmus of Tehuantepec, the Huaxteca region of Papantla, Veracruz, and the Sierra Gorda region of San Luis Potosí.[52] Also, attacks by leagues of rural villagers were made on neighboring haciendas in central Mexico at this time, which the Mexican historian Jan Bazant identifies as an important break with the past.*

Crises in the national government in the late 1860s and early 1870s were also accompanied by insurrections over land and community rights in Jalisco, Nayarit, Zacatecas, Michoacán, and Chiapas. The legitimacy of the national government was endangered in the 1850s and 1860s, not only by its weakness in the face of civil war and French occupation, but also by its attack on the church, which had been the state's traditional ally. A number of the rural uprisings after 1855 were led by disaffected parish priests who made common cause with villagers against the "sacrilegious" reform laws.

The catalyst in transforming local disaffection and loss of faith in national rulers into regional political movements was often an ambitious provincial chieftain who articulated the common fears and grievances of

---

*Bazant, 59. Political homicide and factionalism in communities seem to replace insurrection as a response to these political and economic changes in some areas. Hidalgo's high homicide rate in the nineteenth century may well reflect increased political homicide. A similar change from insurrection to political homicide is recorded by Paul Friedrich for a community in Michoacán.[53]

uprooted villagers and incorporated them into a wider political insurrection against the national government. Whether or not they had the gift of charisma, such leaders emerged from the shadows of earlier leaderless movements as instruments, rather than guiding forces, of the growing conflicts that accompanied the pervasive changes in the Mexican countryside during the nineteenth century. Some regional leaders, such as Manuel Lozada, maintained an impressive hold over their bands of country people clamoring for land and village autonomy. Most would-be leaders, like Miguel Hidalgo in the independence movement in the Bajío in 1810 and Colonel José Cetina in Yucatán in the 1840s, unleashed forces of hatred and despair they could not control. Among leaders of rural insurrections, Emiliano Zapata stands out as uniquely successful—a leader who gained the fellowship of campesinos in Morelos, not because of charisma or personal ambition, but because he understood their cause and was true to it.

The challenge to village boundaries and to the psychic territory of daily and seasonal routine that derived from government support of private estates and new opportunities for commercial agriculture grew in intensity in the last decades of the nineteenth century. But under a strong personalist national government there were few serious insurrections. Rural unrest became a regional and national force once again in 1910, when the legitimacy of the aged Díaz government was challenged by urban and provincial people outside of the government who sought the aid of rural groups that shared their perception of worsening conditions. [Francisco] Madero found potential allies in the rural communities of Morelos that were rapidly losing their lands and their very existence under the Porfirian political system and the expansion of the sugar plantations. But even in Morelos in 1910–11, the village leaders were demanding little more than the right to exist alongside the big estates and the return of the lands that had been taken from them. The rural movement in Morelos spread and became truly revolutionary in goals and methods under the leadership of Emiliano Zapata and less powerful but still independent chieftains; but as Octavio Paz says, "Zapata would have been an obscure figure lost in the solitudes of the south if his insurgency had not coincided with the nation's general insurrection and the fall of the Díaz regime in the capital."[54]

By comparing them with the eighteenth-century peasant rebellions, the nineteenth-century regional insurrections shed some additional light on the earlier uprisings. Regional movements after independence were more frequent and less scattered than the colonial insurrections. Since peasant subordination and perceived abuses of power by district authorities were sources of local conflict and violence in both periods, we should look to changing conditions in the nineteenth century for explanation.

The nineteenth-century revolts seem to have occurred in areas of major new economic incursions during periods of ineffectual national and state government. The national crisis was crucial to rural insurrection in 1910, just as it had been in 1810 and 1846. Such crises at the top were lacking in the eighteenth century. A coincidence of regional peasant movements and national political crises suggests a rupture of trust between villages and the remote high authorities, which began with the overthrow of the Spanish monarchy by Napoleon in 1808. Furthermore, the eighteenth-century villages of central Mexico and Oaxaca were more secure, integrated units in comparison to their late-nineteenth-century counterparts, which apparently were experiencing more factionalism, outmigration, and loss of lands. New taxes on land, the laws against communal property, the pressure of expanding cash crop enterprises, and the spread of debt peonage threatened the very existence of some nineteenth-century villages and were perceived as terminal threats by others, raising the latent potential for revolt. Late colonial villages suffered material distress, but it was not the kind of pervasive, dislocating threat to their existence that might have promoted a concept of struggle between classes or orders and united villages in regional insurrections.

Notes

Abbreviations for works frequently cited:

AEO   Archivo del Estado de Oaxaca.
AGI   Archivo General de las Indias.
AGN   Archivo General de la Nación, Mexico.
CDCh   Centro de Documentación del Museo Nacional,
        Chapultepec Park, Mexico City, Serie Oaxaca.
UT   University of Texas, Austin, Latin American Collection.

1. Charles Tilly, "The Changing Pace of Collective Violence," *Essays in Theory and History: An Approach to the Social Sciences*, ed. Melvin Richter (Cambridge, MA, 1970), 140; Gerrit Huizer, " 'Resistance to Change' and Radical Peasant Mobilization: Foster and Erasmus Reconsidered," *Human Organization* 29 (1970), 303–13, and *The Revolutionary Potential of Peasants in Latin America* (Lexington, MA, 1972); Gerrit Huizer and Rodolfo Stavenhagen, "Peasant Movements and Land Reform in Latin America: Mexico and Bolivia," *Rural Protest, Peasant Movements and Social Change*, ed. Henry A. Landsberger (London, 1974), 378–409; Eric J. Hobsbawm, "Peasant Land Occupations," *Past and Present*, no. 62 (1974), 120–52; Nelson Reed, *The Caste War of Yucatán* (Stanford, CA, 1964); John H. Rowe, "Movimiento Nacional Inca del siglo XVIII," *Revista Universitaria del Cuzco*, no. 107, 2d semester (1954), 17–47.

2. Henri Favre, *Cambio y continuidad entre los Mayas de México* (Mexico, 1973), 269ff.

3. AGN *Criminal* 123 exp. 21, 180 fols. 361–430, 430–75, 155 fol. 111–, 169 fols. 103–43, 210 fols. 189–, 229 fols. 263–, 232 exp. 2, 284 exp. 5, 304 fols. 1–4; *Civil* 865 exp. 9; José Antonio Calderón Quijano et al., *Los virreyes de Nueva España (1759–1808)*, 4 vols. (Seville, 1967–72), I:306–8.

4. Calderón Quijano, I:306–38; AGI *Audiencia de Mexico* 1934 (Papantla, 1767); AGN *Criminal* 54 exp. 14, 57 exp. 1, 75 exps. 3–4, 90 (November 1773), 104 fol. 452r, 117 exp. 7, 123 exp. 21, 180 fols. 361–430 and 430–75, 203 exp. 4, 155 fols. 111–; *Civil* 241 exp. 1, 1599 exp. 9, 865 exp. 9, 2292 exp. 10, 1505 exp. 7.

5. AGN *Criminal* 283 exp. 3.

6. See Robert F. Wasserstrom, "White Fathers and Red Souls: Indian-Ladino Relations in Highland Chiapas, 1528–1973" (Ph.D. diss., Harvard University, 1976), 134, for a critique of the view that the Tzeltal revolt of 1712 was led by members of the Indian cabildo.

7. AGN *Inquisición* 746 exp. 18 fols. 337–56.

8. Wasserstrom, 69, 75.

9. Natalie Z. Davis, *Society and Culture in Early Modern France* (Stanford, CA, 1975), 169–70, makes this distinction.

10. AEO *Juzgados* bundle for 1612–83; "Como los indios se crían en el campo, verse enjaulados lo tienen por mayor pena que la muerte."

11. Teodomiro Manzano, *Anales del Estado de Hidalgo desde los tiempos más remotos hasta nuestros días* (Ixmiquilpan, 1677), 3 vols. (Pachuca, Mex., 1922–27), I:13; AGN *Criminal* 243 exp. 1, 92 exp. 5, 218 fols. 1–19, 229 exp. 231, 107 exp. 1, 307 exp. 2, 202 exp. 1, 151 exp. 1, 306 exps. 1 and 6, 308 (August 31, 1769), 507 exp. 17; *Civil* 241 exp. 1, 865 exps. 8 and 9; AGI *Audiencia de México* 2588 report of Dr. Joseph Ruiz, fol. 4v; CDCh *Oaxaca*, roll 6, exp. 209; roll 8, exp. 286; roll 9, exp. 529; roll 15, exp. 430.

12. AGN *Criminal* 304 exp. 1 fols. 1–4.

13. AGN *Criminal* 79 exp. 1 fol. 6r.

14. AGN *Criminal* 57 exp. 1, 232 exp. 2, 243 exp. 1.

15. AGN *Criminal* 55 fols. 122–, 79 exp. 1 fol. 62v, 304 exp. 1; Calderón Quijano, II:163–75; AEO *Juzgados* bundle for 1806.

16. AGN *Criminal* 304 fol. 366r.

17. AGN *Criminal* 283 exp. 1, 218 fols. 1–19, 54 exp. 14, 230 exp. 15, 203 exp. 4, 166 fols. 185–272, 75 exp. 3, 202 exp. 1, 241 exp. 1, 162 fols. 187–306 exp. 5; *Indios* 54 exp. 85, 70 exp. 69; *Tierras* 381 exp. 5.

18. AGN *Criminal* 306 exp. 6; *Historia* 335 exp. 1.

19. Report on the parish of Tlacochahuaya submitted by Lic. Juan José de Echarri, April 29, 1803, typescript in the possession of Lic. Luis Castañeda Guzmán, Oaxaca, Oaxaca.

20. Herbert I. Priestley, *José de Gálvez, Visitor-General of New Spain (1765–1771)* (Berkeley, CA, 1916), 213–20; AGN *Criminal* 306 exp. 6.

21. AGN *Criminal* 138 exp. 2; R. Contreras, and J. Daniel, *Una rebelión indígena en el partido de Totonicapán en 1820: El indio y la independencia* (Guatemala, 1968), 32.

22. AGN *Criminal* 306 exp. 5.

23. AGN *Criminal* 79 exp. 8 (March 6, 1777).

24. AGN *Criminal* 79 exp. 1 fol. 6r.

25. AGN *Criminal* 308.

26. AGN *Civil* 241.

27. AGN *Criminal* 123 exp. 21.

28. AGN *Criminal* 54 exp. 14, 241 exp. 1.

29. Roland Mousnier, *Peasant Uprisings in Seventeenth-Century France, Russia, and China*, trans. Brian Pearce (New York, 1970), 306; Barrington Moore, Jr., *Social Origins of Dictatorship: Lord and Peasant in the Making of the Modern World* (Boston, 1966), 256–57, 380; Emmanuel Le Roy Ladurie, *The Peasants of Languedoc*, trans. John Day (Urbana, IL, 1974), 265, 269; C. S. L. Davies, "Révoltes populaires en Angleterre (1500–1700)," *Annales: Economies, sociétés, civilisations* 24 (1969), 53, explains the fewer peasant uprisings in England than in France on the basis of lower taxes.

30. AGN *Criminal* 210 fols. 189–205.

31. For example, AGN *Criminal* 166 fols. 354bis–.

32. For example, Calderón Quijano, II:163–75.

33. AGN *Criminal* 166 fols. 320–, 54 exp. 14, 55 fols. 122–, 181 fols. 201–, 163 fols. 295–; *Civil* 865 exp. 8; *Historia* 334 exp. 5; *Indios* 70 exp. 69; CDCh *Oaxaca*, roll 10, exp. 551.

34. AGN *Hospital de Jesús* 307 exp. 4 fol. 5r.

35. AGN *Tierras* 381 exp. 5 fol. 1r–v.

36. AGN *Epidemias* 15 exps. 2, 8, 9, 10 exps. 1, 3, 4, 12 exp. 6.

37. AGN *Tierras* 148 exp. 3, 2384 exp. 1.

38. AGN *Indios* 3 exp. 241; *Criminal* 92 exp. 5; CDCh *Oaxaca*, roll. 21 legajo 2.

39. AGN *Criminal* 180 fols. 361–430.

40. AGN *Criminal* 104 fols. 380–, 123 exp. 21, 180 fols. 430–75, 202 exp. 1, 157 fols. 93–, 507 exp. 17, 55 fols. 122–, 92 exp. 5, 210 fols. 189–, 226 fols. 401–, 229 fols. 263–, 283 exp. 3, 284 exp. 5; *Civil* 241 exp. 1, 2166 exp. 6.

41. For example, AGN *Criminal* 284 exp. 5.

42. AGN *Civil* 241 exp. 1; Manzano, I:13. The 1642 Ixmiquilpan rebellion was surprisingly early and centered in an area of Indian villages. The potential for insurrection there was evident again in 1677 and was momentarily realized in a millenarian movement more than one hundred years later.

43. AGI *Audiencia de Mexico* 2588, report by Dr. Joseph Ruiz, fols. 4v; Bancroft Library, Mexican MS 435 p. 21; UT Mexican MS G-205; AGN *Criminal* 54 exp. 14, 283 exp. 3, 75 exps. 3–4, 306 exp. 5.

44. For example, José Miguel Guridi y Alcocer, *Apuntes de la vida de D. José Miguel Guridi y Alcocer, formados por el mismo en fines de 1801 y principios del siguiente de 1802* (Mexico, 1906), 72–73.

45. AEO *Juzgados* bundle for 1807, January 7, 1744, Santiago Amatepec, jurisdiction of Villa Alta, complaint against Br. Santiago Mariano Villanueva.

46. AGN *Hospital de Jesús* 307 exp. 4; *Criminal* 180 fols. 361–; *Tierras* 318 exp. 5.

47. AGN *Criminal* 306 exp. 5A, 151 fols. 140–, 210 fols. 189–.

48. Moore, 208.

49. The extremely localized nature of rebellion in these two regions is particularly evident when it is compared to the character of peasant uprisings in southern France in the late sixteenth and seventeenth centuries, many of which were true insurrections with far-reaching objectives. Le Roy Ladurie, 192–202.

50. Moisés González Navarro, "Tenencia de la tierra y población agrícola (1877–1960)," *Historia Mexicana* 19 (1969), 63–86.

51. Reed, *Caste War*; Jean Meyer, *Problemas campesinos y Revueltas Agrarias (1821–1920)* (Mexico City, 1973), 11–13, 62–66.

52. Meyer, *Problemas campesinos*, 10–13.

53. Paul Friedrich, "Political Homicide in Rural Mexico," *Anger, Violence, and Politics: Theories and Research*, ed. Ivo and Rosalind Feierabeno and Ted R. Gurr (Englewood Cliffs, NJ, 1972), 269–82.

54. Octavio Paz, *The Other Mexico: Critique of the Pyramid*, trans. Lysander Kemp (New York, 1972), 60.

8

State Power, Indigenous Communities, and Land in Nineteenth-Century Guatemala, 1820–1920

David McCreery

The Indian peoples of Guatemala had retained their lands with little threat of their being seized by non-Indians until the 1870s. In fact, before that decade, most Indian conflicts involved struggles with other native communities. But in the 1870s the sudden profitability offered by coffee production impelled investors—staunchly supported by the new Liberal government—to claim substantial tracts of land that had previously been worked by native communities. These seizures resulted in surprisingly few Indian revolts, for villages were typically able to retain their central plots of land, losing only outlying fields.

The most evident characteristic of nineteenth-century Guatemalan politics was the dramatic increase in the power of the state. This was an outcome of the policies of the Liberal regimes of the 1820s and 1830s and of the coffee-fueled neo-Liberal Reforma after 1871. And it came at the expense of the political and economic autonomy of the rural population, especially that of the indigenous communities of the western highlands and the Alta Verapaz. Remembering that in nineteenth-century Guatemala, as today, land was the chief source of wealth and power for the elite and of subsistence for the rural poor, this chapter will focus on state intervention in the ownership and use of rural property. It questions two widely held perceptions about these years. One involves the way in which and the extent to which export agriculture, and particularly coffee after 1860, invaded and engrossed Indian lands. The other concerns what indigenous communities did when faced with such encroachment. The

chapter traces government land policies, examines the efforts of successive regimes to enforce these, and considers how the population in the
countryside reacted to new demands and pressures.

Perhaps no aspect of the history of Guatemala in the century after
independence is more misunderstood than the fate of the lands of the Indian communities. The general consensus has it that "small holdings and
ejidos (communal lands) were nationalized [or] outlawed," or, specifically, "in 1877, President Justo Rufino Barrios abolished communal ownership of land."[1] This understanding results in part from taking word for
fact: the law passed by the Liberal regime in August 1836, for example,
announced that "all *ejidos* will be converted to private property,"[2] and the
1877 decree mentioned above provided that "when an individual asks for
land from . . . *ejidos* or other community property . . . it will be measured
and put up for public auction."[3] More broadly, it reflects our general ignorance of Guatemalan rural history, a history still to be investigated and
written. In the absence of adequate studies, the tendency is to reason by
analogy, often faulty, with the histories of neighboring or apparently similar
countries or to take law for reality, something few would be so rash as to
do for present-day Guatemala. While it is undoubtedly true that the nineteenth century witnessed a "massive assault on Indian lands,"[4] the process was both more complex and more subtle than is generally recognized.

A second and related idea is that the rural indigenous population reacted violently to Liberal policies and the impact of the market economy:
"Throughout the late 19th and early 20th centuries, highland villages rose
in revolt against Liberal demands on their labor and land."[5] Such a description, however, more accurately characterizes the conflicts of the 1830s
and 1840s[6]—though land disputes were only one among many causes for
these *tumultos* (riots)—than it does that of the turn of the century. If there
were occasional and quite spectacular "rebellions"[7] against some of the
specific results of Reforma policies, what is most notable about the second half of the century is precisely the decline in violent opposition to the
state.[8] The contrary argument (i.e., that violent resistance was the common response) might appear to be rooted in common sense: the state and
the planters, in a harshly exploitative and grotesquely one-sided relationship, took from the indigenous population their land and labor, factors
the Indians themselves needed for survival. Logically, the Indians resisted,
with violence when necessary, as they had in the past. Too, such an interpretation satisfies the need of many historians and social scientists to see
peasants and indigenous populations as positive actors, not simply passive victims, of their own history. The problem for Guatemala is that it
cannot be sustained empirically. Indeed, all evidence suggests few and a
declining number of Indian *tumultos* after mid-century. An interpretation

of the nineteenth century focused on uprisings would require, as the evidence will make clear, a low regard for the abilities of the indigenous population to accurately assess its reality.

Late Colonial Land and Social Relations

To understand how the land situation in Guatemala developed after independence, it is necessary to begin by looking at the last years of the colony. In most areas of what is presently the republic, and particularly in the western highlands where the indigenous communities concentrated, *latifundia* (large estates) hardly existed. A few *haciendas* (e.g., Chancol in Huehuetenango or Chuacorral and Argueta north of Lake Atitlán) survived uneasily in an Indian-dominated highlands, and Creole and *ladino* (people who identify with the local Spanish, rather than Indian, world) cattle ranches had begun to move into lands abandoned by the extinguished towns on the south coast. Hardscrabble farms dotted the Oriente.[9] But the characteristic feature of the colonial period was the failure of the elites to penetrate the countryside as landowners or producers.[10] The profits of the colony, such as they were, were to be had in commerce and office holding or, after mid-eighteenth century, in the indigo fields of El Salvador, not in the *altiplano* (high plain) or the decayed cacao groves of the coast. Thus, much land remained in the possession and use of the indigenous communities. Colonial law in Guatemala recognized the right of each Spanish or Indian, but not *ladino*,[11] *municipio* to an *ejido* (community lands) of one square league.[12] For various reasons some towns never actually obtained this, though most in fact claimed and used much more.[13] Within the community itself, land was held in every imaginable combination of use tenure and private property; *costumbre* (custom) ruled. With a greatly reduced rural population—probably not until the end of the colonial period or even the mid-nineteenth century did populations begin to approximate preconquest levels—and much open space, conflict over land, if more or less traditional between some neighboring communities, was rarely a serious problem for the colonial state.

By the end of the colonial period, the term *"ejido"* had lost its original meaning of village common land. It now applied more broadly to all of the lands a village possessed or claimed or of which it made use. These might include: (1) the *astillero*, strictly community land available to all for wood and water, for the temporary pasture of animals, or, in some cases, for rent in small plots for cultivation by the poorer members of the community; (2) land purchased by and for the community, or by the central state for the community, either from private individuals or from public lands. In the late colonial period this often took the form of *composición*, payment to regularize long-term but technically illegal possession;[14] (3) land owned or possessed by individuals, families, or *parcialidades* (residential clan groups) of the village;[15] (4) tracts claimed for use "since time immemorial" by the village or residents of the village without, at least from the perspective of the state, any legal basis. These latter the state commonly referred to as *excedientes* or *excesos* (i.e., excess land over the community's legal *ejido*), and they technically continued to be state land, called *realenga* in the colonial period and *terreno baldío* after 1821. There were also large tracts of state-owned land that remained unoccupied or only occasionally hosted a transient flock of sheep or a roving woodcutter. Both the colonial and the national state after 1821 recognized rights of de facto possession but, largely for fiscal reasons, sought to induce communities to title the land they used.

All *vecinos* (legal residents)[16] of the village generally had access to community lands for subsistence agriculture and stock raising. Most practiced shifting *milpa* (corn and beans) farming. Land surveyors (*agrimensores*), when they measured *ejidos*, commonly reported crossing large areas of *guatales*, the *monte* or second growth on fallow *milpa* land. Two sets of circumstances, however, might impede free access to and movement across community lands. Local power figures, whether hereditary or self-made *caciques*, Crown-appointed *gobernadores*, or elders (*principales*), and often in collusion with *ladino* officials or the local priest, sometimes conspired to gain control over tracts of community land, whether as legally titled private property or simply in de facto possession.[17] In addition, well-off (by village standards) or particularly well-organized or large families or clans might seek to establish preferential rights to certain areas. These residential groupings not uncommonly solidified into identifiable *cantones* or *aldeas* (hamlets), and reinforced their claims with ancestor crosses as well as surveys, *composición*, and title documents. Eventually they might seek independent *municipio* status.[18]

Outsiders who attempted to gain access to community land usually found this difficult. Under Spanish rule and for most of the nineteenth century prior to 1877, villages could sell land to those from outside the community only with the specific permission of the state.[19] The government, dependent for much of this period on revenue from Indian tribute, generally resisted the alienation of community resources, and before 1821 laws forbade, or discouraged, non-Indians from settling in the towns. The Indians shunned the few that managed to establish themselves there, treating them as a separate *parcialidad de ladinos* (*ladino* district) and specifically excluding them from participation in community land ownership.[20] Only for the most pressing need would a village consider selling land to someone not a native of the town. Within the community, of course, individual property of various sorts existed, parallel to and often intermixed with community-owned tracts. Such parcels, whether held as state-sanctioned private property or as a fixed possession in the peculiar tenure system of the community, had existed at least from the immediate postconquest years.[21] In general, though, and apart from clan claims, individual private property in land made little sense in a regimen of shifting cultivation.

When *ladinos* did penetrate village lands prior to 1877, it was usually through the institution of *censo enfiteusis*, a form of long-term rent available, at the discretion of the community, to *vecinos* and outsiders alike.[22] Towns typically entered into such agreements to raise money to meet tax demands, to fight an epidemic or other natural disaster, or to fund schools and public works. The annual rent for *vecinos* was usually 2 percent of the estimated value of the land; noncommunity members might be charged 3 percent. Contracts typically ran nine years and could be, and commonly were, renewed. Renters might sublet or sell their *dominio útil* (use rights) over the land, as well as any improvements or plantings they had made.[23] Over time, individuals tended and, indeed, some actively sought, to confuse *dominio útil* with legal ownership and to attempt to treat the land as private property. But the law was clear, and where the *municipio* detected and contested this usurpation, the state supported it.[24]

Social Relations before Coffee

The first decades of independence brought a cascade of new land laws notable both for their ineffectualness and for the hostility they engendered. Intent on modernizing their country to conform to the ideas of Bourbon political economy and imported English liberalism, and to meet such specific criticisms of Guatemala's problems as those raised in the famous *Apuntamientos* of 1810,[25] the leaders of the new state, and particularly the Liberals who dominated government policy from independence until 1839, passed law after law meant to convert *ejidos* and *terrenos baldíos* into private property and "family farms": "the small number of property owners is one of the causes of our backwardness."[26] To stimulate the productive use of land, they substituted a land tax, the *contribución territorial*, for the *diezmo* or tithe,[27] and auctioned off to private individuals the properties of the church's regular orders.[28]

Fundamental reform of an institution as deeply rooted in custom as land would have been difficult under the most favorable of circumstances; to undertake it in the midst of the civil wars that wracked Guatemala from the 1820s to the 1840s was suicidal. It is perhaps the best example of the first-generation Liberals' inability to reconcile largely utopian theory with reality, and it accomplished the unlikely feat of bringing many of the large landowners together with the indigenous population in opposition to the state. War, pestilence, and banditry stalked Guatemala in the 1830s, making a mockery of the Liberals' dreams of enlightenment and progress.[29] The stagnation of exports and the effects of the fighting curtailed state resources, while the demands of war drained off what little income was to be had. The state was strong enough to generate opposition but not to put its policies into effect; it could irritate and injure but it could neither protect nor control, especially in the countryside. A flurry of reactionary laws at the end of the 1830s could not save these Liberals, and in 1839 a peasant revolt led by Rafael Carrera swept them from power.[30] Harried by intrigue and revolts, foreign wars, and disease, the Conservatives who succeeded to power were no more able than had been the Liberals to enforce their writ in the rural areas. They simply made less effort to do so.

In a well-known chapter published some forty years ago, Oliver La Farge suggested that the years from the late 1830s through the 1860s were something of a golden age in the Guatemalan highlands for community autonomy and freedom from outside intervention.[31] Recent research tends to bear this out. A fragile and beleaguered state issued laws and decrees but could visit little effective attention on a rural population that resisted paying taxes and for whose land and labor the *ladino* elites had little use. The Conservatives revived the Laws of the Indies but, in fact, more neglected than protected the Indians. The church, weakened by disputes with the state and by declining revenues, lost much of its hold on the village populations. Enlightenment reforms, economic decline, and social chaos combined to strip the community *cofradías* (religious brotherhoods) of many of their resources and properties, prompting a marked decline in church and state interest in these institutions.[32] This situation freed up both the *cabildo* (town government) and the *cofradías* to become more genuinely indigenous political and religious vehicles. The communities, abandoned by the church and the central government and harassed but not overwhelmed by disease and war, were left for a generation largely to themselves to bring to full fruition the institutions of corporate organization associated with the "closed corporate peasant community" and "traditional" society.[33]

It is instructive, if not particularly edifying, to discover that the Indians of the *altiplano* used a good measure of their unaccustomed liberty to fight among themselves over land. Whereas the Spanish colonial regime had been able to enforce a minimum of order, if not justice, in the countryside, with the near collapse of the central state the villages laid into each other with enthusiasm and ferocity. Repeatedly the government sent surveyors to attempt to bring an end to these conflicts by drawing acceptable boundaries. They met with little success. The bewildered head of an 1850s survey commission reported, for example, that just in the area immediately north of Lake Atitlán:[34]

> SOLOLA had *pleitos* (disputes) with Totonicapán, hacienda "Argueta," Santo Tomás Chichicastenango, and Concepción Chirichiapa.
> SANTO TOMAS CHICHICASTENANGO was in conflict with Sololá, Tecpán Guatemala, Chiché, and Totonicapán.
> CHICHE fought with the hacienda "Tululche" and the town of Chinique.
> ZACUALPA disputed boundaries to Canillá and haciendas "Tululche" and "Chuacorral."
> SANTA CATARINA IXTAHUACAN fought, apparently, all of its neighbors, including Zunil, Cantel, and Santa Clara la Laguna.

Every hand was turned, seemingly quite literally, against its neighbor, as well as against any representative of the national government foolish enough to intervene. Prior to mid-century few of these disputes could have been motivated by genuine economic need. Communities such as Zunil or Santiago Atitlán or San Antonio Palopo, located along main travel routes or sited on poor land, probably developed land shortages even before the end of the colonial period.[35] But, generally, war, epidemics, and natural disasters limited population growth;[36] one estimate is of a general annual rate of no more than 1 percent for these years.[37] Except for a few *haciendas* dating back to the colony, outsiders rarely involved themselves as claimants in these conflicts. While some of the disputes between the towns focused on small parcels of particularly good quality land,[38] much of the terrain over which the villages fought was so cold, rocky, and without water that it could have been, in the absence of critical shortages, of little economic interest to anyone. Other motives for land disputes included efforts to control areas and sites linked to the ancestors and to traditional religious practices and to control land in order to dominate populations that might be made to pay service to the *municipio* and to the church in the *cabecera* (chief town). Struggle over land was also a useful mechanism to help construct and reinforce community solidarity.[39] If Spanish colonial policy did not explicitly set one community against another, it sought, in the interest of control and exploitation, to isolate one village from another and to destroy any basis of identification across indigenous society not strictly supervised by the church and the state.[40]

It will not do, of course, to carry this sort of functionalism too far, for the inhabitants of the municipalities fought among themselves with an enthusiasm almost equal to that with which they battled their neighbors. While it is of little use to attempt class analyses of nineteenth-century indigenous society,[41] there were rich individuals and families, and there were conflicts, and commonly these focused on land. Some disputes pitted the general population of *maceguales* (commoners) against their economic or hereditary betters, and others involved conflicting claims by families or *parcialidades* (community districts). The most common disputes, however, were simply boundary squabbles between neighbors of more or less equal situation.⁴² *Aldeas*, too, fell out among themselves, as well as with the *cabecera*.

One example, that of Santa Catarina Ixtahuacán, will do to illustrate these points.⁴³ For more than forty years violence wracked the community, dominating both internal politics and relations with neighbors and the state. One of the most densely populated municipalities of the central highlands and set on generally poor quality land, Santa Catarina began to suffer scarcity even before the end of the colonial period. In response, the inhabitants moved in two directions. They encroached on the lands of neighboring towns, including Santa Clara la Laguna, Cantel, Zunil, Santa María de Jesús, and San Miguel Totonicapán, and resisted violently any efforts to return them to their former boundaries. The *catarinecos* (residents of Santa Catarina Ixtahuacán) also squatted on vacant lands of the adjacent *boca costa* (piedmont), whether state *terrenos baldíos* or the *ejidos* of towns that had died out in the seventeenth and eighteenth centuries. Here they again ran into problems with their neighbors. Zunil, for example, responding to similar land shortages, resettled in the same period several extinguished towns and erected *aldeas* on state land. The claims of these overlapped with those of Santa Catarina, prompting decades of conflict. Hardworking, serious—Santa Catarina was one of the few municipalities able to enforce a ban on alcohol sales—and notoriously ferocious, Santa Catarina terrorized its neighbors and intimidated most of the state's representatives who sought to intervene. Even the priest existed on bare sufferance.

The central regime's lack of control over the countryside is perhaps nowhere more evident than in its inability to bring to an end the decades of conflict during which Santa Catarina tore itself apart. The problems stemmed from differential population growth within the municipality. Though technically only an *aldea*, the community of Nahualá by 1840 had more inhabitants than did the *cabecera*. Nahualá and its satellite communities also supplied the bulk of the population which had settled in the lowland areas colonized by the *municipio*. Thus, by mid-century, Santa Catarina proper increasingly found itself surrounded and outnumbered by a population that, for its part, more and more resented and resisted being forced to give time and taxes for the support of government and religion in the *cabecera*. Characteristically, the *catarinecos* reacted forcefully, attacking and attempting to drive dissidents from the community.

Not only could state authorities not bring this situation under control, but they commonly had little or no idea what was going on. This ineffectualness reached a peak of comic horror in an extended correspondence regarding a head in the possession of government officials. Apparently it had been cut off an individual to punish him for something and as an object lesson to someone, but to whom it had belonged, who had cut it off, and why, no one could discover! When the central government was not otherwise occupied elsewhere in defending itself from one or another band of rebels and bandits that plagued the countryside in these years, it sent troops to pacify Santa Catarina. But these were expensive to maintain in the field and seem to have done little beyond conspiring to smuggle in alcohol. *Ladino* officials ordered to investigate the situation found endless reasons to avoid exposing themselves to the dangers of Santa Catarina, knew little of what was going on, and cheerfully contradicted themselves from one letter to the next.

While the villages thus occupied themselves, Guatemala's export economy began to shift from cochineal (a red dye) to coffee. A series of disastrous cochineal "harvests" in the 1850s, the specter of aniline dyes wiping out the markets for natural dyestuffs, and Costa Rica's success with coffee drew the attention of Guatemalan planters to the new crop.[44] As an export staple, cochineal had always been limited by the precarious nature of the production process and by inadequate transportation facilities, and, as a consequence, it failed to rise above the level of artisan handicraft production or to expand much beyond the areas immediately around Antigua and Amatitlán.[45] Much of Guatemala proved to have ideal soils and climate for coffee, however, and production spread quickly to embrace wide areas of the countryside, from the Alta Verapaz to San Marcos on the Mexican border, previously largely untouched by export production. The result was the most fundamental change in the nation's economic, social, and political structures since the conquest.

Social Relations after Coffee

Coffee provided both the motivation and the wherewithal for the state to assert control over rural Guatemala, as this comparison of budgets from 1870 and 1890 shows.[46]

Budgets	Gobernación (Interior)	Guerra (War)
1870	$113,736	$67,323
1890	$303,167	$307,832

Coffee also prompted the accumulation and investment of unprecedented amounts of local and foreign money capital and credit, the contracting and temporary migration of large numbers of workers, and the construction of modern transport and communications facilities. By 1871 coffee amounted to half, by value, of the country's exports,[47] but planters were certain it had not yet begun to approach its full potential. Increasingly, their dissatisfaction focused on the state.

Central to this dissatisfaction was the inability or the unwillingness of the Conservatives to mobilize or to allow individuals to mobilize the production factors necessary to expand coffee production at the rate and to the extent that the planters deemed possible and desirable. Thousands of acres of state land sat practically useless for want of communications and labor and because inadequate surveys made it impossible to obtain clear title. Promising coffee land existed in the *ejidos* of a few indigenous communities that had survived on the south coast or that Indians from highland municipalities had resettled. Several of these had or sought to control very extensive areas: San Antonio Suchitepequez at one point claimed some seven hundred square leagues, and San Martín Sacatepequez claimed more than one thousand *caballerías* (*caballería* = 112 acres) in the Costa Cuca (the piedmont of the department of Quezaltenango), already singled out in the 1860s as a prime coffee area.[48] Pioneer coffee planters solicited land from the coast communities in *censo enfiteusis*. But most towns resisted, pointing out that permanent crops such as coffee were at odds with the nature of communal ownership and of shifting subsistence agriculture; when pressed, riots threatened or broke out.[49] Existing laws supported such community resistance, and the state generally enforced these. The Conservative regimes of Rafael Carrera (1839–1865) and, especially, Vicente Cerna (1865–1871) took steps to promote coffee,[50] but failed to carry forward such schemes as single mindedly as the planters wished.

It is hardly surprising that many of the coffee growers supported the Liberal Revolution of 1871. General Justo Rufino Barrios, himself a coffee planter from the San Marcos/Mexico border, seized control of the state and within a decade turned the country, with considerable assistance from market demand and foreign capital, into a major coffee producer. His Liberal Reforma built and encouraged private investors to build roads, railroads, ports, telegraphs, and other infrastructural improvements; the state founded an agricultural bank and encouraged the capitalization of private banks and the expansion of merchant banking. State policy swept aside obstacles to the use of land and labor for coffee and other commercial production. Exports boomed.[51]

Although a revised general land code did not appear until 1894,[52] the Liberal regime began almost immediately to issue decrees and new regulations meant to make land more readily and cheaply available for commercial agriculture. Among these was an 1873 provision that facilitated the sale of the lands of the Costa Cuca for coffee. Declared *baldíos*, in spite of various communities' claims, this land was to be sold at fixed prices rather than the generally more lucrative but awkward and time-consuming auction procedures specified for the alienation of state land under existing laws.[53] Other decrees opened public lands in the Alta Verapaz, Izabal, and Zacapa for cattle, rubber, chicle, wood cutting, and similar activities.[54] Potentially most revolutionary of all was Decree 170.[55] Issued in January 1877, this ended *censo enfiteusis*. In the interest of development and the presumed superior efficiency of private property, the law gave tenants who held parcels in *censo* a short time in which to buy them. The selling price was to be calculated by capitalizing the rent, but whereas, for outsiders, for example, the communities had calculated the rent as 3 percent of the estimated value of the land, under Decree 170 for purchase purposes the rent was taken to be 6 percent of the land's worth, effectively cutting the price in half! And the income from these sales went to the central government, not to the communities. Land that renters did not wish to buy or that had not been rented could, under article 13 of the decree, be denounced and purchased by anyone.

The Liberals did not "abolish" or "outlaw" community property. While an 1881 law in neighboring El Salvador declared that "[t]he *ejido* system in El Salvador is abolished," in Guatemala *ejidos* maintained a de facto and a de jure existence.[56] The *ley agraria* of 1894 repeated the guarantees of the 1820s and 1830s land laws, which recognized the rights of legally constituted communities to *ejidos*.[57] Claims to *excesos* received recognition as well. The Liberal Reforma in Guatemala maintained community lands in part because indigenous villages produced most of the country's food; in the late nineteenth century capitalist production of food for the domestic market could not compete with peasant production, even had investors been willing to divert funds from the more profitable fields of coffee and import-export trade. Preserving the *ejidos* also reinforced the communities' role as suppliers and reproducers of seasonal labor for the coffee estates.[58] Where a town lacked adequate resources, the state might intervene to help it acquire more land.[59] The actual situation of given villages at any point in time varied widely, depending upon the specific outcome of several centuries of internal and external struggles.

If the Liberals did not end community lands, they did privilege private property. Specifically, they encouraged, and usually wrote into titles

issued to villages, the conversion of *ejidos* and titled *excesos* into individual plots.[60] Any such transformation from community to private property, however, required a series of positive acts by the individual and/or
the local authorities. Unlike El Salvador, Guatemala proclaimed no blan-
ket decree. Instead, actual or would-be possessors had to apply individually to the state for title and carry forward complicated and expensive
procedures more or less in cooperation with the municipality. Many did.[61]
But in areas where the cultural values of community land ownership and
use persisted and where no internal conflicts or outside speculators seeking land forced a change, the regime of community and clan property
might remain in effect.[62]

The nature of coffee production in Guatemala dictated that, whatever
the law, its expansion did not immediately threaten the survival of most
communities. For towns of the *boca costa* (e.g., Pochuta, Samayac, San
Francisco Zapotitlán, or Coatepequel), of course, coffee hit the local
economy and society as a tidal wave, engrossing land and converting local inhabitants into *colonos* (resident workers) or day laborers on the *fincas*
(coffee plantations).[63] But by the 1870s and 1880s these were a very small
proportion of Guatemala's towns and of its rural population. At the other
pole were those towns wholly contained in the highlands (e.g., much of
central Quiché and the high valleys of the Cuchumatán mountains). Coffee growers initially had no use for or interest in the cold community
lands of these villages. Only gradually did the mechanisms of labor recruiting for coffee prompt planters and their agents to invade highland
ejidos, seeking control over land as a means to control workers and creating the infamous *fincas de mozos*, farms that produced workers.[64] Even
these intrusions resulted not so much in the villages' actually losing land
as in finding the conditions changed under which they had access to the
land.

The largest number of Indian communities fell somewhere between
those with all or none of their lands in the coffee piedmont. Many had
ejidos in the highlands but supplemented these with seasonal corn production on hot country land. Villages that actually bordered the coffee
lowlands—for example, Santiago Atitlán or San Pedro Sacatepequez (San
Marcos)—claimed the right to cultivate land there as part of the *excesos*
of their community *ejidos* or simply on the basis of traditional use rights.[65]
Others (e.g., Momostenango, Zunil, or Rabinal) sent inhabitants to found
new *aldeas* on the coast or north of Uspantán and Nebaj in the "Zona
Reina."[66] The overall effect of the expansion of coffee was to reduce and
constrain the access of these highland Indians to piedmont and coast lands
but not, in most cases, to cut it off abruptly or entirely. Individuals and
communities responded, too, to the new laws and the new competition for

land by titling tracts on the coast or by renting, for money or labor, hot country land. In other cases they simply continued to "squat," buttressed by tradition and need, on land that might technically be *terrenos baldíos* or private property but over which the legal owners were unable or unwilling to assert their rights. The coffee revolution upset the established subsistence equilibrium of towns dependent on part-time cultivation in the lowlands, but it did not immediately threaten the survival of these towns or the economic and social heart of the *común*, the "lands of the ancestors" most closely surrounding the village. Only with the rapid increases in population after 1900 would their plight become evident.

The immediately damaging effects of coffee's demands for cheap land and, especially, cheap labor were nevertheless substantial and readily apparent to the indigenous population. How did they react? Contrary to popular imagination, *tumultos* or revolts were rare after the mid-1870s and their number tended to decline, even as coffee production continued to increase. Violent outbursts did occur, but never on the scale or with the success of the 1830s and 1840s. And of those that did happen and can be linked to coffee, most actually took place in the 1860s before the Liberals took power, or in the early and mid-1870s before the new regime consolidated control. Many of these "revolts," when examined, prove, in fact, to have little or no socioeconomic content or to be outright fabrications growing out of local feuds or *ladino* paranoia. The records of the appeals court at Quezaltenango do reveal a burst of violence in 1898, but most of these resulted not from coffee but from Estrada Cabrera's seizure of power in that year. Perhaps, it might be argued, under the Liberals restive Indians were simply shot out of hand rather than brought to trial; an examination of the records of Gobernación (Ministry of the Interior),[67] however, while it reveals scattered additional examples of conflicts brought on by the invasion of coffee and the summary repression these provoked, just as it shows other instances of conflict for the years before 1871, suggests nothing that significantly alters the angle on the graph on the next page.

An independent measure of the extent to which violence decreased was the fate of the land surveyors who criss-crossed the countryside measuring grants, sales, and *ejidos*. Before the 1870s they commonly worked in peril of their lives. Routinely, surveyors asked for, and occasionally a penurious and preoccupied state provided them, an escort of soldiers. Without this escort, a number had occasion to flee for their lives when their measurements went against local demands and expectations. Less fortunate ones were imprisoned by municipal officials, manhandled, or even killed by enraged mobs.[68] In contrast, by the 1890s even when the villagers felt aggrieved they generally contained their anger and turned instead to petitions to *tata presidente* or to the courts. More and more, in

Appeals Court cases labeled "Rebellions," Quezaltenango, 1820–1900[69]

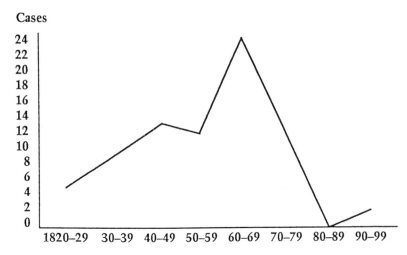

Cases

the words of the inhabitants of Santa Eulalia, they "went before the law" rather than take up arms.[70]

The muted nature of the conflicts that accompanied the spread of coffee after 1871 was the result of several factors. The pressure for land was dispersed over a wide area and for an extended period of time. Few communities faced an immediately identifiable "life or death" situation, and none saw it as an issue around which they could unite with other towns. If a community lost its coast lands, the inhabitants still had the *ejidos* around the village. But, as pointed out above, few towns actually lost access to all of their hot country lands, at least not all at once. More commonly, the villages exchanged vague or traditional claims to a quite extensive area for clear, at least temporarily, title to lesser amounts. For those not yet suffering severe population pressures and land shortages— and few were before the end of the century—this may not have seemed, or indeed have been, a bad bargain. Santiago Atitlán, for example, lost the use of much land between the town and Patulul but titled one hundred *caballerías* of *ejidos*, and many individuals and family groups from the town acquired tracts on the piedmont and lower coast.[71] Atitecos, forced out by the creation of the *municipio* of Chicacao, received in compensation twice as much state land nearby, as did the *vecinos* of Santa Catarina Ixtahuacán made to leave Parraché.[72] If *ladinos* and *ladino* towns, usually led by local militia members,[73] received the lion's share of the new lands to the north opened up in the 1880s and 1890s, indigenous communities were not shut out.[74] Overall, the fate of a community depended on a village's location and population, and the resulting demands for land and/

or labor made upon that particular town, and on how quickly local leaders came to understand the changing situation and to effectively play by the new rules.[75] Broad generalities are of little help. However, in all but the most severe cases, the effects of the coffee revolution were subtle and incremental and extremely difficult for the indigenous communities to mobilize, or to remain mobilized, against.

Too, the Liberal regime sought as much as possible to minimize violence in the countryside. The goal of national leaders and their planter allies was to enrich themselves, which, in a happy coincidence, they equated with national development. It was not simply to harass Indians. Violence discouraged needed foreign and domestic investment, led to destruction of equipment, plantings, and infrastructure, and interrupted the labor supply, as the experience of the 1830s and 1840s clearly demonstrated. In this context, it should be remembered that, prior to the 1930s, labor, not land, was the scarce production factor in Guatemalan export agriculture.

For their part, the indigenous population quickly learned that if violence broke out, the balance of power had turned decisively against them. The days when a community such as Santa Catarina Ixtahuacán could hold the state at bay for decades were past. The Liberals created the modern, centralized state in Guatemala and tied it together with a network of telegraph lines that, by the end of the 1880s, penetrated all corners of the country. *Comandantes locales* (local military chiefs) and *comisionados políticos* (state political agents in the local communities) kept tabs on anything "unusual" in their jurisdiction and reported it up the hierarchy to the president; telegraph operators worked late into the night sending reports on local conditions and receiving orders, circulars, and labor requisitions.[76]

The new regime began professionalization of the military, creating an officers' training school in 1873 and arming the regulars and the militia with modern repeating rifles.[77] Even masses of Indians armed only with rocks, sticks, and colonial-era shotguns were no match for this. The Liberals put in place and organized the means for the central state to project itself into the interior as had never before been possible.

A brief look at one of the better known *tumultos* of the last decades of the century, the outbreak of violence at San Juan Ixcoy in 1898, confirms the new preponderance of state power.[78] Conflict over land arose in the early 1890s between San Juan and members of the *ladino* militia of Soloma to the north and that of Chiantla to the south. These groups presented the government with claims to hundreds of *caballerías*, which they labeled *terrenos baldíos* but which San Juan regarded as traditional community property. In an effort to stave off such claims, San Juan put in its own for 250 *caballerías*. To pay for measuring and titling this land, the *principales* of San Juan sold labor from the community to the coffee *finca* Buenos Aires. But violence broke out between the towns and threatened the *agrimensor*, who fled the area, bringing the measurement process to a halt. When *finca* agents demanded promised labor, the Indians, who linked the labor sale to the titling process, refused to go. Finally, apparently goaded by the *habilitadores* (plantation labor agents), the *sanjuaneros* on the evening of July 17, 1898, set fire to the *cabildo* where a hapless group of labor agents slept and cut them down as they attempted to flee. Hoping to eliminate dangerous witnesses, the Indians then spread out through the village to kill the rest of the *ladinos* living there. One managed to escape to Soloma. Early the next morning the militia of Soloma and, evidently alerted by telegraph, that of Chiantla rode into town, killing unknown numbers of Indians and sending some sixty to Huehuetenango for trial. There could hardly be a more graphic demonstration of the state's capacity for repression.[79]

If the indigenous population less and less commonly rose up in revolt, it did resist. To escape labor demands, individuals and groups fled to other towns and *fincas*, into the wilderness, or across the borders to Belize and Mexico.[80] Towns went to court over land disputes and courted the personalist intervention of the officials and the president. Above all, the communities manifested a constant and well-founded suspicion of and consistent, if usually nonviolent but certainly not passive, opposition to *ladino* and state schemes. Liberal rule, as does that of any state, rested ultimately on the proven ability of government agents to deliver effective violence to communities and individuals in response to unacceptable resistance to the mandates of the state and the classes whose interests that state served. But the regime and, particularly, the planters had no wish to make uninterrupted war on a population whose labor was vital to their prosperity. The result, therefore, was compromise, though, admittedly, a compromise heavily weighted in favor of *finqueros*. Violence by no means disappeared from the countryside. Above all, it permeated the labor recruiting in the villages and labor relations on the *fincas*. What had largely disappeared was the *tumulto* as an effective form of resistance by the indigenous community to the state. The primeval Indian, fire and machete in hand, remained a vivid *ladino* nightmare, though one, at least until very recently, with less and less basis in fact.

Conclusion

This chapter has argued several points. The social, economic, and, particularly, the land situation within and between several communities, and between communities and *ladinos* in nineteenth-century Guatemala, was much more complex than is usually understood. This complexity increased after mid-century under the impact of growing demands for land and labor to service the export economy. There existed vast differences in wealth and security within and between the communities, the result of geography, differential rates of population growth and ecological degradation, family and clan claims, and the accidents of history. Coffee exacerbated these. The uneven development of capitalism in the industrial centers and, as a result, the ebb and flow of the world capitalist system meant that various regions of Guatemala found themselves drawn into the coffee economy at different times and under different conditions.[81] The interaction of these differing circumstances with the peculiar situation and conditions of each community had the result that the process of incorporation, while exhibiting broad similarities, was specific to each case. To discover and examine the regional and local variants of this process of primitive accumulation remains an important object of the rural history of Guatemala.[82]

The efforts of the Liberal state after 1871 to organize the exploitation of land and labor for export production were more sophisticated, more subtle, and more suited to Guatemala's situation than is usually credited. In contrast to the direct assault on village lands characteristic of El Salvador after 1881, which provoked a half-century of uprisings, Guatemala's Reforma Liberals undertook what might best be described as a flank attack on the resources of the indigenous communities. They did this for several reasons. There was some fear, at least early on, of a repeat of the successful peasant-based reaction of the 1830s. Liberal ideology held that the Indian was lazy, dirty, and drunken, but it also portrayed him as sly, vicious, brutal, and prone to violence. The revolt of the Remicheros[83] in the Oriente and a succession of minor risings in the highlands in the 1870s and 1880s linked to the folk memory of Serapio Cruz[84] suggest that fear of a highland-wide *tumulto* was not entirely misplaced, at least until the state reorganized and reequipped the army and consolidated its control. The highland towns also reproduced cheap labor and sustained it in the off season and produced most of the country's food and many necessary handicrafts (e.g., woolen cloth). Most of all, of course, the coffee planters in the majority of cases did not need core community lands for productive purposes and only slowly and indirectly penetrated them as a by-product of labor recruiting. The initial impact of Liberal land policy and coffee was, thus, to cut away at the peripheral community lands while reinforcing control over the core *ejido*.

Far from increasing with the effects of coffee, overt violence, with the exception of that associated with labor recruiting and control, declined in all areas and at all levels of Guatemalan rural society during the course of the nineteenth century. Rural banditry almost disappeared.[85] More to the point, violence between communities and between communities and the state over land, a staple of rural life in the first half of the century, drop-ped off dramatically after 1871. Liberal land laws and state efforts to enforce these touched off no widespread revolts as occurred in El Salvador and Nicaragua in this period. If one wishes to argue that the state is by definition institutionalized violence, and class violence at that, augmented state power may be equated with increased violence, but the very effectiveness of the state meant that this violence remained increasingly imminent rather than manifest. Coffee devastated the indigenous population and communities, but their reaction was muted by the growing power of the state and was, therefore, transmuted or channeled into new vehicles—vehicles probably more effective for indigenous purposes than the old *tumultos* and certainly less likely to bring down the soldiers on the community.

Notes

Abbreviations for works frequently cited:

AGCA   Archivo General de Centroamérica, Guatemala.
AGCA MG   Archivo General de Centroamérica, Ministerio de
                Gobernación.
AGCA-ST   Archivo General de Centroamérica, Sección de
                Tierras.

    1. Susanne Jonas and David Tobis, eds., *Guatemala* (New York, 1974); Edwin Grieshaber, "Hacienda-Indian Community Relations and Indian Acculturation," *Latin American Research Review*, 14:3 (1979), 119. See also Julio C. Cambranes, *Coffee and Peasants in Guatemala* (Stockholm, 1985), for a more subtle vision of land loss still fundamentally in agreement with the argument cited.
    2. Manuel Pineda de Mont, ed., *Recopilación de las leyes de Guatemala*, vol. III (Guatemala, 1869–1872), 679.
    3. J. C. Méndez Montenegro, "444 años de legislación agraria, 1520–1957," *Revista de la Facultad de Ciéncias Jurídicas y Sociales de Guatemala*, Epoca VI (1960), 136.
    4. David McCreery, "Coffee and Class: The Structure of Development in Liberal Guatemala," *Hispanic American Historical Review*, 56:3 (August 1976), 457.
    5. Jim Handy, *Gift of the Devil: A History of Guatemala* (Toronto, 1984), 72. For a more developed argument of the rebelliousness of the indigenous population, see Robert M. Carmack, *Historia social de los Quichés* (Guatemala, 1979), 264–269.
    6. Ralph Lee Woodward, Jr., "Social Revolution in Guatemala: The Carrera Revolt," in *Applied Enlightenment: Nineteenth Century Liberalism, 1830–1839* (New Orleans, 1971), 43–70.

7. William B. Taylor, *Drinking, Homicide, and Rebellion in Colonial Mexican Villages* (Stanford, 1979), 114, writing about colonial Mexico but in terms equally applicable to the late-nineteenth-century highland Guatemala, defines "rebellions" as "localized mass attacks, generally limited to restoring a customary order . . . [S]pontaneous, short-lived outbursts by members of a single community in reaction to threats from outside."

8. AGCA MG, leg. 38595, exp. 39, 51; David McCreery, "Land, Labor, and Violence in Highland Guatemala: San Juan Ixcoy, Huehuetenango, 1893–1945," *The Americas*, 45:2 (October 1988), 237–249.

9. *Alcabala* lists for the last years of the colony give a good indication of the distribution of rural property: AGCA, A3.5 1155 20488 (Quezaltenango), 352 7308 (Huehuetenango and Totonicapán), 352 7309 (Sololá), 352 7314 (Verapaz), and 352 7320 (Chiquimula), among others.

10. Pedro Cortes y Larraz, *Descripción geográfica-moral de la diócesis de Goathemala* (Guatemala, 1958), 115.

11. On the *ladino/mestizo* "agrarian bloc," see Severo Martínez Peláez, *La Patria del criollo: Ensayo de interpretación de la realidad colonial guatemalteca* (Guatemala, 1971), 366–417; and Julio C. Pinto Soria, *Estructura agraria y asentamiento en la Capitanía General de Guatemala (algunos apuntes históricos)* (Guatemala, 1981), 36, note 39; for an example of *ladino* settlement—Zaragosa—struggling with a land shortage see AGCA-ST, Chimaltenango, paquete (paq.)1/ expediente (exp.) 17 (1830), paq. 2/exp. 7 (1840), and paq. 20/exp. 8 (1900).

12. Measurements changed over the three hundred years of the colony, but one square league (*a sitio de ganado mayor*) equaled approximately 38 3/8 "new" *caballerías* (as opposed to 36 "old" *caballerías*); a "new" *caballería* contained slightly less than 112 acres.

13. AGCA, A3.30 2578 37864.

14. AGCA, A1.23, leg. 4570, exp. 39326; Francisco de Solano, *Tierra y sociedad en el reino de Guatemala* (Guatemala, 1977), 114.

15. Robert M. Hill and John Monaghan, *Continuities in Highland Maya Social Organization: Ethnohistory in Sacapulas, Guatemala* (Philadelphia, 1987).

16. By definition this excluded all *ladinos* illegally living in *pueblos de indios*.

17. AGCA, 1855; leg. 28568, exp. 248; & leg. 28619, exp. 254.

18. Hill and Monaghan, *Continuities*, chap. 9.

19. Pineda de Mont, *Recopilación*, 658, 663.

20. AGCA-ST, Huehuetenango 1901: paq. 21, exp. 10.

21. AGCA, "tierras," 6033 53213.

22. Pineda de Mont, *Recopilación*, 661.

23. For examples of *censo* and the sale of *dominio útil* around Antigua during the cochineal boom, see the records of notaries José María Llerena, 1830–1844, and José María Cáceres, 1847–1877, AGCA.

24. AGCA-ST, Chimaltenango 1858: paq. 3, exp. 6.

25. José María García Laguardia, *La génesis de constitucionalismo guatemalteco* (Guatemala, 1971), appendix.

26. Pineda de Mont, *Rocopilación*, 658.

27. AGCA, B. 78.24714 15934; AEG, "Libro de la contribución territorial, 1833–1839."

28. Mary P. Holleran, *Church and State in Guatemala* (New York, 1949), 58–59.

29. See, for examples, the violence cataloged in the AGCA card file under "Asaltos en cuadrilla," box 2–28.

30. Hazel Ingersoll, "The War of the Mountain: A Study of Reactionary Peasant Insurgency in Guatemala, 1837–1873," Ph.D. diss., George Washington University, 1972.

31. Oliver La Farge, "Maya Ethnology: The Sequence of Cultures," in Clarence L. Hay et al., eds., *The Maya and Their Neighbors* (New York, 1940), 282–291.

32. AEG, "Cartas" Feb. 8, 1855, #0042, correspondence of *cura* of Jacaltenango, March 16, 1857.

33. For a review of the literature on the "closed corporate community," see Frank Cancian, "Political and Religious Organizations," in Manning Nash, ed., *Social Anthropology*, Vol. 6 of the *Handbook of Middle American Indians* (Austin, 1967); an extended recent critique of the concept can be found in Robert Wasserstrom, *Class and Society in Central America* (Berkeley, 1983).

34. AGCA MG, leg. 28569, exp. 33.

35. AGCA-ST, Quetzaltenango 1833: paq. 2, exp. 15; AGCA-ST, Sololá 1896: paq. 9, exp. 5; Douglas Madigan, "Santiago Atitlán, a Socio-Economic and Demographic History," Ph.D. diss., University of Pittsburgh, 1976.

36 .One of the worst was the locust epidemic that swept up the west coast from the south in 1801 and lasted until 1806 (AGCA, A1.2.5 2835 25239); locusts remained a problem for Guatemalan food and export agriculture until at least the 1940s (*El Imparcial*, August 16, 1943).

37. Ralph Lee Woodward, Jr., "Population and Development in Guatemala, 1840–1870," *SECOLAS Annals, Journal of the Southeastern Council on Latin American Studies*, 14 (1983), 5–18.

38. AGCA "tierras," 6022 52101.

39. Eric Van Young, "Conflict and Solidarity in Indian Village Life: The Guadalajara Region in the Late Colonial Period," *Hispanic American Historical Review*, 64:1 (February 1984), 55–79.

40. On the transition from indigenous population to "Indians" in Guatemala see Martínez Peláez, *La patria del criollo*, chap. 5; more broadly, see Steve Stern, *Peru's Indian Peoples and the Challenge of Spanish Conquest: Huamanga to 1640* (Madison, 1982).

41. Eric R. Wolf, *Europe and the People Without History* (Berkeley, 1982), chap. 3.

42. AGCA, "tierras," 6022 52101.

43. The following paragraphs are based on a wide range of material, including: AGCA-ST, Sololá, paq. 2, exp. 5 (1853) and paq. 6, exp. 2 (1860); AGCA MG, leg. 28586, exp. 200; leg. 28600, exp. 184, 185, and 186; and leg. 28610, exp. 351; and AEG, "Cartas," January 2, 1854, #001.

44. Ignacio Solís, *Memorias de la Casa de Moneda de Guatemala y del desarrollo económico del país* (Guatemala, 1979).

45. See AGCA MG, leg. 28536, exp. 145 for a description of cochineal production in Sacatepequez.

46. Solís, *Memorias*, 1089–1091; *Memoria del Ministerio de Gobernación, 1891*, 63.

47. Solís, *Memorias*, 911.

48. AGCA-ST, Quetzaltenango, 1815, paq. 1, exp. 15.

49. AGCA MG, leg. 28593, exp. 130.

50. The Conservatives drew up and approved but apparently never published a new land law: AGCA MG, leg. 28623, exp. 159 (1870).

51. David McCreery, *Development and the State in Reforma Guatemala, 1871–1885* (Athens, OH, 1983).
52. Méndez Montenegro, "444 años," 234–238.
53. Ibid., 123–164.
54. Ibid., 150–158.
55. Ibid., 133–141.
56. David Browning, *El Salvador: Landscape and Society* (Oxford, 1971).
57. Méndez Montenegro, "444 años," 234–238.
58. David McCreery, "Debt Servitude in Rural Guatemala, 1871–1885," *Hispanic American Historical Review*, 63:4 (November 1983), 735–759; idem, " 'An Odious Feudalism': Mandamiento and Commercial Agriculture in Guatemala, 1858–1920," *Latin American Perspectives*, 13 (1986), 99–118.
59. Méndez Montenegro, "444 años," 260.
60. AGCA-ST, Huehuetenango, 1989, paq. 11, exp. 10.
61. Compare the experiences of the two neighboring towns of Comalapa (AGCA-ST, Chimaltenango, 1989, paq. 8, exp. 10) and Poaquil (AGCA-ST, Chimaltenango, 1892, paq. 9, exp. 2). For reasons not yet clear, there was a burst of *lotificación* (the conversion of community holdings into lots of private property) in highland towns in the early 1890s, but this still involved only a small percentage of the indigenous communities.
62. A common subterfuge meant to satisfy Liberal laws was for a *principal* or *principales* to title community land in their name(s): AGCA-ST, Quiché, 1893, paq. 7, exp. 7. For some of the problems to which this might lead, see Shelton H. Davis, "Land of Our Ancestors: A Study of Land Tenure and Inheritance in the Highlands of Guatemala," Ph.D. diss., Harvard University, 1970, chap. 4.
63. See, for example, the memories of this experience in Pochuta: Instituto Indigenista de Guatemala, "monografía," #264 Pochuta.
64. McCreery, "Land, Labor, and Violence"; Tani Adams, "San Martín Jilotepeque: Aspects of the Political and Socioeconomic Structure of a Guatemalan Peasant Community," unpublished manuscript, no date.
65. Madigan, "Santiago Atitlán," chap 5; Sandra L. Orellana, "Ethnic Identity and the Tzutujil Maya: A Socio-Political Analysis, 1250–1815," Ph.D. diss., University of California, Los Angeles, 1976.
66. AGCA-ST, Quetzaltenango, 1850, paq. 4, exp. 5; 1878, paq. 9, exp. 17; AGCA-ST. Quiché, 1906, paq. 22, exp. 8; Carmack, *Historia social*, 247–253.
67. There exists a card file index in the AGCA of some use for Gobernación for the years from the 1830s to 1900. Many of the cards inaccurately reflect the contents of the *expedientes*, however, and in some cases *legajos* have been reorganized and/or renumbered, rendering the index useless for these materials.
68. AGCA MG, 1859, leg. 28578, exp. 133; 1865, leg. 28598, exp. 52.
69. These figures come from the indices to *Juzgado de Primera Instancia, criminal*, available in the AGCA. Included in this count are many cases labeled "tumulto," "rebelión," "sedición," and anything that indicated resistance to authority. Each of these was checked for all of the western departments, the south coast, the Verapaz, and the chief departments of the Oriente; for several departments (e.g., Chiquimula or Escuintla), indices are not available or began only after the period treated here. In many cases there was no evident political content to the disturbance but these were, nevertheless, included in the count, as it often was unclear from the documents exactly what was happening. Similar indices are available, and were checked, for the appeals courts.

70. Davis, "Land of Our Ancestors."

71. AGCA-ST, Solalá, 2822, paq. 1, exp. 5; 1894, paq. 2, exp. 7.

72. AGCA-ST, Solalá, 1895, paq. 7, exp. 7.

73. AGCA-ST, Solalá, 1889, paq. 4, exp. 10; McCreery, "Land, Labor, and Violence."

74. For dozens of titles in the Barillas (Huehuetenango) area, see AGCA-ST, Huehuetenango, paqs. 14–30, and for Uspantán, see AGCA-ST, Quiché, paqs. 5–29.

75. It is a mistake to think that the indigenous population of nineteenth-century Guatemala lost land chiefly because they did not understand the new laws or their implications. They disagreed with Liberal views on the nature and proper use of land, but their reluctance to enter into titling procedures stemmed more from problems of the costs involved, distrust of *ladino* officials and courts, and the often shaky basis of their own claims than from ignorance.

76. For a list of telegraph offices and the dates they were established, see *Memoria de Ministerio de Fomento*, 1924, 251–253.

77. Michael McClintock, *The American Connection: State Terror and Popular Resistance in Guatemala* (London, 1985), chap. 1.

78. McCreery, "Land, Labor, and Violence."

79. Robert Carmack, "Barrios y los indígenas: el caso de Santiago Momostenango," *Estudios sociales*, 6 (1972), 264–269, describes a similar revolt arising out of land conflicts in the 1870s at Momostenango. He notes that "[Justo Rufino] Barrios reacted quickly and with force," visiting a "horroroso castigo" (terrible punishment) (p. 267) on the town.

80. McCreery, "Debt Servitude"; idem, " 'An Odious Feudalism.' "

81. The uneven development of capitalism at the center meant that the export sector drew in different areas of Guatemala at different times and under different conditions. See Carol Smith, "Local History in Global Context: Social and Economic Transitions in Western Guatemala," *Comparative Studies in Society and History*, 26:2 (1984), 193–228.

82. The best introduction to primitive accumulation remains Karl Marx, *Capital*, vol. 1, pt. 8: "So- Called Primitive Accumulation" (London, 1976).

83. Manuel Rubio Sánchez, *Los jueces reformadores de milpas en Centroamérica* (Guatemala, 1982), 166ff.

84. These erupted as late as the mid-1880s (AEG, "Cartas," May 20, 1886, #343).

85. Compare travelers' accounts from the 1830s and 1840s, for example, Robert G. Dunlop, *Travels in Central America* (London, 1847) or John L. Stephens, *Incidents of Travel in Central America, Chiapas, and Yucatan* (New York, 1969 [1841]), with those of the 1880s and 1890s, such as William T. Brigham, *Guatemala: The Land of the Quetzal* (Gainesville, 1965 [1887]) or Anne C. M. Maudsley, *A Glimpse of Guatemala and Some Notes on Ancient Monuments of Central America* (New York, 1979 [reprint]).

9

Yaqui Resistance to Mexican Expansion

Evelyn Hu-DeHart

The Yaqui people of northwest Mexico have maintained a remarkable record of ethnic solidarity and resistance to the unwanted demands and incursions of the colonial and national governments of Mexico. Like the Araucanians of Chile described in Chapter 4, the Yaquis accepted some cultural modifications in order to retain their political autonomy.

This selection describes the measures the Yaquis took to combat the unprecedented onslaught on their lands, strongly supported by the dictator Porfirio Díaz, in the late nineteenth century. This struggle resembles a number of others by native peoples in the eighteenth and nineteenth centuries. Often the leaders of these movements were acculturated individuals—such as Cajeme of the Yaqui—who renounced their affiliation with the European sector of society in favor of reinvigorating the autonomy and traditions of their natal peoples.

Many native societies were subordinated by strong national governments that emerged in Latin America in the late nineteenth century. The entrepreneurs of that prosperous era coveted the lands and labor that the natives controlled, and the governments sought to bring all national territory under their effective jurisdictions. Although Cajeme's movement was defeated, the Yaquis continued to resist. Ultimately, through their military participation on the winning side in the Mexican Revolution, the Yaquis attained government recognition of their sovereignty over their lands, some political autonomy, and protection of their traditional cultural and religious practices.

When Vice-Governor José T. Otero addressed the Seventh Constitutional Congress of Sonora in September 1879, he cried out angrily that "there is in this state an anomaly whose existence is shameful for Sonora." He used these words to denounce the Yaquis' "separate nation within the state" and called upon the federal government to give financial and military assistance to destroy such a dangerous situation.[1] Having always considered themselves a separate nation in name and spirit, the Yaquis had made this concept a formal political reality as well. Credit for it belonged primarily to Cajeme, the most extraordinary leader in Yaqui history.

Unusual for the broad experiences he had had outside the Yaqui River before assuming leadership of his people, Cajeme restructured Yaqui society, introduced new methods of waging warfare, and disciplined the Yaquis to rely on their own resources and initiative in confronting the hostile Mexican world. Never since the days of the Jesuit missions were the Yaquis more tightly organized, more secure economically, more prepared militarily, than they were under Cajeme. His goal was not to extend Yaqui hegemony beyond its traditional boundaries, but to strengthen and preserve that autonomy which his people had always claimed was rightfully theirs. That is why his position was essentially a defensive one. His Mexican adversaries unanimously acknowledged their great respect for the man, his intellect and accomplishments, even as they put their heads and resources together to crush his regime.

Born José María Leyva in Hermosillo in 1837, the son of Yaquis Francisco Leyva and Juana Pérez, Cajeme spent the first years of his life in the Yaqui pueblo of Ráum. In 1849, while just a lad of twelve, José María went with his father to California for the gold rush.[2] Not finding the pot of gold that they had dreamed about, father and son returned home after a few years, dejected and disillusioned. But Francisco and Juana Leyva still wanted a better life for their son, so they sent him to school in Guaymas, entrusting him to the guardianship of Prefect Cayetano Navarro. At the age of eighteen, having learned the rudiments of reading and writing in Spanish, José María joined the Guaymas defense forces against the French filibuster, the Count de Raousset Boulbon. Then he drifted south to Sinaloa, where he was briefly apprenticed to a blacksmith before he was drafted into the army. Unwilling to tolerate the harsh life of a lowly recruit, José María escaped to work in a nearby mine. During the wars of the reform (1859–1861), José María volunteered for a Sonoran battalion commanded by Ignacio Pesqueira, who was then defending Liberalism in Sinaloa. After Pesqueira recaptured the crucial port of Mazatlán from the Conservatives, José María returned to Sonora with the governor.

When they arrived in Sonora, the Yaquis were in rebellion; José María immediately signed up for the expeditionary forces sent against the rebels, his own people but with whom he had had practically no contact during his adolescence. Afterwards, he also fought for Governor Pesqueira against the Gandaristas. During these years, when not serving in the military, José María drifted around the state with no stable occupation. In 1867, he again volunteered for the Yaqui campaign, then commanded by Próspero S. Bustamante, and probably witnessed the infamous Bácum massacre of that year. Until mid-1868, José María fought in the Yaqui against his own people and distinguished himself so valiantly in combat that he was elevated to the rank of captain with his own company of one hundred. By the time of the Carlos Conant revolt in 1873, José María Leyva had become a dependable volunteer for the state forces whenever there was a crisis. In recognition of his many services, Governor Pesqueira awarded him the post of alcalde mayor of the Yaqui River, undoubtedly with the hope that he would help the government pacify his indomitable people and obtain their total and permanent submission. There is no indication that the Yaqui manipulated himself into this position of authority.

Soon after he became alcalde mayor, however, José María Leyva betrayed Pesqueira's trust in him and abruptly changed his entire attitude towards the Mexican government. Shocked and dismayed, state officials suggested that Leyva, after returning to the Yaqui River, became "conquered by the Yaquis' imperishable tendency to maintain themselves independent."[3] This brief but insightful observation probably explained the whole story of how José María Leyva became the great Yaqui leader Cajeme, which means in the Yaqui language "He who does not drink."

Cajeme first made himself heard as leader of the Yaquis in the middle of 1875, when Sonora was in the throes of a hotly contested election between Ignacio Pesqueira's puppet José Pesqueira and the caudillo's former protégé Jesús García Morales. Threatening to rebel if his message was not heeded, Cajeme announced he would not recognize the government unless the Yaquis were granted total freedom to govern themselves, because they were the "natural owners" of the Yaqui River. At first the authorities did not view Cajeme with much alarm, because Yaquis had not caused great trouble since 1868. "The Yaquis are not as terrible as they used to be," officials comforted themselves. But they must have had an inkling of what was taking place in the Yaqui, for they also warned that the Yaquis must not be allowed to form "a separate republic."[4]

Granted extraordinary powers of the treasury and war to suppress the insolent Yaquis, Governor Pesqueira immediately raised a forced loan of thirty-five thousand pesos. Before he could proceed to the Yaqui, however, Francisco Serna pronounced against him and José Pesqueira, who was about to take office as the new governor. This delay allowed the Yaqui rebellion to gain momentum, as rebel bands raided and pillaged ranchos and haciendas. Following the orders of Cajeme, they burned to the ground Cócorit, the pueblo which colonists had most infiltrated. Many white families had already fled the Yaqui in fear; traders who customarily did business in the river were afraid to reenter. To make matters worse for the government, Mayos also rose up in rebellion, burning in their turn Santa Cruz, an important port for the Alamos merchants.[5]

Since the rebellion coincided with the Sernista movement, Governor José Pesqueira feared another of the formidable alliances and deemed it imperative to suppress the rebels first. In fact, he had already received reports that Sernista agent Gabriel Monteverde was seen trying to persuade the Yaquis to join the cause. On November 26, Pesqueira marched into the Yaqui with five hundred men, reinforced shortly by a "company of natives" from Huírivis.[6] On December 1, Colonel Eleazar B. Muñoz led three battalions, a cavalry force, and the Huírivis company on the first foray. Hoping to conclude the campaign rapidly and avoid violent open confrontation, he offered Cajeme the chance to negotiate a settlement. Cajeme scoffed at the attempt to make peace with the curt message that he would be waiting for the Mexicans.

At the first battle, government troops engaged Cajeme's five-hundred-man force in forty-five minutes of hard fighting. When the rebels dispersed, they left behind fifty-six dead bodies strewn over the field, according to government reports.[7] Colonel Muñoz stayed in the Yaqui until the last day of December, advancing as far as the middle of the river territory. Although he did not encounter Cajeme again, he had several skirmishes with smaller bands of rebels. In reconnoitering the entire territory, his men found only a few deserted camps and several wandering families, although they did manage to round up several hundred head of cattle, horses, and sheep. The results after a month of the campaign were clearly not encouraging.[8]

With Cajeme deliberately elusive and unwilling to negotiate, and with the Sernista revolt gathering strength throughout the state, José Pesqueira was forced to call off the Yaqui campaign and concentrate his energies on the Sernistas instead. With all the bad news, the governor was perhaps heartened by Cajeme's decision, despite the advice of some of his subordinates, not to join the Sernistas. Nor did Cajeme ally with any subsequent opposition to the Pesqueiras.[9] Because the Yaquis remained uncommitted to any outside political faction, they called little attention to themselves during the next three years, which saw Pesqueira deposed and a new regime come into office. Yaquis spent the interlude quietly but methodically reorganizing their society according to Cajeme's novel ideas.

Cajeme did not shut off the Yaqui River entirely from the outside world, which he needed as much as it needed the Yaqui. He allowed non-Yaquis to enter the river, by foot or by water, for certain legitimate businesses. Ship captains, for example, continued to ply between the port of Guaymas and El Médano, the entrance to the Yaqui River, trading clothes and cheap trinkets for firewood, straw mats, and other products that Yaquis manufactured. Individual traders also came by land, mainly to buy the salt that Yaquis mined on the coast.

On the basis of this trade, Cajeme instituted a tax system, probably the first one in Yaqui history. He charged a duty on imports brought in by ships and exacted a toll from traders and all other travelers. In addition to the money collected in this manner, he imposed another form of taxation: ship captains had to deliver a certain quantity of guns and ammunition on each trip from Guaymas. Moreover, individual travelers who carried firearms had to contribute them to the Yaqui arsenal. Later Cajeme extended this obligation to deserters from the state or federal armies who sought refuge in the Yaqui.

At first Cajeme did not restrict the mobility of Yaquis themselves to and from the river, although his presence most likely attracted many Yaquis on the outside back to their homeland. Individuals or families continued to move about the state, either to trade or to work in the customary places. When they returned, they often brought back guns and ammunition, purchased or obtained through other means from the towns and Mexican communities.[10]

To increase the revenues internally, Cajeme revived a practice that was most effective in the old mission days—the community plots. Each pueblo in the Yaqui had to plant a field of a certain size and maintain a rotation of workers to cultivate these fields. Some of the harvest might have been traded, but most of it was stored. Another ingenious and rather devious source of revenue was the demand of ransoms from hacendados and ranchers who wanted their stolen cattle back.[11]

In addition to the production and storage of grains, Cajeme also laid great emphasis on the buildup of war materials. Although he did not mobilize Yaquis to fight offensively for their independence, he clearly foresaw the day when they would have to defend it. Besides the guns which were confiscated and brought in by the ships, Cajeme called up those war supplies which Yaquis had stashed away from past rebellions. Besides cleaning and repairing the old guns, Yaquis further stocked their arsenal with their own freshly manufactured gunpowder.

As the chief civil, judicial, and military authorities within their pueblos, the *gobernadores* became Cajeme's administrative assistants. Subordinate to them were the captains of war, who were responsible for the mobilization of men in the pueblos: each had to maintain a certain number of men who could be armed and equipped on short notice. Another official role, which had not been noted since the mission days but which received new attention at this time, was that of the *temastian*, or sacristan. As the most important cultural officer, he was in charge of sustaining religious practices and organizing fiestas and ceremonies. Since the Yaqui

River did not have permanent resident ministers at this time, the *temastianes* became in effect the chief guardians of religion and culture.[12]

Even though Cajeme was the obvious brain and motivating force behind the new organization and unchallenged as captain general, he chose to stay in the background. Instead, he pushed into the forefront another ancient Yaqui custom—the popular council, in which every Yaqui man and woman had equal participation. Although these assemblies had been convened spontaneously or on an ad hoc basis in the past, Cajeme institutionalized the council as the major decision-making body and professed to abide by its consensus.

With little difficulty, Cajeme also won the allegiance of some of the Mayos, although he did not reorganize them as thoroughly as he did his own people. He was considerably impeded by the Mexicans' much deeper penetration of the Mayo River. Four of the traditional Mayo pueblos—Navojoa, Tesia, Camoa, and San Pedro—had already been converted into regular municipalities. The other four—Echojoa, Masiaca, Cuirimpo, and Santa Cruz—swore fealty to Cajeme and obeyed his orders to store up weapons and cultivate community plots. To ensure their allegiance, Cajeme himself occasionally traveled to the Mayo to meet with his supporters there.[13]

As Cajeme took control, the state and nation which he confronted also became more organized, more powerful than ever before. For the first time since independence, Mexico attained political unity and stability under President Porfirio Díaz, whose strong, centralized rule destroyed the power of regional caudillos such as Pesqueira of Sonora. In the minds of Díaz and his henchmen, national economic development had to become the country's first priority, given its proverbially abundant natural resources and the anxious foreigners waiting to invest their surplus capital in Mexico. In the particular case of Sonora, its development program entailed Apache pacification, revitalization of the mines, construction of a vast communication and transportation network to improve the state's infrastructure, stimulation of agriculture, industry, and commerce, and finally, colonization and fruitful exploitation of the rich river lands of the Yaqui and Mayo.

Porfirian governor Luis Torres wasted no time in initiating such a program for Sonora. After repeated delays since its original conception in 1860, construction of the Sonoran Railroad finally got under way; by 1881, the American company was hiring some six hundred workers and indicated it could easily employ more.[14] New mining laws and relaxed restrictions brought about a boom in both gold and silver mining in almost every district, with North Americans bringing in most of the capital and technology.[15] Railroads and mines in turn stimulated greater commercial activities. In 1881, Governor Torres approved the establishment of the Bank of the State of Sonora, a joint American-Mexican enterprise.[16] Those interested in agricultural development successfully pushed for the breakup of more indigenous community lands. Pima, Pápago, and Opata pueblos became easy targets as they outlived their usefulness for frontier defense when U.S. and Mexican authorities finally succeeded in neutralizing the Apaches.[17]

Not surprising, colonization of Yaqui land presented the greatest difficulties. Ignacio Pesqueira, who initiated the effort, had made little headway. In fact, many of the colonists who had settled in the Yaqui between 1868 and 1875 fled when Cajeme came to power; those who had been granted land and water concessions found it nearly impossible to take possession of their newly acquired property or to begin work on development projects.[18] In 1879, speaking for the new state government, Vice-Governor Otero reiterated its strong belief in colonization:

> The government under my charge has decided to appeal to that of the Union, requesting its help in organizing these tribes civilly, reducing them to the obedience of the authorities, dividing the land of their pueblos in a manner convenient to the support of life by means of work and forcing them to enter at once onto the road of civilization.
>
> For this objective the Executive hopes that the Congress would lend its efficient and strong support, because a successful colonization of those rivers would result immediately in a great increase of the civilized population and a bountiful production in all the various branches of wealth.[19]

To local developmentalists, colonization became a much broader concept that went beyond Pesqueira's original idea of planting a few agricultural colonies along the Yaqui River. It would include, for example, such a proposal as the "bifurcation of the Río Yaqui with the object of bringing its waters to the valley situated to the northeast of the city of Guaymas."[20] An even more immediate benefit expected from colonization would be to increase the state's labor supply. As Governor Luis Torres explained, by forcing the Yaquis onto "the road of civilization," those displaced from the land would then "provide all the labor necessary for the railroad enterprise and others established in the state, such as agriculture, mining and many others."[21] This would be especially convenient, he continued, since the Yaqui workers could be paid a lower wage than what the other Mexican workers demanded.[22]

The Díaz government, of course, concurred fully with this policy of colonization and development. As early as February 1879, the secretary of development, colonization, industry, and commerce granted Wenceslao Iberri, a leading merchant of Guaymas and one of Sonora's representatives to the national congress, a concession to colonize the island of Ciari in the middle of the Yaqui territory.[23] In February 1881, it approved a comprehensive, three-month contract to Manuel Castro to survey and colonize the *terrenos baldíos*, or unused lands, of the Yaqui and Mayo. The contract expired before any surveying was even begun, however, mainly because conditions in the Yaqui did not permit the entry of engineers.[24] The Mayo was more accessible, especially those pueblos which Mexicans had already substantially expropriated. Since 1880, the Geographic Exploratory Commission, headed by Colonel Agustín Díaz and staffed by army engineers, had been dividing land in some Mayo pueblos into private lots.[25]

Before 1881, however, the federal government was unwilling, or unable, to aid Sonora's efforts at colonization beyond the granting of concessions and contracts. Clearly little progress could be made in this direction if the Yaqui people continued to resist outside attempts to control their persons and land. Having little resources of its own to conduct a full-scale military campaign to crush Cajeme's regime, the state government repeatedly—in 1879, 1880, and 1881—requested soldiers, weapons, and provisions from the federal government.[26] Before Mexico City could promise any substantial aid, an internal power struggle in Sonora precipitated a local crisis, which in turn provoked the Yaquis into armed action.

In July 1881, Luis Torres turned over the reins of government to the newly elected governor, Carlos R. Ortiz, a rich merchant and hacendado from Alamos. This action paralleled a similar peaceful transference of power by President Díaz to his son-in-law and the president-elect, Manuel González. Such gestures were deemed politically necessary, since the Porfiristas had overthrown the old Liberals on the principle of "no reelection." In fact, of course, they merely turned over power to one of their own.

Carlos Ortiz, however, who had been active in the inner circle of Torres, soon broke with the other Porfiristas. At odds was the primacy of state sovereignty, which Ortiz emphasized, and the solidification of a close working relationship between the state government and the federal Díaz regime, which Torres projected. Six months into office, Governor Ortiz suddenly recalled the state of Sonora's National Guards from General Bernardo Reyes's Apache campaign at the frontier, citing the urgent need to defend the state government against an imminent coup by Ramón Corral, Luis Torres, and federal general José G. Carbó. When this unsubstantiated story gained little credibility, Ortiz changed his line. This time he declared a state of emergency, charging that the Yaquis and Mayos were on the verge of open rebellion.[27] In early September, the governor's brother, Agustín Ortiz, led several squadrons of National Guards, totaling some one thousand men, into various Mayo pueblos, purportedly for the reason of gathering information on the alleged rebellion. Actually, there was no disturbance in the Mayo, but the sudden presence of unpopular government troops aroused much resentment. On the nineteenth, Ortiz reported a skirmish between his men and thirteen hundred *indios* led by Jesús Moroyoqui and his sons.[28] Then he spread rumors that Cajeme was preparing the Yaquis to enter the Mayo. When Cajeme still had not appeared by the twenty-seventh, Ortiz extemporized an explanation that Cajeme was delayed because Yaquis were still waiting for more ammunition from Guaymas.[29] His numerous reports during this period were full of alarming news about large gatherings of Mayos in different pueblos, or instructions and promises they had received from Cajeme, and of projected attacks on Baroyeca and other Mexican communities in the vicinity.[30]

General Bernardo Reyes, who had reluctantly released the guards to Governor Ortiz because he had no final authority over them, steadfastly refused to believe that the Yaquis and Mayos were in a state of rebellion. On the contrary, he denounced the movement of troops into the Mayo as a provocation, warning that a full-scale rebellion at this time would be a most undesirable consequence when Apaches were still posing a serious threat to the state.[31] Having apparently seen through Ortiz's scheme of fomenting a Yaqui-Mayo uprising in order to rally statewide support behind himself against his real or imaginary enemies, Reyes instructed his subordinates under no circumstances to lend federal support to Ortiz.[32] This so enraged the governor that he turned around and accused Reyes of being the main instigator of the alleged plot against him.[33]

By this time, if Ortiz had any second thoughts about his scheme, it was too late. Cajeme had indeed arrived in the Mayo with over two thousand Yaquis to take on Agustín Ortiz. On the night of October 15, Cajeme moved his men from their camp at Echojoa to Capetemaya, where they had better access to ranches which could provide food. Thinking that Cajeme had merely divided his forces, and that he could not possibly have more than one thousand men at Capetemaya, Ortiz launched a surprise attack on them, confident of a quick victory. He took with him only a small force of 130 cavalrymen and 150 infantrymen. Instead of one thousand men, Ortiz encountered closer to three thousand, according to his first report. After two-and-a-half hours of hard fighting, the Yaquis and Mayos dispersed towards the Yaqui River, leaving eighty dead comrades, again according to Ortiz's first report.[34] Later, as the Ortiz government unabashedly claimed total victory over Cajeme, it inflated the Yaqui-Mayo forces to four thousand and their casualties to two hundred. It further accused Cajeme and his men of having destroyed and pillaged all the haciendas and ranches within a seven-league radius between the Mayo port of Agiabampo and the city of Alamos. In the same breath, Carlos Ortiz attempted to implicate his political enemies with Cajeme, supplying as evidence that among the dead in Capetemaya were several Mexicans. He accused the federal forces in Sonora, although without specifically naming General Reyes, of having made an accord with Cajeme "to produce a complete disturbance of the public order in the state and force the disappearance of its constitutional powers."[35]

Governor Ortiz's machinations and accusations had so little credibility that, by the end of October, the citizens of Hermosillo and Guaymas, as well as the National Guards, had begun to disavow his authority. Seconding the original analysis by Reyes, they accused Carlos Ortiz and his brother, Agustín, of having "penetrated the territory of the Indians" to provoke them deliberately into a defensive war. To allow Ortiz a graceful exit from what was clearly a political defeat, Reyes provided federal troops to escort him safely into exile in the United States and into political oblivion. Filling out Ortiz's term, Vice-Governor Antonio Escalante immediately ordered that no further action be taken against the Yaquis and Mayos.[36] With Luis Torres returning as governor in March 1883, the Porfirista clique never again relinquished control of the state until it was ultimately overthrown during the Mexican Revolution of 1910.

Besides these general political consequences, the Ortiz incident brought much attention to the Yaquis and Mayos. The confrontation of 1882 demonstrated to the Mexican public the high level of preparedness on the part of Cajeme and his followers in both river territories. When provoked, they were able to mobilize at short notice at least two thousand well-armed, well-trained men, certainly the largest fighting force amassed since Banderas. The maneuvers at Capetemaya had shown Cajeme to be a good strategist; he had learned his lessons well from past experiences as soldier and officer in state and federal armies. No doubt he had been training his men in new techniques of combat and in the use of the modern weapons which they had assiduously collected. Moreover, as their first testing round, the battle gave the Yaquis and Mayos a definite taste of their new strength. It also deepened their mistrust of the Mexicans. It is significant to note that under Cajeme's leadership, the Yaquis and their Mayo allies would rarely venture outside their own territories to take the offensive against the Mexicans. The key to Cajeme's strategy lay in training and preparing his people for the defense of their land and autonomy.

The Ortiz incident had another unforeseen effect: it encouraged the Mayos of Cuirimpo, Navojoa, and Tesia, recently converted into Mexican municipalities, to attempt to regain control of their pueblos. As José Zarapero, *gobernador* of Navojoa and suspected leader of the movement, explained, the Mayos wanted permission "to name their own authorities and to remove the municipal governments."[37] Throughout 1883 and 1884, rumors abounded of plans to attack the municipality of Navojoa and of the imminent arrival of large contingents of Yaqui auxiliaries. But these attacks never took place, nor did the arrival of Yaqui armies.[38] While Cajeme never openly discouraged the Mayos, he was hesitant about sending Yaquis to aid their cause. On one occasion, he reportedly called off a planned attack on Navojoa at the last moment. Another time, a revolt apparently fizzled when Cajeme reneged on earlier promises to send help.[39] The reluctance to become involved suggested a Cajeme policy not to initiate hostilities as long as the government left the Yaquis alone. During these two years, except for the usual complaints of depredations on nearby haciendas and ranches—Yaquis continued to demand ransom from owners for stolen cattle—they directed relatively little attention to themselves. Some of the thirteen thousand residents in the area, however, still felt unsafe and [they] departed.[40]

While the state enjoyed a rare period of uncharacteristic peace, interest in Sonora and its resources grew, especially on the part of North Americans. The *Los Angeles Times* of February 23, 1883, carried a feature story entitled "Seductive Sonora." It recounted the trip to Sonora taken by Mr. John Lowe of California, who was in the "agricultural implement and hardware business." Lowe spoke "in glowing terms of the bright prospects and rapid development" of the state and how Americanized it was fast becoming, observing further that the people are progressive and gladly welcome Americans to their midst, and peace and order are preserved to an extent hardly believed by Americans." With eight hundred to one thousand Americans already living there, Lowe concluded that he expected "to see Sonora an American state within five years if the present influx of Americans continues."[41]

Stories about the real or alleged wealth of the Yaqui territory were particularly attractive. Americans were interested in the carbon fields, salt pits, and oyster beds of the Yaqui.[42] In November 1882, the Mexican secretary of development granted a contract to the American Robert Symon to build a short railroad "from the carboniferous fields of the Río Yaqui to a point called El Morrito on the Bay of Guaymas."[43] Moreover, Mexicans and foreigners alike were obsessed with the thought of discovering large mines in Yaqui-controlled land. Rumors circulated of fabulously rich silver mines in the Sierra de Bacatete, jealously guarded by Yaquis who could not be persuaded to divulge their exact locations; nor would Cajeme permit his people to exploit these mines themselves.[44] There was also the unsubstantiated item carried by the *Arizona Daily Star* of February 14, 1883, on a Mr. Huller of New York selling Yaqui mines to English speculators.[45]

Such growing interest in the Yaqui prompted the state to renew its own efforts to wrest control of the territory from Cajeme. Sonora continued to hound the federal government for cooperation in launching the long-projected campaign. Finally, after an investigation of the Yaqui and Mayo, General José G. Carbó rendered a preliminary report to the secretary of war in October 1884. In it he noted that Cajeme always had three to four hundred armed men around him, but could easily mobilize three to four thousand. He estimated that the Yaquis had two hundred metallic weapons between rifles and carbines, two hundred pistols, and four hundred percussion rifles, all up-to-date war matériel. A fair man, General Carbó offered a personal assessment of Cajeme which agreed with the Yaqui leader's recent conduct: "The character of the jefe Cajeme is very little warlike and his main tendency is not to extend his domain, conquering all the pueblos civilly organized [that is, the Mexican towns] and subjecting them to the obedience of the government which is found between the two rivers . . . but it is to conserve the independence of the territory which they now possess."[46]

For the moment, Carbó concluded in his report, there were only fifty men of the Sixth Battalion guarding both rivers. They had instructions only to defend their position, since they were hardly capable of attacking the much larger Yaqui and Mayo forces.

As the federal government still bided its time in coming to a decision, the more impatient state government searched for other ways to destroy Cajeme. Ramón Corral, secretary of the state government, received the intelligence from Prefect J. A. Rivera of Guaymas of growing discontent among Cajeme's followers. Reportedly, Cajeme was dealing severely with those Yaquis and Mayos who dared oppose him. One of the victims was Loreto Molino, a Yaqui captain expelled from the river [territory] for insubordination. Hoping to take advantage of the schism, Corral directed Rivera "to try to foment diplomatically the divisions in the Río."[47] Accordingly, Rivera successfully persuaded Molino to avenge his ouster from the Yaqui.

One night in January 1885, Molino surreptitiously entered the Yaqui from Guaymas with twenty-nine other men, armed with a plan to assassinate Cajeme at his home at Los Guamúchiles. When they arrived, much to their dismay, they found that Cajeme had departed that very night for the Mayo. In their frustration, Molino and [his] cohorts burned Cajeme's house, terrorized his family members and neighbors, [and] then fled as quietly as they had come.[48]

Immediately notified of Molino's heinous acts, Cajeme rushed back to the Yaqui. His own intelligence network had supplied him with a good inkling of the conspiracy between the renegade Yaqui and the government. Cajeme's first act was to detain all the ships docked at El Médano as hostages, imposing fines of fifty to two hundred pesos on each one. Then he informed the captain of the port of Guaymas that this seizure was necessary because the state had sent Molino to assassinate him and create a crisis in the Yaqui. Finally he demanded that the prefect of Guaymas give him a full explanation of the plot and remit the Yaqui conspirators to him for punishment.[49]

At this tense moment Governor Torres himself communicated with Cajeme to assure the irate Yaqui leader that justice would be done once proper guilt had been ascertained, but not according to Cajeme's methods.[50] Totally unappeased by this answer, Cajeme ordered his followers to begin massive assaults on haciendas, ranches, and stations of the Sonoran railroad in the Guaymas and Alamos districts. Then, by burning the twenty-one ships detained at El Médano, he signaled the beginning of full-scale rebellion.[51]

The government's plot to foment a civil war inside the Yaqui, whereby the people would mercilessly kill each other off, had obviously backfired. Utterly disorganized and unprepared to meet the fury unleashed by Cajeme, it sent all available state and federal troops in the Guaymas and Alamos districts against the rebels, while instructing hacendados to organize their own private forces to defend their properties.[52] The raids, fires, and killings had become so serious that several major mines in Alamos closed down. Mexican residents in the area fled in droves. Soon Mayos joined the Yaqui rebellion, burning the port of Agiabampo. Reports on the size of Yaqui and Mayo rebel bands ranged from five or six hundred to as large as one thousand.[53] The most exposed and raided area was the Guaymas Valley to the northwest of the Yaqui River, between the Sonoran railroad and the Sierra de Bacatete. There were quite a few ranches and haciendas in the valley, engaged primarily in cattle and horse raising and the cultivation of maize, beans, wheat, and cotton. Between twenty-five hundred and three thousand persons lived in that area, some of whom undoubtedly were Yaqui workers.[54]

Only in view of this grave situation did the federal government begin to pay attention to Sonora, much to the relief of local authorities. The secretary of war authorized all available federal forces in Sonora and Sinaloa to engage in the suppression of the rebels.[55] The state government itself began mobilizing its National Guards, as well as raising money in the form of forced loans from merchants and mine owners in Alamos and Guaymas.[56] Finally, on March 31, President Porfirio Díaz authorized his secretary of war to open a formal campaign against the rebels, designating General Carbó, commander of the First Military Zone, to direct it.[57]

By May, General Carbó had gathered in the Guaymas Valley a substantial force of 801 National Guardsmen and 868 federals, with another
500 to join them shortly. General Otero commanded an additional four
hundred men to watch over the Mayo while Carbó conducted the campaign in the Yaqui. Many prominent Sonorans from across the state, including Secretary Ramón Corral and Deputy Rafael Izábal, as well as
several foreign residents, volunteered for the campaign. As the first expedition taken against the Yaquis in many years, it obviously had great popular appeal.[58] The military rosters read like the Sonoran social register.

The campaign formally began on May 8, 1885. Dividing his forces
into two columns, General Carbó led one into the Yaqui from La Pitahaya
and the pueblo of Belém at the mouth of the Yaqui River, while General
[Fausto] Topete went around it to enter from upriver, through Buenavista
and Cócorit. They planned to meet in the pueblo of Tórin, located in the
middle of Yaqui territory. Carbó also armed a two-hundred-man Yaqui
auxiliary force, commanded by the turncoat Loreto Molino, to serve as
explorers, for they alone knew the Yaqui terrain well.[59]

The general arrived at El Médano on the twelfth to set up his campaign headquarters there, choosing this site because it was on an elevation and hence safe from the rains, had easy communication with Guaymas
and the coast, and was a port to which small ships could sail with provisions and other necessities. The small number of Yaquis who usually resided there had all fled. The area near the mouth of the river, from La
Pitahaya to El Médano and including the first three pueblos of Belém,
Ráum, and Huírivis, was rather bare of vegetation. Except for a few families, Yaquis had also deserted this area, leaving their unharvested crops
for the troops to gather.

The rebel stronghold really began with Pótam, situated about two kilometers upriver in a thickly wooded terrain. On the left bank an impenetrable forest stretched towards the Mayo. In its densest part, somewhere
between Pótam and Vícam, Cajeme had build a huge fort, which he named
El Añil. The trees around it were so thick that it took Carbó's scouts a full
day to reconnoitre forty meters of the parapet. They reported that the fort
was surrounded by an immense moat in front of which was a sturdy pali-
sade. From the fort to the river, the Yaquis had constructed a covered path
so that they could travel with some protection to bring in water.

The government located its base of operations in Tórin, which was
considered an excellent military vantage because of its position on top of
a small hill. As with all the other pueblos, it too was deserted. General
Carbó ordered the construction of a small redoubt, where he stationed
five hundred men under Colonel Lorenzo Torres to watch over the entire
river territory. Scout reports revealed that near Tórin, on the Cerro de

Onteme, the Yaquis had built several smaller fortifications. On the left bank facing Tórin, they had dug trenches, which they abandoned when the soldiers arrived. One league downriver was another fortification surrounded by a moat and trenches, and defended by some eight hundred Yaquis. As the scouts continued their explorations, they constantly reported the discovery of still more forts and trenches inside the forests, such as the one near Bácum, five leagues from Tórin and two kilometers inland. Cócorit, the last pueblo, marked the limit of Yaqui territory; beyond it lay Buenavista, the nearest Mexican community.

General Carbó estimated there were twenty-five thousand Yaquis in the river [territory], with another ten thousand Mayos. He calculated that five to six thousand men could be easily mobilized to fight, although not all with firearms.[60] The descriptions of the forts and trenches confirmed that Cajeme had indeed introduced elements of the Mexican or European art of warfare.

With four hundred infantrymen between federals and National Guards, and another two hundred cavalrymen, General Topete marched downriver toward the headquarters at El Médano. On May 16, he engaged in the first battle with Cajeme's forces at El Añil fort. Fixing their only cannon on the fort, Topete ordered his men to attack. Within two hours, the Yaquis successfully repelled the soldiers, causing them twenty dead and fifty-seven wounded. The rebels also recovered the cannon which the troops had abandoned in beating their hasty retreat.[61]

Even though the Yaquis did not totally rout the attackers, they were much encouraged by the results. They celebrated Cajeme as a great military tactician and acclaimed the advantages of the fortifications. With most of the Yaquis barricaded within one of the many forts, only about two hundred of them, armed with firearms, and another three hundred with bows and arrows, moved outside to gather intelligence on the opposition. Consequently the soldiers encountered very few Yaquis in their forays and explorations. Although General Carbó spread the word from the outset of the campaign that any peaceful Indian who went to El Médano headquarters would be well received and pardoned with mercy, few accepted his offers.[62]

In June, several skirmishes and another major battle at El Añil fort took place. This time, General Caamaño and his fourteen hundred men attacked from the Cerro de Onteme facing the fort. Again, they failed to force out the Yaquis or penetrate the well-protected fort.[63]

Obtaining no measurable results militarily, Colonel Lorenzo Torres tried to negotiate a settlement with three Cajeme representatives at Tórin. The rebels offered to end the rebellion if all troops would retreat from the river [territory], but the government considered these demands unacceptable. It in turn offered the rebels guarantees of life and property if they would lay down their guns and submit to the government. The Yaquis deemed these conditions unreasonable. It became clear to Colonel Torres that the rebels, knowing that imminent rains would hinder further troop movements along the swollen river and in the drenched forests, were merely stalling for time.[64] As anticipated, the rains came in July, forcing General Carbó to retire all his men to El Médano, thereby temporarily suspending the campaign.[65]

General Carbó decided not to launch a major attack before the withdrawal, because he was not confident enough that his men could take Cajeme at El Añil. He had discovered from a Yaqui lad who had come from among the rebels that the fort actually had two sections: inside the visible one behind the moat was another. Cajeme and his people were thus double-barricaded within the second wall. Moreover, the lad informed Carbó, the Yaquis planned to fight to the bitter end and never surrender. They even had many of their families with them, along with cattle, horses, and other beasts. Although they were out of ammunition, they had sent for more gunpowder and lead from the Mayo.[66]

Knowing they were coming back, Cajeme nevertheless interpreted the government retreat as a victory for the Yaquis. The temporary letup of the campaign gave him breathing space and a chance to resupply and recuperate from the months of hard fighting. He ordered the Yaquis to return to their fields and prepare seeds for the new planting. He even allowed the resumption of some trade with Guaymas.[67]

Of the troops that had retreated from the Yaqui, the state contingents from Arizpe and Moctezuma went home to help fight the Apaches, who had lately increased their depredations. One section of troops covered designated spots in the Guaymas Valley to prevent raids on haciendas and ranches. Garrisons posted at critical points around the Yaqui and Mayo rivers attempted to block rebels from leaving the area.[68]

Conditions in the Yaqui and Mayo were actually quite miserable, for the months spent holed up inside the forts had depleted their supplies of food, while the new planting could not be immediately harvested. More and more Yaquis and Mayos wanted either to have peace or to leave the river lands. To add to their hardships the yellow fever epidemic, which had been spreading in Sonora since 1883, finally reached the Yaqui in September.[69] In order to affirm his authority in the Mayo, Cajeme went to the extreme of personally executing the leader of a growing peace faction, Andrés Capusari.[70] To prevent the flight of Yaquis, he ordered some of the roads out of the river closed. Only those whom he trusted could go to Guaymas, Alamos, Hermosillo, and Ures to buy guns and ammunition.[71]

In December, a group of citizens from Guaymas, Father Tomás G. de Galdeano, Nicanor Ortiz, and Nieves E. Acosta, entered the Yaqui to try to negotiate a peace with the *gobernadores* and people of the eight pueblos. The only condition they presented to the Yaquis assembled in Pótam was their submission to the Mexican government. Although Cajeme called the meeting, he deliberately remained at an inconspicuous distance, aloof from the actual parleys. When it came time to sign the surrender, the Mexican negotiators asked for Cajeme's signature. Emerging quietly from the background, the Yaqui leader expressed his agreement with the surrender, since it appeared to be the will of the people. But he adamantly refused to sign anything, maintaining simply, "My word is worth as much as my signature and the people have always made peace without signing any piece of paper."[72] Immediately sensing that they had failed in their mission, the three men, dejected, returned to Guaymas. The Mayos refused a similar peace offer that General Otero extended them.[73]

In March 1886, the campaign was reopened. General Angel Martínez, the new commander of the First Military Zone, replaced General Carbó, who had died in October. More federal troops reinforced those already in Sonora. Residents and property owners of the state organized an additional eight hundred auxiliaries to send against the Mayos. This time the campaign was fought on two fronts: General Martínez marched with two thousand men to the Mayo, while General Marcos Carrillo took the remaining two thousand men to the Yaqui.[74]

On May 5, General Carrillo stormed El Añil fort, which Cajeme with just eight hundred Yaquis valiantly but unsuccessfully defended. The rebels had clearly lost much of their morale and vigor from the previous year. As rebels spilled out of El Añil, they fled towards their last refuge, a newly built fort in Buatachive, high in the Sierra de Bacatete.[75] Enclosed by natural protective barriers, Buatachive was thought to be impregnable. Cajeme ordered his men, their families, and all available food and cattle behind its walls. Some religious objects and ornaments stripped from the pueblo churches were also stashed inside for safekeeping.

Noting that Cajeme had in effect entrapped himself with all his people and resources inside Buatachive, General Martínez seized the opportunity to deal him the coup de grace. Leaving the Mayo, he rushed into the Yaqui and ordered the entire campaign force to lay siege to the fort. Four days later, on May 12, the soldiers attacked from all sides. Although the Yaquis defended themselves with their usual valor, there was really no contest. As they scrambled out and escaped into the sierra, the troops stormed inside, there to witness a scene of utmost misery: yellow fever had stricken about two thousand people, women and children, the result of unsanitary and crowded conditions, insufficient food, and lack of fresh water. All of the fighting men, which Martínez estimated to have been two thousand, had managed to escape, except for the two hundred dead scattered over the battlegrounds outside the fort. Not a single piece of weaponry was in sight.[76]

After their disastrous defeats at El Añil and Buatachive, the Yaquis could no longer sustain the rebellion. General Martínez announced the conclusion of the campaign by offering amnesty to all Yaquis and Mayos who presented themselves with their weapons within twenty days of May 15. Hungry, sick, and demoralized, rebels drifted into the military camps established in Tórin, El Médano, Cócorit, and Pótam, as soldiers gathered the old men wandering around the battlefields.[77]

At the camp in Tórin, General Martínez informed the Yaquis who had surrendered that the government's magnanimous policy was to pacify them without destroying them, for they were "intelligent, vigorous and susceptible to civilization and would become a hardworking and useful people, contributing greatly to strengthen the national element on the frontier and develop the public wealth." They would be allowed to keep the land which "pertained honestly to them, according to the law." Furthermore, the *gobernadores* who had served under Cajeme would retain their offices, "because they had been chosen by the people."[78]

After sending blankets, food, and clothing to succor the suffering, Governor Luis Torres personally went to Tórin to accept the surrender. Then he put Colonel Lorenzo Torres in charge of reorganizing the administration of the pueblos.[79] Even though Cajeme was still at large and showed no signs of submission, General Martínez believed that the rebellion had been suppressed. He withdrew a large portion of his men from the Yaqui, leaving three strong detachments in El Médano, Tórin, and Cócorit. Next he marched to the Mayo to arrange the act of surrender there. Mexicans began moving back to the Yaqui to live; traders returned to conduct their usual businesses.[80]

Cajeme made one last major effort to save his faltering regime. He convinced some of the Yaquis who had surrendered in Tórin to rejoin him and those who had not capitulated. As in the past, the Yaquis had salvaged most of their weapons, for those who surrendered their persons seldom gave up their guns. Cajeme had also hoped that the approaching rains would again force the withdrawal of troops from the Yaqui River, as they had a year before. This time, however, the government was determined not to give him a second chance.

First, Cajeme reoccupied the fort of El Añil, but soldiers quickly dispersed his men. The Yaquis regrouped and with a force of twelve hundred tried to take El Médano from Colonel Lorenzo Torres on July 22. Again, they were defeated. Cajeme still did not give up. He divided his men into many small bands, which engaged government troops in minor skirmishes. By October, it became necessary to send more troops back into the Yaqui.

The rebels fled into the Sierra de Bacatete, and when the pursuit became too hot there, they slipped into the Guaymas Valley, where they raided and terrorized the haciendas and ranches. During this whole period, no soldier actually saw Cajeme in person: "He seemed to be an imaginary being, invisible, a myth created by the fantasy of his people."[81] Although he no longer had the total and active support of all Yaquis and Mayos, he had enough loyal men to perpetuate an unstable situation in both river territories.

General Martínez finally concluded that only a war without quarter could force Cajeme into submission. He sent his men like hunters into the forests and the sierra, killing any moving person on sight, confiscating all cattle and food materials. Cajeme was still nowhere to be seen. Many times a soldier thought he had spotted the formidable Yaqui leader, only to find upon approach that the form had simply "vanished like a shadow." Even with all the hardships and intense persecution, Cajeme still had about eight hundred followers, who sustained themselves by traditional plunder in the Guaymas Valley.[82]

At this time Cajeme made an effort to end the hostilities, perhaps again to buy time. He wrote General Juan Hernández, commander of El Médano garrison, offering to surrender if all government troops were withdrawn from the Yaqui territory immediately. Otherwise, he warned ominously, he would fight to the bitter end. The government obviously could not accept these terms, which contradicted its intention to break the Yaqui autonomy. As General Hernández explained it to Cajeme in his reply, the Yaqui was part of the Mexican republic and the republic had a right and obligation to send forces to wherever it deemed necessary. With this answer Cajeme withdrew the olive branch.

Not letting up for one moment, General Martínez ordered his men to increase their search expeditions into the Sierra de Bacatete, into the Guaymas Valley, and into the Mayo, where Cajeme still had some supporters. At first these searches netted only more women, children, and old disabled Yaqui men. But as the persecution intensified, with troops relentlessly chasing after the rebels in their circular flight from the river to the sierras, from the sierra to the valley, and from the valley back to the river, more and more of them surrendered. At the end of the year, the military conducted one last major expedition to the Sierra de Bacatete, along the margins of the Yaqui River, and to the other favorite hideouts of the rebels.[83]

In the final tally, four thousand had surrendered in the Yaqui and another two thousand in the Mayo, but Cajeme was not among them.

Despite the insistence of the commanders, only 140 firearms were recovered.[84] The people in the two river territories had not been able to plant any crops during the year of rebellion; their animals had either been consumed or confiscated. To alleviate their misery, the government sent in food and clothing. Although Cajeme was still at large, General Martínez formally terminated the campaign.

Sonora had spent much of its revenues to pacify the Yaquis. Deputy Rafael Izábal reported that the campaign had cost the state eighty thousand pesos in 1885, and another seventy-four thousand in 1886.[85] Many of the funds were raised through forced contributions. The merchants of Alamos, for example, regularly advanced six to ten thousand pesos a month during 1885.[86]

General Martínez experienced considerable frustration in his first encounter with the Yaquis. During the difficult period of trying to trap the elusive Cajeme and the hardcore rebels, he actually proposed to President Díaz that all Yaqui prisoners be deported out of the state of Sonora. Díaz vetoed the idea because it would "initiate a war of extermination." He demonstrated a sensitive understanding of the Yaqui mentality in explaining: "The Indian prefers death to exile, and before the prospect of being removed from his home, he would fight until he perishes." In view of this, Díaz proposed an alternative, suggesting that once pacification was assured, the leaders of the rebellion be remitted to Mexico to be drafted into the military.[87] Although leaders had been occasionally deported in the past, this was the first time that Mexican authorities seriously considered deportation as a possible solution to the Yaqui problem. While the idea was set aside for the time being, deportation would be discussed again and eventually adopted on a large scale within the next decade.

With peace seemingly assured for the Yaqui River, Mexicans from neighboring communities rushed in. They came mainly from Baroyeca, Quiriego, Rosario, Batacosa, Buenavista, and Cumuripa to trade, to take up land for cultivation, or to raise cattle. This time, three permanent garrisons were posted along the river territory: at El Médano at the entrance, Tórin in the middle, and Cócorit at the end. In addition to the surveillance of the Yaquis, they also supervised the establishment of the first permanent colonies in the Yaqui.[88]

Yet no one felt really safe as long as Cajeme remained free. General Hernández presented to Secretary Ramón Corral a list of thirteen known rebel leaders still at large, headed by the name of José María Leyva Cajeme. Corral circulated this list to all the prefects so that "the greatest vigilance is exercised, for it is not difficult [to see] that some of these Indians, attempting to flee from the forces which pursue them, find refuge in some pueblo or rancho in your jurisdiction, or touch these points during their flight."[89] He included a description of Cajeme: "regular height, rather fat, big eyes, thick lips, beardless, much black hair. Special markings: missing half the index finger on the right hand. Speaks good Spanish and his speech is measured."[90]

It seemed that Cajeme had simply vanished; not even a hint of his presence was detected anywhere. Then one day in April 1887, someone finally spotted the "most wanted man" in Sonora: an Indian who recognized him hiding in a private home near Guaymas. The Indian immediately informed Salvador Armenta, a state official in Guaymas. Before Armenta could ascertain the identity of the suspect, and being afraid that a precipitous move on his part would alert the suspect to escape, he contacted Governor Torres in Nogales by telegraph. The governor in turn notified General Angel Martínez to take the next express train to Guaymas. On the morning of the twelfth, Martínez went with a small escort to the house near Guaymas, confirmed that the man hiding there was indeed Cajeme, and apprehended him. The famous fugitive put up no resistance, seemingly relieved that his long ordeal of flight was over.

General Martínez treated Cajeme with the utmost courtesy, lodging him in his own home like an honored guest, permitting Cajeme's family to visit, and allowing the general public, filled with curiosity or respect, to meet with him. Cajeme received everyone cordially, always with a faint smile on his face. Yaquis especially crowded around General Martínez's house, knowing it would be their last chance to see their fallen leader. Among those who met Cajeme for the first time was Ramón Corral, who interviewed him for a biography and recorded a favorable first impression: "I thought I was going to meet a corpulent Indian, silent and with a ferocious expression on his face. I was never so surprised to see a man of medium height, slim but not skinny, with an astute smile on his wide mouth, friendly and good-natured and communicative as few Indians are."[91]

Cajeme readily answered all of Corral's queries regarding his personal life. With total recollection of dates and details, he also proudly recounted how he had built the separate state in the Yaqui River and how he led his people to defend their independence. But according to biographer Corral, Cajeme had realized since their defeat that the Yaquis must learn to live a new existence, to submit to the government: "Before we were enemies and we fought; now all this is over and we are all friends."[92] To Corral, the Yaqui maintained that he had always been a "patriotic Mexican," recalling how once, when a North American had asked for his cooperation in building a railroad to the Yaqui to facilitate the exploitation of the carbon fields, he had replied: "We Mexicans do not need foreigners to come and take us by the hand and bless us."[93]

Cajeme was the most excited when he talked about the skill and valor of his people. In describing the first battle at El Añil with General Topete, Cajeme told Corral that he had no more than three hundred Yaquis inside the fort. When Corral reminded him that all accounts of the battle would contradict this excessively small number, Cajeme replied with a mysterious smile, "That is because when the Indians are behind a weapon, they become many."[94] When he left the Yaqui prisoner, Corral concluded in his biography, "I was filled with a profound sense of liking for this Indian, so intelligent and so brave."

On April 21, Cajeme was taken by ship to the Yaqui River. When his guard assured him that nothing was going to happen to him, Cajeme chided him, "Do not waste your jokes on a man who is about to die."[95] He had no illusions about his destiny, as he was marched through all the pueblos, arriving at Cócorit on the twenty-fifth. On that day, Cajeme was executed by a firing squad. His own people then solemnly buried him in a quiet ceremony.

An Obituary for Cajeme

Ramón Corral, Sonoran statesman, Cajeme's official biographer, and leading Porfirista spokesman for progress, wrote the words of an appropriate Mexican obituary to the fallen Yaqui leader: "The sacrifice of Cajeme was very painful, but it would give the effect of securing the peace in the [Yaqui and Mayo] rivers, the basis and beginning of a period of civilization for the tribes." In the same optimistic vein, he expressed a personal conviction that Cajeme would be the last Yaqui rebel leader.[96] Corral could not have been more wrong in forecasting the future. Within only a few months of Cajeme's execution, the Yaquis had chosen new leaders and reactivated their armed struggle for their own sovereignty, against a government more powerful and more determined than any previous regime to dispossess and integrate them.

Had Cajeme been able to pen his own obituary, he would have written a more fitting one. He might have provided an inkling of why and how, having spent his early life outside the Yaqui River, apart from the Yaqui people and way of life, in the company largely of Mexicans, his life took such a drastic turn when he finally returned to be among his people. He might have suggested that the brutality of the Mexican military campaigns, some of which he observed and might even have participated in, including the Bácum massacre of 1868, and the compelling persistence of the Yaquis, which he finally came to appreciate, convinced him of the justness of the Yaqui cause. He might have sensed that as a Yaqui—an "Indian"—in Mexican society, he could never have attained great social mobility, so his proper place was with his own kind. He certainly would have lamented the profound suffering his people experienced under his failed leadership in attempting to create a separate Yaqui republic, but he was proud of the fight they had put up against an immense adversary. Finally, he might not have been as contrite at the end as Corral made him out to be. He might have noted that the course of past Yaqui history assured the rise of a new leader and a new form of resistance from the smoulder of the last defeat.

Despite its crushing demise, the Cajeme regime was in many ways the high point of Yaqui history in the nineteenth century. A creative, charismatic leader, Cajeme assumed power at a time when the Yaquis, after a long period of costly alliances, were demoralized, unorganized, leaderless, and unsure about their future. Heeding Cajeme's call, Yaquis who had been living outside the [Yaqui] returned in droves to their traditional pueblos, eager to revitalize their weakened communities. With the goals of autonomy, self-reliance, and self-sufficiency in mind, Cajeme strengthened the Yaquis' economic base by combining innovations, such as the tax system, with traditional practices, such as the community plots. These ensured revenues and surpluses that allowed for the purchase of arms and the stockpiling of food. He sharpened the Yaquis' skills with the white man's war methods, thinking this would enhance their ability to fend off *yori* aggression. Unfortunately, despite initial victories, in the end Yaqui forts, trenches, and maneuvers were an insufficient match for the more experienced, better equipped, and better provisioned Mexican armies which invaded their territory. This was Cajeme's biggest miscalculation.

In spite of, or perhaps because of, his long early absence from the Yaqui River, Cajeme's attention to the revival of traditional Yaqui political and religious institutions was significant. In conjunction with the recall of the dispersed Yaqui population to their traditional pueblos, Cajeme seemed intent to revitalize what he might have perceived to be a sagging commitment to Yaqui culture. While he was indisputably the supreme commander and brooked no challenge to his authority, on public occasions he deferred to the traditional council of *gobernadores* and elders, who represented the will of the people. He emphasized the important role of sacristans, or *temastianes*, and other native religious personnel. Although there is very little information on their precise functions and activities, they were apparently responsible for the upkeep of the village churches and the safeguard of religious objects. In the best days under

Cajeme, Yaqui society probably conformed most closely to its traditional form since the beginning of Mexican independence.

A strong initial unity began to weaken under factional disputes, a problem in part created by deliberate Mexican attempts to foment dissension among the Yaquis and their Mayo allies. Cajeme also had difficulty maintaining high morale, strict discipline, and firm commitment when the regime came under constant Mexican attack. After each military setback, less resolved Yaquis could be seen leaving the river. Yet Cajeme, by force of his personality if nothing else, managed to hold a large portion of his people together until the final rout.

For the larger Mexican state, Cajeme's audacious experiment could not be allowed to succeed, because the state could not tolerate the viable existence of an autonomous Indian state within its boundaries. A strong central government lent massive military assistance to Sonora in crushing what was considered a dangerous anomaly. This marked the beginning of serious federal cooperation in the pacification of the rebellious Yaquis. Beginning as only a local problem, the Yaquis had finally generated national concern, as a potential embarrassment to President Díaz's program of national social integration and a troublesome obstacle to his vision of national economic development.

When the Díaz government finally recognized the gravity of the Yaqui question, it also inherited the dilemma that had plagued local authorities since independence: how to force the Yaquis into submission without having to resort to outright extermination. The government rejected the direct military solution of all-out destructive war, because the Yaquis were not just another Indian group on the frontier, a menace with no redeeming social value. On the contrary, while no Mexican disputed the expediency of killing off the landless, useless, marauding Apaches, all agreed that the Yaquis constituted a potential asset for Sonora's progress and prosperity. Sturdy, hardworking, and talented, they would make valuable laborers for the expanding rural economy or even desirable colonists on their contested homeland. The task facing the Díaz regime was to find some way to change the Yanquis' attitude regarding their integration into Mexican society.

As always, the Yaquis' perception of their condition was markedly different from that of the Mexicans. Cajeme's defeat forced them once again to reassess their position and form of resistance, but certainly not to capitulate. Already in the waning days of Cajeme, they had begun to relearn the effectiveness of small, mobile bands in harassing large contingents of regular army troops. These bands soon grew into a widespread guerrilla movement, hallmark of the next phase of the long Yaqui struggle.

Notes

Abbreviations for works frequently cited:

INAH   Instituto Nacional de Antropologia e Historia. Fondo de
           Micropeliculas. Sonora. Mexico, D.F.
PHS   Patronato de la Historia de Sonora. Archivo de la
           Revolución Mexicana. Mexico, D.F.

1. José T. Otero, Address to the First Session of the Seventh Constitutional Congress, *La Constitución* (official organ of state government), September 18, 1879, INAH Son 7.
2. Ramón Corral, "Biografía de José María Leyva Cajeme," *Obras Históricas*, vol. 1 (Hermosillo: Biblioteca Sonorense de Geografía e Historia, 1959). This biography, first published in 1886, is perhaps the most authoritative and accurate on Cajeme. Corral, a leading member of the new ruling elite, interviewed Cajeme just before Cajeme's execution in 1886 and obtained from him most of the known details on the Yaqui leader's life. Though Corral called Cajeme "el terrible Cajeme," he did not disguise his own respect and admiration for the man, nor deny him recognition for his accomplishments.
3. Corral, "Cajeme," 149–55.
4. *Estrella de Occidente*, May 7, 1875, INAH Son 6.
5. Prefect of Alamos to governor, Alamos, April 29, 1875, INAH Son 6.
6. *Estrella de Occidente*, November 5, 1875, INAH Son 6; José V. Pesqueira, Report, Hacienda del Aguila, November 27, 1875, *Estrella de Occidente*, December 3, 1875, INAH Son 6.
7. Eleazar B. Muñoz, Report on battle at La Pitahaya on December 1 and 3, 1875, El Médano, *Estrella de Occidente*, December 10, 1875, INAH Son 6.
8. Muñoz, Diary of operations in the Yaqui, November 28 to December 31, 1875, Tórin, December 31, 1875, *Estrella de Occidente*, February 4, 1875, INAH Son 6.
9. General José Montijo, Report on failure of Sernistas to win support of Cajeme, *Estrella de Occidente*, January 21, 1876, INAH Son 6. Carlos Conant, who pronounced against Pesqueira in 1873, also reportedly tried to enlist Yaqui support, but apparently failed, because Yaquis were not known to have fought for his cause; see Report on Conant movement, *Estrella de Occidente*, October 10, 1873, INAH Son 6.
10. Corral, "Cajeme," 156; State legislature to Secretary of War, October 12, 1881, in Francisco P. Troncoso, *Las guerras con las tribus Yaqui y Mayo del Estado de Sonora* (Mexico: Tip. Dpto. Estado Mayor, 1905), 70–71. This is an extremely important source, covering the period from Cajeme to the beginning of the twentieth century, since it is essentially a collection of key military documents.
11. Corral, "Cajeme," 155–56.
12. Ibid., 157; Troncoso, *Guerras*, 71.
13. Troncoso, *Guerras*, 70; Agustín Ortiz, Report to prefect of Alamos, May 24, 1881, PHS 2:174.
14. Report on the progress of the railroads, *La Constitución*, February 17, 1881, INAH Son 7.
15. Report on the mining boom, *La Constitución*, June 1881, INAH Son 7.

16. State of Sonora, Decree no. 107, Hermosillo, July 7, 1881, *La Constitución*, July 21, 1881, INAH Son 7.

17. Several examples illustrate how Pimas and Pápagos were unable to prevent the alienation of their community lands. In early 1880, the Pimas of Onavas complained to the government that, contrary to the law, they were not even given their due share of land. They accused the prefect of Ures of indiscriminately selling off their land to hacendados and speculators. Municipality of Onavas, Petition to governor, Ures, March 20, 1880, PHS 2:140.

In 1881, the Pápagos of Pozo Verde lost their land to hacendado Fernando Ortiz when they could not show a clear title of ownership. Prefect of Altar to governor, Report on Pápago complaints, Altar, August 17, 1881, PHS 2:190–91; another complaint lodged by Pápago captain general Jesús Parra to prefect of Altar on a piece of land usurped by an Italian, Altar, August 31, 1881, PHS 2:193–94.

18. "La pacificación del Yaqui," *La Constitución*, February 24, 1881, INAH Son 7.

19. José T. Otero, Address to the First Session of the Seventh Constitutional Congress, *La Constitución*, September 18, 1879, INAH Son 7.

20. Luis Torres to state congress, submitting the project proposal which had been submitted to him earlier, Guaymas, April 21, 1879, *La Constitución*, June 3, 1880, INAH Son 7.

21. Governor to federal government on pacification of Yaquis, Hermosillo, January 19, 1881, PHS 2:167–68.

22. Pedro Monteverde, prefect of Hermosillo, Report on mines in his district, Hermosillo, February 12, 1886, INAH Son 8.

23. Secretary of Development to Wenceslao F. Iberri, Mexico, February 4, 1879, *La Constitución*, April 11, 1879, INAH Son 7.

24. "Colonización del Yaqui y Mayo," *La Constitución*, June 16, 1881, INAH Son 7.

25. Claudio Dabdoub, *Historia de El Valle del Yaqui* (Mexico: Lib. de Manuel Porrúa, 1964), 125, 252.

26. José T. Otero, Address to the First Session of the Seventh Constitutional Congress, *La Constitución*, September 18, 1879, INAH Son 7; Bernardo Reyes, Report to secretary of war on the Yaqui-Mayo situation, May 28, 1881, in Troncoso, *Guerras*, 64–67; Luis Torres, Report to Secretary of War, Hermosillo, November 30, 1881, in Troncoso, *Guerras*, 67–68; Carlos R. Ortiz, Report to Secretary of War, October 12, 1881, in Troncoso, *Guerras*, 72–73; Secretary of war to Bernardo Reyes, July 19, 1881, in Troncoso, *Guerras*, 72; Secretary of War to congress of Sonora, in Troncoso, *Guerras*, 74.

27. It has been difficult to verify the Corral-Torres conspiracy alleged by Ortiz. Torres, Corral, and General José G. Carbó, then commander of the First Military Zone, held a secret meeting in San Francisco, California. When Ortiz learned of this, he immediately declared that the state government was threatened by "enemies"; see Dabdoub, *El Valle del Yaqui*, 125. Ramón Corral, in his otherwise meticulously constructed work on Cajeme, was evasive on the reasons for Ortiz's mobilization of forces against the Yaquis and Mayos and the consequences of these seemingly inexplicable actions; see Corral, "Cajeme," 158. For the exchanges between Reyes and Ortiz regarding release of state troops, see Troncoso, *Guerras*, 75–78.

28. J. S. Quirós, prefect of Alamos, to governor, Alamos, September 19, 1882, PHS 3:182–84.

29. Agustín Ortiz, Report from Navojoa, September 27, 1882, PHS 3:197–98.

30. Agustín Ortiz to prefect of Alamos, Navojoa, September 19, 1882, PHS 3:180–81; Ortiz to prefect of Alamos, Navojoa, September 22, 1882, PHS 3:191–92; Ortiz to prefect of Alamos, Navojoa, September 27, 1882, PHS 3:194–96.

31. Bernardo Reyes to José Carbó, Hermosillo, September 22, 1882, in Troncoso, *Guerras*, 79.

32. Reyes, Circular to his colonels, Hermosillo, September 20, 1882, in Troncoso, *Guerras*, 81.

33. Carlos Ortiz, Report to state congress, accusing Reyes, Hermosillo, October 10, 1882, in Troncoso, *Guerras*, 86; Reyes to President of the republic, answering accusations against him, Hermosillo, October 15, 1882, in Troncoso, *Guerras*, 88.

According to Carleton Beals, the Yaquis rebelled in 1882 because Governor Ortiz "was extending the boundaries of his Navarro hacienda," presumably into Yaqui-held land. Beals, however, does not cite his source for such an allegation, and no other evidence has been found to support it. None of Ortiz's contemporary critics, such as Reyes or Corral, made such a charge in their documents. See Carleton Beals, *Porfirio Díaz, Dictator of Mexico* (Philadelphia: J. B. Lippincott Co., 1932), 310.

34. J. S. Quirós, on Ortiz's report of the Battle of Capetemaya, Alamos, October 17, 1882, PHS 3:214–15.

35. *La Constitución*, October 21, 1882, PHS 3:239–46.

36. Bernardo Reyes to Secretary of War, Hermosillo, November 3, 1882, in Troncoso, *Guerras*, 103–4; Vice-governor to Agustín Ortiz, ordering him to discharge his men, Hermosillo, November 2, 1882, PHS 3:271.

37. E. F. Díaz to prefect of Alamos, Navojoa, January 3, 1883, PHS 4:3–4.

38. C. Gregorio Cháves of Baroyeca, Report on rumors of seven hundred armed Yaquis moving to the Mayo, Baroyeca, June 27, 1883, PHS 4:33; J. de Jesús Salida, prefect of Alamos, Report on rumors of planned attack on Navojoa, Alamos, November 3, 1883, PHS 4:39; General Carbó to governor, on Mayo plans to attack Navojoa on August 7, Mazatlán, August 25, 1884, PHS 4:83.

39. Municipal president of Navojoa, Report to prefect of Alamos on an attack called off by Cajeme, Alamos, August 15, 1883, PHS 4:81; "Sublevación de los indios de Río Mayo," *La Constitución*, August 8, 1884, INAH Son 7.

40. Police commissioner of Batamotal, Report to prefect of Guaymas on Yaqui depredations in his area, Guaymas, August 7, 1883, PHS 4:34; Prefect of Alamos, Report on depredations in the Alamos and Guaymas districts, Hermosillo, April 23, 1883, PHS 4:31; Leonides Hamilton, *Border States of Mexico: Sonora, Sinaloa, Chihuahua and Durango. A Complete Guide for Travelers and Emigrants*, 3d ed. (Chicago: n.p., 1882), 47.

41. *Los Angeles Times*, February 23, 1883, PHS 4:23.

42. Hamilton, *Border States*, 43–47.

43. *La Constitución*, January 19, 1883, INAH Son 7.

44. C. Monteverde, prefect of Guaymas, Report on mines in his district, Guaymas, January 1, 1886, INAH Son 8.

45. *Arizona Daily Star*, February 14, 1883, PHS 4:12–14.

46. José Carbó to Secretary of War, Guaymas, October 6, 1884, PHS 4:89–92.

47. Ramón Corral to J. A. Rivera, prefect of Guaymas, January 7, 1884, PHS 4:68–69.

48. Loreto Molino, Report to J. A. Rivera on his abortive attempt on Cajeme's life, Guaymas, January 30, 1885, PHS 4:110–11; *La Constitución*, February 13, 1885, INAH Son 7; Cajeme's version of the assault, reported to the captain of the port of Guaymas, El Médano, February 3, 1885, in Troncoso, *Guerras*, 111.

49. Cajeme to captain of port of Guaymas, El Médano, February 3, 1885, in Troncoso, *Guerras*, 111.

50. Ibid., 112–13; Corral, "Cajeme," 161.

51. Reports on Yaqui and Mayo assaults in the Guaymas and Alamos districts, *La Constitución*, February 20 and 27, 1885, INAH Son 7; J. A. Rivera, Report on Yaquis in open rebellion, Guaymas, February 16, 1886, PHS 4:117; J. de J. Salida, prefect of Alamos, Report on Cajeme's instructions to the Mayos to mobilize, Alamos, February 17, 1885, PHS 4:120; *La Constitución*, February 22, 1885, PHS 4:132 (this article reports that Cajeme detained twenty-one ships and burned them all, but a Yaqui sailor claimed that only sixteen were detained and fourteen burned).

52. *La Constitución*, February 27 and March 6, 1885, INAH Son 7; J. A. Rivera to Corral, Guaymas, February 22, 1885, PHS 4:131.

53. J. de J. Salida, prefect of Alamos, to governor, March 5, 1885, PHS 4:140; "Los sublevados," *La Constitución*, March 20, 1885, INAH Son 7; J. H. Salazar, prefect of Hermosillo, Report on rebels in his district, Hermosillo, April 4, 1884, PHS 4:184.

54. General Carbó to president of the republic, July 25, 1885, PHS 4:71–84. Haciendas such as La Misa employed about 800 laborers, Noria del Valle 300, San Antonio 200, Santa Rosa 150, and Santa María 100.

55. Secretary of War to General Carbó, Telegram, Mexico, February 28, 1885, in Troncoso, *Guerras*, 113.

56. Lists of contributors to the campaign, March–May 1885, PHS 4:160–62 (almost all the contributors were merchants, including foreign merchants); Corral to José T. Otero, Orders to mobilize National Guards, Hermosillo, March 27, 1885, PHS 4:170.

57. Secretary of War to governor, Mexico, March 31, 1885, PHS 44:178.

58. Description of campaign forces, *La Constitución*, May 1, 1885, INAH Son 7; *La Constitución*, May 8, 1885, INAH Son 7.

59. Corral, "Cajeme," 162; Reports in *La Constitución*, May 15 and 29, 1885, INAH Son 7.

60. General Carbó to president of the republic, July 24, 1885, PHS 4:71–84; Description of Yaqui fortifications, *La Constitución*, July 3, 1885, INAH Son 7.

61. Report on the Battle of El Añil, *La Constitución*, May 29, 1885, INAH Son 7; Corral, "Cajeme," 163.

62. Reports in *La Constitución*, May 8 and July 3, 1885, INAH Son 7.

63. *La Constitución*, July 3, 1885, INAH Son 7.

64. Corral, "Cajeme," 164; *La Constitución*, June 12, 1885, INAH Son 7.

65. *La Constitución*, July 24, 1885, INAH Son 7.

66. *La Constitución*, July 3, 1885, INAH Son 7.

67. Municipal president to Guaymas, remitting testimonies taken from Yaquis who had come from the Yaqui River, September 16, 1885, PHS 5:134–39.

68. *La Constitución*, July 24 and 28, 1885, INAH Son 7.

69. Corral, "Cajeme," 165; Prefect of Guaymas to Corral, Report on epidemic in Yaqui, September 21, 1885, PHS 5: 143; Testimonies of Yaquis on conditions in the Yaqui River, October 16, 1885, PHS 5:168–70.

70. Testimony of a Mayo on execution of Capusari, November 5, 1885, PHS 5:185.

71. Testimonies of Yaquis outside the Yaqui River, Guaymas, October 3, 1885, PHS 5:159–62; October 23, 1885, PHS 5:175–77.

72. Tomás G. de Galdeano, Nicanor Ortiz, and Nieves E. Acosta, Report on their mission, Guaymas, December 21, 1885, PHS 5:202; Corral, "Cajeme," 166.

73. *La Constitución*, March 26, 1886, INAH Son 8.

74. *La Constitución*, February 19, March 26, and April 2, 1886, INAH Son 8.

75. General Angel Martínez to Secretary of War, May 6, 1886, in Troncoso, *Guerras*, 124–25.

76. Angel Martínez to Secretary of War, Report on the Battle of Buatachive, May 9, 12, and 13, 1886, in Troncoso, *Guerras*, 125–29; Corral, "Cajeme," 167–70.

77. Angel Martínez, Report, Tórin, May 15, 1886, *La Constitución*, May 21, 1886, INAH Son 8; *La Constitución*, June 25, July 2, 6, and 9, 1886 (covering the period May 12 to May 30), INAH Son 8.

78. *La Constitución*, July 6, 1886, INAH Son 8.

79. *La Constitución*, May 21 and 23, July 9, 1886, INAH Son 8.

80. *La Constitución*, June 18, 1886, INAH Son 8.

81. Corral, "Cajeme," 171–72.

82. Corral, "Cajeme," 171–80. (For some reason, neither INAH nor PHS contains any documents for this period; similar gaps occur for other short periods.)

83. Corral, "Cajeme," 180–85.

84. List of Yaquis and Mayos who surrendered and the guns that were turned in, in Troncoso, *Guerras*, 148–49.

85. Rafael Izábal, Report on cost of campaign in 1885–86, *La Constitución*, October 14, 1887, INAH Son 8.

86. Many lists of contributors from Alamos, in PHS 4 and 5, for example, for May–April 1885, PHS 4:264, for a total sum of 9,722 pesos.

87. President Porfirio Díaz to General Martínez, Mexico, November 18, 1886, PHS 6:139–40.

88. Corral, "Cajeme," 189.

89. General Juan Hernández, Report, El Médano, January 13, 1887, PHS 6:159; Corral, Circular to all the prefects, Hermosillo, January 18, 1887, PHS 6:160.

90. General Martínez to Corral, Guaymas, December 30, 1886, PHS 6:147.

91. Corral, "Cajeme," 190.

92. Ibid., 190–91.

93. Ibid.

94. Ibid.

95. Ibid.

96. Ibid.

10

Native Cultural Retention and the Struggle for Land in Early Twentieth-Century Bolivia

Erick D. Langer*

In his study of a failed uprising by the Chayanta of southern Bolivia in the 1920s, Erick Langer illustrates how native peoples endeavored to use distinct practices on the one hand to invoke their traditional cultural unity and on the other to appeal effectively for help from the national authorities. Throughout Latin America, indigenous societies, even those that enjoyed considerable autonomy, appreciated the importance of national governments and their officials in determining the outcome of native efforts to retain their lands and customary leaders.

For years the Chayanta had engaged in boundary disputes with surrounding haciendas. When they finally rebelled, they believed that they had simultaneously to assert their ethnic identity—to demonstrate their legitimate claims to the contested lands in terms both they and neighboring native groups would recognize—and to follow legal formulas that they realized government officials would insist upon before acknowledging a claim as rightful. The Chayanta thereby accepted the authority of certain non-Indian procedures even to ratify their seizure of a hacienda during a revolt.

*The author wishes to acknowledge the helpful comments of members of the Mentalities Seminar of the Pittsburgh Center for Social History, to whom this article was first presented; his thanks go particularly to Donald Sutton and Daniel Resnick for their suggestions. This article also benefited from the comments of James Lockhart and two anonymous readers and from discussions with Philip M. Keyes. Financial support for the research was provided by a Maurice Falk Semester Leave Grant, a Fulbright-Hays Faculty Research Grant (CIES), an American Philosophical Society Research Grant, and an Albert J. Beveridge Grant for Research in the History of the Western Hemisphere.

It is inherently difficult to uncover the motivations of peasants in revolt. Many of the sources available to the historian are quite removed from the thought processes of the protagonists. In the case of the Andes, most interpretations of the motives of rebelling peasants (who were usually monolingual Aymara—or Quechua-speaking Indians) come from newspaper accounts written by Spanish urban dwellers, reports by government officials, trial records, or, in the most exceptional cases, documents written by or for the rebels themselves. While all of these sources are to a certain extent helpful, they reveal only small fragments of the motivations and consciousness of the peasants when used in conventional ways.

The inherent difficulties of revealing the mental constructs and assumptions of an overwhelmingly nonliterate people can in part be overcome by analyzing the rituals that were an integral part of the revolts. For rituals, as actions endowed with special symbolic meaning, organize perceived reality in certain ways. These often repetitive actions express ideal social and political arrangements as well as relationships with the supernatural. As David Kertzer suggests, "Ritual helps give meaning to our world in part by linking the past to the present and the present to the future."[1] Thus, not only the motivations of revolt but also the kind of world the peasants see around them and the world they want to construct can be revealed through the rituals in which the rebels try to deal with and make sense of this time of momentous stress in their society. In this article, two rituals from the 1927 Indian rebellion in southern Bolivia are compared and contrasted to arrive at a more profound understanding of how peasants perceived their world and how they thought it should be changed.

The 1927 rebellion can be seen as the culmination of a number of long-term trends and tendencies in the region. In the southern Bolivian highlands, the twin institutions of Indian communities and haciendas (large landed estates) predominated, although there were also a significant, albeit much smaller number of individual smallholdings owned largely by mestizo town dwellers. The peasant communities, called ayllus in the Andes, were the remnants of preconquest ethnic groups. Although the Spanish colonial government had reorganized the communities in an effort to control and evangelize the conquered population, provide for efficient tribute collection, and make possible the extraction of labor resources (in this region, primarily for the silver mines), the ayllus maintained most of their aboriginal organization and culture. The communities continued to control much of the region's land, especially in the uplands of the department of Potosí. In turn, owners of the haciendas were typically members of the elite, descendants of the Spanish. Haciendas were generally concentrated in the valleys, where the warmer climate and access to irrigation made land more productive and valuable. The estate's resident labor force was for the most part indistinguishable from the population of the surrounding communities. Thus, the vast majority of the southern Bolivian highland population (even on the haciendas) was Indian and, in one sense or another, imbued with Andean rather than European culture.[2]

The patterns of land ownership changed rapidly in the half century prior to the revolt, and this can be seen as one of the prime reasons for the 1927 uprising. As a result of legislation introduced in the 1870s that abolished Indian communities, the haciendas expanded dramatically at the expense of the former communities. Despite the abolition of the communities' legal status, the Indians of southern Bolivia attempted to keep their communal organization and authority structures intact, often locally resisting the measurement and later the acquisition of their lands by outsiders. They succeeded to a larger extent here than in northern Bolivia, for the decline in silver mining, the region's economic mainstay, weakened the southern Bolivian landlords and precluded their wholesale usurpation of complete communities. Thus the assault on community lands took on a piecemeal character; nevertheless, in certain areas, such as northern Chuquisaca, it severely weakened some communities. In northern Potosí, on the other hand, the loss of Indian lands, through hacienda expansion and acquisition by mestizo townspeople, was relatively slight and did not completely disrupt the traditional predominance of the Indian communities. One observer noted in 1921 that in Potosí the better part of the aboriginal population continued to live in Indian communities, whereas in Chuquisaca most of the land and the rural population were under the direct control of the white landlords.[3]

Although their effects were greater in certain areas than in others, the laws abolishing the indigenous communities clearly worked to the detriment of the Indian peasants of southern Bolivia. The principal legislative bills, adopted in 1874 and the early 1880s, anticipated that the Indians, through their participation in a free land market and through the abolition of the archaic institution of the community imposed by colonial circumstances, would become full citizens of the nation. The reality was rather different from the legislators' ideal of turning the Indians into yeoman farmers. Not only did land purchasers and government officials often use fraudulent means to acquire land very cheaply, but in no other way were the community members enfranchised to participate in national life and utilize the opportunities that the liberal laws gave them in theory. In southern Bolivia most Indians continued to pay the traditional tribute. Although the name of the tax had been changed to *contribución territorial* and was collected by departmental rather than national authorities, the reality of a discriminatory tribute exacted on one ethnic group because of its earlier conquest by the Spanish remained.[4] In other ways community members remained outside national society as well; they could not speak Spanish, the official language of Bolivia; received no schooling; did not vote; were generally the poorest members of society; and were disdained by all other groups within the country.

On July 25, 1927, one of the largest peasant rebellions of the twentieth century erupted in Chayanta province, in northern Potosí. The Indians attacked a number of estates there and elsewhere, sacking hacienda houses, killing cattle, and destroying gardens and orchards. Peasants in four of the country's nine departments rose in revolt, but in only a month troops armed with machine guns were able to suffocate the rebellion. All told, about ten thousand peasants participated in the revolt; hundreds were killed. Although the revolt was suppressed, it effectively halted the expansion of the hacienda onto Indian community lands and prompted the government to replace corrupt local officials.[5]

On July 27, 1927, in the midst of the rebellion, a revealing ritual took place. On the recently conquered Hacienda Peaña, in the presence of all the members of Jaiguari allyu, the *ilacata*, or community official, solemnly took declarations from a number of witnesses about the abuses committed by the owner of Peaña and Hacienda Murifaya. Taking a transcription of the proceedings in the correct legal form was the corregidor (highest political authority), Néstor Sotomayor, recently captured by the Indians. After declarations had been taken, Sotomayor and another minor official, the *juez parroquial* J. Villalta, drew up a document giving Peaña and Murifaya to the "surrounding community members" from Macha and Pocoata. They were forced to copy this document four times onto other sheets, as well as a paper signed by another landowner that gave all his land to the Indians.[6]

Two days later, the Indian rebels stormed Hacienda Guadalupe. A very different ritual took place there. The attackers captured the owner of the estate, Julio Berdeja, who had valiantly fought them off with a pistol and even managed to kill one Indian. The Indians took Berdeja to the river and killed him. Marcelino Burgos, one of the leaders of Jaiguari ayllu, ate portions of the dead man; according to court testimony, other Indians from that community joined Burgos in the act. Afterwards, the rest of Berdeja's body was sacrificed to the god residing in the mountain known as Condor Nasa by interment at the mountain.[7]

The Meaning of Judicial Ritual

What can these rituals tell us about the Indians and their motivations and about the world they wanted to construct? Let us first examine the first incident, which resulted in the officials' signing over Hacienda Peaña and Murifaya to the rebels. The format of this "judicial ritual" was a trial, but without the usual European authorities presiding. The Indians did not usually imitate European forms to resolve their disputes, but in this case they minutely observed the various legal formalities of a regular court. The papers that document this incident look almost exactly like the record of the Indians' later trial for subversion, in which these documents served as some of the authorities' prime inculpatory pieces of evidence. Other than the lack of stamped official paper, the documents are the same as those from the subsequent trial. The Indians reproduced the same phrases that one would hear in the criminal cases in even the most backward village court; witnesses were called, and all those testifying against the landowner were asked the same questions, just as in regular court proceedings. Unfortunately, other than the documents inserted into the later trial to back the charge against the rebels of subversion, we have no other source for this ritual. This means that we cannot decipher from the records exactly how the trial was set up, the position of the accusers, the Indian judge, and the captured officials, nor the ceremonies surrounding this event. Nevertheless, the extant documents are sufficiently rich to provide important insights into key aspects of the rebels' mindset.

In certain ways, this trial was very different from those that occurred daily in the many small town courts throughout the country. Perhaps most obvious was the fact that an Indian community official presided as judge, unlike the normal hierarchy, in which the judge was always a city-bred member of the elite and any lawyers were of the same ethnic heritage or were small-town mestizos. Nevertheless, the presence of local officials to take down the proceedings and sign documents points to the Indians' continued acknowledgment of Europeans as legal specialists (and the only ones who could speak and write Spanish, the official language of all court documents).

The use of legal forms even during rebellions and uprisings is much more common than might be supposed. Witness, for example, E. P. Thompson's discovery that crowds in eighteenth-century English bread riots acted in a legalistic manner when attacking price gougers and setting what they considered to be fair prices.[8] There are numerous Andean examples as well, particularly in the much-studied case of the Tupac Katari/ Tupac Amaru rebellions in the late eighteenth century. In 1780, one of the first acts of Tupac Amaru's rebellion had been the public trial and execution of the hated corregidor Antonio Juan de Arriaga. Likewise, Sergio Serulnikov has recently argued that the Indian rebel leaders of the 1780s in northern Potosí (the same area where the 1927 rebellion occurred) were only trying to enforce the edicts of the Buenos Aires courts, at least as the

Indians interpreted them.[9] Certainly, the Indians in early twentieth-century southern Bolivia were also familiar with the trial setting and the legal forms, as the multitude of cases in the local courts that dealt with community members shows.

What was innovative, however, was the content of the legal proceedings themselves, namely, the reasons for the expropriation of the haciendas. One would have expected, after the tremendous expansion of the Bolivian hacienda just prior to the rebellion, that the Indians would assert that the land had simply been theirs to begin with. In fact, direct evidence from many sources confirms that one of the main tenets of the rebel leaders was that all land belonged to the Indians and the haciendas should all be turned back into community land.[10]

Despite these precedents, this was not the reason cited for expropriation. Instead, the community Indians based their claims to the haciendas on the abusive treatment that the hacienda peons, or *colonos*, had received at the hands of [Andrés] Garnica, the hacendado. The eleven *colonos* who testified at the trial described three basic abuses. The most common complaint was that the landlord treated his laborers unfairly. Garnica "abusively entered the sheep corrals and takes one and does not pay a fair price"; "the cost of taking a [loaded] donkey costs us one Boliviano, and he pays [only] forty *centavos*."[11] The second complaint was the rapid rise in rental costs for the land that the peons occupied. According to one *colono*, "Garnica charges for my plot what once cost five *pesos febles* [debased coins worth 80 percent of the Boliviano] but today charges 40 Bolivianos."[12] The last major complaint was that he "was accustomed to raping the married and single women" of the estate, both in the hacienda house and in the fields, where he "committed abuses to those women and girls who went to pasture the cattle or sheep." In fact, rape of women and girls who watched the family livestock in the hills alone was (and still is) rather common (moreover, courtship rites among Indians were frequently accompanied by violence). However, Garnica's position as outsider and the impunity with which he allegedly committed these crimes were reprehensible enough to merit inclusion among the abuses that led to the forfeiture of his properties.[13]

It is remarkable that throughout the trial the only reason given for the hacienda expropriations was the abuse of the *colonos*. Why did the Indians not even mention the Spanish conquest and that the hacendados had abusively taken the land in the past forty years? There are a number of possible answers. For one, witnesses in the government trial against the rebels asserted that Manuel Michel, the self-styled "Casique [Chief] General de Chuquisaca" and the prime mover of the revolt, claimed that there were "only three properties or estates and the others were all Indian lands."[14] Perhaps Peaña and Murifaya were those non-Indian lands that Michel referred to, and so another reason than aboriginal rights had to be adduced. This is unlikely, however, given the fact that the properties were handed over to the Macha and Pocoata communities and were not kept by Michel himself, as others alleged. The other possibility is that these estates had been part of the Indian lands so long ago that they were not considered community lands anymore. This possibility, however, argues against much of the thrust of the rebels' apparent call for the abolition of all haciendas and their return to Indian ownership.

What is interesting is that despite the *colonos'* collaboration in this judicial ritual, it seems that Peaña and Murifaya were turned over not to them but to the Indians of the nearby communities of Macha and Pocoata who had stormed the properties. Moreover, instead of burning the hacienda books, as the rebels did on other estates, the Indians preserved them. Perhaps the books were seen as icons (given the almost universal illiteracy of the rebel leadership and its army), which could also prove the claims of possession by communities. In any case, both of these facts suggest that the communities wanted merely to switch ownership of the estates and maintain the hacienda workers in some kind of dependent status. In fact, this was already occurring. Evidence from the early twentieth century in the region points to the creation or transformation of a group within the ayllus to *colonos* of other community members, mirroring the categories on the haciendas.[15]

Although analysis of the content of this judicial ritual by itself leaves important questions unanswered, an understanding of who the intended audience was can help determine why the rebels proceeded as they did. Ritual is frequently directed not only at those present but also at audiences elsewhere, and the ending is certainly preordained. The ending in this case probably reflected quite accurately how the community members felt when they entered the official court system in Bolivia.

The rebels undoubtedly used a trial format to assert legitimacy of their actions. As Steve Stern has shown, Andeans soon after the Spanish conquest had accepted the colonial legal system, though at first they used it to play various factions within European society against one another and mitigate their condition.[16] By the late colonial period, as mentioned above, the Indian rebels of the 1780s had also utilized the public trial to legitimate the execution of a hated official. The Indians' use of the court system to settle disputes accelerated after the 1874 laws abolishing the Indian communities. Once ayllu officers lost their officially sanctioned roles as arbiters within the communities, the courts increasingly became involved in the myriad intra-ayllu disputes, particularly over land rights. Thus the courts—and, by extension, the legal procedures themselves—

became the standard for settling these types of matters even among the Indian population.

The legitimacy of this particular proceeding was also confirmed through the presence of the two officials who had been captured. As those arrested during the rebellion testified, rebel leaders emphasized that they had "through the corregidor and the juez parroquial made them give us the above-mentioned properties [Peaña and Murifaya], driving out the landlords" in meetings, and they brandished the carefully preserved hacienda account books to prove it.[17] Although these officials did not participate voluntarily, they were important legitimating agents not only because of their presence but also because they produced the documents used to extend this air of legitimacy.

The procedures the rebels used suggest that the trial was directed at three principal parties. First of all, it was directed at fellow rebels, to show that the movement had made significant gains. It was the first time since 1871 that the Indians had gained rather than lost land.[18] Interestingly enough, one of the copies of the documents transferring the properties to the Indians (the only one bearing the seal of Manuel Michel, the leader of the rebellion) contains a curious addition. After the certification by the two captured officials, it states that "now there is news here so that all the community members of the Copavilque Valley know of this."[19] This phrase was put there either to strengthen the Macha and Pocoata ayllus' claim to these properties, to the exclusion of the other major groups that participated in the uprising in the area, such as the members of the Condo ayllus who had lands in the Copavilque valley, or simply to indicate to whom the copy of the document should be sent. In either case, it is clear that the ritual—and its end result, the certificate transferring property rights—was directed internally.

The trial ritual was also directed at the larger society, in particular at the hacendado whose properties were expropriated; by using the formulas which the landowners themselves accepted when they fought their legal battles with the communities, the rebel leaders appealed to the legitimacy that the judicial ritual implied. There even remained an implication that there was some room for negotiation of the terms of this transfer, since the document promised that the community members "will make formal arrangements with the *patrón* Andres Garnica."[20]

The Indians considered the papers of the trial and the certificates themselves powerful artifacts. As James Lockhart has found for central Mexico in the late seventeenth and eighteenth centuries, villagers created their own "primordial titles" to assert their rights to land, though these titles were not accepted by colonial society as legitimate documents. By the early twentieth century, the Zapatista peasants were still preserving these types of titles and attributing the same values to them.[21] Similarly, in the agitation prior to 1927, the Indians engaged in a kind of "paper war," using "official" documents to assert their rights to land and causing real consternation among the hacendados. One of the tactics was the pasting of fliers, which mimicked some broadly worded governmental resolutions in favor of Indian rights, on the walls of landlords' hacienda houses.[22] This tactic of psychological warfare was certainly effective, for it greatly upset the landowners. As the overwhelmingly illiterate Indians thought, these relatively meaningless fliers possessed a certain efficacy as pieces of paper; though crudely written, they invaded the very center of the landlord's power and symbolically challenged the legitimacy of his rule. They also suggested that the national government identified with the Indians' cause, emboldening the peasants to take matters into their own hands.

The trial and the documents written during this ritual also aimed at reaching some kind of understanding with the national government, perhaps the most important audience inasmuch as its army controlled the forces of repression. For this reason, the transfer document stated that the change of ownership was provisional until ratified by petition to "higher authorities."[23] Further indicating that this ritual was directed at the larger society and at the government in particular was the fact that the documents were written in Spanish, not Quechua or Aymara. It is clear from the trial records of the Indian rebels that few of their leaders even spoke Spanish. That their accusations were translated into a foreign tongue, a troublesome procedure, implies that the rebels were addressing the national government, composed exclusively of members of the urban Europe-oriented elite.

Imitating the legal forms of a trial, in which witnesses brought charges against a defendant, also provided a basis for legal action by the government on behalf of the Indians. Perhaps the rebels felt that claims based on aboriginal rights to the land would be rejected because in the past fifty years the state had sanctioned the sale of Indian land to outsiders and was dedicated to the preservation of private property. In this fashion, the rebels were trying to gain the high moral ground and impress upon the government the justice of their cause. Only a year earlier the government had supported a failed effort by the Catholic church to prevent abuse against the Indians.[24] By making the abuse of the hacienda labor force the crux of the communities' right to take over the hacienda land, the rebels put the whole governmental reform effort to the test as well.

Why were the Indians so anxious to legitimate their actions in front of the national government in this ritual, when they in fact were breaking the law? After all, the rebels had taken two government officials prisoner and threatened them, attacked the private property that the government was sworn to protect, and expropriated land from local elites. One possible answer is that the rebels conceived of the country's political organization differently than the Europeanized members of Bolivian society. The national government, and the president in particular, were seen to be distinct from corrupt local officials and the urban-based European society. Frank Salomon has recently asserted that the Indians in late eighteenth-century Arequipa (Peru) considered society to be divided into two human groups, the Spanish and the Indians. The Indians' segmentary view of society, in which kin groups were divided into moieties and other discrete units, corresponded rather closely to the organization of the early Spanish colonial state. Thus, according to Salomon, the Indians felt that they were part of the "Indian republic" (*república de indios*) overseen by the Spanish king, who was above both Europeans and Indians.[25] The argument can be made that these conceptions of society remained in force into the twentieth century because they dovetailed very nicely with Andean ideas of social organization. For example, Catherine Allen has shown recently how the quintessentially Andean idea of complementary but opposing pairs, such as the Indians and non-Indians, is still evident in the present-day Andean peasants' conception of society.[26]

There is considerable evidence that the Indians conserved a conception of the Bolivian state that echoed colonial rather than early twentieth-century political realities. For example, even after the de facto capital had moved to La Paz, Indians went to Sucre, the colonial administrative capital, to petition the national government. Manuel Michel's self-styled title, "Casique General de Chuquisaca," had these colonial resonances, as Indians still saw Chuquisaca, with Sucre as its capital, as the center of legitimacy in the national political system.[27] Thus, the conceptions of social and political organization remained filtered through the prism of Andean standards (in which the three centuries of colonial experience naturally loomed large), which helps us to understand why so much care was taken in this judicial ritual to follow procedures used by the national court system.

The issues of this ritual's audience and the need for legitimacy, primarily among fellow Indians and the national government, inform an understanding of the goals and motivations of the rebels. The trial is very suggestive about the kind of society the Indians had in mind after the uprising. The trial probably reflected not only the ideas of the rebel leaders but, to a certain extent, those of their followers, who, after all, participated or at least acquiesced in this ritual. Moreover, the leadership had been winnowed during the numerous smaller incidents that had taken place in the previous two or three years. Thus, those who led and those who followed probably had roughly congruent goals, hammered out during the lengthy phase of rebellion leading up to 1927.

Quite clearly, the trial showed that the Indian did not conceive of a world without non-Indian elites. The rebels' scrupulous regard for the forms of judicial procedure shows that they were willing, in some way, to accept the legitimacy of the national government. Their incessant petitions and requests for legal relief both in La Paz and in Sucre also suggest that the communities accepted the government's prerogative to dispense justice, one of the primary functions of any government.

A common cry among many revolutionaries, at least in the beginning, was that only the local representatives were corrupt; if only the president (earlier, the king) heard of these matters, they would be straightened out.[28] In fact, the national government's actions had encouraged this belief; virtually every time the Indians had petitioned the higher levels of government on some matter, they had received a favorable *resolución* (which in practical terms was so vague as to be useless). Thus, the rebels saw the national government as on their side; the problem was that local authorities refused to carry out the national authorities' orders. This ambivalence towards government was common among peasants throughout the Spanish empire and, in fact, among peasant populations throughout the world—it amounted to a modified version of "Long live the king but down with the local officials."[29] In the Spanish American case this propensity had much to do with the colonial administrative structure (and its republican successors), where ordinary countryfolk had little access to high officials. The judicial ritual, in which local authorities were forced to accept the Indians' verdict, confirms this.

Implicit in the judicial ritual, and its insistence on maintaining many legal forms, was an appeal by the rebels for the support of the national government. The rebels were quite aware of the power the state could muster. The many incidents prior to the 1927 rebellion (most notably the siege of the town of Tarabuco during Carnival in 1925) showed the repressive power of the state, when it mobilized police forces and soldiers armed with machine guns and cannons, arms which the Indians could never hope to match.[30] By keeping to legal forms even within a potentially revolutionary setting and recording these acts, the rebels undoubtedly were aiming at an eventual accommodation with the state. That they thought these legal forms and these papers could help achieve this goal, or at least keep this possibility open, shows the power that the judicial ritual was thought to possess.

In the Andean case, this apparently contradictory behavior—accommodation within a revolutionary setting—was amplified by the Indians' perceptions of two divergent societies, one European and the other

Indian, ruled over by a common sovereign.[31] Of course, the perception of dual societies was based on many concrete realities which the liberal reforms of the nineteenth century had done little to change. Indians still paid tribute in many cases (although it was now called something else), were treated as second-class citizens by non-Indians, and spoke a different language. On the other hand, the division of the world into Indian and non-Indian spheres did not necessarily mean that the Indians accepted contemporary roles within society. With their actions, the rebels clearly showed that they felt that hacendados were illegitimate usurpers of Indian land and should lose their land if they mistreated their laborers.

These *colonos'* complaints and the verdict of the trial, which gave the land to the communities, also suggest a certain hierarchical conception of society. Clearly, the community members knew of the abuses the hacienda peons had suffered under their landlord. This, however, was insufficient for the abolition of *colono* status. Rather, as mentioned above, the mistreatment justified the hacendados' loss of authority over the *colonos* and the territory they worked to the presumably more benevolent Indian community members. Equality for all was not one of the rebels' goals; the invading community Indians were content to maintain a hierarchical society with the *colonos* as their inferiors, even though they shared virtually the same ethnic heritage. This attitude manifested itself in the structure of the trial, in which an official from the Macha ayllus, not one of the *colonos*, acted as ritual leader. Furthermore, many of the hacienda workers suffered abuse at the hands of the community Indians during the hacienda takeovers.[32] This situation was a far cry from the accusations hurled by the landowners and certain officials, who claimed that the Indians were inspired by communist ideas and wanted to wipe out all distinctions between the wealthy and the poor.[33]

Human Sacrifice, Mountain Gods, and Ritual Limits

Prior to the rebellion, Julio Berdeja, owner of Hacienda Guadalupe, who also happened to be the corregidor of *canton* (county) Guadalupe, had apparently harassed the Indians from Tinguipaya who traveled to the valleys to take care of the fields they owned there. He made them work without pay on his hacienda by taking their pack animals and tools until they had finished the tasks that he assigned them. In addition, the hacendado had acquired some Indian lands. Using a common strategy, Berdeja apparently had lent some money to an Indian and later had taken over his property, claiming that he had not been paid back. The hacendado also disputed water rights over an irrigation ditch with the Indian residents of the Guadalupe Valley.[34]

As the rebellion spilled into Guadalupe on July 29, Berdeja killed an Indian and cabled for help from Sucre to contain the revolt. However, before the government could mobilize its troops, three hundred Indians attacked Berdeja's hacienda with clubs and sticks, took him to the small stream in the middle of the valley, and killed him. His fingers were cut off and put in the rebels' coca bags. Marcelino Burgos, one of the rebel leaders, began to eat the body; according to one witness, "all of Burgos's ayllu ate the cadaver." Another witness testified that Burgos had asserted afterwards "that Berdeja's flesh had been stringy." The Indians then buried the bones at Condor Nasa, on the border between Antora and Pitantora counties, offering him to the mountain god who dwelled there.[35]

For this set of rituals we unfortunately have no records written as they happened. Most of the information about the human sacrifice comes from police records, which only contain answers to leading questions. Moreover, none of the accused was willing to admit that he had participated in this ritual, though many claimed that they had heard of it from a third person and were quite sure of the names of the instigators. The other source of information is the accounts of anthropologists who have worked in the northern Potosí area and tapped into the apparently rich oral traditions that record this event.[36]

What can we tell from this ritual? Certainly, the few details that we have suggest an affair very different from the first ritual described. Most striking is the violence displayed; there apparently was no attempt to employ the forms of the national justice system. An obvious explanation of the ritual, compared to the previous one, might be that the Indians by now realized that their actions would bring about violent repression from the government and thus were willing to leave aside legal niceties. This, however, is not borne out by the facts. A group of the revolt's leaders was not captured until the night of August 3, fully five days after the murder. Among the captured leaders were Manuel Michel and members of the Jaiguari, Janina, Condo, Quilaquila, Copavilque, and Pitantora ayllus. The main purpose of the meeting at which the leaders were captured, from what we can gather from the interrogations, had been to show off the success of the revolt by asserting that the rebels had gained legal ownership of Haciendas Murifaya and Peaña. Thus, the leaders were still trying to insist on the legitimacy of their actions, since all those who confessed to having been at the meeting asserted that the rebel leaders had displayed the papers transferring the estates to the communities as well as the hacienda records at that time. The police in fact found these documents in the possession of their prisoners, and they thus entered the record of the proceedings against the Indians involved in the rebellion. Moreover, the Indian leaders held the meeting in the suburbs of Sucre (where they were

captured), far beyond any territory controlled by rebel bands. The choice
of location suggests that they were hoping for some kind of support from
high government authorities.[37]

There are reports that episodes of cannibalism also occurred in earlier revolts, such as the great Tupac Katari/Tupac Amaru rebellion, which
engulfed what is now southern Peru and Bolivia at the end of the colonial
period, and the most important Indian rebellion in republican Bolivia before the 1927 rebellion, which occurred in 1899 at the end of the Federal-
ist War. The latter episode of cannibalism occurred during the massacre
of a troop of soldiers in the church at Mohoza in the Bolivian altiplano.
During the trial of the Indians involved at Mohoza, the Indian leader's
attorney, Bautista Saavedra, asserted that the rebels

> ripped out the [soldiers'] eyes, cut the tongues off and mutilated the
> testicles, to eat them with undefinable pleasure . . . inclined face down-
> ward, over the puddles and rivulets of blood [the Indians] drank it. . . .
> This type of cannibalism is very common among the Aymaras, because
> it is based on the superstitious belief that drinking the blood of the en-
> emy gives one great courage and satisfies fully [their desire for]
> revenge.[38]

Saavedra sensationalized the incident in the courtroom and, to help make
his case, claimed a greater frequency for ritual cannibalism among Aymaras
than probably existed. It is probably more useful to think of cannibalism
as an "occasional" ritual associated with rebellion and violence. What
was apparently new in the 1927 ritual was, as we shall see, the association
of ritual cannibalism and human sacrifice to indigenous deities with claims
to land rights and ethnic identity.

The most likely explanation is that this ritual was directed primarily
toward the Andean sacred sphere, although there were also a number of
very concrete intentions and consequences directed toward outsiders.
Fernando Montes Ruiz has postulated that during rebellions after the Spanish conquest, the Aymara frequently renounced Christianity and sacked
churches and other Catholic religious shrines. This in fact occurred during the 1927 rebellion, for the rebels sacked the pilgrimage site of Pumpuri.
Rejection of Catholicism and its representations provided a symbolic
means of rejecting Spanish conquerors and promoting a specifically
Andean ethnic identity.[39]

Anthropologists have documented that an Andean belief system has
persisted among the Aymara peasantry, despite the efforts of
Christianization, since the Spanish conquest. Although the Indians consider themselves Catholic, their world is inhabited by a hierarchy of aboriginal gods and spirits closely associated with geographical locations
and natural phenomena. The most important spirits live in high moun-

tains, streams, lakes, and the like; the next order of spirits are place spirits; the least important are house guardians. Some of these spirits are wholly good or bad, whereas others can be benevolent or evil, depending upon their treatment by the Indians. Lightning is also greatly feared, since it is a source of supernatural power.[40] It was to these most powerful supernatural beings that the rebels were primarily addressing themselves when they sacrificed Berdeja.

To understand this event, it is necessary to examine both the act of cannibalism and the act of sacrifice to the mountain god of Condor Nasa. Fernando Montes Ruiz, in a generally lucid analysis, postulates that the Indians ate Berdeja because they were afraid that the victim and other hacendados might bewitch them and punish them for the murder. Thus, according to Montes, the hacendado was treated like a malignant witch whose power (and perhaps symbolically that of other hacendados, the Indians' declared enemies?) could be nullified through ritual cannibalism. In addition, as also in the 1899 episode noted above, it gave the rebels the courage to fight against superior forces.[41]

The sacrifice of the hapless hacendado's bones is related to cannibalism but, according to Montes, had a different purpose. Condor Nasa is one of the highest peaks in the region and thus possesses extraordinary powers. Moreover, this mountain was traditionally associated with lightning, the ancient Aymara god of war. After the Spanish conquest, however, the European invaders appropriated lightning as a symbol of Santiago, the saint who led the Christians against the Moors during the long *reconquista* in Iberia. Even today lightning is associated with Santiago, who is sometimes described as wearing a silver revolver (much like some of the hacendados of the period), killing anyone he pleases. Montes asserts that the sacrifice of Berdeja's bones was a propitiation of the mountain god and so of the lightning deity. This rite thus served as a way of reappropriating an Aymara god and ensuring success against the Europeans.[42]

While this interpretation makes some sense, Montes ignores other elements which give the episode a much wider significance and show that both the cannibalism and the human sacrifice combine to make a powerful symbolic statement for the rebels. According to Tristan Platt, who complements but also expands upon Montes's analysis, the Indians of northern Potosí equated the act of cannibalism with the doctrine of transubstantiation, which the Franciscans imported into the region. The eating of the Host was thus reinterpreted in terms of the Andean solar cult, in which the consumption of the human body was related to the propitiation of the sun. In turn, the burying of the bones at the base of Condor Nasa (significantly, the mountain bases are called *saphis*, or "roots," in the region) also nourished the other part of the world under the earth; it was part of the characteristic effort by Andeans to maintain a natural balance at all times.[43]

More importantly for our purposes, both rites incorporated powerful assertions of territorial rights, and closely related ethnic identity, against the European society that had been insinuating itself into the northern Potosí countryside. To understand how these are related, it is necessary to examine *tinkus*, ritual battles between different kinship groups, because it is during the *tinku* that cannibalism probably occurs most frequently in the northern Potosí. In these battles, drunken community members from different ayllus or from the two moieties within an ayllu fight against each other, men against men and women against women. Tristan Platt has interpreted the *tinkus*, in which outright "winners" are never declared, as representing the affirmation of boundaries between the various levels of ethnic group organization and rights to land. According to Platt, *tinkus* can occur between different kinship-based subgroups, also called ayllus, within the larger ethnic unit, which he calls the Great Ayllu. However, if the members of one Great Ayllu attack members of another, then the various subgroups unite behind their Great Ayllu to fight against the others, who are even more different. Verb forms with the root *tinku* also mean "to fit together." (The *tinku* has sexual connotations and is a fertility rite as well.[44])

Tinkus are also closely related to *ch'axwas*, or battles between ethnic groups over land. In fact, at times the *tinku* and the *ch'axwa* can scarcely be distinguished, for both types of battles relate to struggles over the control of land, are highly ritualized, and put into play essentially the same underlying ideologies. In both, cannibalism occurs. The *ch'axwa*, however, is usually even more ferocious and is engaged in only with those defined to be outside the larger segmentary organizations (the Great Ayllus) and thus outsiders far removed in human society from the particular ethnic group. In many ways, of course, the 1927 rebellion can be defined as a *ch'axwa*, since the dispute was over land and involved, as we have seen, an ethnic group (Europeans and perhaps also mestizos) viewed as outsiders in the northern Potosí countryside.[45]

It has generally been assumed that people engage in cannibalism because it appropriates the victim's strength and emasculates him.[46] This, to a certain extent, is the case in northern Potosí, where only those who fight well during the *tinku* are sacrificed; the cannibals want to imbibe the victim's fighting abilities.[47] In the case of Berdeja, the hacendado undoubtedly earned a reputation as a powerful man and a good fighter from his desperate resistance, during which he managed to kill one of his attackers. But the powers of the victim were only a minor consideration. More importantly, the rites served to distinguish the cannibals from their victims. Jan Szemiński asserts that the rebels during the Tupac Amaru rebellion of the late eighteenth century only killed and mutilated Spaniards because they were identified as *nak'aq* (devilish and evil hominoids), but this interpretation is too limited. Berdeja might have been considered an evil creature, but in the Andean case many different types of outsiders—witches, members of other ayllus, and Europeans—are consumed.[48]

The act of cannibalism, an extraordinary rite that is taboo during "normal" times, serves to bring this group together. Thus, the fact that "all of Burgos's ayllu ate the cadaver" helped unite the rebels (and probably even those who until then had participated only halfheartedly) in a powerful common bond, or, at the very least, in a shared guilt. On the other hand, the consuming of a hacendado, as Tristan Platt has asserted, showed the enmity of the Indians toward those whom they considered the usurpers of their land and, as in the case of Berdeja, toward the abusers of power (both as local officials and as hacendados), the representatives of European society who penetrated into the countryside. Thus, I disagree, at least in part, with Szemiński, who believes that "Andean tradition condemns cannibalism." Andean tradition permits cannibalism of powerful but evil individuals under special circumstances of war or in ritual battles.[49]

As Olivia Harris and Xavier Albó have pointed out, the subsequent sacrifice to the mountain god served essentially the same purpose. They suggest that the location of the burial, along the boundaries of two counties, "underlined symbolically the ancestral right of the ayllus over land usurped by landlords."[50] Of the two *cantones* in question, Pitantora was the one in which the hacienda predominated; in Antora, it did not. Harris and Albó suggest that perhaps the boundaries of the two counties were also based on territorial divisions among local elite groups. Thus, the ayllus asserted the predominance of the communities over both types of *cantones* and also perhaps reaffirmed the territorial coherence of the region divided among the different ethnic groups. As we have already seen in the *tinkus* and the *ch'axwa*, land rights and ethnic identity were closely interwoven, as is natural in a peasant society. The Indians in a sense restricted the landlords, members of the urban elite, to their own sphere in the cities, thus liberating the countryside in favor of the autochthonous population. This the landlords undoubtedly also understood, though perhaps on a different symbolic level. The killing of one of their compatriots, combined with the Indian "savagery," almost certainly made the estate owners think twice about venturing out into the countryside, which the Indians now claimed for themselves.

Conclusion

A comparison between these two rituals can help us understand the motivations of the Indian rebels and how they conceived of the world around them. In a sense, rituals describe how participants perceive the world or how they would like the world to be. Each ritual also creates a rich symbolic language that speaks not only to participants but to observers and outsiders alike. Certainly, it is likely that to each group these rituals mean different things, but they are nevertheless important for understanding the discourse between groups within a society. The revolutionary politics of peasants, especially that of a nonliterate population that does not even communicate in the language in which records are kept, is difficult to disentangle without recourse to extralingual behavior. A look at rituals and how certain forms were utilized to make radical demands can help overcome this problem.

The rituals examined above, especially when taken as different expressions of the same political program, reveal many aspects of the rebels' goals shorn of the interpretations which outsiders attempted to impose on them during and after the uprising. The judicial ritual, with its almost slavish imitation of legal forms, showed that the peasants were concerned about the legitimacy of their actions and attempted to enlist the national government on their side or at least to co-opt it into not repressing the movement. By emphasizing the abuse of workers, a political issue on which the government had already declared itself on the side of the peasants, the rebels hoped to justify their radical expropriation of the haciendas. The abduction of local officials and their forced participation in the trial do not contradict this intent, since the Indians considered these individuals part of a different "republic"; in any case, only in this fashion could the Indians force the landlords to follow what they interpreted as the intentions of the government all along. Even the murder, consumption, and sacrifice of a hacendado did not, in the Indians' view, negate the efficacy of the judicial ritual, since the sacrifice of Berdeja was directed primarily towards the supernatural sphere. One issue which connected the two rituals and provided the rationale for both was the abuse of Andeans, though in the case of Berdeja the shooting of a rebel probably triggered the murder and sacrifice of the hacendado.

Both the expropriation of the haciendas and the rituals surrounding the killing of Berdeja were intimately tied to the issue of land ownership and ethnic identity. It is difficult, in fact, to make distinctions between these issues, because in the Indians' cognitive framework land and ethnic identity were two sides of the same coin. As the connections between ritual cannibalism and the *tinku* (and by extension, the *ch'axwa*), as well

as the location of the landlord's sacrifice, indicate, the Indians were symbolically delineating the boundaries between (to use sixteenth-century
terminology) the "república de españoles" and the "república de indios."
This ritual and other pronouncements indicate that the Indians were asserting their rights to the countryside. After all, one of their slogans was
that all haciendas, whether they had in recent memory been ayllu property or not, be turned into *terrenos de origen* (community lands). Non-
Indians were presumably restricted to the towns and cities.

What is interesting to note is that the trial showed no efforts toward
revolutionary egalitarianism, as urban elites, alarmed over the rebels' ties
with the Socialist party and the spread of communism, claimed. Rather,
the rebels' actions reflected an ideology in which the communities asserted the right to a determined place within the larger social and political hierarchy. The Macha ayllu's *ilacata*, or community official, who
presided as judge, resumed a sense of superiority, in particular in reference to the haciendas' *colonos*, who appeared only as witnesses and (at
best) indirect beneficiaries of the hacienda expropriation procedure. The
ilacata's authority rested ultimately on the consent of the community
members and the prestige accumulated through reciprocal (and, to a certain extent, redistributive) ties to the other members, ties maintained by
progressing through a series of ritual offices and their abundant festival
expenses. Few such links existed with the *colonos* from the haciendas,
who were only peripherally involved in the communities' moral and material economy. Thus, the *colonos* remained outside the communities' networks, in an inferior position. Whether or not they spoke the same language
or had originally come from the same ethnic groups mattered little. While
other evidence suggests that many hacienda workers joined the conspiracies preceding the 1927 rebellion and initially welcomed the rebels with
open arms, the actions that the community members took made it clear
that the *colonos* were to remain in more or less the same inferior position
even if the Indians permanently occupied the haciendas.[51] The judicial
ritual confirms this view. In effect, in the eyes of the *colonos*, the rebels
were reproducing the old hierarchical society. But now their masters were
to be the community members, the new owners of the haciendas.

The *ilacata*'s judgeship also implied a certain competence and equality with judges in the European world. At the same time, the imitations of
national legal forms and the promise to negotiate with the national government to make the expropriation documents effective show that the Indians were willing to work within the larger society's legal framework,
which the communities had utilized since the early colonial period. Perhaps this can be subsumed into the framework of Aymara political thought,
which Tristan Platt has tried to develop. Aymara "justice" involves two

parts that maintain a state of equilibrium; one side, however, is also superior.[52] Accepting the national state as the superior member, the rebels at the same time tried to reestablish a new equilibrium between both "republics." This did not imply that high national authorities ultimately were not in some sense superior to Andean ethnic authorities.

The episode of cannibalism and its attendant rituals were in the main internally oriented. Unlike the trial, put on for the benefit of the national government (and perhaps for other ethnic groups as well), this episode of cannibalism was oriented primarily towards the Indians' own supernatural sphere. Again, it is difficult to separate the concern for the supernatural from the issue of ethnic identity, for if Fernando Montes Ruiz is correct, the reappropriation of the supreme lightning god by the Indians and the repudiation of Christian symbols were attempts to reconstitute the Aymara cultural sphere independently of European intrusion. Thus, as in the land question, the Indians attempted to assert their own autonomy and delimit their world from that of their oppressors. In this fashion they tried to reverse the penetration of the hacienda into the northern Potosí countryside that had taken place in the previous forty-odd years and the exploitation that followed. To do this, the rebels utilized a new combination of rituals to assert their dominion over the land and the outsiders who had abused them and to revive their own gods. Their goal was to bring about a new equilibrium, in which old wrongs were righted and each portion of human society remained within what the rebels considered its proper boundaries.

Concurrently, the act of cannibalism might be interpreted as an act of psychological warfare as well. It is unclear whether the rebels had publicized this incident or, for that matter, wanted to do so. Nor is it evident, though it is certainly possible, that the community members and their leaders had heard or thought of the implications of the well-publicized trial of the Mohoza massacre a few decades earlier. In their dealings with national society, community members frequently used their status as Indians to their advantage; might they not have used this incident, which proved them "savages," to strike fear into the hearts of hacendados and mestizo smallholders? It is difficult to ascertain whether this had been an intention of the rebels, because the leadership was captured before it made public its motivations.

There are a number of apparent contradictions in the messages contained within these two rituals. Most obvious is the contrast between the scrupulous abandonment of them in the second. However, as I have argued, this might not have appeared contradictory to the rebels, for their conceptions of the Bolivian political and social systems were quite coherent and in many ways reflected the realities of life. Catholicism and its

symbols had penetrated into the countryside but had achieved meaning for the peasants only through the prism of Andean ideology. Ethnic identity was still framed within the crucibles of links with fellow community members, territory, and the reciprocal relationship with the earth, mountains, sky, and weather. Local officials exploited the Indians according to their own interests. Hacendados were abusive in their relations with community members and even with their own workers and thus merited punishment as evil, though very powerful, personages. In a real sense, Indian and non-Indian societies were two different worlds held together only by the unequal relationships between mestizos and hacendados (who also were the local officials) on one side and the Indians on the other, in combination with the very tenuous hold of the government on the countryside. The rebels saw the national government as a distant but potentially benevolent institution, to which they appealed in the judicial ritual. No such effort could be made for the hacendados, who had to be eliminated from the rural setting (symbolically and concretely) so that the community members could achieve their rightful ownership over the land.

These rituals reflected, in many ways very accurately, the historical movement in which the southern Bolivian community members found themselves. The Indians had what might be considered "archaic" conceptions of society, in that they presumed a social and political order not far removed from the colonial period. Ironically, as we have seen, these conceptions were quite true to the way in which Bolivian society treated the Indian population. Even after decades of liberal reforms by the state, in which (at least in theory) the Indians were to be integrated into society as equal members and full citizens, this important segment of the nation's inhabitants remained alienated and largely disenfranchised. The Indians countered the forces of hacienda expansion and exploitation by outsiders with rebellion, which included these types of rituals. In many ways, the rebels reacted in this fashion because they were conditioned to do so through their relationship with the other parts of Bolivian society.

Nevertheless, the rebels failed to bring the national government over to their side in their fight against the hacendados. Although some groups within the larger society were willing to support the Indians' demands, such as the small Socialist party and certain reformist politicians, once the Indians had committed themselves to a violent course of action against the hacendados, the national government, inevitably, repressed the movement. While the panic-stricken government misunderstood the rebels' actions and demands, the Indians themselves possibly misunderstood the revolutionary implications of their actions. Thus, the leaders of the rebellion were easily captured, and hundreds of Indians lost their lives when the government troops began a concerted campaign against them, bringing the revolt to an end by late August. Nevertheless, the Indians achieved some success; the bloody uprising did bring to a halt the wholesale usurpation of community lands by outsiders.

Notes

1. David I. Kertzer, *Ritual, Politics, and Power* (New Haven, CT, 1988), 9–10. There is a vast literature on defining ritual; most of it deals with the connection between ritual and the supernatural. For an introduction to "secular ritual" and its meanings, see also Sally Falk Moore and Barbara G. Myerhoff, eds., *Secular Ritual* (Assen, 1977), passim.

2. For an overview of nineteenth- and twentieth-century southern Bolivian social and economic history, see Tristan Platt, *Estado boliviano y ayllu andino: Tierra y tributo en el Norte de Potosí* (Lima, 1982); Erick D. Langer, *Economic Change and Rural Resistance in Southern Bolivia, 1880–1930* (Stanford, CA, 1989). For the purposes of this article, I have defined the southern Bolivian highlands as comprising Yamparaez province in Chuquisaca, the old province of Chayanta in Potosí, and the region between Lake Poopó and northern Potosí in Oruro.

3. George McCutchen McBride, *The Agrarian Indian Communities of Highland Bolivia* (New York, 1921), 19–25. For maps of ethnic boundaries, see Tristan Platt, "Mapas coloniales de la provincia de Chayanta: Dos visiones conflictivas de un solo paisaje," in *Estudios bolivianos en homenaje a Gunnar Mendoza L.*, comp. Martha Vrioste de Aguirre (La Paz, 1978), 113; Erick D. Langer, "Persistence and Change in Southern Bolivian Indian Communities in the Nineteenth Century," paper delivered at the Ninth International Symposium of CLACSO, "Las comunidades campesinas en los Andes del siglo 19," Quito, Ecuador, July 27, 1989, 6.

4. Nicolas Sánchez Albornoz, *Indios y tributos en el Alto Perú* (Lima, 1978), 187–218; Tristan Platt, "Liberalism and Ethnocide in the Southern Andes," *History Workshop* 17 (1984), 3–18; Erick D. Langer, "El liberalismo y la abolición de la comunidad indígena en el siglo 19," *Historia y cultura* 14 (1988), 59–95.

5. For an overview of the ramifications of the 1927 revolt for Potosí, see René Danilo Arze Aguirre, *Guerra y conflictos sociales: El caso rural boliviano durante la campaña del Chaco* (La Paz, 1987), 11–25; Olivia Harris and Xavier Albó, *Monteras y guardatojos: Campesinos y mineros en el Norte de Potosí*, rev. ed. (La Paz, 1984), 59–71; Fernando Montes Ruiz, *La máscara de piedra: Simbolismo y personalidad aymaras en la historia* (La Paz, 1986), 339–42. For a discussion of its impact primarily in Chuquisaca, see Erick D. Langer, "The Great Southern Bolivian Rebellion of 1927: A Microanalysis," paper delivered at the symposium "Peasant Resistance and Rebellion: New Perspectives," Forty-sixth International Congress of Americanists, Amsterdam, July 7, 1988. Philip M. Keyes is presently working on an important analysis of the rebellion.

6. "Sublevación Indigenal" (1927), vol. 2, Criminal, Corte Superior de Chuquisaca (Sucre), fols. 100–104. My thanks to Philip Keyes, who found and made available this important document.

7. Although it is clear from the trial records and newspaper accounts that Berdeja was killed and parts of his body eaten (see ibid., fols. 19, 2; Claudio Andrade P.,

"Sublevación Provincia Chayanta 1927," unpublished manuscript in the author's possession, 1985, 3), the actual sequence of events is provided only in oral traditions uncovered by anthropologists Olivia Harris and Tristan Platt, who have worked extensively in the northern Potosí area. See Harris and Albó, *Monteras y guardatojos*, 61–62; Platt, *Estado boliviano*, 145–47.

8. E. P. Thompson, "The Moral Economy of the English Crowd in the Eighteenth Century," *Past and Present* 50 (1971), 76–136.

9. For standard, though somewhat dated, accounts of the Tupac Amaru rebellion, see Lillian E. Fisher, *The Last Inca Revolt, 1780–1783* (Norman, OK, 1966); Boleslao Lewin, *Túpac Amaru: Su época, su lucha, su hado* (Buenos Aires, 1973); Sergio Serulnikov, *Tomás Catari y la producción de justicia* (Buenos Aires, 1988); Serulnikov, *Revindicaciones indígenas y legalidad colonial: La rebelión de Chayanta (1777–1781)* (Buenos Aires, 1989).

10. This tenet is mentioned throughout the trial, both by suspects interviewed and by the landowners bringing suit. For the development of this radical idea, see Langer, "The Great Southern Bolivian Indian Rebellion," passim.

11. "Sublevación Indigenal," vol. 2, fols. 101, 103.

12. Ibid., fol. 101v.

13. Ibid., fols. 101v–102. For the courtship and sexual practices of the peasants in the region under discussion, see the pathbreaking work of Javier Isko, "Condores y mast'akus: Vida y muerte en los valles nortepotosinos," in *Tiempo y muerte: Estudio de caso en dos contextos andinos de Bolivia*, by Javier Isko, Ramiro Molina, and René Pereira (Cochabamba, 1986), 11–168.

14. "Sublevación Indigenal," vol. 2, fol. 56v.

15. See Erick D. Langer, "La comercialización del siglo 20," in *La participación indigena en los mercados surandinos*, ed. Olivia Harris, Brooke Larson, and Enrique Tandeter (La Paz, 1987), 583–601. The community Indians' neglect of the hacienda peons' demands that they be given the hacienda lands in northern Potosí and elsewhere led to the dissolution of the temporary alliance that both groups had formed prior to 1927 and was one of the main reasons for the movement's disintegration into local units. See Langer, "The Great Southern Bolivian Indian Rebellion."

16. Steven J. Stern, "The Social Significance of Judicial Institutions in an Exploitative Society: Huamanga, Peru, 1570–1640," in *The Inca and Aztec States, 1400–1800: Anthropology and History*, ed. George A. Collier, Renato J. Rosaldo, and John D. Wirth (New York, 1982), 289–320; Stern, *Peru's Indian Peoples and the Challenges of Spanish Conquest: Huamanga to 1640* (Madison, WI, 1982), esp. chap. 5.

17. "Sublevación Indigenal," vol. 2, fols. 1–13v. The quote is from fol. 13v.

18. For the retaking of Indian lands from the haciendas during the revolution against the Melgarejo regime in 1870–71, see Langer, "El liberalismo," 72–73.

19. "Sublevación Indigenal," vol. 2, fol. 104.

20. Ibid., fol. 100.

21. James Lockhart, "Views of Corporate Self and History in Some Valley of Mexico Towns: Late Seventeenth and Eighteenth Centuries," in *The Inca and Aztec States*, ed. Collier et al., 367–93. For the Zapatista experience, see John Womack, Jr., *Zapata and the Mexican Revolution* (New York, 1970), 371–72.

22. For a discussion of this point, see Langer, "The Great Southern Bolivian Indian Rebellion," 20.

23. "Sublevación Indigenal," vol. 2, fol. 100.

24. The "Great National Pro-Indian Crusade" by the Bolivian Catholic church in 1926 and its failure are chronicled in Herbert S. Klein, *Parties and Political Change in Bolivia, 1880–1952* (Cambridge, 1971), 90–91.

25. Frank Salomon, "Ancestor Cults and Resistance to the State in Arequipa, ca. 1748–1754," *Resistance, Rebellion, and Consciousness in the Andean Peasant World, Eighteenth to Twentieth Centuries*, ed. Steve J. Stern (Madison, WI, 1987), 148–65. For another, albeit flawed attempt at explaining the apparently contradictory actions of Andean rebels, see Jan Szemiński, "Why Kill the Spaniard? New Perspectives on Andean Insurrectionary Ideology in the Eighteenth Century," ibid., 166–92.

26. Catherine J. Allen, *The Hold Life Has: Coca and Cultural Identity in an Andean Community* (Washington, DC, 1988), 107–12. Part of this analysis is based upon Tristan Platt's seminal study of a northern Potosí community, "Symétries en miroir: Le concept *yanantin* chez les Macha de Bolivie," *Annales: Economies, sociétés, civilisations* 33 (1978), 1082–84.

27. Michel undoubtedly selected this title in large part for these connotations. In fact, he lived in the neighboring department of Potosí and could claim adherence to an ethnic group whose residential center lay in that department. Moreover, even today many Indians refer to Sucre as Chuquisaca, the aboriginal name of the city's location.

28. Soon after the Spanish conquest the colonial government had used its monopoly on the dispensation of justice to make various ethnic groups rely on non-Andean authorities to ensure the smooth functioning of society, thus fatally dividing the Andeans. See n. 16 for references.

29. For the Mexican case, see William B. Taylor, *Drinking, Homicide, and Rebellion in Colonial Mexican Villages* (Stanford, CA, 1979), 133–34. See also John L. Phelan, *The People and the King: The Comunero Revolution in Colombia, 1781* (Madison, WI, 1978). Of course, this was also a common sentiment during the early phases of the wars for independence throughout Spanish America.

30. Langer, "The Great Southern Bolivian Indian Rebellion," 16–20.

31. The substitution of the president of the nation for the Spanish king is also documented for the Ayacucho region in Peru and probably was common elsewhere in the Andean region as well. See, for example, John Earls, "La organización del poder en la mitología quechua," in *Ideología mesiánica del mundo andino*, ed. Juan M. Ossio (Lima, 1973), 393–414.

32. Langer, "The Great Southern Bolivian Indian Rebellion," passim. In fact, after 1927 the quite substantial support the rebel community members garnered from the *colonos* evaporated.

33. The Socialist party had attempted to integrate the peasant movement into its struggle and had invited many rebel leaders to its 1927 convention in Oruro, where the Indians gave speeches and in return received certificates of attendance and other paraphernalia from the Socialists. It is clear, however, that the Socialists had a very different agenda, according to which they attempted to subordinate the peasants to their labor movement. Despite the scare tactics of the right wing and the landowners, who tried to tar both with the same brush, all evidence points to the Socialists' failure to integrate the Indians effectively by 1927.

34. See Andrade, "Sublevación Provincia," 3–4; Harris and Albó, *Monteras y guardatojos*, 61.

35. This account, which comes largely from oral traditions, is contained in Harris and Albó, *Monteras y guardatojos*, 61–62; Platt, *Estado boliviano*, 145–46. The quotations come from "Sublevación Indigenal," vol. 2, fols. 19, 21.

36. See in particular Harris and Albó, *Monteras y guardatojos*; Montes, *La máscara de piedra*; and Platt, *Estado boliviano*. Both written and oral sources must be treated with caution; however, they are generally consistent internally and with each other. Other than the caveats expressed in the text, I feel that the information can be given credence. On another level, of course, what the Indians imagined this ritual to have been is as important as the actual sequence of events, which is impossible to reconstruct in detail in any case.

37. In fact, as Philip Keyes has found, the rebel leaders earlier had received support from the president of the university in Sucre, as well as from other prominent members of the southern Bolivian society, for building schools in the countryside.

38. Bautista Saavedra, *El ayllu* (La Paz, 1903), 185. Saavedra later became president of Bolivia (1921–1925). Curiously, Ramiro Condarco Morales, in *Zárate, el "temible" Willka: Historia de una rebelión indígena de 1899* (La Paz, 1966), the standard account of this rebellion, makes no mention of cannibalism. Incidents of cannibalism during the 1780 rebellion are summarized in Leon G. Campbell, "Ideology and Factionalism during the Great Rebellion, 1780–1782," in *Resistance*, ed. Stern, 124–26.

39. Montes, *La máscara de piedra*, 356–84. The sacking of Pumpuri is mentioned in Harris and Albó, *Monteras y guardatojos*, 61. An interesting view of shrines and the roles they play in Andean society is contained in Michael J. Sallnow, *Pilgrims of the Andes: Regional Cults in Cusco* (Washington, DC, 1987). Unfortunately, we lack the information on Pumpuri necessary to analyze the burning of the shrine based on Sallnow's hypotheses. Was Pumpuri considered a "mestizo shrine" and so open to attack?

40. Harry Tshopik, Jr., "The Aymara," in *Handbook of South American Indians*, vol. 2, ed. Julian H. Steward (Washington, DC, 1946), 558–60. Also see Tristan Platt, "The Andean Soldiers of Christ; Confraternity Organization, the Mass of the Sun, and Regenerative Warfare in Rural Potosí (Eighteenth–Twentieth Centuries)," *Journal de la Société des Américanistes* 73 (1987), 139–92.

41. Montes, *La máscara de piedra*, 378–79. The need to consume part of the witch's body to render it harmless is confirmed by another incident during the 1927 rebellion. An accused witch who had earlier aided hacendados in acquiring land from the Indians was imprisoned by rebels. According to witnesses, the Indians threatened to kill her and drink her blood. See Criminal Juzgado de Instrucción (Tarabuco), 1927, vol. 1, fol. 16v.

42. Montes, *La máscara de piedra*, 236–38, 379–80. For the most detailed analysis of the mountain gods, see Gabriel Martínez, "Los dioses de los cerros en los Andes," *Journal de la Société des Américanistes* 69 (1983), 85–115.

43. Platt, "The Andean Soldiers of Christ."

44. Tristan Platt, *Espejos y maíz: Temas de la estructura simbólica andina* (La Paz, 1976), 17–18; Platt, "The Andean Soldiers of Christ"; Thérèse Bouysse-Cassagne and Olivia Harris, "Pacha: En torno al pensamiento aymara," in *Tres reflexiones sobre el pensamiento aymara*, ed. Thérèse Bouysse-Cassagne, Olivia Harris, Tristan Platt, and Verónica Cereceda (La Paz, 1987), 29–31; Platt, "Entre

Ch'axwa y Muxsa: Para una historia del pensamiento político aymara," ibid., 82–93. Ludovico Bertonio, *Vocabulario dela lengua aymara* (Cochabamba, 1984 [1612]), 350, in addition to the various meanings related to meeting in battle, interprets *tincusitha*, for example, as "conformarse una cosa con otra; venir bien, ajustarse."

45. For an explanation of the *ch'axwa*, see Platt, "Entre Ch'axwa y Muxsa."

46. See Montes, *La máscara de piedra*, 376–77; Fritz John Porter Poole, "Cannibals, Tricksters, and Witches: Anthropophagic Images among Bimin-Kuskusmin," in *The Ethnography of Cannibalism*, ed. Paula Brown and Donald Tuzin (Washington, DC, 1983), 6–32; Gillian Gillison, "Cannibalism among Women in the Eastern Highlands of Papua New Guinea," ibid., 34–50; I. M. Lewis, *Religion in Context: Cults and Charisma* (Cambridge, 1986), 63–77.

47. Javier Isko, pers. comm. March 29, 1989.

48. This line of reasoning, of course, stands William Arens's argument, that cannibalism does not exist, on its head. See Arens, *The Man-Eating Myth: Anthropology and Anthropophagy* (New York, 1979); see also Lewis, *Religion in Context*, 63–72. I am not implying that cannibalism functions in this way everywhere; see, for example, Gillison, "Cannibalism among Women." Moreover, in some religions within the Andes foreigners are seen as vampires and cannibals. This occurs even today in places such as Ayacucho province, Peru. See Szemiński, "Why Kill the Spaniard?" 170–71; Jean-Marie Ansion, *Demons de Andes: La pensée mythique dans une région des Andes péruviennes (Ayacucho)* (Louvain-la-Neuve, 1984). For the Cuzco region, see Allen, *The Hold Life Has*, III.

49. The quote is from "Sublevación Indigenal," vol. 2, fol. 19. Platt, *Estado boliviano*, 145–46; Szemiński, "Why Kill the Spaniard?" 169.

50. Harris and Albó, *Monteras y guardatojos*, 62.

51. See n. 32.

52. Platt, "Entre Ch'axwa y Muxsa."

11

Ethnic Identity and Its Attributes in a Contemporary Mexican Indian Village

Alan R. Sandstrom

A repeated visitor to a Nahua village (to which he gives the pseudonym of Amatlán) in northern Veracruz province, Mexico, in the 1970s and 1980s, Alan R. Sandstrom provides a cogent description of the salient features of native community life in modern times and of those factors promoting change. He directly addresses the crucial issues of what defines an Indian in the late twentieth century and of how Indians differentiate themselves from the mestizo culture that dominates most of Mexico. He points out that many Indians and mestizos share some aspects of the other group's culture and discusses the process by which some Indians gradually become mestizos.

Defining who is an Indian—and who is not—is a surprisingly difficult task. Most Mexicans distinguish between *mestizos*, people of mixed American Indian and European racial stock who possess a Hispanic cultural outlook, and *indios*, who are identified with the remnants of the traditional American Indian races and cultures that existed at the time of the Conquest. In general, urban Mexicans recognize that rural *mestizos* share some Indian cultural traits, but they know that *mestizo* culture is basically that of urban national Mexico. The term *indio* has pejorative connotations for most Mexicans because many urban people consider Indians to be backward, and Indians are overrepresented in the lowest socioeconomic levels of Mexican society. A more neutral phrase in use is *gente indígena*, or indigenous people. Urban Mexicans generally identify these indigenous people as those who live in or originate from small villages, speak Native American languages, and have a traditional culture that differs from theirs. However, this commonly held distinction between people of mixed versus aboriginal heritage is highly misleading.

The first problem is the use of the term *race*. Virtually all Mexicans are of mixed racial stock. A few people consider themselves to be "white," claiming to have a pedigree going back to the *peninsulares*, or Spaniards from the Iberian Peninsula, with no Indian admixture. These individuals are exceedingly rare and in most cases probably mistaken. People with Indian features, including black straight hair, dark brown eyes, brown skin, and relatively short stature, can be found at all levels of Mexican society. This fact has led some observers to claim that Mexico is thus free from racism and that social distinctions are based solely on ethnic and class affiliation. Although it is true that overt racial discrimination such as that often found in the United States is rare and would be impossible to maintain in such a mixed population, definite racial biases exist in Mexico. Indian features are widely held to be unattractive and thus undesirable. Even in Amatlán I found that people admired children born with lighter skin or brown, as opposed to black, hair. In Mexico to be *güero*, or light complexioned, gives a person advantages over his or her darker peers. But being darker does not necessarily mean the person is more Indian. An Indian can be *güero,* too.

This confusion is not totally eliminated if we focus on strictly sociocultural factors to distinguish Indians from *mestizos*. In one sense all Mexicans are *mestizos* and, in fact, scholars and writers sometimes say "we are a nation of *mestizos*." Indians have influenced many aspects of Mexican urban national culture including diet, art and architecture, language, religious belief, and ritual. In turn, there are virtually no Indians in contemporary Mexico who have escaped the influence of urban national culture. Thus, from the viewpoint of the outsider, defining what it is to be Indian is a matter of degree rather than of kind. Nor can the criterion of language always distinguish Indians from *mestizos*. Many rural *mestizo* people speak Indian languages bilingually, and in some cases Spanish is actually their second language. Individuals who are monolingual in a Native American language, however, can almost certainly be said to be Indian by whatever criteria are applied.[1]

The difficulty of distinguishing Indians from *mestizos* is a problem faced by the Mexican government as it tries to settle land disputes, develop policies to encourage economic development, and deliver services to Indian populations. In the past, officials needed a quick measure of "Indianness," and they settled on the criterion of footwear as one distinguishing feature. People who wear shoes are *mestizos*; those who do not are Indians. This solution helps to explain the oddity about the Mexican national census. Like many countries, the federal government conducts a census every ten years. The surveys normally contained questions regarding language affiliation that were designed to identify Indians. It eventually became obvious that language alone as a measure of Indianness is too crude to be of much use. As a consequence, beginning with the sixth national census in 1943, additional cultural data were collected from people, including whether or not they wore shoes.[2] The question was intended to keep track of the Indian population and measure its growth or decline relative to *mestizos*. Interestingly, by the 1980 census the question had been deleted.[3]

The example of Julio Martínez of Amatlán will help to clarify some of the problems in distinguishing Indians from *mestizos*. Julio was born in the village and, like all other residents, learned Nahuatl as his native language. His wife is from a neighboring Indian village and she, too, is a native Nahuatl speaker. Both Julio and his wife speak competent Spanish, and in fact are probably among the most fluent villagers. Julio is a farmer like other villagers, but he is distinguished by being one of the few people who owns cattle as well. His herd is large, and he has constant dealings with neighboring ranchers to ensure access to pastures and water. Out of a small counter at the side of his house he runs one of two functioning *cantinas* (bars) in Amatlán. He carries an assortment of dry goods, but most of his business comes from selling cane alcohol to the villagers. His wife peddles bread she bakes in a stone-and-mud bread oven, and his children wait on customers at the *cantina* counter. Julio is a true entrepreneur who, in addition to his village life, operates a clothing and dry goods stall at the weekly markets in Ixhuatlán de Madero and in Llano de Enmedio. In 1986, when electricity reached Amatlán for the first time, he purchased a small refrigerator that he had transported by burro to the village. He now sells *hielitos*, the Spanish term for Popsicle-like frozen bags of water mixed with sugar, coloring, and flavoring, in addition to cold soft drinks and beer.

When I first entered the village in 1970, Julio was one of the few men to wear Western-style clothing as well as shoes. He was curious about the United States and asked many questions about our farming practices and how much farm workers are paid in wages. He is extremely well off by comparison to the other villagers, and it is clear that he intends the same for his several children. In 1986, his eldest daughter was attending secondary school in a distant town, an expense most villagers cannot afford. In addition to his entrepreneurial activities, Julio had by 1986 become an active force for change in the village. He is on a committee to petition the *municipio* government to have a road constructed connecting Amatlán to the outside, and he worked diligently to have electricity brought to the village. In sum, his outlook, many economic activities, dress, speech, and other characteristics would seem to link him to the *mestizo* world. And yet in many ways, he is thoroughly Indian.

Julio and his wife speak Spanish well and yet, for them, Nahuatl is the language of everyday use. With the exception of the refrigerator (purchased in 1986) and the *cantina* counter, nothing distinguishes their house from any other in the village. In addition, both Julio and his wife participate actively in the communal activities of the village. He never misses a communal work party, and he willingly serves on village committees. Moreover, Julio and his family participate actively in the traditional religion. He has an altar in his house watched over by a paper cutout of a witness spirit, and he calls in traditional curers when a member of his family falls ill. He acts as sponsor to major rituals such as the yearly ceremony to *tonantsij*, an important fertility spirit. Julio does not appear to engage in these activities to mollify jealous neighbors or fend off criticisms by others less successful than he. He fervently believes in the Nahua pantheon of spirits, follows the traditional customs, and actively participates in his culture. He strives for the benefit of himself and his family, but does not remain aloof from his neighbors nor attempt to accrue power at their expense. He is one of those rare people little written about in social scientific literature: an Indian who has achieved substantial prosperity, while staying within the Indian system of values.

The complexities of distinguishing Indians from *mestizos* derive from the fact that no clear and stable dividing lines exist between the two groups. Although the cultural orientations of the two are different, from the perspective of the outsider they shade imperceptibly into one another. As in any sliding scale, the extremes are easy to distinguish. The in-between cases pose the difficulty. I would like to add here that the people of Amatlán do not appear to have any difficulty in determining a person's identity. Only an outsider, unfamiliar with the symbolic means of distinguishing the two groups, has difficulty.[4]

For the reader unfamiliar with ethnic divisions in Mexico, I would like to indicate some general features that distinguish Indians from *mestizos*. Ethnicity is often situational in that people decide when and how to assert their identity using different strategies at different times. An added complicating factor is that over time a group's self-definition changes to meet new challenges, and the symbols people choose to represent their identity may be modified, created anew, intentionally eliminated, or resurrected from a previous period. Thus, any listing of traits poses the danger of oversimplifying and thereby falsifying a complex and constantly shifting multiethnic situation. With these cautions in mind, I will identify some features of Nahua ethnicity recognized by both Indians and *mestizos*, and also meaningful to the outside observer.

Julio's example provides insight into how we might establish minimal criteria for defining Indian status that are valid for the period of my fieldwork. Such a definition should include the following characteristics: the person must (1) define himself or herself as an Indian; (2) be a native speaker of an indigenous language that is the language of choice in everyday speech; (3) participate freely in the communal activities of a village; (4) revere a pantheon of spirits and participate in rituals that, although influenced to a greater or lesser extent by Spanish Catholicism, derive from Native American traditions; (5) attempt through ritual and other means to enter into a balance or harmony with the social and natural worlds as opposed to striving for strict control over them. This last characteristic is difficult to apply, but it refers to the fact that most *mestizos* partake of the Euro-American world view, with its injunction to master the natural and social universes. Being Indian is not a state of wealth, nor is it antithetical to entrepreneurship or a progressive outlook that sees some benefits in adopting Western technology. Julio and his family are solidly Indian by their own assessment and by the five characteristics listed above.[5]

Two features of this list are important to note. First, none of the criteria is biological. Second, with the possible exception of the first (self-definition as an Indian), each characteristic allows for a range of adherence by the participants. For example, a person may engage in communal village activities in only a minimal way or perhaps remain a background figure during rituals. Individuals divide their time and energies differently, but to be Indian, they must meet to some extent all five criteria. The characteristics cannot be applied rigidly, and each is difficult to measure. However, if one or more of them is not met, the chances are good that the person is on the way to becoming a *mestizo*. It is mobility from the Indian to the *mestizo* sector that contributes to the blurring of the distinction between the two social categories. Also, the Indians have an interest in keeping the cultural border area between themselves and the dominant *mestizo* population ill defined.

Another way to appreciate the differences between Indians and *mestizos* is to view the situation from a regional perspective. Indians live in villages with distinctive social structures, whereas *mestizos* live on ranches, in towns, or in cities. Wherever *mestizos* live in small, even isolated, farming communities they retain the basic outlook and values of their fellow *mestizos* who live in the towns. On a regional basis, Indians and *mestizos* interact under very special conditions. The Indians may work for the ranchers on a temporary basis, or they may trade with *mestizo* middlemen at the market, but there is virtually no socializing that occurs outside of well-defined situations such as these. Even when Indians invite *mestizo* cowboys to their villages for a bull-riding (*jaripeo* in Spanish), the cowboys ride the bulls and the Indians simply observe from outside the corral. The line separating Indian from *mestizo* is clearly recognized by the people in the region, and this is reflected in the rules of engagement followed by both groups when they interact.

The people of Amatlán are fully aware of their status as Indians, and this awareness is reflected in the terms they use to describe themselves and outsiders. They call themselves by the general term *masehualmej*, which in Nahuatl means "Indian farmers" or "countrymen." This is the same term used by the ancient Aztecs to refer to commoners, and so the word has an association with pre-Hispanic Mexico.[6] When wishing to be more specific, the villagers refer to themselves by the Nahuatl term *mexijcaj* (sing. *mexijcatl),* which is the same word used by the ancient Aztecs to refer to themselves. They call all *mestizos,* whether farmers or not, by the Nahuatl term *coyomej* (sing. *coyotl*) that has been translated by some anthropologists as "gentlemen" but which also has a derogatory connotation. Although James Taggart translates the term as "gentleman," he does point out that the Nahuatl word *coyotl* ("coyote" in English) is an animal the Nahuas view as a mischiefmaker and back-biter as well as being clever and self-serving.[7] The *coyomej* are seen as aggressive and arrogant, people who exploit others when allowed.[8] Older villagers will occasionally use the Spanish-Nahuatl word *caxtiltlacamej* ("Castilians") or the Spanish phrase *gente de razón* ("people of reason") to describe *mestizos,* obvious legacies of the colonial epoch. Villagers occasionally use the Spanish word *indio* ("Indian") when describing themselves or other non-Nahua Indians, but they will modify the word by adding the diminutive suffix *-ito.* So they may talk about *inditos,* but never *indios.* They use Nahuatl names to refer to their non-Nahua Indian neighbors: *huaxtecatl* for a Huastec, *otomitl* for an Otomí, and *tepehuatl* for a Tepehua. All of these people would be referred to as *masehualmej* (or "Indian farmers") as well.

The way the villagers use these terms depends largely on the context in which they are speaking. In distinguishing Indians from *mestizos,* they employ the general terms *masehualmej* and *coyomej.* In other contexts they may choose to distinguish Nahuas from other Indian groups, and they will use the appellation *mexijcaj.* As suggested above, use of these ethnic labels is situational and depends upon the speaker's position relative to his or her listeners and upon how inclusive or exclusive the speaker wishes to be. How villagers use ethnic labels is complicated by the somewhat ambiguous distinctions between Indian and *mestizo* and the slow but steady migration of Indians into the *mestizo* world. Local people who relocated to the city always maintain their positive Indian identity in the eyes of those who stay behind. Villagers reserve the disparaging term *otomimej* (sing. *otomitl*) for Indians who disguise themselves by dressing or acting like *mestizos* in order to put on airs or to take advantage of other Indians.[9] The use of the term *otomimej* in such a negative context reveals the degree of hostility in interethnic relations among Indians. The most significant social cleavage in the Huasteca, however, is between Indian and non-Indian. In virtually every situation, Indians from differing ethnic affiliations will unite to face the common *mestizo* threat.

Nahua Social Character

The Nahuas exhibit a range of personality types that one might expect to find in a relatively small group of people anywhere in the world. Some are serious, private, and inwardly directed. Others are outgoing, witty, and charismatic. But there exist in all societies a set of unspoken or rarely articulated guidelines for how a person should present himself or herself to others. Successful individuals express their personalities within these guidelines, and those who deviate too widely experience stress and will be pressured by others to conform. It is these socially shared guidelines that I call "social character." There is no doubt that most villagers possess personalities that fall within the range of Nahua social character, and thus they share many personality traits. It is also clear that Nahua social character is quite different from that of neighboring *mestizos* and from that of most Anglo-Americans. My observations about Nahua social character derive from my long-term residence in Amatlán where I was able to witness numerous occasions in which individuals, both in public and in private, played their social roles, handled adversity, and discussed the deviations of others. I did not administer psychology tests to the villagers nor employ other methods for gathering systematic data on personality, and so my observations must remain tentative.

Anthropologist Paul Jean Provost conducted a study of a Huastecan Nahua village in which he outlines five basic "cultural principles" that underlie social interaction and reflect something of social character.[10] I found these principles to be an accurate description of the interactional patterns in Amatlán. The first principle he calls "indirectness." Nahuas generally value social interaction that is oblique and avoids direct confrontation. Pointed questions, authoritative assertions, commands, or direct requests are considered rude and aggressive. Social interaction requires patience as participants communicate through circumlocution and gentle suggestion. As an outsider I had to learn indirectness before my interactions with villagers went smoothly and I was able to elicit accurate information from them. A second cultural principle, related to the first, Provost calls "attrition." Villagers persuade not by the direct argument that would contradict the first cultural principle, but rather by wearing the listener down with subtle and persistent suggestion. No excuse or evasive action can turn back the tide of entreaties, and in the end the listener is overwhelmed and forced to capitulate.

A third cultural principle among the Nahuas is "informality." Most areas of Nahua life are free from rigid rules and strict procedures, and many village activities are accordingly carried out in a relaxed and flexible way. Religious rituals, village meetings, and communal work crews appear almost disorganized to the outsider. But informality does not mean disorganization, and the villagers are very efficient at accomplishing cooperative tasks. One exception to the principle of informality is in the area of Nahua hospitality. A visitor is always provided with a special chair, food is prepared, and the guest is treated very cordially. The Nahuas are renowned throughout the region for their hospitality, politeness, and the respect they show others. The fourth principle discussed by Provost is "individuality." Villagers view themselves and others as individuals, and each person is expected to behave accordingly. Even in matters of kinship a great deal of individuality is permitted and encouraged within the group. The final cultural principle is "reciprocity." The villagers see themselves at the center of a complex network of obligations and expectations involving other villagers, *mestizos*, and even the spirits in their pantheon. The ideal of exchange permeates the way they think about the world and their place in it. Village life is largely organized around gift exchange, labor exchange, and ritual offerings to spirits in return for health, food, and well-being.

These five principles—indirectness, attrition, informality, individuality, and reciprocity—combine to create a social character that differs markedly from that of the *mestizos*. To many *mestizos* the Indians appear dull-witted, slow, and uncooperative. In contrast, once I became aware of their style of interaction I found them to be curious and quick learners. I taught many people a few words in English while I was there in the early 1970s, and they were able to repeat them perfectly in 1986. To the villagers, many *mestizos* lack proper reserve and are overly direct and blunt. *Mestizos* thus appear rude, aggressive, demanding, and overbearing. When Indians and *mestizos* interact with each other, one may easily see that both are acting properly according to the guidelines of their own ethnic groups and yet are reinforcing each other's negative stereotypes.

Decision Making in Amatlán

I wish to identify the four major features of economic life in Amatlán. The first is that villagers must be able to generate cash income in order to meet the needs of the household. This means that they must grow crops for money and that they must depend on the *mestizo*-controlled sector of the national economy to supplement their incomes. The second feature is that even the inhabitants of remote villages like Amatlán are largely dependent on economic and political forces that derive from the power centers of the nation. Indians work hard to avoid direct domination by *mestizo* elites, but in the end they can succeed only partially in extricating themselves from being ensnared in the lower reaches of the national socioeconomic hierarchy. In all cases power is wielded by non-Indians, and so the villagers' situation differs from that of most poor Mexicans only in that the power gap is exacerbated by a cultural gap. Third, the village does not operate communally despite some appearances to the contrary. The household is the focus of consumption and production activity in Amatlán. Finally, like people everywhere, the people of Amatlán are compelled to economize. Villagers must make decisions on how to allocate their scarce means to satisfy diverse ends. They must make strategic decisions all the time, and they are fully aware that they are doing so.

There are three features of Nahua culture that give their participation in production and consumption activities a style that is distinct from that of most *mestizos*. The first is that consumption patterns are similar from household to household regardless of the unequal levels of household wealth. For the Nahuas, the purpose of wealth is to have a sense of security, or perhaps simply a degree of stability in a changing world. Wealth is not used to prove self-worth, nor is it paraded in any way to impress neighbors. Quite the opposite is true. Villagers feel that displays of wealth cause envy and that feelings of envy can cause disease to spread throughout the village. People do like to dress well and to display jewels or adornments and, more rarely, gold dental work, but they always dress within a fairly narrow range of fashion. Clothes that are new and clean are valued, but anything flashy or expensive is thought to invite envy. The same value applies as well to houses and possessions. An image of genteel poverty is the ideal presentation of self in Amatlán.

In fact, in some cases, the wealthier a villager is, the more likely that he will make an effort to appear poor. Tomás used to visit me quite often during my research in 1972–73, but I really came to know him in 1986. He is pleasant enough, but he always is the most ragged person in the village. For a long time I attributed his dress to the fact that he drinks to excess, but I learned later that he owns half a dozen head of cattle. Another friend, Juan, dresses in new Western clothing, wears a silver ring, and plays the guitar for rituals. He is a *vecino* (a resident of the community with no claim to its common-held land) and among the poorest people in the village. In this case and many others, quality of dress is actually inversely correlated with level of wealth. Demonstrating wealth can not only bring on dangerous feelings of envy, but it also makes one fair game for requests to borrow money. Ranulfo graduated from a teachers' training program, and he now teaches elementary-school children in a neighboring *municipio*. He once told me that he hates to visit Amatlán because everyone thinks he is rich and they always ask to borrow money from him. Rich people are expected to pay more for things such as village "cooperations," and they are expected to be very generous with all visitors.

Wealth invites trouble, and so it is in the interest of those who are better off to conceal their superior positions. This cultural feature has led some scholars to propose that Indians in Mexico have a strong attitude of "shared poverty,"[11] or that they subscribe to an image of "limited good."[12] Wolf notes that, "in Mesoamerica, display of wealth is viewed with direct hostility."[13] He states that surplus wealth is redistributed within the village and that resignation to poverty is praised. This attitude of shared poverty siphons off surplus wealth and works against the purchase of new goods. George Foster holds that villagers in Mexico see a fixed amount of good in the world and that one individual's success is seen by others as reducing their own chances to derive benefits for themselves. Thus, villagers exhibit hostile feelings toward wealthy individuals and assume that those who are better off must have gained their property through dishonesty. This image of the limited good, according to Foster, stymies wealth accumulation and, ultimately, economic development.

These viewpoints only partially describe the situation in Amatlán. Although all villagers identified themselves as poor people, and I did find some jealousy among individuals, I found no evidence that these attitudes contributed to village poverty. Feelings of envy or shared poverty apparently do not stop people from striving to enter the level of wealthier cattle-raising families in the village; nor others, like Julio, from opening up a *cantina* and becoming a merchant in the market. Generosity is valued and the rich are expected to pay more, but mechanisms for internal redistribution of surplus wealth do not destroy differences in wealth among village families. Despite the fact that everyone knows who is actually wealthy and who is not, the point seems to be to avoid behavior that places one person above another. A cherished value for the Nahuas is a sense of equality and community, and these traits would be destroyed in their view by the show of arrogance and hierarchy that would result if the rich paraded their wealth. In short, villagers strive for economic success, but they are careful not to flaunt it.

I do not wish to exaggerate this egalitarian value nor its effect on people's behavior. Individuals do own items that set them apart from others. A few men have purchased corrugated tarpaper roofing material for their houses. Others have work animals for turning the sugarcane press or for transporting crops to the market. Some households have transistor radios, and I noticed in 1986 that a few people had purchased crank grinders for the first and most difficult step in preparing cornmeal. Small differences do exist among households in quantity and quality of possessions, but the important point is that these differences are not of the same magnitude as the actual differences in wealth in the village.

The second Nahua cultural feature is related to the first. When the villagers talk about *mestizos*, the characteristic they most disparage is how aggressive and hierarchical they are. Many *mestizos* do indeed look down upon the Indians and do not seem to realize how much the Indians resent it. When villagers leave to work for a while on a local ranch or in a more distant city, they frequently return with stories of how they had to quit because the boss (*patrón* in Spanish) was so bad. In fact, the villagers are generally good employees who are willing to work very hard for what appears to be minimal compensation. And yet I have talked to many local *mestizo* ranchers who told me that the Indians are lazy and not to be trusted. Part of the cause of this problem of perception is the different attitude villagers have toward work, and the fact that villagers resent the way *mestizos* set up the work situation. Although there are many reasons why Indians leave jobs, the one they talk about most frequently is that they hate working for a boss. The *mestizo* workplace for them is a contradiction of the democratic and egalitarian values of village life. Of equal importance, villagers resent being dependent on outsiders for their livelihood.

The third feature of Nahua culture that affects their production and consumption activities is more difficult to characterize. It is manifest in an approach to work and an attitude toward time that differs somewhat from that of *mestizo* Mexico.[14] The people of Amatlán are task oriented in that they work diligently to finish what needs to be done. They attack and complete projects that appear to the outsider to require almost superhuman endurance. Clearing thick tropical brush in the humidity and scorching heat, or carrying loads of firewood or corn for great distances over steep and broken trails, are two minor examples of the hard work they do without complaint. But for them the purpose of work is to accomplish tasks, and it is not particularly valuable in itself. Although villagers take pride in the work they do, they do not feel lost or empty if, after a task is completed, no further work presents itself. This approach to labor works fine if a person is hired by a local rancher on a temporary basis to complete a specific task. It does not lead to success, however, for more permanent positions where long-term consistent work for its own sake is required.

Differing concepts of time are another element of incompatibility between *mestizo* entrepreneurs and villagers. The villagers tend to take the long view of things compared with most Westerners. Like the growing seasons, things unfold in a measured way, and the people of Amatlán have a high tolerance for periods of waiting. Patience is not a virtue for them; it is a way of life. When returning to the village for more research, it always takes me several days to slow down my pace so that it is compatible with theirs. One of the big shocks at returning to the United States after a long stay in the village is how quickly everyone appears to talk and move. People on a city street appear almost comical, like figures gesticulating in a film that has been speeded up. Most American tourists comment on the slower pace of life in Mexican cities, but even the cities are fast-paced compared to life in the villages. This different perception of time sometimes causes problems for Indians in the *mestizo* workplace.

Individual men may go to the city or surrounding ranches and work on a contractual basis for several months at a time. From the point of view of the employer, the man holds a permanent job and has a responsibility to continue working. The villager, on the other hand, had a long-term plan to return to the village and continue farming. When the time comes to leave, the villager, who always thought that the job was temporary, just quits. The employer is reaffirmed in his judgment that Indians cannot be trusted and that they are too lazy or lack motivation to work. From the point of view of the villager, three or four months is more than enough time to spend on a job, and the employer is unreasonable in his expectation that it be longer. Additional problems arise over deadlines of any type, the imposition of strict work schedules according to the clock or even days of the week, timetables for beginning and ending work, or any requirement in which timing takes priority over the work itself. From the villagers' perspective, the employers are simply trying to force their will on the workers, and they are usually glad to leave when the time comes.

Some villagers leave Amatlán for good, of course, and they adapt quite well to the alien conditions in the work world. For them, working in the city is no longer a strategy for supplementing farm income but is an end in itself. Changes required for life on the job mean adopting *mestizo* traits and leaving the traditional culture behind. The villagers know this, and a number are willing to make the changes for the greater opportunities present in the city. Many who leave do so because they have been cut off from land and they have no chance of living a normal life in the village. A few return from the city complaining about air pollution, traffic, and the unpleasant features of urban living. Some of these returnees even become *vecinos* and begin the long wait for the opportunity to obtain land. Most who make up their minds to leave, however, never come back. Both Indians and *mestizos* must plan, economize, and work in order to maintain their lives. At the same time, each occupies a different world.

Notes

1. See Jane H. Hill and Kenneth C. Hill, *Speaking Mexicano: Dynamics of Syncretic Language in Central Mexico* (Tucson, 1986), for a sociolinguistic study of language and ethnicity among Nahuas of central Mexico.

2. Anselmo Marino Flores, "Indian Population and Its Identification," in Manning Nash, ed., *Social Anthropology* (Austin, 1967), 12–25, Vol. 6 in Robert Wauchope, gen. ed., *Handbook of Middle American Indians*.

3. George P. Castile, "On the Tarascanness of the Tarascans and the Indianness of the Indians," in George P. Castile and Gilbert Kushner, eds., *Persistent Peoples: Cultural Enclaves in Perspective* (Austin, 1981), 171–191.

4. See Alfonso Caso, *La comunidad indígena* (Mexico, 1971), 83ff., for a discussion of the complexities of defining Indians.

5. Gregory Reck, *In the Shadow of Tlaloc: Life in a Mexican Village* (Prospect Heights, IL, 1986 [1978]), has written a novel that seeks to illuminate the distinction between Indian and *mestizo* world views.

6. Jacques Soustelle, *Daily Life of the Aztecs on the Eve of the Spanish Conquest* (Stanford, 1961 [1955]), 70ff.

7. James M. Taggart, *Nahuat Myth and Social Structure* (Austin, 1983), 260.

8. See Joaquin Romualdo Hernández, *Relaciones políticas entre indígenas y mestizos en Xochiatipan, Hgo.* (Mexico, 1982), and Rosa Reyes Martínez, *La comunidad indígena de Tlacolula, Veracruz: La tierra y sus problemas* (Mexico, 1982), for Nahua descriptions of *coyomej*; also Eric Wolf, *Sons of the Shaking Earth* (Chicago, 1959), 237.

9. Reyes Martínez, *La comunidad indígena*, 93, 176; Romualdo Hernández, *Relaciones políticas*, 158.

10. Paul Jean Provost, "Culture and Anti-Culture among the Eastern Nahua of Northern Veracruz, Mexico," Ph.D. diss., Indiana University, 1975, 138ff.

11. See, for example, Eric Wolf, "Closed Corporate Peasant Communities in Mesoamerica and Central Java," *Southwestern Journal of Anthropology*, 13:1 (1957), 1–18.

12. George Foster, *Tzintzuntzan: Mexican Peasants in a Changing World* (Boston, 1967), 122ff.

13. Wolf, "Closed Corporate Peasant Communities," 5.

14. Marie-Noëlle Chamoux, "The Conception of Work in Contemporary Nahuatl-Speaking Communities in the Sierra de Puebla," Paper presented at the Annual Meeting of the American Anthropological Association, 1985.

Glossary

Aclla
Women assigned to religious centers under the Incas.

Alcaldía mayor
Mayoralty office.

Altiplano
The high plain heavily populated by Aymara-speaking Indians that dominates western Bolivia.

Arcabuz
An early musket, or arquebus.

Ayllu
A Peruvian term for a kinship group and the land it controls.

Cabecera
The head town of an indigenous province.

Cabildo
A municipal council.

Cacicazgo
The lands controlled by a native lord.

Cacique
A term that the Spaniards apply broadly to native rulers.

Caciquismo
Political bossism.

Calpixqui (calpixque, pl.)
A Nahuatl term for a tax collector and administrative official.

Cargo system
A common practice in rural communities whereby men attain prestige and power through sponsorship of religious festivals.

Cofradía
A religious confraternity.

Composición
Legalization of a land title.

Común
Community, or the total population of a settlement.

Corregimiento
The colonial political jurisdiction for an Indian province.

Curaca
See **Kuraka**

Denuncia
Legal term for a land claim.

Ejido
A collective landholding in Mexico.

Escribano
A notary public.

Forastero
Spanish term used in the Andes to refer to outsiders living in native communities who have no access to communal land but are exempt from labor service as well.

Güero
A person with blond hair or a light complexion.

Huaca
See **Wak'a**

Jacal
A hut.

Juez (jueces, pl.)
A judge.

Kuraka (curaca)
A native ruler or lord in the Andes.

Labrador
A market-oriented farmer who works his own land.

Ladino
A Hispanized Indian, or person of mixed blood.

Latifundium (latifundia, pl.)
A large estate or a system of landholding dominated by large estates.

Macehual
The native term in Mexico for an Indian commoner.

Merced
A royal grant, commonly of land.

Mestizo
A person of mixed European and Indian ancestry.

Mit'a
The Andean term for required rotary labor service.

Mitaq (or mitmaq) (mitimae, pl.)
Colonists from different ethnic groups under the Incas.

Nahua
The people of the largest indigenous language group in Mexico.

Obraje
A large workshop, often producing textiles and utilizing forced laborers.

Originario
Spanish term used in the Andes for a person residing in his native community and who therefore has access to a share of its communal lands, but who must perform labor service and perhaps pay tribute as well.

Panaqa
A royal lineage under the Incas.

Parcialidad
Spanish term for a large subdivision of a sizeable native town.

Pardo
A person of mixed European and African ancestry.

Peninsular
An immigrant from Spain (the Iberian Peninsula).

Principal
A native noble.

Puna
High mountain grasslands in the Andes.

Ranchero
The owner of a private farm or ranch.

Sujeto
A village or hamlet under the jurisdiction of a head town in an Indian province.

Swidden
Slash-and-burn agriculture.

Tepache
A crude fermented drink derived from the maguey cactus.

Tierra Baldía
Vacant or public land.

Tributario
A tribute payer.

Wak'a (or huaca)
A sacred site or object in the Andes.

Yana (or yanacona)
A personal retainer in the Andean region.

Yori
The Yaqui term for a European.

Suggested Readings

The cultural achievements of the Aztecs, Maya, and Incas, reinforced by the relative abundance of documentation that we have on their civilizations both before and after the arrival of the Spaniards, have understandably drawn the attention of scholars more than have those of other peoples of the Americas with important but less majestic histories. Further, researchers have devoted themselves primarily to the colonial period, largely for two reasons. First, many of the most dramatic events and developments transpired during this period. Second, Indians as corporate groups are more difficult to trace in most Latin American countries following independence, while they likewise have seemed to most investigators as rather peripheral to the primary trajectories and issues in these national histories. This view is currently being modified, and, as we shall see, several fine books have recently examined the role of native peoples in the modern period.

Abundant archaeological remains, a few surviving codices, and a diverse body of postconquest chronicles written by both indigenous intellectuals and interested Spaniards (mostly clerics) provide a rich repository of evidence that reaches deeply into the pre-Hispanic history of Mesoamerica and the Andean highlands. The best single volume that outlines the salient characteristics of the great civilizations that punctuated Mexican history for perhaps three thousand years before the coming of Cortés is Nigel Davies, *The Ancient Kingdoms of Mexico* (New York: Penguin Books, 1983). A thorough and persuasive study of patterns of Aztec warfare and the growth and structure of the Aztec empire is Ross Hassig, *Aztec Warfare: Imperial Expansion and Political Control* (Norman: University of Oklahoma Press, 1988).

Charles Gibson, *The Aztecs under Spanish Rule: A History of the Indians of the Valley of Mexico, 1519–1810* (Stanford: Stanford University Press, 1964), represents one of the abiding moments in the history of the natives of Latin America. It examines the indigenous communities of central Mexico in the colonial period to portray not only how diverse external forces brought about important transformations but also how native ethnic identity and certain crucial beliefs and practices were maintained.

Many of the concepts and relationships that were first enumerated in this lengthy work remain central to our vision of this advanced culture zone.

More recently, scholars, especially some who have learned to read documents in Nahuatl, the primary native language to this day in Mexico, have penetrated more deeply into cultural change at the local level and have probed adaptations inside the indigenous community and even within the family after the arrival of the Europeans. Louise M. Burkhart, *The Slippery Earth: Nahua-Christian Dialogue in Sixteenth-Century Mexico* (Tucson: University of Arizona Press, 1989), analyzes how Christian concepts were translated into Nahuatl and were understood by native converts. S. L. Cline, *Colonial Culhuacan, 1580–1600: A Social History of an Aztec Town* (Albuquerque: University of New Mexico Press, 1986), utilizes a set of wills generated in Nahuatl just a few generations after the conquest in a community close to Mexico City to study change in such vital institutions as landholding, inheritance, and the position and activities of women.

The most comprehensive examination of the transformation of native life and culture within central Mexican communities during the colonial period is James Lockhart, *The Nahuas after the Conquest: A Social and Cultural History of the Indians of Central Mexico, Sixteenth through Eighteenth Centuries* (Stanford: Stanford University Press, 1992). It analyzes social, political, and family relationships and even explores changes in belief systems and language use.

Much acculturation and race mixture transpired in urban settings. John K. Chance, *Race and Class in Colonial Oaxaca* (Stanford: Stanford University Press, 1978), which examines social and ethnic change in a city in southern Mexico, represents the best systematic study of such phenomena over an extended period.

Of course, not all aspects of pre-Hispanic religious belief systems were eliminated over time. In isolated areas that avoided systematic Spanish social and economic penetration, earlier traditions were maintained. Serge Gruzinski, *Man-Gods in the Mexican Highlands: Indian Power and Colonial Society, 1520–1800* (Stanford: Stanford University Press, 1989), looks at four natives who declared themselves to be God incarnate, examining their beliefs and what their existence says about the kind of cultural transformation that took place.

Steve J. Stern, the author of one of the contributions in this collection, has composed a more fully rendered book on the social and cultural changes that took place among the Andean peoples during the first century of colonization, *Peru's Indian Peoples and the Challenge of Spanish Conquest: Huamanga to 1640* (Madison: University of Wisconsin Press,

1982). Karen W. Spalding, *Huarochirí: An Andean Society under Inca and Spanish Rule* (Stanford: Stanford University Press, 1984), is an equally distinguished study of a native province, this one located closer to Lima, the center of Spanish settlement. It also offers careful consideration of the impact of the Inca empire on this subjugated people in the century before the coming of the Europeans.

Sabine MacCormack, *Religion in the Andes: Vision and Imagination in Early Colonial Peru* (Princeton: Princeton University Press, 1991), constitutes a modern classic. In a careful and thorough manner, it depicts the penetration of Christian ideas into the Andean world of the sacred, showing how some major writers and common people reconciled the two belief systems, their symbols, and their shrines. Kenneth Mills, *Idolatry and its Enemies: Colonial Andean Religion and Extirpation, 1640–1750* (Princeton: Princeton University Press, 1997), examines the nature of Andean religious practices in the mid-colonial period and discusses a major Spanish campaign to eradicate enduring pre-Hispanic beliefs.

Ann M. Wightman, *Indigenous Migration and Social Change: The Forasteros of Cuzco, 1570–1720* (Durham: Duke University Press, 1989), addresses the issue of native migration into the important regional center of Cuzco. She considers which types of people moved to the city, for what reasons, and what impact they had both on the communities they left behind and on the city they moved to. A penetrating examination of indigenous migration patterns in colonial Ecuador is Karen Vieira Powers, *Andean Journeys: Migration, Ethnogenesis, and the State in Colonial Quito* (Albuquerque: University of New Mexico Press, 1995).

The Indian peoples of the Andes maintained a tradition of violent resistance to external rule that was even more vibrant than was the case in Mexico. This endemic protest peaked in the massive Tupac Amaru revolt that broke out in 1780. Scarlett O'Phelan Godoy, *Rebellions and Revolts in Eighteenth-Century Peru and Upper Peru* (Cologne: Böhlau Verlag, 1985), carefully examines the larger tradition of resistance in which this great revolt occurred. Steve J. Stern, ed., *Resistance, Rebellion, and Consciousness in the Andean Peasant World, Eighteenth to Twentieth Centuries* (Madison: University of Wisconsin Press, 1987), offers a series of case studies of violent protests in this culture zone over the last three centuries. This pattern of violent resistance of subordination by outsiders continues to the present day. Michael F. Brown and Eduardo Fernández, *War of Shadows: The Struggle for Utopia in the Peruvian Amazon* (Berkeley: University of California Press, 1991), is a fascinating consideration of one people's continuing search for a messiah to lead them away from oppression, from colonial times to the present.

The extended resistance of the various Maya peoples to Spanish colonization has recently attracted the attention of a new generation of scholars who have rendered sensitive depictions of the military and cultural conflict that took place in the Yucatán. Two of the very best of these are Inga Clendinnen, *Ambivalent Conquest: Maya and Spaniard in Yucatán, 1517–1570* (Cambridge, Eng.: Cambridge University Press, 1987), and Grant D. Jones, *Maya Resistance to Spanish Rule: Time and History on a Colonial Frontier* (Albuquerque: University of New Mexico Press, 1989). An innovative and comprehensive study of Maya community and family life in the three centuries following 1550, which makes great use of numerous Maya-language documents that had been previously ignored, is Matthew Restall, *The Maya World: Yucatec Culture and Society, 1550–1850* (Stanford: Stanford University Press, 1997).

The Spanish experienced a greatly different situation among the tribal societies and hunting-and-gathering peoples found throughout much of Latin America. Some of these societies were able to resist very resolutely. Philip Wayne Powell, *Soldiers, Indians, and Silver: The Northward Advance of New Spain, 1550–1600* (Berkeley: University of California Press, 1952), lays out the series of Spanish initiatives against the nomadic peoples of northern Mexico in the late sixteenth century and the reasons for the failure of so many of them and for the limited success that finally occurred. A modern treatment of some of these peoples, which places them in their physical environment and under the influence of missions during the final century of the colonial period and the early decades of the independence era, is Cynthia Radding, *Wandering Peoples: Colonialism, Ethnic Spaces, and Ecological Frontiers in Northwestern Mexico, 1700–1850* (Durham: Duke University Press, 1997).

A very different trajectory in native-colonist relations is treated in Elman R. Service, *Spanish-Guaraní Relations in Early Colonial Paraguay* (Ann Arbor: University of Michigan Press, 1954). Here the Guaraní and the Spaniards, both vulnerable to depradations from the warlike peoples who surrounded them in central Paraguay, entered into an understanding in which they intermarried and joined forces in mutual protection. Spanish colonists gained access to the Indian labor that could bring about prosperity only through their relationships with senior females of this ethnic group, the people who had privileged claims on labor service from their male relatives.

As previously noted, the volume and overall quality of books on Latin American Indians in the national period are distinctly inferior to those for the colonial period. Nonetheless, some very valuable work has appeared, particularly in the last decade or so. Mexico is heavily represented in both the colonial and the national periods. Nelson Reed, *The Caste War of*

Yucatán (Stanford: Stanford University Press, 1964), is a sophisticated examination of the character of a massive Maya revolt against the provincial government that broke out in the late 1840s and persisted into the early twentieth century. Deep racial animosities and the sanction given by a new local religion to the revolt's leaders fueled this enduring uprising. A recent, multidimensioned study of the causes of this major revolt is Terry Rugeley, *Yucatán's Maya Peasantry and the Origins of the Caste War* (Austin: University of Texas Press, 1996). Even after the Mexican Revolution of 1910 to 1920, Maya communities far in the interior of the peninsula aspired to gain munitions and international support to initiate a new insurrection. They even sought to draw American archaeologists into their struggle, a facet well explored in Paul Sullivan, *Unfinished Conversations: Mayas and Foreigners between Two Wars* (New York: Alfred A. Knopf, 1989).

The Mexican Revolution itself included Indian participation, perhaps no place more than in the Zapata movement. This key aspect of the larger revolution is beautifully described in John Womack, Jr., *Zapata and the Mexican Revolution* (New York: Alfred A. Knopf, 1968). The subsequent twentieth-century history of the native peoples in this same region is explored in Arturo Warman, *We Come to Object: The Peasants of Morelos and the National State* (Baltimore: Johns Hopkins University Press, 1981). Paul Friedrich, *Agrarian Revolt in a Mexican Village* (Chicago: University of Chicago Press, 1970), offers a marvelously well-developed yet succinct examination of the struggle for agrarian reform in an Indian community in another region of Mexico in the decades following the revolution.

Two distinguished studies have appeared recently on the responses of indigenous peoples in the Andean highlands to the economic transformations brought to the region in the late nineteenth and early twentieth centuries. Florencia E. Mallon, *The Defense of Community in Peru's Central Highlands: Peasant Struggle and Capitalist Transition, 1860–1940* (Princeton: Princeton University Press, 1983), looks at changes that transpired within communities brought about first by a foreign invasion of the nation and later by the installation of a modern copper smelter. Erick D. Langer, *Economic Change and Rural Resistance in Southern Bolivia, 1880–1930* (Stanford: Stanford University Press, 1989), treats the impact of the emergence of commercial agriculture on diverse communities of native peoples in southern Bolivia, a region previously long divorced from the market economy.

Mallon's new book, *Peasant and Nation: The Making of Postcolonial Mexico and Peru* (Berkeley: University of California Press, 1995), argues that rural peoples—generally Indians—themselves shaped a model of the nation in the nineteenth century, particularly as they organized into military units to resist foreign invasions. But with the withdrawal of the enemy, these peasant bands in turn had to combat forces marshalled by the urban elites, who had their own image of the emerging nation-state. Another interesting work on the position and role of Indian peoples in the formation of the Peruvian nation is Mark Thurner, *From Two Republics to One Divided: Contradictions of Postcolonial Nationmaking in Andean Peru* (Durham: Duke University Press, 1997).

Frans J. Schryer, *Ethnicity and Class in Conflict in Rural Mexico* (Princeton: Princeton University Press, 1990), looks at the mutability of ethnic identity in contemporary Mexico and the role of ethnic identity in the distribution of land and the organization of local government. Howard Campbell, *Zapotec Renaissance: Ethnic Politics and Cultural Revivalism in Southern Mexico* (Albuquerque: University of New Mexico Press, 1995), considers a recent major drive for cultural and political autonomy among the Zapotecs of Oaxaca in southern Mexico.

For more than three decades, Guatemala endured a civil war, recently ended by a peace accord, in which several distinct guerrilla forces operated in the countryside. These troops enjoyed broad support from the rural dwellers, many of whom are Maya, in their fight against a brutal national army. Military engagements—but especially army massacres of civilians—resulted in the deaths of several hundreds of thousands of peasants. In the midst of this desolation, Maya culture enjoyed a substantial rebirth. Richard Wilson, *Maya Resurgence in Guatemala: Q'eqchi' Experiences* (Norman: University of Oklahoma Press, 1995), recounts one example of this resurgence. Robert M. Carmack, *Rebels of Highland Guatemala: The Quiché-Mayas of Momostenango* (Norman: University of Oklahoma Press, 1995), is the culmination of the author's career spent studying this Maya ethnic group. It covers the history of Momostenango from pre-Hispanic times to the present, although nearly half of the book is devoted to consideration of the last fifty years.

Suggested Films

Valuable fictional and documentary films about the history and culture of Latin American Indians have been produced over the years. One of several films that portrays the subjugation of native peoples, *The Conquest of Mexico* (1988), is a thirty-five-minute documentary that describes Cortés's conquest of Mexico and how it has been viewed by individuals in different eras. *Conflict of the Gods* (1992, program two in the series The Buried Mirror: Reflections of Spain and the New World), retraces in one hour the world of pre-Hispanic Mexico, the nature and impact of the conquest, and the transformed world of the Indians in the early colonial period. *Francisco Pizarro: Inca Nation, Peru, 1532* (1976) is a sixty-minute fictional re-creation of Pizarro's expedition into Peru through the capture and execution of Atahualpa and the Spaniards' entrance into Cuzco, the Incas' capital city.

Aguirre: The Wrath of God (1972), the acclaimed German director Werner Herzog's full-length fictional version of a sixteenth-century expedition into the headwaters of the Amazon, concentrates on the deterioration of the Spaniards as they ventured deep into a lush natural setting populated by elusive natives, neither of which they could understand, let alone subdue. In addition to the compelling story and quality acting and production, the movie is evocative of the most ill-fated Spanish undertakings against the tropical hunting-and-gathering societies. A marvelously effective Brazilian fictional film, *How Tasty Was My Little Frenchman* (1973), closely examines the beliefs and way of life of the Tupinambá, a major Brazilian people who practiced cannibalism, by studying the fate of a sixteenth-century Frenchman captured by them and awaiting execution.

Perhaps understandably, little of value has been produced on Latin American Indian history in the colonial period and the nineteenth century; these developments are not well known by the general public, and they often lack compelling dramatic interest. The significant exception is Roland Joffé's popular film *The Mission* (1986), which, although it possesses considerable pedagogical value, greatly overstates and romanticizes an episode between Jesuits and the Guarani Indians in the Paraguayan region in the mid-eighteenth century.

Elia Kazan's *Zapata* (1952), from a screenplay by John Steinbeck, regards this central figure of the Mexican Revolution as a spokesperson for the nation's suffering peasantry. It does not fully appreciate the fact that Emiliano Zapata's revolt emerged from one of the most Indian regions of Mexico, but it remains useful for depicting the nature of the revolution and the social and racial attitudes of the time. Of note is the fine historical documentary *Martin Chambi and the Heirs of the Incas* (1990), which, in fifty minutes, examines the career and work of an Indian of Peru who ran a photography studio in Cuzco during the early part of this century and recorded the lives and rituals of both rural peoples and city dwellers.

Two one-half-hour productions in the series Faces of Culture significantly enhance our understanding of the position and values of Latin American Indians in the modern world. Number 14, *The Aymara: A Case Study in Social Stratification* (1983), depicts the lives of two interdependent communities in highland Bolivia, one a mestizo market town and the other an Indian peasant village. The marketplace, religion, education, labor systems, and health care are among the subjects covered. Number 16, *The Highland Maya: A Case Study in Economic Anthropology* (1983), studies the role of the cargo system and fiestas in a Guatemalan community, showing their economic impact and how individuals utilize them to attain higher standing and authority in local society.

Sacred Games (1989) provides a rich treatment of an annual carnival in a Mayan community in southern Mexico. One hour in length, it displays the merger of Catholicism with traditional Mayan rites and focuses on the activities of one of the sponsors of the week-long festival. A more multidimensional examination of a contemporary Mayan community is *Todos Santos Cuchumatan: Report from a Guatemalan Village* (1983). In forty minutes it treats local rituals and ways of life, and examines the impact of the seasonal migration of people from the community to cotton plantations in the lowlands. Its sequel, *Todos Santos: The Survivors* (1989, fifty-eight minutes), examines the community after it has been devastated by warfare between left-wing guerrilla forces and the national army.

The Earth Is Our Mother (1986, fifty-five minutes) compares two Indian tribes in modern Colombia and Venezuela as they respond to intensive missionary campaigns. In one case the people have become heavily dependent on the religious order and cannot maintain their traditional way of life. The other society eventually runs the missionaries off its land and continues to maintain a vibrant, autonomous culture and control over its own territory.

About the Contributors

THOMAS C. PATTERSON is a professor of anthropology at Temple University. Noted as an archaeologist, he has written *Archaeology: The Historical Development of Civilization* (1994), among other books.

STEVE J. STERN is a professor of history at the University of Wisconsin, Madison. He is the author of *The Secret History of Gender: Men, Women, and Power in Late Colonial Mexico* (1995).

NANCY M. FARRISS is the Walter H. Annenberg Professor of History at the University of Pennsylvania. She has long researched the Maya cultures of the Yucatán Peninsula in the colonial period.

ROBERT CHARLES PADDEN is a professor emeritus of history at Brown University. His writings include *The Hummingbird and the Hawk: Conquest and Sovereignty in the Valley of Mexico, 1503–1541* (1967), a study of the struggle between the Aztecs and Spaniards in the conquest era.

ROBERT HASKETT is an associate professor of history at the University of Oregon. Skilled in Nahuatl, the primary language of the natives of central Mexico, he is currently investigating the use of indigenous laborers in the important silver mining center of Taxco.

PAUL CHARNEY is a lecturer at Frostburg State University, Maryland. His 1989 dissertation examines the transformation of Indian life in the Lima Valley of Peru from 1532 to 1824.

WILLIAM B. TAYLOR is the Muriel McKevitt Sonne Professor of History at the University of California, Berkeley. He is the author of the prize-winning *Magistrates of the Sacred: Priests and Parishioners in Eighteenth-Century Mexico* (1996).

DAVID MCCREERY is a professor of history at Georgia State University. He has authored *Rural Guatemala, 1760–1940* (1994).

EVELYN HU-DEHART is a professor of ethnic studies and the director of the Center for Studies of Ethnicity and Race in America at the University of Colorado, Boulder. She has written *Missionaries, Miners, and Indians: Spanish Contact with the Yaqui Nation of Northwestern New Spain, 1533–1820* (1981).

ERICK D. LANGER is an associate professor of history at Georgetown University. He is the author of *Economic Change and Rural Resistance in Southern Bolivia, 1880–1930* (1989).

ALAN R. SANDSTROM is a professor of anthropology at Indiana University-Purdue University, Fort Wayne. Among his books is *The Image of Disease: Medical Practices of Nahua Indians of the Huasteca* (1978).

ISBN 0-8420-2822-6

9 780842 028226

90000